Child's Play

Child's Play

*Multi-Sensory Histories of Children and
Childhood in Japan*

―――

Edited by Sabine Frühstück and Anne Walthall

中

UNIVERSITY OF CALIFORNIA PRESS

University of California Press, one of the most distinguished university presses in the United States, enriches lives around the world by advancing scholarship in the humanities, social sciences, and natural sciences. Its activities are supported by the UC Press Foundation and by philanthropic contributions from individuals and institutions. For more information, visit www.ucpress.edu.

University of California Press
Oakland, California

Suggested citation: Frühstück, Sabine and Walthall, Anne. *Child's Play: Multi-Sensory Histories of Children and Childhood in Japan*. Oakland: University of California Press, 2017. doi: https://doi.org/10.1525/luminos.40

Library of Congress Cataloging-in-Publication Data

Names: Frühstück, Sabine, editor. | Walthall, Anne, editor.
Title: Child's play : multi-sensory histories of children and childhood in Japan / edited by Sabine Frühstück and Anne Walthall.
Description: Oakland, California : University of California Press, [2018] | Includes bibliographical references and index.
Identifiers: LCCN 2017022291| ISBN 9780520296275 (pbk. : alk. paper) | ISBN 9780520968844 (ebook)
Subjects: LCSH: Children—Japan—History. | Children—Japan—Social conditions. | Japan—Social conditions. | Education—Japan—History. | Parent and child—Japan—History.
Classification: LCC HQ792.J3 C47 2018 | DDC 305.230952—dc23
LC record available at https://lccn.loc.gov/2017022291

27 26 25 24 23 22 21 20 19 18
10 9 8 7 6 5 4 3 2 1

CONTENTS

ILLUSTRATIONS AND TABLE

FIGURES

TABLE

ACKNOWLEDGMENTS

Earlier versions of the essays published in this volume were presented at a workshop held at the University of California, Santa Barbara on 27–28 February 2015. Erika Imada and Kimio Itō gave two additional papers that could not be included here but have been published in Japanese.[1] We would like to extend special thanks to Machida Kumi who agreed to a panel discussion about her art, much of which features childlike figures. Jennifer Robertson and Dick Hebdige made this component of the event most interesting.[2]

We are grateful for the generous support of the Japan Society for the Promotion of Science, the main sponsor of the conference and, with Sabine Frühstück, its co-organizer. Also essential were the support of the Society for the History of Children and Youth, the Division of Humanities and Fine Arts, and the Division of Social Sciences at the University of California, Santa Barbara. We are also delighted to acknowledge the generosity and enthusiasm with which the following academic units at UCSB supported the event: Interdisciplinary Humanities Center, East Asian Center, and the departments of Art, East Asian Languages and Cultural Studies, History, Sociology, and Anthropology. We couldn't have done it without our brilliant conference assistant, Dr. Silke Werth, the unwavering support of Japanese language instructors Akiyo Cantrell and Yoko Yamauchi, and the dedicated interpreters, sound and visual technicians, and mini-crisis managers we found in graduate students Cade Bourne, Erika I-Tremblay, Ema Parker, Christoph Reichenbächer, Emily B. Simpson, and Kai Wasson.

We acknowledge our gratitude to Machida Kumi for allowing us to use her work "Relations" (2006) for the cover of the book. A contribution by the Dean of Humanities and Fine Arts and an Open Access Fund at UCSB, as well as support from University of California, Irvine, Humanities Commons, home of coeditor Anne Walthall, made this publication possible. As always we owe a debt of gratitude to Reed Malcolm for his interest and enthusiasm, Caroline Knapp for her brilliant copyediting, and Zuha Khan for expertly ushering the manuscript through the production process.

NOTES

1. Slightly modified versions of both papers have been published in Japanese. Imada's is included in *Sekushuariti no sengo-shi: Henyō suru shinmitsuken kōkyōken,* ed. Koyama Shizuko, Akaeda Kanako, and Imada Erika (Kyōto: Kyōto Daigaku Gakujutsu Shuppankai, 2014). Itō's can be found in *Dansei no hibōryoku senden—howaito ribon kyanpēn,* ed. Taga Futoshi, Itō Kimio, and Andō Tetsuya (Tokyo: Iwanami Shoten, 2015).

2. In 2016, Machida's work was exhibited at Asia House (London), the National Art Center (Tokyo), Ohara Museum of Art (Kurashiki), and the Museum of Contemporary Art Tokyo.

Introduction

In September 2016, the Twitter hashtag "*Tsukamotoyochien*" attracted a series of comments on the practices of the Tsukamoto kindergarten, where three- to five-year-olds are educated "according to prewar ideals" (Ha 2016). Apparently, the pupils at the kindergarten are taught to recite the Imperial Rescript on Education (1890) and to bow to the Shōwa emperor's (r. 1926–1989) photograph in the hallways; they are also routinely taken to military bases—all with the explicit aim of preparing them to "protect their nation against potential threats from other countries." One tweet pronounced Japan's democracy to be dying. Another expressed concern that these children were being groomed for direct recruitment into the Self-Defense Forces. Many other comments highlighted a new urgency surrounding issues of children's education and their relationship to the nation-state, all the while commenting on how "sweet," "innocent," and "pitiful" these kindergarteners were.

Since the early 1980s, Japanese media have teemed with intense debates about bullying at schools, child poverty, child suicides, violent crimes committed by children, the rise of socially withdrawn youngsters, and, most recently, forceful moves by the Abe Shinzō administration to introduce a decisively more conservative educational curriculum (Ogi 2013). While the Twitter storm mentioned above was partly informed by Japan's widely noted right turn, signified in part by the introduction of new security legislation, it also speaks to issues debated in global conversations about the nature of children and how to raise them, the forces and pressures impinging on children, the rights that should be accorded to them, and the responsibilities with which they should be entrusted (Cunningham 1998: 1195; Arai 2016).

1

Emotions often erupt when the topic of children is discussed, particularly when further provocations are added to the mix. Across a range of media, in Japan and around the world, current debates reflect and fuel concerns about whether, for instance, children lend themselves particularly easily to the "politics of distraction" (Arai 2016); children are merely "born to buy" (Schor 2005); or, indeed, whether "babies [have come to] rule the world" (Dubinsky 2012: 7). Another set of key questions oscillates along a continuum of concern: why children don't want to grow up (Miller and Bardsley 2005; Kinsella 2013; Cross 2010), whether childhood has dramatically changed to the degree of being irrevocably lost (Field 1995; Fass 2016), or whether the loss is not just that of childhood but, due to an unprecedented demographic crisis, the loss of Japanese children themselves.

THE HISTORY OF CHILDREN AND CHILDHOOD

Since the time of its 1960 publication, Philippe Ariès's *L'Enfant et la vie familiale sous l'ancien regime* and its several subsequent translations have been a touchstone for historians of childhood. Within the discussions the book inspired, one (mis) reading of Aries's "discovery of childhood" was frequently reproduced: that there had been a particular moment at which that discovery occurred. Challenging that interpretation, Michael Kinski (Kinski, Salomon, and Grossmann 2015: 24–25) proposed that the "discovery of childhood" signifies no more (or less) than the dissolution of "the child" and "childhood" as natural and unquestioned things, and challenged us to identify and examine the sites and moments in Japanese history where and when children were thought of, described, and represented as both distinguishable and distinguished from adults. As the chapters in this volume will make apparent, the further back in history one reaches, the harder that moment is to pinpoint. It is the more difficult precisely because the moderns insisted so vehemently on *their* discovery of childhood. In fact Stefan Tanaka goes so far as to argue that childhood has become a significant symbol or a metaphor for processes inherent to the modern nation-state. In his discussion, the child, children, and childhood become abstractions through which to think about the state's imposition of responsible citizenship on the Japanese people (1997, 2004). In addition, contemporary policymakers, educators, and others worry that true childhood has been lost, and that the conditions under which it supposedly flourished need to be resurrected.

That said, thus far the historiography and ethnography of children and childhood have remained heavily tilted toward the Euro-American sphere. With respect to the historiography of children and childhood in Asia, our fellow scholars in China and Korea studies have begun to overcome this limitation.[1] Together with a formidable body of scholarship in Japanese (Moriyama and Nakae 2002 and others cited below), the Western-language Japan field has produced a handful of pioneering works, almost all firmly situated in modern/contemporary times. Among them are Kathleen Uno's *Passages to Modernity: Motherhood, Childhood, and Social Reform in Twentieth-Century Japan* (1999); David R. Ambaras's *Bad Youth: Juvenile Delinquency and the Politics of Everyday Life in Modern Japan* (2005); Mark Jones's *Children as Treasures: Childhood and the Middle Class in Early Twentieth-Century Japan* (2010); and, more recently, Andrea Arai's *The Strange Child: Education and the Psychology of Patriotism in Recessionary Japan* (2016). Two recent issues of *Japan Forum*—"Geographies of Childhood: Japanese Versions of Global Children's Culture" (2006, issue 1, guest ed. Alissa Freedman) and "Children, Education, and Media in Japan and Its Empire" (2016, issue 1, guest ed. Peter Cave)—further demonstrate an emerging field of inquiry. Thus far, the lone exception to the modern/contemporary bias is the volume *Kindheit in der japanischen Geschichte / Childhood in Japanese History* (2015), which was edited by Michael Kinski, Harald Salomon, and Eike Grossman and written partly in German and partly in English. Charting the history and historiography of childhood in Japan from the Heian (794–1185) to the Heisei era (1989 to the present), the book highlights the wide spectrum of case studies that demonstrate the preoccupation of Japan scholars with children and childhood during the modern/contemporary periods.

With this book we strive to broaden the disciplinary frame of the debate on children and childhood, not least by assembling the views of scholars in the fields of history, anthropology, religion, film, and cultural studies. Throughout these essays, we also make two interventions. First, we comb prior periods of Japanese history, seeking the feelings and disciplines to which children were subjected in order to highlight modes and conventions of distinguishing children from adults in ways that differ from modern and contemporary preoccupations. And second, we tie the study of children and childhood to analyses of emotions, affects, and sensibilities.

Regarding the first intervention—the historical and anthropological breadth of this volume—we track children's footprints in medieval monasteries and early modern samurai households, inquire about their memories of child's play during war and peace, listen to their quests for family in child welfare institutions, observe them in kindergartens for autistic children, and quietly cheer for them on soccer fields. Taking such a *longue durée* approach introduces unique challenges with regard to the source bases of our analyses. Our explorations—some traveling far into the early modern past—are made possible by both reading and reading between the lines of letters, diaries, memoirs, family and household records, and religious polemics about promising, rambunctious, sickly, happy, and dutiful youngsters. The literature by people writing about themselves, including their own childhoods and those of their children and grandchildren, constitutes a particularly abundant source.

The further back into the historical record we delve, the more limited is our access. It is worth noting that it was monks, not family members, who first found it necessary to call attention to children in the aggregate in admonitory texts.

While children are not absent from medieval accounts, they by no means appear as frequently or figure as prominently as they do today. They appear most often in literary accounts, often in ways that expose the workings of the gods in human affairs, sometimes taking on unexpected roles or performing superhuman deeds. In early modern Japan, the publishing industry started producing textbooks and childrearing manuals, woodblock prints and fiction that took children as their themes. Letters and diaries too get us much closer to childhood experiences than ever before. Nonetheless, it is only in modern Japan that magazines for children appear and writings by children survive. Sometimes, representations of children in discourse and film are as close as we can get to comprehending either their experience or how adults might have viewed them at the time, be that as burdensome or useful, or as worthy of love, care, education, reform, or control.

Another difficulty in accessing children's genuine responses to their worlds derives from the source materials themselves, which can embed true expression in the demands of educational institutions, social norms, and the molding power of certain forms of expression. For example, consider school essays and diary entries that children knew would be read by their teachers—and possibly by their parents as well. Of course there is danger in taking such writings as unmediated expressions of their authors' intentions; and yet, it is also true that such expressions do not actually exist. Even if they were made, they were never recorded—or were not preserved in historical documents. Efforts to gain a comprehensive understanding of the young writers' true experience can be additionally limited by the fact that the ethics of fieldwork currently restrict scholars' communication with children (Robertson 2009). Regardless of these methodological and ethical problems, some contributors in this collection have aimed to bring out children's voices. Collectively, we hope that this volume will be followed by many more concerning children and childhood in non-Western parts of the world and in Japan more specifically.

WHEN IS A CHILD A CHILD?

A history of children and childhood must begin with the question "When is a child a child?" But we could focus our discussion even further by asking, for greater specificity: "At what point does a baby become a child?" "At what point does childhood end?" "When childhood does end, does the child become an adolescent or an adult?" And what of the answers? Even they inspire additional questions. The famous folklorist Yanagita Kunio popularized the notion that in traditional Japan, people believed that children belonged to the gods until age seven—and therefore it behooved parents to not get too attached to them. Historians such as Shibata Jun have argued that Yanagita created this notion, as they can find no evidence for it in the historical record (Shibata 2013; Tanigawa 1996; Kinski, Salomon, and Grossmann 2015). Instead the importance of age seven is that it marks the dividing line between the immature child, who is kept close to home, and the more mature child, who is sent out to school, to work, to play. Also, it is worth noting that the *seven* being referred to is not the Western *seven* but the old Japanese *seven*. If a child is one year old *(sai)* at birth and turns an additional year old at each subsequent new year, then the "seven-year-old" discussed by Yanagita is approximately five or six Western years old.

The question of the age-defined parameters of childhood is particularly fraught for earlier periods. For example, the paucity of viable sources limits the conversations we can have about children before the Edo period (1600–1868). In his chapter, "Nasty Boys or Obedient Children? Childhood and Relative Autonomy in Medieval Japanese Monasteries," Or Porath addresses this difficulty by examining negotiations over what constituted a "child" in religious texts that centered on "children's" behavioral flaws. The Edo period is the setting for two chapters—Luke S. Roberts's "Growing Up Manly: Male Samurai Childhood in Late Edo-Era Tosa" and Anne Walthall's "For the Love of Children: Practice, Affect, and Subjectivities in Hirata Atsutane's Household"—that question our modern assumption that age is the first determinant in defining a child. Both historians propose that age was fungible, that the "end of childhood" for samurai boys and girls varied greatly. Roberts alludes to a trend that finds its exact opposite in the twenty-first century: at the beginning of the nineteenth century, in an effort to mark their sons' social status ever earlier in life and to extend adulthood ever deeper into childhood, young samurai boys were made to wear two swords as markers of adulthood.

From such early modern perspectives, a number of contributors thus question both the modern understanding of the "natural age" of the child and the equally taken-for-granted progression from child to adult through more or less clearly delineated stages. Instead, they propose that the rules of delineation and how these were defined—and, in some cases, defied—have differed dramatically. In some eras, occupational and social status, not age or not age alone, determined what most constituted the boundaries of the child (see also Kawahara 1997). And what of adolescence? Some of the authors in this volume pursue evidence for childhood into the teenage years, suggesting that the boundaries for defining childhood are porous.

Yet another question: How did children learn to be children? Although the documentation is scanty for medieval Japan, it seems likely that, in the monks' eyes, boys learned how to misbehave from other boys. And we should not forget the violence that pervaded seventeenth-century boys' books at a time when the outré behavior they celebrated was already in the past (Kimbrough 2015). Different documents shed different light on this question. W. Puck Brecher (2015) has analyzed images of commoner schoolchildren in late eighteenth- and early nineteenth-century Japan that depict them making faces behind the teacher's back, chatting, and playing games rather than studying (see also Williams 2012). He reads other sources for examples of children's pranks and mock battles—in which though the fighting was pretend the injuries could be all too real. In such games, violence was never far beneath the surface. And since, in his eyes, "childrearing among commoners was intentionally hands-off" (97), the result was that many children got hurt.

Other historians disagree with this "hands-off" assessment, at least for some eras and social statuses. Shibata Jun argues that over the course of Japan's long history an important change emerged in the relationship between adults and children. In medieval Japan, children were essentially ignored, left to grow up on their own. But in the late seventeenth century, the custom of educating children began to spread. By the turn of the eighteenth century, commoner households had become stabilized and their continuity became possible. The famous educator Kaibara Ekiken stated that children are treasures above all else, a belief that pervaded most parts of Japan by the late nineteenth century. And even though scholars of Tokugawa Japan urged parents not to dote on their children, but to raise them with due regard for the future, accounts by foreigners just before and after the fall of the Tokugawa shogunate in 1867 considered Japan a paradise for children, noting how the Japanese neither scolded nor chastised their progeny (Shibata 2013). Not surprisingly, child abuse, of which there was a considerable amount, remained hidden from them as it does from most contemporary Japanese (Mishima 2005).

At the beginning of the twentieth century, we find a new approach to the question of what constitutes a child and how children should be treated. Thanks to advancements in pedagogy, psychology, and medicine, as well as the successes of modern nation-state building, the child became increasingly recognized and embraced as a creature different from the adult. This recognition subsequently set into motion the ongoing tendency to extend childhood as long and as deeply as possible into what used to be considered adulthood. This development in turn brought about the aforementioned emphasis on adolescence as being an essential transition period from child to adult.

In the 1910s and 1920s a range of literary figures, intellectuals, scholars, educators, and reporters proclaimed the child as inherently innocent, and thus demanded and wrote children's literature, founded children's magazines, invented children's toys, and imported (and then produced in Japan) children's clothes that furthered this stance.[2] Yuan Xu devoted an entire book to the study of prewar children's comics printed in newspapers (2013). Koresawa Hiroaki did the same for modern educational toys (2009). In her chapter, "Consumer Consumption for Children: Conceptions of Childhood in the Work of Taishō-Period Designers," Jinnō Yuki describes the role of the child and childhood within the flourishing new culture of urban consumption, a theme she has developed at greater length in her book on children and the material culture of modern consumer goods (2011).

Given the unavoidably partial nature of all records, another question we ask is: Why not observe children at play? Monks of the medieval period (1185–1600) looked upon play with scorn: in their view, acolytes played too hard and too often. Throughout the Edo period (1603–1868), the play of children was rarely noted in diaries written by adults—though they did report gifts of toys that suggest play was encouraged, even if it was deemed not worthy of mention. In the early twentieth century, it was necessary to observe children at play, since unsupervised play could be physically and ideologically risky if children subverted the messages they were taught at school. In a range of documents, play was dismissed as an impediment to children's maturation, exploited as preparation for war, or even embraced as an "arena of propaganda" (Kushner 2009: 245).

Institutionalized child play today contrasts dramatically with that of earlier times. Child play in religious and educational institutions, for instance—never trivial, always ambiguous (Sutton-Smith 1997)—is open to adult direction and indoctrination, and yet it is also a site of (perpetual) child resistance and self-reinvention. And so several contributors have examined sociocultural norms that govern a wide range of children's experiences—as well as how they are reproduced, challenged, and modified within institutions designated for childhood education. Elise Edwards's chapter, "From Grade Schooler to Great Star: Childhood Development and the 'Golden Age' in the World of Japanese Soccer," steps into one of the many centers of contemporary negotiations about both how child players might eventually morph into adult workers and how proper play at the right age might produce competitive adult players on the soccer field. Play and games, together with affect and emotion, are essential to the reproduction of the norms that other institutions adhere to as well. They are promoted and performed in the child welfare institution that Kathryn E. Goldfarb analyzes in her essay "Food, Affect, and Experiments in Care: Constituting a 'Household-like' Child Welfare Institution in Japan"; they are also central to the educational and therapeutic efforts that preschools for autistic children engage in, as Junko Teruyama describes in her chapter, "Treatment and Intervention for Children with Developmental Disabilities."

CHILDHOOD AND THE STUDY OF EMOTIONS

In this collection we have viewed the study of children and childhood through a second lens as well. We aim to provide readers with opportunities to engage with the affective education, management, and exploitation of children across different centuries and institutions; to, as it were, put themselves in the shoes of a medieval monk, an early modern samurai grandmother, a mobilized citizen during the Asia-Pacific War, or a victim-critic of nuclear policy in twenty-first century Japan. In so doing, readers can get even closer to historically specific meanings of childhood while also appreciating a twin difficulty that is central to analyses of both childhood and emotions: the assumption of their naturalness and their fleeting quality. Even within the same individual, emotions change over time. And, no matter where and when, the child is a liminal figure who moves in and out of her/his own work and that of adults.

In 1943, Lucien Febvre proclaimed that one could not fully comprehend a period of history without taking into account the emotional character of workaday existence in that period, a standpoint that has been renewed and transformed many times since.[3] Around the new millennium, a new interest in the study of emotions emerged, manifested, for example, in Ute Frevert's monumental project at the Center for the History of Emotions within the Max Planck Institute for Human Development in Berlin. The two fields of inquiry—the history of childhood and the history of emotions—became explicitly intertwined in the United States when Peter N. Stearns and Timothy Haggerty (1991) described the role of fear and transitions in American "emotional standards for children" in the wake of Stearns's (1985) proclamation of "emotionology" as a new field of inquiry, and their study was advanced by the foundation of the Society for the History of Children and Youth in 2001. Subsequently, challenging the modern bias of "emotionology" that aims to identify emotional standards across American society, Barbara H. Rosenwein (2002, 2007, 2015), by contrast, has coined the notion of "emotional communities." In this volume, we aim to answer her call for "new narratives that recognize various emotional styles, emotional communities, emotional outlets, and emotional restraints in *every* period," for narratives that "consider how and why these have changed over time."

This volume engages the new history of emotions, particularly children's emotions and emotions that are directed at children, whether by other children or by adults. Our interests parallel those of a growing group of historians around Ute Frevert, a key pioneer in the field, who have examined the various paths, strategies, and conventions that mold the ways children have "[learned] how to feel" (Eitler, Olson, and Jensen 2014; Frevert and Wulf 2012; Frevert 2011).[4]

The studies in this collection address how individual children expressed, managed, and were taken by surprise by their emotions—while also inquiring how ordinary adults, families, media, and other institutions, in aiming to shape how children learned, felt, and formed adult personae, exploited emotions associated with children and childhood for various political goals. Can such expressions ever be simply personal and biographical and *not* at the same time social and cultural? What of those displays of emotion that can be *either* genuine *or* feigned? When people broadcast emotion to the world is it an expression of their internal state? Or is it contrived in order to fulfill social expectations? It might seem that our attention to the senses inevitably leads to children, whose experiences and expressions have often struck adult observers as less mediated, more natural, and more uninhibited by the norms of language (Eustace et al. 2012). After all, one of our key challenges is getting direct information from children themselves rather than relying on adult perceptions, recommendations, and adult-created artifacts.

In this field, too, the existing body of research regarding things Japanese is distinctly modest. As much as the stoic suppression of emotion is widely associated with Japanese culture in the broadest terms, we know little about even the ritualized expression of emotion in religious contexts—and we know next to nil about emotions related to or expressed by children (Ebersole 1989, 2000, 2004; Bolitho 2003). For instance, Walthall finds that, though samurai grandparents might be well aware of the necessity of controlling their feelings as one of their class's key conventions, their training did not keep them from writing of the tears they shed over missing their grandchildren. The concept of loving children, something that today feels uncomplicated, was previously often tied with status and the future of a household, feared as a weakness (particularly in men), and yet expressed in letters and diaries. The language of love among children, according to Roberts, was freely used when boys were in love with each other, but not in heterosexual constellations. Only in the modern period was the love of children contemplated as a natural bond that connected children to their parents—to their mothers in particular—while also rendering loving mothers politically and legally powerless (Burns 2014).

And yet, the child's symbolic value increased to become hyper-visible as a figure that represents humanity and modernity, as Tanaka proposes for childhood more generally (1997). Harald Salomon argues as much in his chapter, "'Children in the Wind': Examining the Golden Age of Childhood Film in Wartime Japan." At the same time, perhaps more than during any other time in the twentieth century, children became political actors—or, at least, were exploited as such; this is the proposition of both Koresawa Hiroaki, in a chapter titled "Children and the Founding of Manchukuo: The Young Girl Ambassadors as Promoters of Friendship" and Sabine Frühstück in "'And my heart screams': Children and the War of Emotions." Frühstück then carries her analysis into the postwar period. Yet even during the 1930s and 1940s children continued to embody remnants of human wildness and antimodernity, resisted adult supervision and control, and did not assume their place in society without a fight or, at least, vivid expressions of resentment, according to Aaron William Moore in "Reversing the Gaze: The Construction of 'Adulthood' in the Wartime Diaries of Japanese Children and Youth."

Similarly, in "Outdoor Play in Wartime Japan," L. Halliday Piel finds that aging adults who were children of the Asia-Pacific War remember the joys of outdoor play as children of any time might—despite ever-present fear and sorrow and anguish concerning death and the possibility of death. Piel's findings also highlight that, though children prior to the modern period frequently experienced the death of young siblings, we know next to nothing about their emotional responses to those experiences—other than through the recollections of adults (Childs 1991).

Norma Field has aptly noted how, during the Asia-Pacific War, the notion that children were children to their parents and "little citizens" of the empire, at the same time that their parents were "children" of the emperor father figure, symbolized "an obliteration of childhood through its universalization" (1995: 66; see also Yamanaka 2002). But what about the encouragement "to think and feel like a child" in the anti-nuclear movement of the twenty-first century, as Noriko Manabe asks in her essay, "Monju-kun: Children's Culture as Protest." Worth noting as well is that this important symbol of winsome suffering is gendered male, which leads us to Imada Erika's (2003) insights on what it means when children's gender is left unspecified. One consequence is that boys come to the fore, whether the discussion is of impressing human emotions on nuclear power plants or of rallying the children of China, Manchukuo, and Korea to the Japanese cause, as in prewar propaganda. Perhaps the modern propensity to assume that children's expressions, sentimentality, and emotionality are "natural" is precisely why they are easily exploited for political effect.

Defining the boundaries of "childhood" is an ongoing project, one that is continuously modulated by entrepreneurs of children's products, scholars, and educational, legal, and political institutions, as well as by children themselves. Within these modulating definitions, two angles remain front and center: the assumed inherent innocence of the child, and the adult will to exploit the versatility of the child in the service of a range of problems and positions. Within this process, no matter how much adults strive to sympathize with the child, the delineation between children and adults increases all the more. As such, all inquiries about children's experiences necessitate an unbiased examination of the ways that children's emotional lives have been appropriated as ideological and symbolic manifestations of power.

. . .

The diverse essays in this volume—which for the most part cluster around certain periods, in particular the second half of the Tokugawa period, wartime Japan, and the present—are presented chronologically. We begin with three essays that move from Buddhist monasteries in medieval Japan to the multigenerational homes of samurai families in the early modern period. Covering the early twentieth century, another set of essays sheds light on how interior design, film, and the efforts of what we might call "soft power colonization" have envisioned children. Under the specter of the Asia-Pacific War, diaries and children's books and magazines provide clues about how children envisioned adulthood, how they played, and how their "emotional capital" became a concept that survived both war and defeat. Finally, speaking to the concerns of contemporary Japan are four essays that center on play and discipline, norms, and, again, the political uses of not quite "the child" but the remnants of the modern conception of "the child": innocence, harmlessness, and vulnerability. In thus traversing this collection through the chronologic lens, the reader is able to spend time in different emotional communities at work in the same historical moment, in and outside different institutional frameworks and constraints, and across a range of textual records—all with the aim of getting as close as possible to the multifaceted, elusive and changing natures of children and childhood.

NOTES

1. Key works include those by Anne Behnke Kinney (2004), Ping-Chen Hsiung (2005), Vanessa R. Sasson (2013), Orna Naftali (2014, 2016), David M. Promfit (2015), and Dafna Zur (2017).

2. Kristin Holly Williams (2012) has recently suggested that not only were children much more often represented in Edo-period pictures than previously thought, there were also books written for them.

3. More often than not memories of one's childhood are saturated with sensual impressions. They have been the object of study in the longstanding history of the senses and have reemerged within the new history of emotions (Jay 2011; Flint 2014; Reddy 2001). They are loosely intertwined with the history of the senses once contemplated by such thinkers as Lucien Febvre (1938, 1941) and Michel Serres (1985) and more recently charted by Alain Corbin (2005).

4. The journal *Passions in Context: International Journal for the History and Theory of Emotions* emerged from the increased attention to the study of emotions in a wide variety of disciplines including anthropology, history, sociology, political science, legal theory, criminology, economics, cultural studies, and media studies as well as literature.

BIBLIOGRAPHY

Note: Unless noted otherwise the place of publication for Japanese books is Tokyo.

Ambaras, David. 2005. *Bad Youth: Juvenile Delinquency and the Politics of Everyday Life in Modern Japan.* Berkeley: University of California Press.

Arai, Andrea. 2016. *The Strange Child: Education and the Psychology of Patriotism in Recessionary Japan.* Stanford, CA: Stanford University Press.

Bolitho, Harold. 2003. *Bereavement and Consolation: Testimonies from Tokugawa.* New Haven, CT: Yale University Press.

Brecher, W. Puck. 2015. "Being a Brat: The Ethics of Child Disobedience in the Edo period." In *Values, Identity, and Equality in Eighteenth- and Nineteenth-Century Japan,* ed. Peter Nosco, James E. Ketelaar, Yasunori Kojima, 80–109. Leiden: Brill.

Burns, Susan L. 2014. "Introduction." In *Gender and Law in the Japanese Imperium,* ed. Susan L. Burns and Barbara J. Brooks, 1–19. Honolulu: University of Hawai'i Press.

Childs, Margaret Helen. 1991. *Rethinking Sorrow: Revelatory Tales of Late Medieval Japan.* Ann Arbor: Center for Japanese Studies, University of Michigan.

Corbin, Alain. 2005. "Charting the Cultural History of the Senses." In *Empire of the Senses: The Sensual Culture Reader,* ed. David Howes, 128–46. London: Bloomsbury.

Cross, Gary. 2010. *Men to Boys: The Making of Modern Immaturity.* New York: Columbia University Press.

Cunningham, Hugh. 1998. "Review Essay: Histories of Childhood." *American Historical Review* 103(4): 1195–1208.

Dubinsky, Karen. 2012. "Children, Ideology, and Iconography: How Babies Rule the World." *Journal of the History of Childhood and Youth* 5(1): 5–13.

Ebersole, Gary L. 1989. *Ritual Poetry and the Politics of Death in Early Japan.* Princeton, NJ: Princeton University Press.

———. 2000. "The Function of Ritual Weeping Revisited: Affective Expression and Moral Discourse." *History of Religions* 39, no. 3 (February 2000): 211–46.

———. 2004. "The Poetics and Politics of Ritualized Weeping in Early and Medieval Japan." In *Holy Tears: Weeping in the Religious Imagination,* ed. Jon Hawley and Kimberley Patton, 25–51. Princeton, NJ: Princeton University Press.

Eitler, Pascal, Stephanie Olsen, and Uffa Jensen. 2014. "Introduction." In *Learning How to Feel: Children's Literature and Emotional Socialization, 1870–1970,* ed. Ute Frevert et. al., 1–20. Oxford: Oxford University Press.

Eustace, Nicole, Eugenia Lean, Julie Livingstone, Jan Plamper, William M. Reddy, and Barbara Rosenwein. 2012. "AHR Conversation: The Historical Study of Emotions." *American Historical Review* 117(5): 1487–1531.

Fass, Paula. 2016. *The End of American Childhood: A History of Parenting from Life on the Frontier to the Managed Child.* Princeton, NJ: Princeton University Press.

Febvre, Lucien. 1938. "Psychologie et histoire," *Encyclopédie francaise,* vol. 8, *La vie mentale.* Paris: Société de gestion de l'Encyclopédie francaise.

———. 1941. "La sensibilité et l'histoire: Comment reconstituer la vie affective d'autrefois?" *Annales d'histoire sociale* 3, no. 1/2: 5–20.

Field, Norma. 1995. "The Child as Laborer and Consumer: The Disappearance of Childhood in Contemporary Japan." In *Children and the Politics of Culture,* ed. S. Stephens, 51–79. Princeton, NJ: Princeton University Press.

Flint, Kate. 2014. "The Social Life of the Senses: The Assaults and Seductions of Modernity." In *The Cultural History of the Senses: In the Age of Empire,* ed. Constance Classen, 25–45. London: Bloomsbury.

Frevert, Ute. 2011. *Emotions in History: Lost and Found.* Budapest: Central European University Press.

Frevert, Ute, and Christoph Wulf. 2012. "Die Bildung der Gefühle." *Zeitschrift für Erziehungswissenschaft* 16: 1–10.

Frevert, Ute, et al. 2014. *Learning How to Feel: Children's Literature and Emotional Socialization, 1870–1970.* Oxford: Oxford University Press.

Ha, Kwiyeon. 2016. "Japanese Kindergarten Teaches Students Pre-war Ideals." *Reuters,* 8 December. www.reuters.com/article/us-japan-education-idUSKBN13X1UV.

Hamilton, Walter. 2013. *Children of the Occupation: Japan's Untold Story.* New Brunswick, NJ: Rutgers University Press.

Hsiung, Ping-Chen. 2005. *A Tender Voyage: Children and Vhildhood in Late Imperial China.* Stanford, CA: Stanford University Press.

Imada Erika. 2003. "Jendā-ka sareru 'kodomo'" [Gendered 'children']. *Soshioroji* 48(1): 57–74.

Jay, Martin. 2011. "In the Realm of the Senses: An Introduction." *American Historical Review* 116(2): 307–15.

Jinnō Yuki. 2011. *Kodomo o meguru desain to kindai: Kakudai suru shōhin sekai* [Design for children and modernity: The expanding world of goods]. Kyōto: Sekai Shisō-sha.

Jones, Mark. 2010. *Children as Treasures: Childhood and the Middle Class in Early Twentieth-Century Japan.* Cambridge, MA: Harvard University Asia Center.

Kawahara Kazue. 1997. *Kodomokan no kindai* [The modern view of childhood]. Chūō Kōron Shinsha.

Kimbrough, R. Keller. 2015. "Bloody Hell! Reading Boys' Books in Seventeenth-Century Japan." *Asian Ethnology* 74(1): 133–61.

Kinney, Anne Behnke. 2004. *Representations of Childhood and Youth in Early China*. Stanford, CA: Stanford University Press.

Kinsella, Sharon. 2013. *Schoolgirls, Money and Rebellion in Japan*. London: Routledge.

Kinski, Michael, Harald Salomon, and Eike Grossmann, eds. 2016. *Kindheit in der japanischen Geschichte / Childhood in Japanese history*. Wiesbaden: Otto Harrassowitz.

Koresawa Hiroaki. 2009. *Kyōiku gangu no kindai: Kyōiku taishō toshite no kodomo no tanjō* [Modern educational toys: The birth of the child as an educational phenomenon]. Nara: Bunkyōdō.

Kushner, Barak. 2009. "Planes, Trains and Games: Selling Japan's War in Asia." In *Looking Modern: East Asian Visual Culture from Treaty Ports to World War II*, ed. Jennifer Purtle and Hans Bjarne Thomson, 243–64. Chicago: Center for the Art of East Asia, Art Media Resources.

Miller, Laura, and Jan Bardsley. 2005. *Bad Girls of Japan*. New York: Palgrave MacMillan.

Mishima Akiko. 2005. *Jidō gyakutai to dōbutsu gyakutai* [Child abuse and animal abuse]. Seikyūsha.

Moriyama Shigeki and Nakae Kazue. 2002. *Nihon kodomo-shi* [A history of children in Japan]. Heibonsha.

Naftali, Orna. 2014. *Children, Rights and Modernity in China: Raising Self-Governing Citizens*. Studies in Childhood and Youth. New York: Palgrave Macmillan.

———. 2016. *Children in China*. Cambridge: Polity Press.

Ogi Naoki. 2013 (2000). *Kodomo no kiki o dō miru ka* [How to view the child crisis]. Iwanami.

Promfit, David M. 2015. *Youth and Empire: Trans-colonial Childhoods in British and French Asia*. Stanford, CA: Stanford University Press.

Reddy, William M. 2001. *The Navigation of Feeling: A Framework for the History of Emotions*. Cambridge: Cambridge University Press.

Robertson, Jennifer, ed. 2009. *Politics and Pitfalls of Japan Ethnography: Reflexivity, Responsibility, and Anthropological Ethics*. London: Routledge.

Rosenwein, Barbara. 2002. "Worrying about Emotions in History." *American Historical Review* 107(3): 821–45.

———. 2007. *Emotional Communities in the Early Middle Ages*. Ithaca, NY: Cornell University Press.

———. 2015. *Generations of Feeling: A History of Emotions, 1600–1700*. Cambridge: Cambridge University Press.

Sasson, Vanessa R. 2013. *Little Buddhas: Children and Childhoods in Buddhist Texts and Traditions*. Oxford: Oxford University Press.

Schor, Juliet B. 2005. *Born to Buy: The Commercialized Child and the New Consumer Culture*. New York: Scribner.

Serres, Michel. 1985. *Les cinq sens*. Paris: B. Grasset.

Shibata Jun. 2013. *Nihon yōji-shi: Kodomo e no manazashi* [A history of Japanese children]. Yoshikawa Kōbunkan.

Stearns, Peter N. 1985. "Emotionology: Clarifying the History of Emotions and Emotional Standards." *American Historical Review* 90, no. 4 (Oct. 1985): 813–36.

Stearns, Peter N., and Timothy Haggerty. 1991. "The Role of Fear: Transitions in American Emotional Standards for Children, 1850–1950." *American Historical Review* 96, no. 1 (Feb. 1991): 63–94.

Sutton-Smith, Brian. 1997. *The Ambiguity of Play.* Cambridge, MA: Harvard University Press.

Tanaka, Stefan. 1997. "Childhood: Naturalization of Development into a Japanese Space." In *Cultures of Scholarship,* ed. S. C. Humphreys, 21–56. Ann Arbor: University of Michigan Press.

———. 2004. *New Times in Modern Japan.* Princeton: Princeton University Press.

Tanigawa Kenichi. 1996. *Nihon minzoku bunka shiryō shūssei dai 24-ken: Kodomo no minzoku-shi* [Collection of sources on Japan's folklore culture, vol. 24: Children's folklore]. Sanichi Shobō.

Uno, Kathleen. *Passages to Modernity: Motherhood, Childhood, and Social Reform in Twentieth-Century Japan.* Honolulu: University of Hawaii Press, 1999.

Williams, Kristin Holly. 2012. "Visualizing the Child: Japanese Children's Literature in the Age of Woodblock Print, 1678–1888." Ph.D dissertation, East Asian Languages and Civilizations, Harvard University.

Xu Yuan. 2013. *Nihon ni okeru shinbun rensai kodomo manga no senzen-shi* [A prewar history of children's comics printed in Japanese newspapers]. Duan.

Yamanaka Hisashi. 2002. *Kodomo ga shokokumin to iwareta koro* [When children were called "little citizens"]. Asahi Shinbunsha.

Zur, Dafna. 2017. *Figuring Korean Futures: Writing the Child-Heart in Modern Korea.* Stanford, CA: Stanford University Press.

PART ONE

Premodern Period

Nasty Boys or Obedient Children?

Childhood and Relative Autonomy in Medieval Japanese Monasteries

Or Porath

The aim of this chapter is to explore how children in Buddhist monasteries have been construed and to make sense of the conceptual boundaries of the male child in medieval Japan (twelfth to sixteenth centuries). The *chigo* and *dōji* were representative figures of child monastics. The former is often defined by scholars as a young assistant involved in sexual affairs with older Buddhist priests, while the latter resonated with the broader imaginary role of children as sacred entities. However, there are important caveats to bear in mind. First, we must consider that the notion of a child in medieval Japan was not determined by biological age but by cultural demands, as we see as well in chapters 2 and 3, which deal with the Edo period. Therefore, some of the male acolytes I discuss would not be considered children by today's standards. Also, even though Buddhist monasteries were not confined to male-male social interaction, the focus of my study will be male children due to their distinctive ontological status in the medieval world.[1] Ultimately, I contend that the child category in medieval Japan was a fluid one, with boundaries dictated by social, occupational, and religious factors. Although its complexity cannot be fully understood through pedagogical materials, such documents reveal porousness in the child's moral restrictions. Though tempered by institutional imperatives and constraints of the monastic environment, the fluidity allowed the child a certain amount of freedom, or what I call "relative autonomy."

By "relative autonomy," I do not mean that acolytes enjoyed "full liberty" or "rights" in monasteries that would have allowed them to exercise what scholars call "agency." Instead, I argue that there was an opportunity for some acolytes to diverge from behavioral norms and reject cultural expectations within the power relations that the monastery imposed.[2] In my definition of relative autonomy, the concept does not rule out corporal punishments or sexual abuses inflicted upon children, nor does it imply that children had control over their fate; rather I posit that within the specific medieval historical context, certain situations permitted children to circumvent regulations and behave as they wished.[3]

Few primary sources exist that shed light on the conceptual category of the child or the issue of a child's autonomy. Also rare are sources regarding power relations between monk and disciple. This is because monks produced texts whereas children had little opportunity for textual expression. Therefore, the only way to examine the concept of children in the medieval era is through texts written by adult monks. This in itself indicates that children were not agents, but rather individuals who attempted to negotiate their freedom when possible while constantly subjected to imaginary manipulation by their superiors. Nonetheless, representations of children in monastic texts reveal much about their behavior. I selected the texts analyzed below because they explicitly describe both the idealized and actual behavior of children in medieval monasteries, including disobedience. The texts present didactic attempts to instill compliance and decorum in acolytes, but they also reveal that novices resisted the establishment and created a space to assert relative autonomy. Monks feared that acolytes would further exercise their ability to ignore monastic injunctions and deviate from the Buddhist curriculum by engaging in nonreligious pursuits that challenged the monastic lifestyle.

The following analysis will examine two didactic and pedagogical texts that provide rationalization for accepting monastic rules. The first, *Instructions for Children* (Dōji-kyō), was written within a Buddhist and Confucian epistemological framework and is falsely attributed to the monk Annen (841–?), an important priest in the Tendai tradition. Similar to other didactic texts, it prescribes and proscribes how acolytes should behave and attempts to impose social order in the monastery by employing Buddho-Confucian concepts while also implying a certain codependence between master and acolyte. The Confucian elements of the texts mostly lionize the teacher (Buddhist priest) and contribute to the overall aggrandizement of the authority of monks. The second text, *Education for Acolytes* (Chigo kyōkun) is attributed to the monk-poet Sōgi (1421–1502) and was written much later than *Instructions,* in the Muromachi period. Here, Sōgi laments the bad behavior of monastic children and implies that children should show moral integrity. The first text establishes the boundaries of proper monastic behavior, but posits an impossible ideal for education when measured against the second. The second text reveals the relative autonomy of unruly acolytes through their disobedience. In other words, *Education* is a magnified and negative evaluation of what the first text would consider a "worst-case scenario," in which children completely ignore monastic injunctions and show their own initiative. Even if this is an overly exaggerated picture of social reality, it exposes a concern that one of the scenarios depicting mischievous boys might come to fruition. Thus, *Education* indicates that some acolytes could, in theory, enjoy a certain amount of freedom.

CHILDREN IN MEDIEVAL JAPANESE MONASTICISM

Within the socio-historical context of monk-acolyte relations in medieval Japan, textual tradition presents a complex array of children that remain unclassified. The monastic environment contained extensive terminology for children, and each child-category can be read using multiple theoretical lenses. This fluidity of the child is evident in a wide corpus of medieval prose, temple records, ritual manuals, and various treatises. In other words, the figure of the *chigo* or *dōji* is always in flux and his image contested by diverse semiological considerations.

In the Middle Ages, temples were the primary locus of children's education, and sources show that pedagogical relations were accompanied by close social inter-action, including various forms of intimacy. For example, in Esoteric Buddhism *(mikkyō)* in both of its Shingon and Tendai varieties, master-disciple relations were a key component in edification, and some religious texts established that intimate affairs, whether sexual or emotional, were conducive to the attainment of rebirth in heaven (Porath 2015). These intimate relations placed the young monas-tic child in a lower social position vis-à-vis the monk, as the "passive" or "violated" partner (Tanaka 1997: 18–23), but there were certain occasions that required egali-tarianism between the two parties, specifically religious initiations. For example, an *abhiṣeka* (Esoteric ritual consecration) in the Tendai tradition, called *kaikanjō* (the Ritual Consecration of Precepts), constituted a rite-of-passage in which stu-dent and master achieved union with Śākyamuni Buddha and the cosmic Bud-dha Many Jewels. In the ritual, master and disciple held hands intimately with the disciple alternating in assuming the role of the teacher (Tanaka 1999: 69). Another *abhiṣeka, Chigo kanjō* (the Ritual Consecration of Acolytes), raised children into the altar to be sexually penetrated so that they could be deified as the bodhisattva Kannon and the Mountain King Avatar (Sannō gongen). While the sexual act can be seen as violent and coercive, it is also evident that the child became socially empowered given the ritual's strong symbolical connection with Emperorship and important divine figures such as Shōtoku Taishi, Kannon, and Sannō (Abe 1984a, 1984b; Matsuoka 1991). This coexistence of egalitarianism and mistreatment also existed within the context of the Buddhist educational episteme, which elevated the status of the Buddhist teacher and attempted to shape the child into a well-behaved individual and socially conformed youth who was positioned bellow his superior, yet cherished as an individual. But where did the acolyte category come from, and what are its conceptual boundaries?

The etymological origin of *chigo* is *chichigo,* a word that means "an infant who sucks from the breast" (Moriyama and Nakae 2002: 13). Thus, the word *chigo* contains the original meaning of "newborn." The word *chigo* first appears in doc-uments from the tenth century, such as *Tale of the Woodcutter* (Taketori monoga-tari, tenth century), *Tale of the Hollow Tree* (Utsuho monogatari, tenth century), and *Japanese Names [for things] Classified and Annotated* (Wamyōshō, 938). In later medieval writings the usage and structure shifted, and infants were clearly seen as preceding the *chigo* category. *Chigo* contains two Chinese characters that denote child, yet the signification was not limited to young children. Instead *Chigo* became a monastic category designating preadult male attendants who performed various chores in temple life. This category included both children and adolescents who attended their superiors and engaged in performances. The *chigo* also partook in important religious activities and the performing arts, and these two fields were not often mutually exclusive. For example, *chigo* sometimes operated as mediators between this world and the other, a kind of a human replacement for the *yorimashi* (a "Shinto" receptacle into which kami descend). In the Child Dancing *(warawa mai)* at Daigoji temple in Kyoto, held as part of the *Sakura-e* ceremony, the *chigo* dancers were possessed by gods and delivered oracles. As noted previously, *chigo* also functioned as sexual partners for adult priests, a point I will expand on shortly. Thus medieval texts attached occupational, religious, and social (including sexual) meanings to the denomination of *chigo*. Rather than simply being biologically determined, the monastic child became a social category and was recognized as a specific rank in the lower stratum of Buddhist society.

However, *chigo* was not the only term used to describe children. As Tsuchiya Megumi demonstrates in her research on social stratification in medieval monastic society, the acolytes were also called *dōji* (child) and *warawa* (child). Tsuchiya conducted a rigorous study on child categories in monastic cloisters *(in* and *bō)* using historical documents in temples such as Daigoji and Ninnaji in Kyoto and elaborates a typology of child monastics as follows: upper-child *(uewarawa)*, middle-child *(chūdōji)*, and great-child *(daidōji)*. The *chūdōji* and *uewarawa* were generally preadult males from the age of twelve to sixteen as Tanaka Takako claims. With regards to *chigo*, the precise boundaries of age are underexplored, but Tanaka concludes (most likely based on Kuroda's general discussion on the boundaries of childhood) that *chigo* are young boys over the age of seven who correspond roughly to adolescents (Tanaka 2004: 15). Tsuchiya shows that *chigo* were children of the *seigake* ministers (officials who could be promoted to the highest position of chancellor). They were also children of administrators *(bōkan)*, bureaucrats who ran the *monzeki* (temples governed by an imperial prince) and came from a noble rank. At the lower echelons, *chigo* were sons of the North Guards *(hokumen)* that served the Retired Emperor *(in)*, as well as children of the warrior elites or samurai. Tsuchiya argues that the *chigo* were roughly parallel to the upper-child rank. For example, according to one extant record from Ninnaji temple, although *chigo* of Ninnaji Omuro were children of administrators, they are also mentioned as performing the role of upper-children in processions. Children who came from families with lower social rank such as North Guards or samurai were able to outrank their fathers as *chigo*, as seen by their relatively loftier position in processions (Tsuchiya 2001). The role of the middle-child (also called *warabe*) was to decorate the processions with his lavish physical appearance (a role that was also shared by *chigo*) and to set the table *(baizen)*.

Nonetheless, the third category of great-children who served as attendants and errands differed significantly from the first two. The *daidōji* denoted an adult male who wore the hairstyle and attire of a monastic child, but modern definitions do not recognize him as a child per se (Tanaka 2004: 9–10). This means that an attendant could, theoretically, wear the hairstyle of a child and live in a state of perpetual childhood. The implication is that they were individuals outside normative social progression. Another category for adults who disguised themselves as a child was *dōjisugata*, who are often depicted in medieval illustrated scrolls or *emaki* (Kuroda 1986). Tsuchiya argues that the representative figure of the "adult-child" phenomenon was the *daidōji*, and contests Kuroda's emphasis on the *dōdōji* (Tsuchiya 2001). The *dōdōji* also served as an attendant and, especially in Buddhist rituals *(daihōe)* and consecrations *(kanjō)*, in the role of delivering flower baskets *(keko)* for flower-scattering. Scholars agree that it is more likely that a superior adult determined the acolyte's fate as an everlasting youth. By becoming a child forever, the *daidōji* could remain in a fixed ontological and social position, but also pay the price of occupying a low social status.

Social background, rank, and age determined an acolyte's social designation in the monastery. For example, the *chigo/dōji* were normally students sent from noble families and warrior elites. The *chūdōji* and *daidōji* were sometimes synonymous with the attendants of low-ranking families, or *sanjo*. The *uewarawa* possessed the most social prestige and were allowed to both serve adult priests in general and study under an individual monk (Tsuchiya 2001). This situation granted easy access to erotic intimacy with the priest (Tanaka 2004). It goes without saying that the age of these different child members determined their physical appearance. Normally, when acolytes reached a certain age (fifteen, seventeen, or eighteen) they underwent a rite of passage called *genbuku* through which they became adults. In this ceremony, they would replace their unlined robe *(hitoe)* or short-sleeved garment *(kosode)* with adult's outfit. Also, their juvenile haircut would be cut and braided, and they would usually be bestowed with a cap. Following this initiation, the new adults would leave the monastic precincts and rejoin their aristocratic or samurai families. Alternatively, they could choose to stay in the monastery, shave their pates, and take the tonsure. According to Tanaka, until the *genbuku*, the acolytes embodied a cultural identity of childhood through their aesthetic appearance—putting on makeup, adorning themselves with exquisite attire, and wearing long hair. In artistic depictions, they are recognizable by their plump faces, groomed eyebrows, and extravagant outfits, all reminiscent of women. Although scholars have also noted the acolytes' alleged androgynous quality and their stylistic proximity to women in the arts (Abe 1998; Tanaka 2004), they were still distinctive in appearance and cannot be simply aligned with femininity. In all of these different categories, children had a set of embodied practices that differed from those of monks and women.

Beyond the embodiment of "quasi-feminine" characteristics, children also possessed a "nonhuman" quality. Some scholars claim the monastic child held a position outside the boundaries of the human hierarchy (Kuroda 1986: 224). Intellectual historian Kuroda Hideo, through analyzing various textual and pictorial sources, posits that in medieval times children were seen as an ontological category distinct from people *(hito)*. According to Kuroda's formulation, medieval society can be divided into four categories: children *(warawa)*, people *(hito)*, monks *(sōryo)*, and outcastes *(hinin)*, which can be distinguished by visual markers. For example, the child usually sports dangling hair, whereas the "person" (adult man) has his hair in a topknot *(motodori)* and wears the *eboshi* cap or *kanmuri* hat common to bureaucrats and other state officials. As mentioned earlier, a child could enter "personhood" by participating in a rite of passage, when his haircut was altered and the *eboshi* placed on top of his head. In fact, a child would undergo several sartorial transformations before becoming an adult.

In some cases, children were thought of as similar to "outcastes," or defiled people, such as lepers. In the medieval encyclopedia *Chiribukuro*, the young *chigo (shōni)* was categorized among beings considered "nonpeople" *(hito naranu mono)*, but this does not necessarily mean that he was as inferior as those in the "outcastes" category (Kuroda 1986: 187–88). Historian Amino Yoshiko notes that adults who used children's names, such as *yase-dōji* (workers who carried palanquins and coffins of aristocrats in Northern Kyoto) were connected with *hinin* due to their association with impurity and alleged descent from demons (Amino 2012: 190–94) and that any adults who used the name or form of children, including cow-herders *(ushikai)*, possessed magical powers and were closely related to the world of kami and buddhas (Amino 2005: 94–117). Because of this confusion between the sacred and profane nature of various individuals labeled as a children *(warawa)*, it is easy to understand why Kuroda sees them as "either lacking essence or as intermediary beings." This also has to do with the fact children precede gender differentiation. As Kuroda notes, they are not yet male or female. Abe Yasurō calls them "middle-sex" entities. In other words, one can see the *chigo/dōji* as intermediary beings who are continuous with the divine realm.

Kuroda argues that children, together with old men and women, were considered sacred precisely because they stood on the fringes of society and were never seen as fully adult (men). They belonged to the order of chaos, rather than that of nómos ("the law"). Children in particular carried a significant symbolical weight as sacred entities. The word for children—*dōji*—has a religious origin and some non-Japanese etymological connotations that associate children with sacrality. The term is a translation of the Sanskrit word *kumara*, which alludes to both prince and child. This term has a pre-Buddhist history, originally appearing in Hindu sources. The feminine equivalent is *kumāri*, which designates a virgin in the Indian Tantric tradition. Although an understanding of purity was maintained in the transition to Japanese culture, the Hindu tradition also speaks of *kumāra* as an epithet for Skandha/Vishakha, the god of war, representing violence, which was also carried to Japan in the form of wrathful youths.

In the Buddhist context, the term still carries a divine connotation. In Japan, the *kumāra* or *dōji* figure is identified with a cohort of boy attendants who often accompany Buddhas, bodhisattvas, and Buddhist wisdom kings *(myōō)*. For instance, the Wisdom King Fudō Myōō (and sometimes the bodhisattva Monju) is depicted in texts and iconography as being surrounded by eight acolytes who serve him, and in many cases commonly flanked by the duo Kongara-dōji and Seitaka-dōji. Similarly, the goddess Benzaiten has fifteen or sixteen boy attendants as her retinue who function as her disciples. Another type of *dōji* is an avatar in child-form of Buddhas and bodhisattvas, such as Vajra-Kumāra *(kongō-dōji)* and Konpira *(konpira-dōji)*. Dōji can also stand for child figures of kami and Buddhas, like Hachiman-dōji, the young form of the popular god Hachiman. In addition, there are many cases in which *dōji* refers to divinities who exist solely as "children," neither an attendant or a child-version of another being. Some are not recognized as children so clearly. These "stand-alone" children are suprahuman beings, for example, Shuten-dōji, Sessen-dōji, and Uhō-dōji (although the last of these is clearly a child and conceived as a Buddhist version of Amaterasu, the sun goddess). Other deities are known as children without the labeling of *dōji*, such as Jūzenji, a placenta deity that is a manifestation of the Mountain King Avatar (Sannō-gongen), who was an important icon in the Sannō Shinto tradition of Mt. Hiei and Hie Shrine. There are also other denominations for sacred children, for example *wakamiya*, the attendants at Kasuga and Hachiman shrines. The "stand-alone" children form a pantheon of heavenly beings with close connection to the acolyte.[4] It is certain that children partook of sacrality because they enjoyed a denomination identical to these lofty beings, and that the two categories overlapped occasionally.

Based on painstaking research, Kuroda uses additional labels for children in monastic settings. For example, Kuroda speaks of *warawa* ("children") and, as I mentioned before, *dōji-sugata* ("adults who were forced to wear children's clothes"). *Dōji-sugata* sometimes appears in sources as *dōgyō*. *Warawa* is the Japanese pronunciation for the first Chinese character of *dōji*, essentially meaning children. Unlike *dōji*, which has a Buddhist etymological background, *warawa* is a category devoid of any Buddhist meaning, denoting messiness or laughter. Nevertheless, *warawa* is still commonly used to refer to monastic children, as we have seen earlier with *uewarawa*. The monastic child was not only an attendant and an apprentice, but also served a ritualistic and performative function in the performing arts. The dancing *chigo* were termed *dōbu* or *waramai* and, according to Kuroda and Tsuchiya, became the love objects of monks. Some acolytes joined various thespian performances, such as Noh, Ennen, Fūryū, where they fulfilled religious roles as mediums that summon kami. . Rather than a unified system of child taxonomy, scholarship generally points to an ontological state of the *chigo/ dōji* that was fluctuating, intermediate, and negotiable (Lin 2001).

Although the categorization of children remains indistinct, the sexual configuration of acolytes, that of male-male love, is relatively stable in textual and artistic representations. The *chigo* is mostly known for its association with male-male love from the *chigo monogatari* genre, a corpus of tales that recounts love affairs between *chigo* and other males (and less often, females too). Many of these relations are described as taking place between adult monks and young acolytes, and end with the demise of the *chigo* or his separation from the loved monk, while monks enjoy the fruits of awakening resulting from a sexual encounter with the *chigo*-turned-bodhisattva. Abe Yasurō noted that the trope of the suffering or dying *chigo* is a common thread running through the *chigo monogatari* and *setsuwa* genres (Abe 1998). The sexual construction of male-male sexual relations can also be found outside of this genre, and is also asymmetrical. In sexual relations, the junior partner typically fulfilled the role of insertee in anal intercourse (Hosokawa 2000; Tanaka 2004). The structure is clear in several medieval sources, such as *The Scroll of Acolytes* (Chigo no sōshi), *The Solicitation Book of the Way of Youths* (Nyakudō no Kanjinchō, 1482), and the sexual ritual *Chigo kanjō* and its commentaries. Texts that make an appeal to perform these rigid sexual roles suggest that some acolytes were not following the sexual conventions expected of them, so it is possible that there was a certain amount of flexibility in sexual engagements (Porath 2015). This flexibility is also observed in the response to general monastic exhortations. Children were not always obedient to their senior monastic partners, and some of them could enjoy a sense of freedom, even though they were expected to participate in asymmetrical socio-sexual relations. For that reason, this paper points to child disobedience that extends beyond sexuality to general behavior.

OBEDIENT CHILDREN: INSTRUCTIONS FOR CHILDREN

Instructions for Children (Dōji-kyō) is well-known as a part of a primer that includes another text called *The Teaching of the Truthful Words* (Jitsugokyō). Both *Instructions* and *Truthful Words* were taught in the medieval period and they were published together as primers for children throughout the Edo (1603–1868) and Meiji periods (1868–1912). Both were composed in ancient and medieval times, and in monasteries they were taught separately. Tsuji Zennosuke claims that *Instructions* became extremely popular in the Muromachi period (Tsuji 1951: 362), and it is well known that in the Edo period the text was used in homeschooling and in the widespread temple schools *(terakoya)* that catered to commoners, villagers, and townsmen. *Truthful Words* was written around the Heian period (794–1185) and is attributed to Kūkai (Kōbo Daishi, 774–835), though the exact date and authorship is unknown. *Instructions* was written in 1377. Although tradition identifies the author to be the eminent monk Annen, the lack of an extant manuscript from the ninth century makes this doubtful.

According to a study on medieval Japanese education by Sugawara Masako, *Instructions* was taught to monastic children from around the age of thirteen. A retainer of Aki province who served the Mori warrior clan, Tamaki Yoshiyasu (1552–1633), for example, used this text when he was studying at Shōraku-ji (Sugawara 2014: 30–31, Yuki 1977). According to Tamaki's biography, in the first year of study, he was assigned to read the Heart Sutra and the Kannon Sutra in the morning, and in the evening, in addition to Chinese character practice, he would read *Instructions* and *Truthful Words* along other didactic material. The second year entailed the study of the *Analects,* the Confucian classics, and others. The third was comprised of Japanese poetry and literature such as the *Man'yōshū,* the *Tale of Ise,* and *the Tale of Genji.* Yuki Rikurō claims that Tamaki's depiction of the curriculum reflected the general pedagogical structure for *chigo* in temples (Yuki 1977: 162–63), but Yonehara Masayoshi (cited in Sugawara 2014) argues that it was identical to the study program of *sengoku* samurai and mirrored the general education and knowledge that warriors pursued. Whether the curriculum was restricted to children of samurai descent or not, what is certain is that the texts were taught in temples to young children. Another source edited by the Shingon monk Zonsei displays a catalogue of texts that served as necessary tools for learning for late-Muromachi monks. Zonsei highlights texts that children need to study by the age of fifteen. The genres are quite diverse and include *setsuwa* (didactic tales), *denki* (biographies), *gunki* (military tales), *engi* (origins of temples), *emaki* (illustrated scrolls), and others, but among them a group of primers *(ōraimono)* is mentioned, which includes *Instructions* and *Truthful Words.* Similarly, the Tendai-turned-Nichiren-shū monk Nichi'i (1444–1519) classified various texts into a collection of study materials. In the section on "what children should read," *Instructions* and *Truthful Words* remain part of the core curriculum (Takahashi 2007). As such, *Instructions* and *Truthful Words* became a crucial part of the monastic learning experience for children.

The content of both texts was regarded as complementary to the edification of children. Both are written in classical Chinese and in lines of five characters that are readable in Sino-Japanese or *kanbun. Truthful Words* was ostensibly written by Heian-period nobles and directed to aristocratic elites using a Confucian episteme, but it cannot be ruled out that the text might be a copy of an earlier Chinese source. It places an emphasis on the importance of learning, the distinctions between a wise and a foolish man, and includes excerpts from Confucian classics. *Instructions for Children,* on the other hand, was formulated by Buddhist clergy for temple children of varying social backgrounds and it contains rich Buddhist pedagogical elements. *Instructions* is not so systemized and covers a jumbled assortment of theological and pedagogical concerns. It includes passages instructing proper demeanor and etiquette, but also exhorts children to study and cultivate their motivation for learning. In addition, the text is embedded in a Buddho-Confucian episteme, presenting a unique synthesis of dogmas.

It is precisely the Buddho-Confucian system of knowledge that provided a convenient theoretical frame for instilling proper conduct in children. The two doctrines were employed to position the child in a lower social standing so that he respected the authority of the priesthood. The role of Confucianism in *Instructions* was to impart to children a mode of behavior informed by the five human relationships model (Ch. *wulun,* Jp. *gorin*) that ensures an orderly patriarchal structure. Buddhism, in turn, assured attainment of Buddhahood. Both Confucian and Buddhist norms of obeisance were emphasized so that respect was channeled to the clergy.

The teachers mentioned in the texts undoubtedly refer to Buddhist clerics. Buddhism expanded the five human relationships concept to add a monastic layer as the supreme authority. The Buddhist teaching also served as a warning to children of the punishments they would endure in their next lifetime should they choose not to obey monastic orders. The text manipulates the symbolic significance of the two traditions to inspire awe and fear among disciples.

Instructions quickly makes it clear that rank is an important notion in the monastic social landscape. The text establishes correspondence between this-worldly authority and the divine realm, and establishes a hierarchy of ordinary beings vis-à-vis their masters: "Do not speak without being asked. If you are issued a command, listen carefully. When you approach the Three Treasures, bow three times. When facing the divinities, bow twice. When facing an ordinary person, bow once. When seeing masters and gentlemen, bow low in respect" (Pseudo-Annen 1931: 9). The general etiquette between a child/acolyte and his superior restricts the child by prohibiting him from complaining about hardships and urging him to obey instructions. The narrative shifts to divine authority, which imparts that the "Three Treasures" are to be worshipped with the highest respect, the kami close behind. The "Three Treasures" include the Buddha, the Buddhist teachings, and the entire priestly community (Sk. *saṃgha*). The immediate implication is that the Buddhist symbols and clergy deserve higher respect than autochthonous deities. When the text refers to human relations, the teacher/master stands at the top of the social pyramid with the common people at the bottom. This was reflected in the monk/acolyte relationship in which monks assume the teacher status and acolytes are situated at a level lower along with common people not worthy of receiving homage.

Therefore, if the monastic hierarchy can be read in the deference one earns, it can also be judged from one's level of authoritative expression:

> People have manners; the court necessarily has protocols. People without manners will cause trouble among the *saṃgha*. If you mingle, you should not use foul language.

When you're done [with your affairs], withdraw immediately. When you handle an affair, do not turn your back to friends. Words should not cause separation. People who talk a lot accomplish little, and are like an old dog that barks at friends. Lazy people who eat in a rush are like a tired monkey that covets fruit. Brave people necessarily encounter danger. They are like a summer insect that enters the flames. Dull people don't meet trouble, like a spring bird playing in the forest. (Pseudo-Annen 1931: 9)

The Buddhist establishment or the *saṃgha* cannot allow a poorly mannered individual within its cloister, for this can endanger the wholesomeness of the community. In demanding the obeisance of children, *Instructions* wishes to limit their freedom of interaction by forbidding them to use coarse or obscene words. Also, it requires that social interaction be minimal. A child should make an effort to avoid conversation, and the child should leave at once if he meets another person while undertaking a chore. At the same time, in conformity with the five Confucian relations, the child is advised not to hurt his friends. Of course, monastic leaders could not limit all types of social bonding. A good friendship defined in Confucian terms was a desired interaction, to be maintained because it ensured harmonious stability.

Monks established strict boundaries for communication, and they were also interested in controlling movement. Monastics worried that children would engage in risky adventures and neglect their monastic duties. By demonizing bravery and encouraging insipidness, monks could prevent unwarranted behavior. Dullness should be understood as humbleness rather than stupidity. This interpretation is supported elsewhere via yin-yang theory: "People with *yin* virtues will necessarily have *yang* rewards" (Pseudo-Annen 1931: 10). In Chinese philosophy, *yin* is normally equated with humility and modesty, whereas *yang* refers to clear or evident benefits earned in this lifetime. The text also limits students' activities, for it emphasizes the virtues of learning and scholarly life. It bursts with praise of erudition: "Even on a winter night, wearing a thin silk robe, you should withstand the cold and recite throughout the night," and "even on a summer night, suffering from malnourishment, you should study all day regardless of your hunger" (12). Such obedience has an ascetic tinge. There were also physical limitations on movement of children: "A student should be seven feet *(shaku)* away from a master; he must not even step in his shadow" (11). In this way, the hierarchy between children and monks was transmuted into spatial terms. The monk was too exalted to stand near a child, indicating the social prestige of the clergy and the physical boundaries in monasteries.

Apart from imposing limitations on movement, the text uses "scare tactics." The monks' pedagogical enterprise involved fear and promoted tameness: "If a master does not teach his disciple, this may be called a violation of the precepts. If a master punishes a disciple, this may be called adherence to Buddhist precepts. If [a master] rears a bad student, both master and disciple fall to hell. If you are a good student, both master and disciple achieve Buddhahood. A student who does not follow the teachings should be quickly sent back to his father and mother" (Pseudo-Annen 1931: 11). Monks not only promise spiritual benefits to obedient students, but they also use intimidation to convince disciples to follow the rules. The violation of precepts *(hakai)* is, at least ideally, a serious transgression for Buddhists (even if they were often contravened in Japan). These violations include committing forbidden sexual acts, stealing, killing a person, and lying. A monk who instructs children poorly commits an offence equal to these transgressive behaviors. A similar reference can be found elsewhere in the text: "The master hits the student, not because he hates [him] but because he wants to cultivate his skills" (11). This passage suggests that monks performed corporal punishment. Punishing a student is not only mandatory for educational purposes, but it is also a Buddhist obligation. That said, corporal punishing was not considered abusive in medieval Japan, nor was it considered abusive anywhere in the world at that time. There is an equal responsibility for both parties to work hard to achieve proper cultivation of a student's character. The stakes are high. If education fails, then both student and master will end up in hell.

Both the scare tactics and the promise of enlightenment are colored by Confucian and Buddhist ideals. The text cleverly uses religious eclecticism to enhance the authority of adult superiors and to make it easier to elicit obedient behavior on the part of children. This is especially clear in numerous passages where teachers and parents are glorified: "Kannon, out of filiality to her father, had crowned Amida with a Buddha Crown. Seishi, out of filial devotion, put the bones of his father and mother on his head, and placed the [rest of their] bones into a precious vase" (Pseudo-Annen 1931: 11–12)." While these figures are carrying out filial duties, their parents are construed as Buddhist divinities, and the lineage that children worship is the divine lineage of Buddhas rather than ordinary human ancestors. Such amalgamation of Confucianism with Buddhist doctrine is also demonstrated in a passage on the gestative process leading to the birth of a child: "The white bone is the father's 'sexual liquid,' the red flesh is the mother's 'sexual liquid.' The red and white drops being united, the body is realized in five limbs" (13). The text employs the sexual ontology of Esoteric Buddhism in order to explain the rationale behind the Confucian notion of filial piety. In Buddhist Esotericism, the notion of the twin-fluids *(sekibyaku nitai)* constructs the semen and menstrual blood as the Buddhist virtues of male wisdom and female compassion. The seminal and menstrual discharges are seen as the key components that create the mind and its contents, and eventually the human body. The child is created out of these two bodily fluids as red flesh and white bones, and since he embodies in his corporal existence his own parents, filial obligation constitutes loyalty to oneself. This type of reasoning displays an overarching Buddhist vision of the cosmos in which nonduality permeates all physical and mental phenomena, including father and mother. Confucian notions are thus subsumed within a larger Buddhist ontological system in which priestly authority was deeply embedded.

There are many more occasions in which Buddho-Confucian doctrine is used to legitimize the teacher priest as an authoritative figure. Advising children to respect their masters, the text reads: "Even a teacher for a day should not be shunned, not to mention a teacher who has taught for numerous years. The teacher is a vow of Three Realms. The ancestor is a glance at one realm" (Pseudo-Annen 1931: 11). Therefore, the teacher, a Buddhist priest, "is a vow," and is coextensive with all temporalities, an ontological condition only rivaled by the cosmic Buddha. The "Three Realms" from a Confucian perspective are the "Three Generations": father, son, and grandson. If the term is read in Confucian terms, the teacher is already loftier than a parent because he expresses the entire familial lineage in his bodily existence, whereas the ancestor constitutes a glimpse into one generation. It follows that no one else enjoys the teacher's prestige, and children ought to respect the divine authority of their priestly superiors, even more than that of their parental figures.

If children follow the above-mentioned behavioral protocol, then they will be rewarded. The text ends with important exhortations indicative of Buddhist soteriology:

> First, one has to aspire to become Buddha.
> Second, one has to reward the Four Benevolences that one receives.
> Third, everywhere in the Six Destinies every individual should altogether attain Buddhahood.
> In order to guide children, one should inform them on the laws of Karma. These [obligations] come from Buddhist and Non-Buddhist scriptures alike. (Pseudo-Annen 1931: 15)

The most significant goal for a child is to become a Buddha. The access to Buddhahood is premised on obedience to priestly teachers; for disruptive children, there is karmic retribution. For this reason, monks are instructed to edify children on the workings of karma to prevent youth from straying from the Buddhist path. Carrying out idealized behavior will result in karmic fruition for all. Children who exhibit humbleness, learning, and good nature will necessarily benefit all sentient beings. Hence, well-mannered behavior is deemed an expression of Buddhist compassion.

Instructions does not stop with connecting good behavior to compassion. Obedience to monks is an act of gratitude to one of the Four Benevolences. Even if the Four Benevolences seem rooted in Confucian ideology, because they are based on a relationship model, by the time the text was written, the concept amalgamated Buddhism with Confucianism. In *The Great Mahayana Sutra of Contemplating the Mind Ground* (Ch. *Dasheng bensheng xindi guan jing*), the Four Benevolences are the four objects of compassion—parents, sentient beings, rulers, and the Three

Treasures.[5] The "Three Treasures" include the symbolical authority of the monastic community, as seen above. Another important sutra, *The Sutra of Refuge in the True Dharma* (Sk. *Saddharma-smṛty-upasthāna-sūtra*, Ch. *Zhengfa nianchu jing*) describes obligation to the father, the mother, the Tathāgata (Buddha), and the Dharma teacher.[6] Thus two logics for conforming to priestly authority are operative in *Instructions:* following the principles of Buddhism in order to be rewarded, both for worldly desire and for the attainment of awakening; following the higher authority of Buddhists and parents because they embody sacrality, with obedience intimately tied to the fulfillment of Buddhist goals. The text urges full obeisance, but we would be wrong to construe monastic social structure as an inflexible hierarchy. The text hints at mutual dependence between monks and acolytes and prioritizes the attainment of Buddhahood for both. Further, as we shall see below, another medieval text presents evidence of children challenging priestly authorities in various ways.

NASTY BOYS: THE EDUCATION OF ACOLYTES

In *Instructions for Children*, it is evident that monks set clear rules for instilling obedient behavior in children, and that respecting priestly authority was essential for achieving the end of Buddhist practice—Buddhahood. On the other hand, *The Education of Acolytes* sheds light on the reality that departs from this ideal monastic world. *The Education of Acolytes* is a satire on the unruliness of temple novices. It was composed in the form of five-seven *morae* verses *(shichigo-chō)* sometime in the Muromachi period (1337–1573) and functioned as a popular pedagogical poem-essay. It saw a further variant in the Azuchi-Momoyama period (1573–1600) under the title of *The Dog Short-Poem* (Inu tanka, Keichō era 1596–1615) and was later republished in the Edo period under the label of *Tales of Youths* (Wakashū monogatari, 1657). The *Education*, in its many iterations, was likely targeted at acolytes from samurai families, and provided moral instruction for young warriors well into the Edo period. It contains a long series of poems in which the narrator lists the misbehavior of acolytes, often complaining about their disobedience to priestly authority. The fact that the children were not conforming to Buddhist constraints and had little desire to participate in monastic activities shows that they could enjoy a relative freedom. The majority of their social activities are described as nonreligious, indicating that their disobedience was even more disturbing to clerical elites.

Not much is known about *The Education of Acolytes*. Although it is said to have been written by the monk-poet Sōgi, it is not found in most of the collected compendia of Sōgi's writings. However, that absence can be explained by a homophobic tendency on the part of religious and literature scholars of the modern period, who often ignored works that allude to male-male sexual engagements. Indeed, the work is classified as a *nanshoku* ("male-male eros") text in the authoritative bibliography of male-male love written by the folklorist Iwata Jun'ichi even though it is difficult to find references to actual male-male erotic intimacy in the text (Iwata 2002: 347). Sōgi may play on ambiguity that is found in the work, but there is no conclusive evidence that allows us to claim that *Education* is indeed homoerotic. I will go into detail in my examination of passages that may be construed as homoerotic, but I will also show that there is no clear-cut instance. Instead I will underscore that the obligations stated in *Instructions for Children* are reported in *Education* to be ignored by acolytes. The text problematizes the notion that monks were successful in exerting full control over acolytes.

The title of *The Education of Acolytes* suggests it is pedagogical text explaining how to edify acolytes. Yet, the title does not fit the contents. The tone in this text is not normative in nature but descriptive, and the prose style is more typical of a comical narrative than of didactic literature. Be that as it may, one cannot assume that the content was merely the product of the writer's imagination. The text speaks to issues analogous to those found in *Instructions* and provides readers with a glance at how acolytes deviated from the norms for conduct.

As in many other medieval works, the child category in *The Education* is not coherent. While the title mentions *chigo* or temple acolyte, the opening passage makes it clear that acolytes under discussion are designated differently in the body of the text: "Today, considering carefully in the rain, I am writing here in an idle fashion and in detail about the bad behavior of youths [*wakashu*] in this world. Even a master of brush would sound foolish. To begin with, they dislike the refinement of the Way, they act obstinately, and as they speak they make fun of other people" (Sōgi 1959: 336). The term *wakashu* ("youth") refers to a preadult partner in a male-male sexual relationship. This hints that the young boys under discussion are objects of erotic intimacy. The proximity of the word "Way" to the *wakashu* category might imply that this is the "Way of Youths" *(shudō)*, a disciplinary tradition of male-male love that was especially prevalent in the Edo period and had antecedents in medieval times.[7] The labeling of male-male love as a "Way" says something significant about the larger concept, because the term has a rich and complex cultural history. The word *dō* or "Way" as it relates to a doctrine or a discipline bestows a concept with a religious or ethical nuance. This understanding derives from Daoism, Confucianism, and other continental traditions that refer to their own body of knowledge as a "Way" as well. Thus, in medieval Japan, the major religious ideologies of Confucianism *(judō)*, Buddhism *(butsudō)*, and Shinto *(shintō)* all receive the denomination of a way. Secular activities such as calligraphy *(kadō)* and martial arts *(budō)* would later be associated with spirituality by being labeled as "ways." As the historian Gregory Pflugfelder argues when he discusses the "Way of Youths," it is possible to "conceive of a 'way' as a discipline of mind and body, a set of practices and knowledge expected to bring both spiritual and physical rewards to those who choose to follow its path" (Pflugfelder 1999: 28). In this regard, mention of the term *tashinami,* which stands for "refinement"

or cultivation of physical and spiritual capacities, renders unambiguous the connection to a path of self-cultivation that needs to be perfected. When Sōgi says
that acolytes dislike the refinement *(tashinami)* of the "Way," it is possible that he
means novices do not adhere to the general and normative order of male-male
love as practiced in monasteries.

Most information on the disciplinary nature of male-male love comes from
the Edo period, when the term *wakashu* formed a crucial part of the "Way of
Youths." As described in existing scholarship on male-male sexuality in Japan, the
"Way" can be understood as a disciplined sexual relationship between two males
who belong to different age groups: the young lover is the "youth" *(wakashu)* and
the mature lover the adult *(nenja)*. The relationship between the two in various
early-modern media was asymmetrical; it was characterized by power relations in
which the subject *(nenja)* and the object *(wakashu)* occupied unequal positions.
The nature of these relations is expressed in sexual terms: sexual activities are
mostly confined to anal penetration in which the *nenja* is the penetrative partner,
whereas the *wakashu* is the penetrated (Pflugfelder 1999: 29–44). But did such an
understanding exist in medieval times?

Medieval sources such as *The Scroll of Acolytes* (*Chigo no sōshi,* 1321) describe
a sexual paradigm that is similar to the Edo understandings of male-male love
(see also chapter 2). For example, the medieval scroll shows monks and acolytes
engaging in anal intercourse in which the adults are almost always the inserters
and acolytes the insertees. In addition, the commentary on the *chigo kanjō* ritual
includes a detailed discussion of the varieties of names given to the buttocks of
young *chigo,* within which the active role of penetration is mentioned.[8] Further,
the connection with a spiritual path is evident in the *Chigo no sōshi* text, for it
describes a monk who could not control his desire and was unsuccessful in aban-
doning the "Way" (Leupp 1995: 44; Dōmoto 1985: 167–88). Another indication for
asymmetrical sexual relations between monks and acolytes is found in an oath
(kishōmon) written by the monk Sōshō (1202–1278), dated 1237. In it, Sōshō writes
that he has slept with more than one hundred acolytes, and that he wishes to resist
his lascivious desire by not penetrating them in the future. He swears to have only
one "love-boy" *(aidō)* and makes an oath not to become a *nenja* of upper-children
(uewarawa) and middle-children *(chūdō),* the different occupational positions of
child acolytes (Matsuo 2008: 75). That the senior monk could have dozens of lov-
ers, and that he occupied the penetrative role as the *nenja,* reveals much about
power relations in temples. There are at least two other texts dated from the fif-
teenth century (and a third that was lost) that are titled *Nyakudō no Kanjinchō* or
Nyake Kanjinchō and that hint at the penetrative and receptive roles of anal intercourse while also discussing male-male sexuality as a religious path that can lead
its adherents to rebirth in paradise (Porath 2015). Already in medieval times one
can recognize male-male love as a sacred pursuit, one that advocates asymmetrical

sexual relations between monks and their acolytes and is sometimes framed by phrases later dominant in the Edo period.

By declaring the author to be an adult monk, associating acolytes with a "Way" that is worthy of refinement or cultivation, and addressing acolytes as *wakashu*, *The Education of Acolytes* points to a construction of sexuality prevalent in medieval monasteries that informed later early-modern understandings of sexuality. Sōgi's criticism of acolytes might be understood as dissatisfaction with children's behavior on the grounds that they do not adhere to proper conduct associated with the "Way of Youths." Nonetheless, such a reading can only be carried out by monks who are informed about male-male sexuality as a religious path. One could interpret the "Way" as "the Buddhist Way" *(butsudō)*: though *tashinami* is often used in an erotic context, it can refer more generally to the fact that monks do not abide to some behavioral decorum. But the term is suspicious. We cannot conclude with certainty that the text is explicitly about *wakashu* as objects of male-male love, but the possibility exists.

The Education complicates further our understanding of the taxonomy of children. There were types of acolytes who wore the attire of children and remained in everlasting childhood without undergoing a rite of passage into adulthood. At one point, the text indicates that these children are older than adolescents. When Sōgi complains about the wild behavior of acolytes, he muses: "If they were youths of the age of twelve, thirteen, or around fourteen and fifteen years old, and had a childish heart, I would have let it pass. But it is far worse, they are adults" (340). The word for adult *(otona)* did not usually refer to an older youth but to a mature man. The passage shows that the acolytes here are not children per se, but rather that they embody childhood via their occupational and social status. In other passages, Sōgi refers to the same acolytes as children *(kodomo)*: "Isn't it shameful that even if you raise many children, if you bring them up in the rice fields, they will carry out mischiefs to themselves and in their homes, and end up being no different than the uncouth people of the mountains?" (344).[9] It is possible these children are "adults" according to modern understanding, but for Sōgi that does not make a difference, and he continues to call them children. The boundaries between adults and children become blurred for today's readers. Even if acolytes were considered adults by their biological age, they could still constitute part of a monastic continuum of childhood. Sōgi's conceptualization of children thus echoes the scholarly discussion on the ontology of childhood.

Regardless of his hazy age categories for acolytes, Sōgi unambiguously describes the conduct of children. Throughout the text, he resents the acolytes' bad behavior. He remarks they cannot be trusted, and that they generally act in an immoderate and insolent manner (336). As mentioned earlier in the analysis of *Instructions for Children*, monks expected children to use verbal communication only when asked and not to use language against their friends. In Sōgi's treatise, however, children do the opposite.

Sōgi writes that acolytes ridicule other youths (*wakashu,* Sōgi 1959: 336). At the same time, he laments that young novices "criticize the way people dress" and "they gossip about people and laugh at their appearance" (337). Children say pointless things and engage in casual talk and very often burst into laughter (339). As he puts it, "They have no time to answer the questions of others . . . . One cannot describe in written words the unbelievable things they say as they gamble [when playing board games]." Acolytes clearly used their verbal capacity not to sustain harmony in the way priestly monks expected, but to cause dispute and malcontent.

Just as acolytes digressed from proper means of communication, they also ignored the Buddho-Confucian ideal of scholarly dedication. As we saw in *Instructions for Children,* monks wanted to guarantee that children would discipline themselves to hard work and diligence. They especially wanted to prepare acolytes who would later lead a monastic lifestyle, which was challenging and required many years of learning, recitations, and familiarization with scripture. However, Sōgi's text shows that acolytes did not even complete the designated curriculum: "One should at least spend four or five years in the temple. If one resides in the temple, there should be some indication [of accomplishment], and yet they cannot even pass three years [in the monastery]" (Sōgi 1959: 336–37). Acolytes do not seem to favor scholarly life in general: "They despise that which they learn" (336), and their routine is marked by laziness. For example: "They wake up late, and have an afternoon nap" (336). The text abounds with these accusations of laziness. It seems that children preferred to dedicate their time to leisure instead of to the study of religious doctrines and the performance of ritual practices.

Indeed, most acolytes in these texts seem to prefer a nonreligious, leisurely lifestyle. They are preoccupied with various forms of amusement. There are ample references to children engaging in occupations such as martial arts, banquets, board games, and obscene behavior. At one point, Sōgi criticizes children who "draw the swords of others along with their sword guards, and judge whether the swords can cut well or not" (Sōgi 1959: 339). He does not admire children who cultivate the skills of swordsmanship. To the contrary, he comments that their obsession with unimportant matters goes so far as appreciating the sharpness of their weapons. Familiarity with the art of the sword is often tied to violent behavior: "They draw their long sword and short sword as they barge into the tatami rooms of other people unannounced" (339). Other passages include mention of acolytes drinking as many as three cups of sake in banquets, which suggest they breached monastic rules, and that they were often invited to feasts outside monastic precincts (338).[10] In addition, the acolytes are described as addicted to board games (*go, shōgi, suguroku*), and Sōgi expresses displeasure with their gambling habits and the unfair techniques they use in competitions (339). He complains that acolytes cuddle close to their masters, which could be an allusion to male-male love (336). Similarly, he critiques acolytes for not showing proper respect when senior monks get up from their tatami mattresses (338). These complaints can also be interpreted as disrespectful of personal space or just reflective of bad decorum, not necessarily eroticism.

In addition to behavioral mischief, Sōgi measures the acolytes' acts by other less objective factors. When he observes the behavior of children, he reveals a distinctive sensorial aversion to their demeanor. In some cases his unease, sometimes reaching the level of repugnance, is particularly perceptual, emotional, and judgmental. He despises the visual, aural, and, less often, tactile qualities of the acolytes' conduct. His expressive and aesthetic reactions are ones of revulsion. In his mind, children deserve to be criticized because they do not show sensibility and refinement in their daily life.

Among the various sense impressions that evoke Sōgi's unease, visuality occupies a major space. For example, in discussing poor sartorial style, Sōgi complains that acolytes "roll their sidelocks to the back . . . and make them grow like reeds in the summer fields" (Sōgi 1959: 337). He is clearly unsatisfied with their unappealing appearance, claiming that they look like "fourteen-year-old young falcons" (337). He comments on their unaesthetic choice of wardrobe: "They wear paper-garment jackets . . . . they cover themselves with layers of vibrantly colored sleeves" (337). This may sound aesthetically appealing to modern readers, but Sōgi may have perceived flashy colors to be distasteful and distracting. The monk-poet also bemoans other uncivilized habits: "They do not use toothpicks [to clean their teeth], nor do they tie their hair, and neither do they cut their fingernails" (337). In addition to deviating from the normative sartorial style of the monastery, acolytes exposed unwanted views of their bodies. For instance, Sōgi writes: "The belts of their *hakama* are loosely tied, which causes the front [of their pants] to fall down" (337). Beholding such acolytes made him uncomfortable. This exposure should not be mistaken as an erotic act. Eroticism on the part of an acolyte would more likely take the form of showing off the buttocks or upper thigh. Exposing a penis is a threat.

In the same way that Sōgi finds the clothing and physical displays of temple pages disagreeable, he considers their style of eating to be repugnant: "They make it a habit to grind their teeth as they please when chewing the bones of fish and chicken . . . . when they eat they make loud noises, and this is a painful sight for both old and young" (338). Sōgi adds, in this context: "They shove kelp into their mouth in its entirety, and while chewing they start talking without being asked to do so" (338). The action of grinding one's teeth or swallowing food uninhibitedly grated upon Sōgi. Since acolytes were expected to serve food for many ceremonial events, it was all the more surprising to Sōgi that they did not follow food etiquette.

The passage above not only betrays Sōgi's visual sensitivity, but also expresses his aural aversion to the sounds of misbehaving children. For example, he announces that "when they speak it's painful to the ears" (338). He bristles when they vocalize "silly" sounds (339). He often repeats his discontent with the tendency of youths to laugh out loud when they gossip and tease (337, 338, 339). In other words, laughing deserves reproach not merely because it is inconsiderate, but also because the loud sounds that laughter produces betray a lack of refinement. For this reason, the subsequent passages of *The Education of Acolytes* are dedicated to a poetic sophistication that embraces accepted sensory norms and ideals of elegance and pathos *(mono no aware)*. The crafting of poetry and admiration of natural imagery could hardly evoke any visual, aural, or tactile aversion on Sōgi's part.

CONCLUSION

What can *Instructions for Children* and *The Education of Acolytes* reveal about children in medieval Japanese monasteries? The two documents represent different visions of childhood. It would be misguided to read *Instructions* as replicating the actual behavior of children, and it would be wrong to assume that Sōgi's descriptions in *The Education* are an accurate reflection of historical reality. It cannot be discounted that both texts were written by monastics reflecting on their discipline and describing their subalterns, whether seriously or humorously. What we know of the way children acted in medieval Japan is always mediated by the conceptualization of their superiors. The value of these texts lies in their representations of how medieval Japanese conceptualized childhood in Japan.

Instructions was taught within the monastic educational system, which aimed at shaping acolytes into mature monks or adult aristocrats/samurai. It was one of many texts that described how paradigmatic acolytes should behave by way of religious and ethical injunctions that, ideally, could infuse a sense of morality that an individual would carry for the rest of his life. Certainly, the text is self-serving for monks; the doctrinal and normative elevation of Buddhism, and the limitations imposed on young acolytes emphasized the authority of the priesthood. However, even though *Instructions* does not ascribe much liberty to child acolytes, it does not reflect attempts to altogether suppress or subjugate children. For example, the text challenges the understanding that the monastic hierarchy was inflexible. Subordinates were subject to behavioral restrictions, to be sure, and perhaps verbal and physical retaliation, but there is also room for codependence between monks and children. They share equal soteriological possibilities, they are made out of the same ontological substance, and they are influenced equally by karmic forces. In fact, the text reflects the structure of medieval Buddhist epistemology and monasticism, in which all members of the system were seen as interconnected parts of an integrated whole.

Interpreting *The Education of Acolytes* is far more difficult. It represents a reverse-image of the exemplary acolytes described in *Instructions*. The majority of the text cannot be said to be prescriptive. It highlights negative behavior and assumes the reader will infer that positive behavior is antithetical to the conduct of the acolytes described. Furthermore, the style of the text suggests an effort to be funny. Nevertheless, whether humorous or serious, *Education* reflects how older monks conceived of acolytes as unruly, uncouth, and playful individuals who did not follow monastic orders and etiquette—simply put, as nasty boys. Although acolytes were not involved in the production of the text, the setting of the text is realistic. One cannot dismiss the evidence that acolytes could have enjoyed some freedom in their actions.

By reading these texts, it is easier to make sense of the trajectory that the monastic child traveled in the social landscape of medieval Japan. A child is one who is assigned a low social status in the monastery, albeit in some cases a higher one than people with noble pedigree. He has the responsibility to fulfill his institutional obligations by allegiance and conformity to Buddhist and monastic orders. There is an institutional attempt to transform the child into an ideal, adult priest by instilling in him the virtues of learning, politeness, moderation, humbleness and obedience. In addition, the child's role in the larger Buddhist epistemology is instantiated. He is encouraged to act as a Buddhist to contribute to the harmony and wholesomeness of the monastic community. However, the child is sometimes able to transcend his own social limitations when monastic regulations of decorum and discipline are not enforced properly. When enforcement slackens, the child is given leeway, and he is capable of navigating the monastic setting according to his wishes. Ultimately, the limitations on expression, movement, and behavior are futile if the child ignores authority and goes his own way.

Children in monasteries could afford to follow their own initiative if authority was lax, and they could direct attention to secular enjoyment forbidden by Buddhist doctrine. However, the escape from religious obligations was not the acolytes' decision, since the monks themselves introduced nonreligious activities into the monastery. As is evident from Sōgi's descriptions, acolytes were invited to banquets outside temples, they had a variety of board games in the monastery, and those of samurai descent were given the liberty to carry swords. We also know from other sources that sexual relations were institutionalized by adult monks. In this regard, it is important to acknowledge that relative autonomy was in some cases reproduced by monks themselves, and not by the sudden impulses of renegade acolytes. What bothered Sōgi (and perhaps many other monks) was not that acolytes had these activities at their disposal, but the manner in which they overindulged in these various forms of amusement. It is one thing to drink a cup of sake, but it is another to drink too much alcohol in a vulgar manner, while ignoring one's responsibility to study. Be that as it may, the monastic child was a fluid mode of being, oscillating between extremes of sacred and profane, occupying multiple social roles and age categories, and preoccupying himself with a variety of joyful yet morally conflicting activities. Given these circumstances, certain children could afford for themselves a relative autonomy.

NOTES

I thank Devon Cahill for his useful editorial comments on this chapter.

1. This leaves the treatment of female children to a future study.

2. It is unclear whether children consciously resisted monastic ideals, or whether the conditions provided fertile ground for creating a culture that allowed for disobedience. Following Dorothy Ko and Sabah Mahmoud, Lori Meeks studies female nuns in the medieval restoration movement of Hokkeji temple and acknowledges the polyvalence of agency, noting that nuns would sometimes maneuver around patriarchal and androcentric norms but also, at times, cultivated them. The common point of departure in these studies is that scholarship should go beyond notions of resistance and oppression and attempt to bring into focus the cultivation of new cultures that challenged dominant ideologies, whether willfully or unconsciously (Meeks 2010: 10–14).

3. Brecher maintains that child disobedience was a social reality in the Edo period (1600–1868). He premises his argument on the wealth of literary and artistic representations that depict this type of behavior (Brecher 2015). However, I remain unconvinced by Brecher's contention that this behavior was celebrated. Rather, it seems disobedience was used as satire in school settings precisely because it served as an effective pedagogical tool for showing behavior that was antithetical to what was deemed ethical.

4. For a discussion on artistic representations of divine boys and their cultural significance, see Guth 1987: 1–23.

5. *The Great Mahayana Sutra of Contemplating the Mind Ground* (Dasheng bensheng xindi guan jing), in Takakusu and Watanabe 1924–34, 3.297a.

6. *The Sutra of Refuge in the True Dharma* (Zhengfa nianchu jing), in Takakusu and Watanabe 1924–34, 0.0001a.

7. For the historical genealogy of male-male sexual discourse and its production as a discipline in early-modern Japanese history, see Pflugfelder 1999.

8. See my "The Apotheosis of Youths: The Chigo kanjō Consecration of Acolytes and its Ritual Commentaries" (Porath, forthcoming).

9. The poet's mention of "rice fields" suggests that he refers to children in general, since the vast majority of the population at the time lived in farm villages. But judging from the general vocabulary used in the text, the majority of children discussed in the text are acolytes from a samurai background.

10. Although the banquets mentioned in *Education* seem to take place outside of monasteries, during medieval times, banquets were not an unusual occurrence inside as well. See for example Itō, Brisset, and Masuo 2015.

BIBLIOGRAPHY

Note: Unless noted otherwise the place of publication for Japanese books is Tokyo.

Abe Yasurō. 1984a. "Jidō setsuwa no keisei: Tendai *Sokui hō* no seiritsu o megurite" [The figuration of the Tale of Jidō: Concerning the formation of the Tendai *Sokui hō*] (Part 1). *Kokugo kokubun* 53(8): 1–29.

———. 1984b. "Jidō setsuwa no keisei: Tendai *Sokui hō* no seiritsu wo megurite" [The figuration of the Tale of Jidō: Concerning the formation of the Tendai *Sokui hō*] (Part 2). *Kokugo kokubun* 53(9): 30–56.

———. 1998. *Yuya no kōgō: Chūsei no sei to sei naru mono.* [The empress of the bathhouse: Medieval sexuality and the sacred]. Nagoya: Nagoya daigaku shuppan kai.

Amino Yoshihiko. 2005. *Chūsei no hinin to yūjo* [Medieval outcastes and prostitutes]. Kōdansha gakujutsu bunko.

———. 2012. *Rethinking Japanese History.* Translated by Alan S. Christy. Ann Arbor: University of Michigan.

Brecher, W. Puck. 2015. "Being a Brat: The Ethics of Child Disobedience in the Edo Period." In *Values, Identity, and Equality in Eighteenth- and Nineteenth-Century Japan,* edited by Peter Nosco, James Edward Ketelaar, and Yasunori Kojima. Leiden: Brill.

Childs, Margaret H. 1980. "*Chigo Monogatari:* Love Stories or Buddhist Sermons?" *Monumenta Nipponica* 35, no (Summer): 127–51.

Dōmoto Masaki. 1985. "Chigo no sōshi: Honbun shōkai" [*The Scroll of Acolytes*: Introduction to the primary source]. *Yasō* 15: 167–88.

Faure, Bernard. 1998. *The Red Thread: Buddhist Approaches to Sexuality.* Princeton, NJ: Princeton University Press.

Guth, Christine M. E. 1987. "The Divine Boy in Japanese Art." *Monumenta Nipponica* 42, no. 1 (Spring): 1–23.

Hosokawa Ryōichi. 2000 [1996]. *Itsudatsu no Nihon chūsei* [Deviant medieval Japan]. Chikuma gakugei bunko.

Ijiri Matakurō Tadasuke. 1917. *Nyakudō no kanjinchō* [The solicitation book of the Way of Youths]. In *Misonoya*, vol. 4., edited by Ōta Nanpo et al., 477–78. Kokusho kankōkai.

Itō Nobuhiro, Claire-Akiko Brisset, and Shin'ichirō Masuo. 2015. "*Shuhanron emaki*" *eiin to kenkyū: Bunkachō-bon, Furansu Kokuritsu Toshokan-bon to sono shūhen* [The Facsimile and research on "The Picture Scroll of the Debate over Rice and Sake": The Cultural Agency manuscript, the National Library of France manuscript and their environs]. Kyoto: Rinsen shoten.

Iwata Jun'ichi. 2002. *Honchō nanshoku kō: Nanshoku bunken shoshi* [An investigation into the male eros in our land: A bibliography on male eros]. Hara Shobō.

Kōbō Daishi. 1931. *Jistugokyō* [The teaching of the truthful words]. In *Kokumin shisō sōsho: Minshū hen,* edited by Katō Totsudō, 3–8. Tōkyō: Daitō Shuppansha.

Kuroda Hideo. 1986. *Kyōkai no chūsei: Shōchō no chūsei* [The borders of the medieval: The borders of the symbol]. Tōkyō: Daigaku Shuppansha.

Leupp, Gary. 1995. *Male Colors: The Construction of Homosexuality in Tokugawa Japan.* Berkeley: University of California.

Lin, Irene Hong-Hong. 2001. "Traversing Boundaries: The Demonic Child in the Medieval Japanese Religious Imaginaire." PhD diss., Stanford University.

Matsuo Kenji. 2008. *Hakai to nanshoku no bukkyōshi* [The Buddhist history of breaching the Precepts]. Heibonsha.

Matsuoka Shinpei. 1991. *Utage no shintai: Basara kara Zeami he* [The body of the banquet: From Basara to Zeami]. Iwanami shoten.

Meeks, Lori Rachelle. 2010. *Hokkeji and the Reemergence of Female Monastic Orders in Premodern Japan*. Honolulu: University of Hawai'i Press.

Moriyama Shigeki and Nakae Kazue. 2002. *Nihon kodomo shi* [The history of children in Japan]. Heibonsha.

Pflugfelder, Gregory M. 1999. *Cartographies of Desire: Male-Male Sexuality in Japanese Discourse, 1600–1950*. Berkeley: University of California Press.

Porath, Or. 2015. "The Cosmology of Male-Male Love in Medieval Japan: *Nyakudō no Kanjinchō* and the Way of Youths." *Journal of Religion in Japan* 4(2): 241–71.

Pseudo-Annen. 1931. *Dōji-kyō* [Instructions for children]. In *Kokumin shisō sōsho: Minshū hen*, edited by Katō Totsudō, 9–27. Daitō Shuppansha.

Sōgi. 1959/60. *Chigo kyōkun* [The education of acolytes]. In *Gunsho ruijū*, vol. 17 edited by Hanawa Hokiichi et al. Zoku Gunsho Ruijū Kanseikai, , 336–46.

Sugawara Masako. 2014. *Nihon chūsei no gakumon to kyōiku* [Scholarship and education in medieval Japan]. Dōseisha.

Takahashi Shūjō. 2007. "Yōdō no keiko: Tokyo Daigaku Shiryōhensanjo-zō 'renren ni keiko seshimuru sōshi ige no koto' ni miru bungaku-sho to fu'ei'in" [The practice of young children: Literary texts and their attached facsimiles as seen in the manuscript *The Scroll that Makes [Children] Practice Continuously and Other Texts* in the repository of Tokyo University's Historiographical Institute." *Chisan gakuhō* 56, no. 3: 545–67.

Takakusu, Junjirō, and Watanabe Kaikyoku, eds. 1924–34. *Taishō shinshū daizōkyō* [The Taishō-era Buddhist canon]. 100 vols. Tōkyō: Taishō Issaikyō Kankōkai.

Tanaka Takako. 1999. *Muromachi obōsan monogatari* [Tales of Muromachi priests]. Kōdansha gendai shinsho.

———. 2004. *Seiai no Nihon Chūsei* [Sexual love in medieval Japan]. Chikuma Shobō.

Tsuchiya Megumi. 2001. *Chūsei jiin no shakai to geinō* [Society and the performing arts in medieval Japan]. Yoshikawa Kōbunkan.

Tsuji Zennosuke. 1951; reprint 1970. *Nihon Bukkyō shi* [The Buddhist history of Japan]. Vol. 6. Iwanami Shoten.

Yūki Rikurō. 1977. *Ransei no kodomo* [Children in Trouble Times], Vol. 2 of Nihon kodomo no rekishi . Tokyo: Daiichi Hōki Shuppan.

2

___

Growing Up Manly

Male Samurai Childhood in Late Edo-Era Tosa

Luke S. Roberts

"*Previously young samurai of the household still wore the round forelock hairstyles of children until around age fourteen or fifteen, and none of them walked around wearing two swords. Instead, they wore just one short sword when they left the house. It was proper for all of them to start wearing two swords when they trimmed corners into their forelocks and sewed up the open underarms of their kimonos in a 'half-adulthood' ceremony showing they would soon take on the appearance and duties of an adult. But in recent years, little boys aged five or six with their hair still up in toddler-like buns cannot go out of the house for even a minute without wearing two swords. Their parents and elder brothers say that of course it is a sign of being born into a warrior house, that they are born into precocious excellence and should wear two swords like adults.*"

—TOSA SAMURAI MINOURA YUKINAO, WRITING IN 1803
AT AGE SEVENTY-EIGHT

The warrior-bureaucrats known as samurai constituted the ruling class in the Edo period (1600–1868) and filled the highest levels of both government and military. The head of each samurai household was a male who held a particular rank and received a specified fief or stipend in his lord's household. This position conferred on him a house and its property, a guaranteed annual income, and high social and legal status that set him above the villagers, townspeople, and other commoners who made up over 95 percent of the population. This position was inherited, and if a samurai lost it as punishment for a crime, he became a *rōnin*: a lordless samurai without income, without a house, and of low social standing. Not having a son ready to inherit might see the end of the family's position as well. Such loss was a disaster for the whole household of family members, dependents, and servants, and also threatened a decline in influence and prestige for people in the kin network. Naturally families put a disproportionate amount of resources into maintaining the male head and raising his heir, and children were raised to learn their several roles in ensuring the household's continuance (Ōta 2011: 55, 72–120).

Family strategies shaped the experience of childhood for both samurai boys and girls. Daughters were raised to marry a samurai household head and serve as wife and mother. They were trained to take on a large degree of household management and contribute to economically productive activities such as weaving. Women were not allowed to be official household heads, but if there were no sons in the household, then one of the daughters would be expected to remain in the house and marry a man who was willing to be adopted into the household and take on the family name and position. Such adoption was a frequent and relatively easy matter in samurai households because household continuance was much more important than paternal bloodline, but sons sired by the male head of the house were generally desired as the ideal way to maintain the family lineage. One elderly retainer in Tosa domain, Kusunose Ōe, wrote in his diary upon the birth of a son in 1831: "Up to now I have had six daughters. Now that the seventh child is a son I can somewhat justify myself to my ancestors. There is no happiness greater than this!" (Ōta 2011: 85–86) Samurai sons were raised to be heir and then master of a household, either in their own home, by being adopted into an heirless household, or—more rarely—by having the domain lord hire them directly as retainers and thereby to set up a new household. The family goal was to make sons capable family heads, good retainers of their lords, and men respected by their peers and others.

How did families relate to their children and raise them, and what specifically did they regard as good, capable, and respectable? Analyzing such family goals is well suited to highlighting the socially constructed nature of samurai childhood because the goals of samurai childrearing were focused on maintaining the family's institutionally well-defined hereditary status and economic class.

However, one of the inherent limitations in a family strategies approach to childhood is that it produces narratives of children as the objects of adult action and desires and reduces their subjectivity (Cunningham 1998: 1196). One way to compensate for this and to more fully grasp a child's experience and active place in the family is to explore the emotions involved in the familial relationship. The rules of emotional communication are, like family strategies, constructed historically, but they have a strong biological basis that puts children and adults on more equal footing as individuals (Rosenwein 2002: 837). Emotions were used communicatively in the deployment of family strategy. Records of emotional expression or of states of attachment and alienation can help us better understand how people experienced its effects and inherent tensions, and in particular how children related to their parents and peers as they grew ("AHR Conversation" 2012: 1496–1500). What were the rules regarding emotional expression and function (what Solomon calls the emotional repertoire; see chapter 5), and did these rules change along the way to adulthood?

This chapter addresses these questions through a close look at childrearing and commentary on samurai-class boys in the Yamauchi clan, who ruled Tosa domain in southwestern Japan. Numerous memoirs and diaries by various Tosa domain samurai who lived from the mid-eighteenth century to the mid-nineteenth century, roughly the final century of the Edo period, survive and they contain many records of children and their upbringing. The memoirs relate their authors' own childhood experiences as well as the childhood experiences of others, and are especially rich in the expression of emotional narratives. Being written by adults they have the advantage of containing an interpretive and reflective understanding of the past, but the disadvantage of reflecting highly selective and edited views of the experience of childhood. The diaries contain parents' records of childrearing and children's behavior and occasionally reveal emotional expressions. Three of the documents come from three generations of the Mori family, who were an upper-rank, if not elite, samurai household in Tosa domain. The first ("Nikki") is the mid-eighteenth-century diary by Mori Hirosada (1710–1773), who raised two sons and two daughters. His income was enough to maintain a household of ten to fifteen people including the servants. The next ("Nichiroku") is the diary of his son Mori Yoshiki (1768–1807), who raised four sons and two daughters. One of Yoshiki's sons, Mori Masana (1805–1873), compiled a type of biography of Yoshiki that consisted of excerpts from his father's letters and diary and, more importantly, many stories told about Yoshiki by Yoshiki's wife, relatives, friends, and chief retainer ("Sendai gyōjo"). Additionally, a samurai contemporary of Hirosada and Yoshiki, Minoura Yukinao (1726–1813), began writing a set of memoirs in 1803 when he was seventy-eight years old, reflecting on how customs in Tosa had changed since he was a child. It contains many observations on samurai childrearing practices and childhood experience (Minoura 2010).[1] Finally, the early pages of the memoir-diary by Sasaki Takayuki (1830–1910), a man who started life as a samurai of low status and income, contain a rich record of experience and emotive language regarding childhood in the mid-nineteenth century (Sasaki 1970).

MARKING STAGES OF CHILDHOOD GROWTH AND ENTRY INTO ADULTHOOD

Edo-era childhood was differentiated into various stages, each of which had its expectations and goals for advancement. Movement into each succeeding stage was socially marked by ceremonies involving family and friends and entailed changes in dress and hairstyle that indicated clearly even to strangers what stage the child had achieved. Reception into the social world as a baby happened about a week after birth with a naming ceremony. Having had their heads shaved as babies, sons and daughters became toddlers around age three with a *kamioki* ceremony allowing their hair to grow out. They might begin education outside the home around age six or seven. A son would receive a new set of pleated pants *(hakama)* and became a youth around age ten to twelve when he gained a hairstyle and clothing transitioning towards that of an adult. The *sodedome* ceremony marked the change from childhood to adulthood for a female samurai, when the long sleeves of her kimono were shortened, usually soon after her first marriage. For a male samurai the public ceremony that marked him as an adult *(genpuku)* meant a new hairstyle. This usually happened around age sixteen or seventeen but there was much variation. This ceremonial adulthood was the endpoint of a long process of development and education that brought the child stage by stage to becoming a full-fledged person. However, the actual age was much less important than many other considerations. What mattered most in the social sense were the various rites of passage for each new stage, as shown also in chapter 3. And even these social stages alone were not the whole story in achieving adulthood. A male samurai had the legal right to adopt an heir only from his seventeenth calendar year (around age sixteen)—which made this a crucial stage of adulthood in terms of securing household continuity. He might also be adult but not inherit his father's position and rank until his father retired at an advanced age, or conversely he might have to legally inherit while still a child because of his father's sudden death.

Passing through the stages of childhood fostered a strong claim to identity as a person of samurai status and inculcated masculinity in contradistinction to femininity. Half of the samurai were women, and half of the residents in most samurai households were commoner servants, so even within the home these two issues were confronted daily. Therefore although the focus of this paper is the socialization of samurai boys, it will also explore their relationships with samurai girls and with servants to highlight the development of status and gender distinctions.

Status issues were particularly important in the last century of the Tokugawa period. The commercial transformation of society and culture that began in the seventeenth century had, by the eighteenth century, grown long fingers that scrabbled away at the proper place of samurai in this peaceful world. Economic change engendered increasing protests, and samurai acknowledged that generally declining respect for them was in part associated with increasing criticism of "corrupt and lax" samurai behavior. Minoura Yukinao railed against the "decline" that he saw in samurai society, and in the introductory quotation to this chapter he notes one of the effects of status anxiety on the raising of samurai children: Families wished to mark their sons' social status ever earlier in life by, for example, having even very little children wear two swords. He also commented that parents were having all of the ceremonies marking a child's growth and even marriage take place much earlier than in the past (Minoura 2010: 64), suggesting that having the children find their place as samurai adults was a cause of much anxiety for parents. Parents may also have hurried them along the stages of maturity because they worried about their chosen children's survival. Children too had much to be anxious about as they wended the perilous path toward adulthood amid family plans and an uncontrollable world.

STAYING ALIVE

Children had many obstacles to overcome early in life, including some related to issues of family strategy. In the days before effective contraception, families world-wide had to confront the issue of what to do when there were too many children for the household economy. Abandonment, abortion, and infanticide were much more common than in modern times (Cunningham 1998: 1203–4). In some parts of Japan parents tended to raise many children but sent most of them out into indentured servitude. In other parts of Japan the practices of abortion or infan-ticide at the time of birth were relatively common. Tosa was such a region, not merely for reasons of poverty but as family strategy (Drixler 2013: 26–27, 78). It was commonly said that samurai families in Tosa generally desired to have no children after they had two sons, raising the "second son as a reserve in case some-thing should happen to the heir" (Yamakawa 1992: 174). Nevertheless, there was continual moral debate over this practice. In 1759 the domain lord issued an order that abortion and infanticide should stop, which drove the practice into hiding (Ōta 1997: 584). The samurai Mori Hirosada copied this order in his diary ("Nikki" 1759.7.29).[2] It became relevant years later in 1772 when in his own home he already had an adopted male heir and his own late-born son, Yoshiki, who was three years old. Hirosada's wife, Ume, gave birth that year in what he described as a "very easy birth," but Hirosada finished by writing a phrase that might be understood as "but there was no child" or possibly "but we got rid of the child" ("Nikki" 1772.11.28). He made no mention of subsequent burial, prayers, or rites, writing instead about his wife's process of recovery. We cannot really know if the cryptic description indicates parental decision or if it meant that a stillbirth occurred. At any rate, limiting the number of potential heirs to two was hardly a uniform custom. Some families raised more. Mori Yoshiki's second wife, Tachi, bore six children: two daughters and four sons. According to a story related by Yoshiki's manservant, she was sickly and raising them was difficult for her, especially after her mother-in-law died. When she was pregnant with the sixth, she told Yoshiki she was unable to raise it. This was either a request for an abortion or for help. Yoshiki opted for the latter saying, "'Even if there are tens of them children should be raised. If you can't do it, I'll take care of it, protect it, and raise it.' Indeed even though Yoshiki had many older sons he never carried them as babies or did things like that, but he was always holding Shirō. Because there was no grandmother he often made rice milk and fed it to Shirō himself" ("Sendai gyōjo": folio 94). In terms of family strategy, having four sons meant that three of them would have to hunt for positions as adults, perhaps to end up as an unplaceable younger brother living in the home. As it turned out, all three of the younger sons lucked out by being adopted as heirs of houses in the Mori kin group ("Mori-shi kafu," vol. 4).

Children were ushered into social reality with a party and naming ceremony that occurred on the seventh night after birth. This was done for both daughters and sons of the master of the house regardless of whether the mother was the legal wife or a servant. The childhood name given at that ceremony was generally used until the child's coming-of-age ceremony, when he or she received a new name. When Mori Hirosada's daughter Mase was born to his servant girl, he invited many relatives to a celebratory dinner, along with the midwife, doctor, and wet nurse. The relatives brought baby clothes, and Hirosada gave gifts of money and celebratory foods to everyone present and to others who could not come ("Nikki" 1765.11.23–12.1). An almost identical set of events and gift presentations happened when his son Yoshiki was born and given the childhood name Saihachi, suggesting that gender had little to do with this first ceremony of life ("Nikki" 1768.11.1–11.8). Expressions of emotion are rare in the Mori family diaries, but one can sense Hirosada's pleasure at his children's first smile. "Saihachi first smiled this morning. Mase first smiled on the fortieth day after her birth. Saihachi first smiled on his fortieth day, today!" ("Nikki" 1768.12.10). He also devoted equal attention to recording their illnesses, occasional accidents, and visits to the houses of relatives or festivals.

Various ceremonies were gender specific from early on. After having their heads shaved from birth until around age two, hairstyles for infants gradually differentiated their gender. Mase celebrated her first Girls Day by receiving gifts of dolls and flowers ("Nikki" 1766.3.3). Saihachi (Yoshiki) would likely have received traditional manly gifts such as swords and folding fans on his first Boys Day (1769.5.5) and a particular type of colorful flag would have been flown on the family property. Unfortunately the diary for that year no longer survives (Kōchi Chihōshi Kenkyūkai 1980: 43–44; Ōta 2011: 95–107).

The parents would also have to choose whether or not to register the children with the domain. Any child born to a servant or concubine would be recognized only if the samurai father acknowledged it. Yoshiki's mother, Ume, had a more complicated status than Mase's mother, Riso, though both had entered the household as servants. Hirosada had held a wedding ceremony and party to designate Ume as his wife. However, because she was of commoner origin, she legally remained a concubine in the eyes of the domain, which accepted only samurai women as legal wives (Roberts 2002: 27–28). Hirosada acknowledged Yoshiki but already had adopted a nephew, Sanpachi (Hirotake), as his heir. It seems as if an agreement had been made early on that Hirotake would in turn adopt Yoshiki as his son. However Hirotake had married a samurai woman and they had a son. By domain law Hirotake could not adopt a concubine's son in preference to his own by a samurai wife. Therefore what the family chose to do was to not register Hirotake's son at all. He lived in public anonymity until he chanced to die at age ten ("Mori-shi kafu," vol. 4).

Parents knew that the children they chose to raise would have to confront many diseases. Mortality was high, and illness caused much anxiety. Children frequently encountered the death of siblings, but the documents that relate their feelings are mostly the memoirs of adults. In his early teens Sasaki Takayuki saw a little sister die at seven months and a brother die at three days. "It was a boy, and we were happy, but it immediately turned into an unhappiness" that sent his generally difficult father into a long period of deep depression (Sasaki 1970: 15, 17). Mori Yoshiki's son by his first wife died after living only a month and a half, and his fourth child, his daughter Aya, died at age three ("Mori-shi kafu" vol. 4, "Nichiroku" 1801.9.7).

Diseases such as smallpox and dysentery often ravaged Tosa, like the rest of Japan, regardless of status and class, but some health issues particularly affected children of samurai status because of the diet associated with their status. Beriberi is a disease caused by a deficiency in thiamine, which generally harms nerve function and results in weakness, body pains, confusion, emotional disturbance and—especially in children—weight loss and death. In East Asia at this time it commonly occurred when people maintained a diet overly dependent on polished rice from which the thiamine, present only in the bran and germ, had been removed. Commoners tended to have more varied diets that included whole grains and were less affected by beriberi than samurai. Although this disease was common and caused great problems in late Tokugawa Japan, its cause was not discovered until the late 1880s (Bay 2008). Writing in 1803 the samurai Minoura Yukinao noted that the disease had seldom occurred in Tosa in the 1740s, but that in recent decades it had become common among samurai. Although this suggests to us that the samurai diet may have been changing, Yukinao's explanation was that, because it was rare among farmers, laborers and active people, its emergence among samurai must be because they had become less physically active in recent decades (Minoura 2010: 68–69). Many young children died from or struggled with this disease.

Another disease peculiar to children of the samurai class was lead poisoning (Nakashima et al. 1998), which can be said to result from family strategies of status differentiation. This was because the white skin cosmetic with which women of higher status painted themselves was lead-based, and breasts offered to infants were often covered with the cosmetic as a sign of respect. Analyses of lead levels in the bones excavated from samurai graves reveal that female samurai levels of lead were much higher than those of males, and that infants' levels were much higher than adults, probably brought about by ingestion of lead through suckling (Nakashima 2011). The levels were high enough to suggest widespread lead poisoning that would have led to many neurological, emotional, and learning disorders and forms of weakness. These common diseases, beriberi and lead poisoning, not only had long-term implications for personal development but also posed problems when affected children were put up as heirs. Mori Yoshiki once became involved as a consultant in a difficult situation in which a dying man wanted his son to be recognized as his heir even though the three-year-old child could not yet manage to stand up on his own legs. Although this troubled relatives and officials, ultimately Yoshiki, a key official at the time, recommended inheritance in the hope that things would turn out all right ("Nichiroku" 1800.8.2).

The diaries reveal that families commonly responded to a child's illness by calling on the help of relatives, doctors, gods, and Buddhas. Women often traveled between homes to assist with caring for the sick. When Sasaki Takayuki fell gravely ill at age two, his family made offerings for prayer at the famous Gion shrine in distant Kyoto (three hundred kilometers away) for his recovery. When he became better the family changed his name to Matsunosuke according to the oath they had offered to the shrine (Sasaki 1970: 6). When Mori Hirosada's adopted son, Hirotake, contracted smallpox at age seven he was seriously ill for two weeks. Hirosada called numerous doctors, and many relatives and friends from the neighborhood and even villagers from the fief in Takaoka showed up to offer sympathy and assistance. Following a common religious custom, the family set up a special altar *(hōsōkamidana)* in the household that would be taken down only when the child had recovered. When Hirotake was deemed safe, signaled by pus collecting in his pox, Hirosada immediately called over many relatives to celebrate with a feast, and he sent fish and red beans as celebratory foods as a way of informing others in town. Thirteen villagers from the fief brought a barrel of sake a day later, which they all drank to celebrate. All of this worry, work, and celebration integrated a large community of family, kin, and friends around Hirotake and his presence in the house ("Nikki" 1759.2.26–1759.3.12). One might be tempted to think that the celebrations were particularly lavish because of Hirotake's social importance as Hirosada's adopted heir, yet when Hirosada's daughter Mase, whom he had by a servant, became ill with smallpox the course of events was quite similar. They ended with a grand party of friends and relatives for which professional female entertainers were hired, and everyone "celebrated festively" late into the night ("Nikki" 1772.12.15–12.26).

When the children of the servants of the household were ill, Hirosada's response was much more limited. He mentioned their births and the outcome of their illnesses but recovery was not an occasion for a full household celebration ("Nikki" 1760.8.7, 1765.3.28, 1765.11.13). A slight exception was when the son of his hereditary chief manservant was ill with smallpox. Then the family set up a shrine and held an internal household celebration when he recovered ("Nikki" 1765.11.5). The graduated levels of status that derived through relationship to the father of the household were thus marked clearly on these occasions of sadness, anxiety, and joy.

LEARNING DESIRABLE PERSONAL QUALITIES

Mori Yoshiki's mother told her grandchildren about how good he was when he was little: "When he was just a toddler he was different from most children in that he understood things well. He would ask me to go to bed with him, and if I were preparing cotton for spinning I would say, 'After I have prepared so many rolls of cotton.' Even if it took some time he would not press me but instead counted how many rolls to go while he waited" ("Sendai gyōjo," folio 66). This introduces us to a common scenario of children pressuring their parents to lay down with them while they go to sleep, and the parent training the child in the virtues of self-restraint and cooperation. One of the leading Japanese scholars of early modern childhood, Ōta Motoko, argues that teaching the denial of self-interest and personal desire in order to be able to perform one's duty was typical of Edo-period education for samurai children (Ōta 2011: 74).

The Tosa documents reveal many examples of how samurai taught self-denial and self-control while educating their children. One nineteenth-century retainer writing about notable people of the domain said of Mori Yoshiki, "He was always saying that wearing a *haori* jacket showed a lack of resolute preparedness, and even in the cold he would not let his children and servants wear them" ("Shikishō, Chōnai hikki"). Yoshiki also tried to raise his children to express emotions in ways he thought proper. His manservant recalled, "When his boys sniffled [holding back tears], he would scold, 'When you cry, cry fully! Men don't sniffle!' and with that they always stopped crying" ("Sendai gyōjo," folio 93). Whether the goal was to encourage emotional restraint or intentional expressiveness is unclear but it fits his ideal of a controlled but assertive masculinity.

Yoshiki died relatively young at age thirty-nine, but his wife Tachi frequently used stories about his behavior to authorize her instructions to her still-young children in the importance of self-control and family identity. According to an account told by their son Harue,

> My dear mother was always saying to us, "No matter how hot it became, your father never passed time without his clothes on, he did not take afternoon naps, and if he was not laboring, he did not drop his kimono off his shoulders. When he sat he neither stretched his legs out nor put his knees sideways. When he slept he did not use just a thin informal belt and he did not let his hair get messed up. No matter the time, if something came up he would respond appropriately, and he always made sure to be ready to meet guests immediately. He learned these things from the house lessons of his own father, Hirosada, and indeed those who are his descendants should take these to heart" ("Sendai gyōjo," folio 58).

In his later years Yoshiki was assigned to the post of caretaker of the daimyo's son, and he even chided this exalted person about being tough and prepared like a warrior. As he told this eight-year-old heir, "Daimyo are warriors! Even when the situation calls for proceeding in a carriage or a horse, walking is the proper form for a daimyo!" His words surprised the young lord who was accustomed to being treated with more deference. Later that night at his bath the young lord confided to his attendant, "No one has ever spoken to me like that before" ("Genshin-kō iji," folios 2–3).

Yoshiki may have been a bit extreme, but the basic values he tried to instill in his children were common and well recognized. Sasaki Takayuki described in his memoirs how family members, particularly his father, praised him for behavior that showed self-control, confidence, and resolve enacted on behalf of the household, values that were promoted by samurai authorities who rewarded precocious filial piety displayed by children (Van Steenpaal 2016). When Takayuki was only five, he had his first audience with the domain lord. Most families provided a relative to accompany small children, but his father sent him alone. Takayuki behaved "as if there were nothing at all to be fearful about; just another normal thing to do. . . . When I came home my father and others all praised me, and I remember how happy I felt" (Sasaki 1970: 10).

Tadayuki's father had greater trouble with his own emotions. He blamed himself for causing his brother's suicide, and became sleepless, visiting the brother's grave nightly. His emotional disturbance caused young Takayuki much anxiety: "My childish heart felt this, and I worried much" (Sasaki 1970: 9). The following year his father became suicidal and slashed his face with a blade. Young Takayuki had to run to the neighbors to ask for help to prevent his father from killing himself. Ultimately the relatives built a cage in the house to keep him in until he recovered. The family finances became so bad at that point that the family sold all of the weapons and armor except for one set that had belonged to his great grandfather Chūsaburō. Chūsaburō was a particularly revered man who had restored the fortunes of the house in the 1780s (Roberts 1997: 581–83, 594–96), and this armor had heirloom significance. Yet eventually finances became so tight that even this armor had to be used to get money. The relatives found a wealthy samurai who would buy it with the promise of reselling it to Takayuki when Takayuki was able. He was still just six years old but he was deeply moved and declared to his elder relatives, "Without doubt, I will one day buy it back!" for which he remembers them praising him (Sasaki 1970: 10–11).

A collective endemic anxiety over the continuity of the household was instilled in children at an early age. Samurai households were only one sad crime or untimely death away from destruction, and incidents of household termination occurred often especially among the poorer, more marginal households. Takayuki's father was deemed better after a year. The family let him out of his cage and he returned to performing his duties. He nevertheless remained an extremely sensitive and difficult person, often so depressed that he could hardly do anything. All the relatives commented on it, one of them saying, "There is a bolt of lightning waiting over the Sasaki household day and night. When it will fall we don't know, but there is nothing one can do but hold our breath and wait for the moment." Takayuki writes about how often he became anxious about his father and the family on this account, but nevertheless said that despite his own status as an adopted son, his father "loved and cared for me deeply. His difficulties were because of his illness" (Sasaki 1970: 18). Takayuki's status as adopted son made him, early on in life, all the more aware of the problems of household continuity. His adoptive father too likely loved and cared for his heir all the more because Takayuki represented the fulfillment of his duties to maintain household continuity.

The sons of samurai in the late eighteenth century were educated into becoming members of the warrior class during an era of extended peace. This involved a delicate mix of expressing a willingness to use violence to defend one's honor while nevertheless showing restraint. The domain often meted out punishments following violent incidents to serve as a warning to encourage restraint, yet samurai who were not ready to be violent were seen as somehow not proper samurai. Many samurai commonly expressed such anxieties, such the seventy-seven-year-old samurai Minoura Yukinao, who wrote in 1803 about how young samurai were increasingly unlikely to punish a person of equal or lower status for being rude. In the old days, he said, they would often use their swords in response to rudeness. These days they would go home angry and discuss the event with family members who would usually arrange for a monk or a doctor to be a go-between to make peace between the parties even when one was of lower status. "This is because the customs of our domain have declined terribly, and samurai forget their way" (Minoura 2010: 77). This suggests that civility and restraint were becoming more important socially in the late Edo period even among samurai youth. Mori Yoshiki himself was deeply invested in a military identity and often wrote about his worries that samurai were losing their martial character, using such phrases as "Daimyo these days don't know what it means to be a warrior!"

Yoshiki's chief manservant told a number of stories related to childrearing that make Yoshiki appear to be a severe figure who encouraged a tough manliness. On one occasion in 1806, Yoshiki's six-year-old son, Komaji, came home crying after being teased by a neighborhood samurai boy. Yoshiki was furious and sent out a manservant with his son saying, "It isn't over if you just come home crying. Go cut down your opponent, and I won't let you back in the house until you do!" ("Sendai gyōjo," folio 92). Fortunately some women of the house overheard this and quickly ran over to the neighbors to garner polite apologies so that the day ended without violence. It is likely that Yoshiki's intent was performative—not really a hope that his son would kill a neighbor—and that he depended on others to smooth things over. Still one must wonder what went on in the mind of his six-year-old son at that time.

Indeed Yoshiki chides himself for his concern for his children. During a lengthy government trip inspecting the villages of the domain he worried about reports from home that his eldest son had dysentery: "Here I write about the House Elder being weak when traveling, and yet my heart is so weak about just one child that I write thoughts just as they come to me." He both fears and acknowledges his love for his son. The fear is that parental affection will make his son undisciplined and unwilling to face hardship, qualities which Yoshiki saw as important to being a manly samurai.

FINDING ONE'S PLACE AMONG OTHER YOUTHS

An important component to growing up was learning how to interact with superiors, peers, and inferiors as well as developing a network of friends and rivals that might endure over a lifetime. After samurai sons reached the age of six, they began learning to read outside of the home and by their mid-teens they were learning many military arts as well, gradually socializing them into the values of the community of peers that they would join as adults. These interactions resulted in the formation of memories both collective and individual that structured friendships and created enemies.

Diaries and memoirs are filled with accounts of children's interactions with one another. Hirosada and Yoshiki's diaries reveal that they and their male children participated in classes and the informal practice of many military skills. Sasaki Takayuki noted how this made him aware of the importance of status distinctions: When he was seven he began commuting to a school that happened to have many high-status retainers in it. He could not afford his own books because of his family's low status and income. He remembers frequently being slighted and treated with contempt, noting some of the worst offenders by name. "I felt so mortified and hoped for a future day when I could push them down" (Sasaki 1970: 14). He had friends though and remembers how when he was seven he listened with interest to letters read aloud by one of his fourteen-year-old friends describing the fighting at the time of Ōshio Heihachirō's 1837 rebellion in Osaka. Two months later he was invited to the home of a wealthier friend where in the garden they had set up figurines and fired off miniature cannons recreating the rebellion. "It was so interesting to my child's heart. I eagerly hoped that war would occur" (Sasaki 1970: 13). Starting at age ten he and his friends began reading military texts and stories of fighting on their own. A friend of his had a copy of the famous tale *Revenge Killing at Tenka Teahouse* (Tenka Chaya no adauchi) and read it to Takayuki, who consumed it with interest (Sasaki 1970: 19). He began studying military skills such as swordsmanship and the spear when he turned fourteen (Sasaki 1970: 23), and entered horsemanship school at age seventeen. However this latter experience became yet another disappointing lesson in the ways of the samurai world. The teacher would only actually teach students who gave him gifts and provided him with dinners. Poor students such as Takayuki found themselves left out, and he soon quit (Sasaki 1970: 30). It is little surprise that when he reached adulthood he became part of a political faction that actively resisted the power of the traditional elite houses.

Other forms of socialization were less structured. Youths often ran around together unsupervised and they commonly created gangs. In these gangs they began forming lifelong friendships and learned about modes of aggression, competitive manliness, obedience to hierarchies, and group unity—qualities important in adulthood. According to Minoura Yukinao, "Samurai children and younger brothers gather themselves into gangs with names. They make new members sign strict oaths and become very close to each other, so as to maintain what is righteous. I hear that the young ones are ordered around by the older ones who are reaching adulthood" (Minoura 2010: 73).

Mori Yoshiki described in his diary how such gangs competed with each other at a Dragon King festival on the bay by the castle town in 1799. One gang embarked on two large houseboats decorated with dozens of lanterns and crossed to the opposite shore, where the other gang was waiting in many small boats. It attacked the larger boats in an attempt to cut down the lanterns while also launching fireworks from the land. The two large vessels fired their own "shooting stars" at the little boats as well. When the fireworks ran out, the smaller boats closed, and the youths on them began cutting down the lanterns with their short swords. Just as the brawl began turning into a more serious fight, both sides retreated, yelling that they would meet again ("Nichiroku" 1799.6.15). Such rowdiness would not have been tolerated between adults, but it helped bond the youths socially to each other in forms of aggressive masculinity and team building that constituted a preparation for the usually more restrained behavior of adulthood.

Of course there were times when such behavior went too far, and groups of unruly youths ended up punished by the domain for causing disturbances. On such occasions the fathers were punished as well for the crime of "not properly managing their households." In the late Tokugawa period such incidents occurred in the castle town every few years ("Okachū hengi"). For example, when the youth Teshima Kihachi and a number of his friends suddenly approached his father, who was a government official, and appealed "in an overly forceful and disrespectful manner" about governmental matters—both rude in itself and beyond their station in politics—this caught the attention of other domain officials. The father's punishment was comparatively light—a period of "circumspection" that was lifted after a few days—but such public shaming became a part of the permanent record of the household lineages maintained by the domain ("Osamuraichū senzo sho keizu chō," vol. 54). If the youth's crimes were too severe, the punishments rose in severity even to disenfeoffment and banishment, thus effectively ending the household.

Youths often formed intimate bonds, and individual exchanges of oaths testifying to devotion between senior and younger youths who developed romantic and sexual relationships were quite common (Moriguchi 1996). These relationships often deeply involved the parents, whose permission was sought by suitors. This permission was important because it helped to ensure a serial monogamy in these relations and thereby to prevent disruptive conflicts between suitors that might lead to domain punishments. The evidence of Mori Hirosada's diary suggests that such relationships were common among youths from their early to late teens. At age sixteen, his adopted son, Hirotake, "became infatuated with Watanabe Yakuma's son and heir, Kichitarō." While Hirotake waited at home with seven friends, two others went to Yakuma to declare Hirotake's love. Yakuma said that although he had no objections, his son might already be involved with someone else. He would check with his son and respond later. As it turned out, Kichitarō, who was fifteen, already had a lover in another youth who was unwilling to let go, so the father told Hirotake to "please stop thinking about" Kichitarō. Hirotake did so, and the matter ended peaceably ("Nikki" 1768.10.23, Moriguchi 1996: 49–50).

A similar incident in another Mori household in the kin group, one that did not resolve so cleanly, reveals how extensive kin networks could be affected by youthful emotions. In that case nineteen-year-old Mori Jūjirō showed up at the house of Ishikawa Sōzaemon and stated his desire to have a lover's relationship with his son Ichinosuke. The father said he was favorable to the idea and "thought highly" of Jūjirō but he was presently busy with domain business. He promised to check later with his son and sent Jūjirō home. As it turned out, his son was already in a relationship with a youth from the Kataoka family. Jūjirō thought that the father told him at this point that he should "wait until a way could be opened up," suggesting perhaps that the Kataoka would give up the relationship, but this only complicated the situation. Soon members of the Mori, Ishikawa, and Kataoka kin groups gathered to discuss the situation, but none gave in. The was the kind of conflict that would attract domain attention. When punishment appeared in the offing, the kin groups invited in outside mediators who resolved things by having the Kataoka youth give up his relationship with the young Ichinosuke and Jūjirō promise not to press his suit: in effect a divorce all around ("Nikki" 1762.1.21). Personal honor was bound up in these youthful love relationships (Schalow 1990: 27–32). This honor might lead to fights, and a youth's honor was also tied to that of his kin group, both factors that encouraged families to become deeply involved in the management and outcomes of these relationships.

Intimate relationships were thus made in familial and social contexts but they were generally understood to be temporary, usually ending when the younger partner grew into adulthood. Although such relationships often created long-term bonds of friendship even after they ended, one more incident from Hirosada's diary reveals complications that might arise when a youth exited a relationship. In 1769 when Fukuoka Kyūhachirō "had his *genpuku* ceremony and became a man," he sent notice via a friend to his adult lover that he wished to end the relationship. The lover did not want to end the relationship, and it took a number of people to finally get him to agree. However he still would not return the written oath that Kyūhachirō had given him, and this oath "had many ridiculous things in it. Allowing it to remain [in the lover's hands] would be very problematic for Kyūhachirō's future" ("Nikki" 1770.i6.14). Quite possibly it contained promises to obey the lover even if the lord's government ordered otherwise—a display of ultimate devotion, but one that could prove fatal if made public during adulthood. Finally after much negotiation the lover returned the oath.

Although Hirosada's diary frequently refers to the emotions of intimate friendship, infatuation, and love (*chiin, shūshin, nengoro*) that male youths had for each other, it is significant that no such language is used for the relationships between youthful men and women—or for that matter between adult men and women, although records of heterosexual relationships abound in his life and diary. This probably had to do with notions of masculinity that were tied to a gender hierarchy that demeaned women and to a large degree turned them into men's property. Social norms promoted a feeling that it would be degrading to display affection for a woman too publicly (Schalow 1990: 4–5, 49–56). For a man to express his close relationship with another young man made him manly, while to do so concerning women put him in danger of becoming "womanly."

Male relationships with women seem to have been handled with much more public emotional restraint. Hirosada's diary contains many discussions of marriage negotiations but the only word signifying attachment was *shomō* which means "want to have" or "desire to have," and can be applied to objects as well as people. Furthermore, the desiring party was the youth's father rather than the youth himself. Unlike in male-male relationships, individuals did not carry out the negotiations. No son would suddenly show up at a man's house asking for his daughter. Instead negotiations would begin with the arrival of a third party who would say "so-and-so's son wants your daughter in marriage." In Hirosada's case his daughter Otsune was first engaged that way to Inoue Saemon, whose father sent a messenger ("Nikki" 1760.2.19). Later her fiancé died, and a different family likewise sent Hirosada a request. The request on behalf of Hirosada's son Hirotake, made via Sasaki Kurōemon, for the hand of Hayashi Seigo's daughter was likewise unemotional—the Hayashi family's response that "we have no difficulty with it" led to marriage ("Nikki" 1764.2.24).

This is not to say that youths might not have feelings of attachment to women, but rather that it was unseemly to express such feelings. Sasaki Takayuki wrote that samurai youths used to tease each other by walking in groups around town and singing the names of something or someone that a youth loved in front of his house gate as if they were selling them, including sometimes the names of commoner women (Sasaki 1970: 37). He does not mention teasing about feelings toward women of samurai status. That would likely have been too sensitive a topic to families to tease about publicly even if such feelings existed, and they would have been dangerous to honor. At any rate in this homosocial world, youthful males and females of samurai status had little opportunity for interaction outside the family. Decisions about marriage were much more a matter between the young people's families than between the young people themselves and might even happen in their childhood. This does not mean that youthful emotions were ignored, and youthful divorce was quite common.

Minoura Yukinao wrote that by the start of the nineteenth century, families were rushing everything for their children, including arranging their marriages at younger and younger ages. "Because they do not yet know the way of adulthood, the husband looks askance at his wife and then they divorce, leading to relations between hitherto friendly families suddenly ceasing in a morning" (Minoura 2010: 64). One strategy that families used to deal with this was to have the daughter live informally in the groom's home for some months beforehand to see if the couple was compatible. Sasaki Takayuki writes that the daughter of a fellow samurai came to live with him in informal marriage when he was sixteen, but even so after four months they divorced. His second marriage, begun at age seventeen, lasted only until he was nineteen (Sasaki 1970: 30–31, 33, 47). In 1760 Mori Hirosada engaged his thirteen-year-old daughter Otsune to Inoue Saemon, the son of a close friend, but she remained at home until she was old enough to actually marry.

CONCLUSION

Samurai children were highly valued particularly for their roles in maintaining family continuity, and emotional bonds were shaped in tandem. Only males could attain the employment with the lord that permitted the continuance of the house, and eldest sons were particularly treasured. However, the widespread use of adoption among samurai families, including the possibility of adopting the husband of the family daughter, meant that all children could play a key role in the continuance of the family. Families devoted substantial resources to the health and life-stage ceremonies of all of the children regardless of gender and whether they were born to the wife or a concubine or were adopted.

Family members strove to train children into behavior that would sustain the continuance of the household, but children also had their own occasionally disruptive desires and plans. Youthful love or dislike might end up embroiling families and kin groups in troublesome conflicts or conversely might help to create friendly associations. Additionally, adults and children alike confronted the frequent vicissitudes of accident and illness that sometimes emerged from family strategies and sometimes randomly intruded into plans for success. But the goal of keeping household status and income from one generation to the next remained, and the legal framework required successful inheritance and transition to a new male heir who would achieve adulthood.

It is impossible to define a clear end to samurai childhood in a generalized way because the many markers of adulthood in samurai society did not occur in coordination or at rigidly prescribed ages. The *genpuku* adulthood ceremony in which sons had their hair cut according to adult fashion was certainly an important moment, but it might happen so early as to make it only a partial marker of becoming a full-fledged man, as happened with Sasaki Takayuki, who was fourteen and still just finding his way in school among peers (Sasaki 1970: 22). Marriage also might happen young but end quickly. Perhaps it was increasing anxiety over status and familial success, evident in the latter half of the Tokugawa period, that led to the earlier enactments of such markers of advancement toward adulthood. Seventeen was an age that legally allowed a man to adopt an heir but he did not become family head until his father retired or died. Family headship might occur at an earlier age than adulthood as we have seen in the case of the three-year-old child who still could not yet walk becoming the head of samurai household. Hiro-sada became legal head of his house at age fourteen and Yoshiki at age nine. Even though family life was filled with ceremonies marking stages of childhood and finally entry into adulthood, life itself was infinitely complex and samurai families adjusted in the interest of maintaining the legal samurai household upon which so many people depended.

NOTES

1. Japanese in the Edo period counted age differently than in the modern era, counting not by birthdays but by how many calendar years one had lived in. A person born in November was im-mediately 1 *sai* and next January was 2 *sai* because he or she had lived in two calendar years. I present approximate Western ages in this chapter, made by subtracting one year from the *sai*.

2. Dates refer to those in the documents, based on the Tokugawa period lunar-solar calendar, pre-senting the year, month, day, but with the year converted to the approximate Gregorian calendar year. 1772.11.28 corresponds to the Gregorian December 22, 1772.

BIBLIOGRAPHY

Note: Unless noted otherwise the place of publication for Japanese books is Tokyo.

"AHR Conversation: The Historical Study of Emotions. Participants: Nicole Eustace, Euge-nia Lean, Julie Livingston, Jan Plamper, William M. Reddy, and Barbara H. Rosenwein." 2012. *American Historical Review* 117, no. 5 (December): 1487–1531.

Akizawa Shigeru et al., eds. 1998–2011. *Tosa no kuni gunsho ruijū* [Categorized collection of documents of Tosa province]. 13 vols. Kōchi: Kōchi Kenritsu Toshokan.

Bay, Alexander. 2008. "Beriberi, Military Medicine, and Medical Authority in Prewar Japan." *Japan Review* 20: 111–56.

Cunningham, Hugh. 1998. "Review Essay: Histories of Childhood." *American Historical Review* 103(4): 1195–1208.

Drixler, Fabian. 2013. *Mabiki: Infanticide and Population Growth in Eastern Japan, 1660–1950.* Berkeley: University of California Press.

"Genshin-kō iji" [Records of lord Genshin]. Document K289 yama-2, Kōchi Prefecture Library.

Kōchi Chihōshi Kenkyūkai. 1980. *Kusunose Ōe nikki: Hiuchibukuro.* Vol. 13. Kōchi: Kōchi City Library.

Minoura Senpachi (Yukinao). 2010. "Kokuzoku henkō mokushiki roku" [A record of changes in the customs of the province that I have seen and understand]. In *Tosa no kuni gunsho ruiju* (Categorized collection of documents of Tosa province), edited by Akizawa Shigeru et al., vol. 12, 62–99. Kōchi: KōchiPrefecture Library.

Moriguchi Kōji. 1996. "Tosa hansei kōki ni okeru 'chiin' kō: Wakasamurai no 'koi' no shūzoku" [Thoughts on "intimacy" during the latter half of the era of Tosa domain: Customs of love between young samurai]. *Tosa shidan* [Discussions of Tosa History] 200 (Jan.): 45–52.

"Mori-shi ate sekitokushū" [Collection of letters sent to the Mori family. Document 903, Ban Bunko collection, Kōchi City Library.

"Mori-shi kafu" [Mori family lineages]. 9 vols, uncatalogued, Kōchi Prefecture Library.

Mutō Munekazu. 1990–1998. *Nanro shi* [History and geography of the southern provinces], edited by Yorimitsu Kanji, Akizawa Shigeru, et al. 10 vols. Kōchi: Kōchi Kenritsu Toshokan.

Nakashima Tamiji, H. Hayashi, H. Tashiro, T. Matsushita. 1998. "Gender and Hierarchical Differences in Lead-Contaminated Japanese Bone from the Edo Period." *Journal of Occupational Health* 40, no. 1 (January): 55–60.

Nakashima Tamiji, Koji Matsuno, Masami Matsushita, Takayuki Matsushita. 2011. "Severe Lead Contamination among Children of Samurai Families in Edo Period Japan." *Journal of Archaeological Science* 38(1): 23–28.

"Nichiroku" [Diary of Mori Yoshiki]. 12 volumes (1788, 1791, 1793, 1798–1807). Document K289 mori, Kōchi Prefecture Library.

"Nikki" [Diary of Mori Hirosada]. 20 volumes (1731–1749, 1751–1768, 1770–1772). Document K289 mori, Kōchi Prefecture Library.

"Okachū hengi" [Disturbances in the household], Vols. 20–26 in "Nanrōshi yoku," 50 vols., document 4141.84/.5/.51, Tōkyō: Tōkyō Daigaku Shirōhensanjo.

"Osamuraichū senzosho keizuchō" [Lineages and service records of all of the samurai of Tosa domain]. Document K288 osa, Kōchi Prefecture Library.

Ōta Motoko. 1994. *Edo no oyako: Chichioya ga kodomo wo sodateta jidai* [Parents and children of the Edo period: An era when fathers helped raise children]. Chūō kōron-sha.

———. 1997. *Kinsei Nihon mabiki kankō shiryō shūsei* [Collected documents on the custom of infanticide in early modern Japan]. Tōsui Shobō.

———. 2011. *Kinsei no "ie" to kazoku: Kosodate o meguru shakaishi* [The early modern "household" and family: A social history of childrearing]. Kadokawa Gakugei Shuppan.

Roberts, Luke S. 1997. "A Petition for a Popularly Chosen Council of Government in Tosa in 1787." *Harvard Journal of Asiatic Studies* 57(2): 575–96.

———. 2002. "Mori Yoshiki: Samurai Government Officer." In *The Human Tradition in Modern Japan,* edited by Anne Walthall, 25–44. Wilmington: Scholarly Resources.

Rosenwein, Barbara H. 2002. "Worrying about Emotions in History." *The American Historical Review* 107, no. 3 (June): 821–45.

Sasaki Takayuki. 1970. *Hogohiroi: Sasaki Takayuki nikki* [Gathered bits of discarded things: The diary of Sasaki Takayuki]. Vol. 1. Tokyo University Press.

Schalow, Paul Gordon. 1990. "Introduction." In *The Great Mirror of Male Love,* by Ihara Saikaku, translated by Paul Gordon Schalow, 1–46. Stanford, CA: Stanford University Press.

"Sendai gyōjō" [Life and letters of my father], by Mori Masana and Ichihara Genzō, Kōchi Museum of History and Culture.

Shibata Jun. 2013. *Nihon yōjishi: Kodomo e no manazashi* [A history of childrearing in Japan: Perspectives on children]. Yoshikawa Kōbunkan.

"Shikishō, Chōnai hikki" [Excerpts from personal records, writings in my notebook], by Ōmachi Masayoshi. In "Tosa shiryō" [Documents of Tosa], vol. 6., Seki S6, Tosa Yamauchi Family Treasury and Archives.

Van Steenpaal, Niels. 2016. "Conflicting Paradigms of Moral and Biological Childhood: The Biography of Tomematsu the Filial Boy." In *Childhood in Japanese History: Concepts and Experiences / Kindheit in der japanischen Geschichte: Vorstellungen und Erfahrungen,* edited by Michael Kinski, Harald Salomon, and Eike Grossman, 215–36. Wiesbaden: Harrassowitz.

Yamakawa Kikue. 1992. *Women of the Mito Domain: Recollections of Samurai Family Life.* Translated and with an Introduction by Kate Waldman Nakai. University of Tokyo Press.

3

For the Love of Children

Practice, Affect, and Subjectivities in Hirata Atsutane's Household

Anne Walthall

If grief is one response to the loss of a loved one, then Hirata Atsutane's reaction to the sickness and death of his three-year-old granddaughter from smallpox in 1829 suggests that he indeed loved her: "Atsutane stayed up all night watching over her . . . . The next day he put her into the bath, but her condition worsened . . . . Asking us to keep vigil over her, he put her care in our hands while he shut himself in his study and prayed to the gods. He allowed no one to enter and refused food lest it interrupt his prayers . . . . She died around three in the afternoon. We made preparations for her funeral, and everyone spent the night at her pillow" (Watanabe 1942: 1059–61). For the twelve days that Fuki suffered, she absorbed her parents' and grandparents' energies and time. They tried everything: medicine, baths, moxa, prayers. After she died, they held a funeral, paid visits to the temple on the appropriate days, distributed steamed buns on the forty-ninth day after her death, commemorated her hundredth-day death anniversary, and remembered her on her death day for the next seven years.

There is a long-running debate in the Western historiography of childhood as to whether parents in the past grieved for their dead children (Cunningham 1998: 1198). Drawing on legal codes, mourning regulations, and other publicly disseminated documents, Shibata Jun argues that in the case of Japan, a transformation in views of children took place between the medieval and early modern periods. Instead of young corpses being placed in sacks and abandoned in the woods or mountains, they were given proper burials, although parents were still warned against the sort of extended mourning that the Hirata family performed for Fuki. Medieval children had been left to grow up on their own; early modern children came to be seen as treasures to be carefully raised and educated. As reasons for this change, Shibata points to political, social, and economic factors such as the late seventeenth-century laws of compassion, a society that promoted more stable families with property that could be maintained from one generation to the next, and an intellectual shift from reliance on either Buddhas or gods to reliance on one's own efforts and knowledge (Shibata 2013: esp. 189). In his book on infanticide, Fabian Drixler provides a different explanation. He posits that adherents of True Pure Land Buddhism were much less likely to kill newborn children than those who practiced funerary Buddhism (Drixler 2013). I think that the nativists such as Atsutane and his disciples took a third path: they abhorred infanticide and saw children as gifts from the gods to be cherished and trained for the good of family and nation (Hirano 1983: 93). In short, a number of emotional communities existed in early nineteenth-century Japan, each with its own perception of childhood (Rosenwein 2002: 842). To study even one of them, it is necessary to get below the surface of public pronouncements by examining private records.

My evidence for the place of children in the emotional community of nativists comes from the voluminous collection of documents left by Hirata Atsutane (1776–1843) and his family in the first two-thirds of the nineteenth century. Children wrote none of them; indeed, it is difficult to find any record of what children thought. Because Atsutane became famous for promoting Japanese exceptionalism based on his understanding of cosmology and the afterlife, his adopted son preserved materials relating to his father and his own efforts to promote his father's teachings. This being a family enterprise, he kept a diary and saved letters that incidentally shed light on the milestones in children's lives, their activities and opportunities as children, and the relations between parents and children and among the children themselves. Although Atsutane is known as a thinker and religious figure, he never forgot his samurai heritage, and he tried to raise his grandchildren as samurai. On the other hand, as a scholar, he shared with other proponents of the Japanese tradition a particular configuration of attitudes toward family and children that at least in their eyes differed from the strands of Chinese thought then prevalent in Japan.

In the status-bound world of early modern Japan, inculcating children with the skills appropriate to their status and performing appropriate childhood rituals attested to and validated a family's position. At the cost of considerable financial strain, the Hirata family tried to match practice to expectations. The family diary provides year-by-year, sometimes day-by-day records of milestones in the lives for boys and girls alike, although it does not always record them consistently. A useful comparison for the norms surrounding the rituals of childhood and attitudes toward children comes from the pen of Tachibana Moribe (1781–1849), Atsutane's close contemporary, like him a nativist scholar, and as such a member of the same emotional community.

Whereas diaries provide information regarding a child's process of maturation, letters speak to the emotional bonds that nativist scholars celebrated as tying the family together, what can be called the affect at play in the family game. Note that here I use "play" and "game" metaphorically to suggest that parents and children enjoyed interacting with each other in playful pursuits that demonstrated and deepened their mutual love and affection. Like Moribe's correspondence with his disciple and patron in the weaving center of Kiryū, which addresses the rearing of children, the letters sent by Atsutane and his wife to the family in Edo when he was sent into exile offer tender glimpses of their grandchildren and the children they encountered. Later letters by his grandson Nobutane delimit a different scenario: the difficulty of raising a boy who rejects everyday norms of samurai and scholarly behavior.

Letters also offer occasional glimpses of how men remembered their own childhoods. As he grew older, Atsutane recollected conflicting accounts of how he grew up that, by acknowledging the norms of childrearing practice and calling them into question, shed light on periods of strain in a family history. In a letter to his mother, Nobutane idealized his childhood in a way that reduced it to what it took to make him a man. The various perspectives afforded by these materials make it possible to address questions of what made a child a child and what constituted childhood for early nineteenth-century boys and girls in terms of practice, affect, and subjectivity.

A note on age: In early modern Japan, children were considered to be one year old *(sai)* at birth and turned another *sai* at the beginning of each subsequent year, even if they had been born at the end of the twelfth lunar month. Based on their birth dates, I have converted *sai* for the children I discuss to the Western concept of age. This does not always work, however, when particular *sai* have meaning. For example, on his fifth *sai,* a nineteenth-century samurai boy would put on the pleated pants called *hakama,* a practice still followed by boys in Japan today, though only for the purpose of a shrine visit and formal photograph (see figure 1).

RITUALS AND PRACTICE

One way to uncover the play of norms versus behavior is to map the patterns of childhood rituals recorded in the Hirata family diary. A caveat: Atsutane kept a diary to remember milestones in his school's development, not in his grandchildren's lives. After he adopted Kanetane as his son-in-law in 1824, he had Kanetane perform this task. Kanetane kept an inconsistent chronicle of his children's lives; many rituals that we can assume the family must have performed go unmarked. Instead he tended to record the children's activities only when they occurred in conjunction with those of adults—going on an excursion, for example. Despite these lacunas, the diary provides a useful introduction to the children and how they grew up.

O-Chō, Atsutane's daughter who married Kanetane, bore seven children, a large number for that era, especially considering the family's straitened finances. As Atsutane's disciple Miyaoi Sadao wrote, "true wealth lies in having many children" (Hirano 1983: 94). A survey of childbirth rates among warrior households done by Isoda Michifumi indicates that the average number of children per household was between two and four, hardly enough to maintain the warrior population. When

FIGURE 1. Nakai Tomochika dressed in *hakama* for the celebration of his fifth *sai* on 15 November 2015. Photo courtesy of Nakai Maki.

class differences are taken into account, it appears that higher-ranking warriors had 5.13 children apiece; lower-ranking warriors had 3.86 children, in part because the higher ranks married earlier—in the early twenties for men and late teens for women.[1] Kanetane and O-Chō got a late start: he was twenty-six when they married in 1825; she was twenty. She then spent the next twenty years frequently pregnant and always surrounded by children and infants.

Table 1 below summarizes significant childhood events as they are recorded in the family diary. Note that the lives of the eldest daughter and son are better documented than those of the children born later. This constitutes but one indication that birth order mattered, no matter what the family's status. In the diary kept by a wealthy farm family, the Kitahara in the Ina valley, for example, the father noted his age and that of his eldest son at the beginning of every year, ignoring his other children. When his eldest son was murdered on his way to Kyoto, he then recorded the age of his second son who had under these unfortunate circumstances became his heir (Kitahara-ke monjo). Even though the keepers of the Hirata family diary were more inclusive in their recordkeeping, the possibility remains that some milestones were observed without being recorded, even in the case of the oldest son.

As the first-born son, Nobutane received special attention. Relatives came to celebrate his birth, and the family distributed gifts widely. It celebrated the casting of his horoscope, his first solid meal, and the first time he put on a loincloth. Atsutane started taking Nobutane with him to view the cherry blossoms when Nobutane was only two years old, and a year later they went on an excursion to the mountains. Pleasure trips, usually in the company of his grandparents, continued throughout Nobutane's childhood. When Nobutane was three years old, family friends gave him his first adult-style clothing. He received a new *hakama* from a different man when he was four in celebration of his fifth *sai*. To signify his status to strangers, no warrior was supposed to leave his gate without wearing *hakama,* although by the 1830s wealthy merchants ceremoniously dressed their five-*sai* sons in this formal wear as well (in Tosa boys first put on *hakama* much later; see chapter 2).[2] Now properly clothed, Nobutane began preparation for his life as a warrior and scholar: his parents took him with them when they paid courtesy calls, one example of how he acquired the social skills that matched his station through imitation. In 1837, the year he turned nine, the family sent him out on his own to make New Year's visits on its behalf, a practice it continued thereafter.

When children began schooling, their studies varied according to gender, status, and opportunity. Moribe had his son Fuyuteru start writing Japanese and memorizing Chinese at age four (five *sai*). In Kiryū, the Yoshida daughter and son both began their studies at the local temple school some months before their seventh birthday, once they had turned 8 *sai,* the age at which most children started schooling (Shibata 2013: 81, 131). He also attended a private academy to study Chinese whereas she practiced the *koto.* In the year Nobutane turned six, he began

TABLE 1 Significant childhood events recorded in the Hirata family diary, 1826–56

	Fuki	Nobutane	Kaneya	Kanesaburō	Mika (Iku)	Suzu	Taneo
Birth	1826.2.12	1828.9.13	1830.7.6	1833.2.13	1835.6.3	1840.9.7	1843.8.7
First bath	1826.4.14				1835.6.9	1840.9.13	
Seventh night	1826.4.18	1828.9.17		1833.2.19; haircut	1835.6.9		
Prayers to kami	1826.4.21				1835.7.5		
First shrine or temple visit	1826.5.14	1828.11.20				1840.10.10	1843.9.15
First girls' or boys' day	1827.3.5, age 1	1829.5.5, age 8 months		1833.5.5, age 2 months			
Birthday party	1828.4.12, age 2		1831.7.6, age 1				
First solid meal		1829.3.8, age 6 months				1841.2.13, age 5 months	
Begin schooling		1834.2.15, age 6	1836.3.25, age 6				
First loincloth		1836.12.3, age 8					
Horse riding lessons		1842.5.15, age 14	1842.5.15, age 12				
Coming of age ceremony		1842.8.2, age 14	1844.11.25, age 14	1847.11.24, age 14*			
Begin koto lessons					1843.4.7, age 8	1850.8.10, age 10**	
Spear practice		1845.7.1, age 17	1844.12.16, age 14	1845.5.13, age 12			
Sword practice			1845.5.7, age 15				
Archery practice		1848.2.25, age 20	1848.2.25, age 18	1848.2.25, age 15			
Marriage or adoption		1853.2.20, age 25	1848.6.5, age 18		1851.12.27, age 16	1856.3.19, age 16	1855.4.9, age 12

SOURCE: The Hirata family diary has been published in three separate places: the early years are in Watanabe 1942: 967–1072; the middle years are in Miyachi 2005: 4–65; and the last years are in Miyachi 2006: 17–388.

* The term used is maegami tori (cutting the forelocks), rather than the standard genpuku (coming-of-age ceremony).

** Suzu must have started lessons earlier; it is on this date that she received a license.

to learn to read and write, and the next year read a text written by Atsutane. In a later letter from Akita, Atsutane noted that "all of the warriors here right down to the children know at least the Four Books and Five Classics," the fundamental texts in the Chinese tradition (Watanabe 1942: 574). We can assume that Atsutane's male grandchildren were equally well educated, even though like Moribe, Atsutane lauded the superiority of all things Japanese over the Chinese.

Although the Hirata family had warrior pretensions, its lack of official standing during the years while Nobutane was growing up curtailed his opportunities. The point of being a warrior was to serve a lord, but until Atsutane received status, rank, and salary from Akita in 1842, the Hirata had no lord to serve. This meant that Nobutane did not have his first audience with a lord until after he had gone through his coming-of-age ceremony. At one point Atsutane suggested that it be postponed in order for Nobutane to meet the requirements for being a page. Some months later, he proposed adding two years to Nobutane's age to quality him for a larger stipend (Nakagawa 2014: 71). Most warrior boys had their first audience between the ages of seven and nine, and those of high enough status then became the lord's pages and wore a long-sleeved kimono. At 12.5 *sai*, they performed the sleeve-shortening ceremony and become apprentices; at 14.5 *sai* they cut their forelocks and came of age (Isoda 2013: 183–84). Most began practice in the martial arts well before that time. In the kabuki play *Tweezers* (Kenuki), for example, Hata Hidetarō, the boy sent to keep the lecherous hero Kumedera Danjō company, announces that he has studied spearmanship and archery. Hearing that Hidetarō has not yet learned to ride a horse, Danjō announces that "the way of horse and bow is what the warrior must learn first of all." When he offers to teach the boy how to ride and demonstrates what he intends, Hidetarō calls him lewd and runs off (Kokuritsu gekijo 2012: 15). Although Nobutane studied the martial arts, he did so as a latecomer; for him, textual studies came first. In his case, the norms that governed samurai upbringing mattered less than family circumstances in determining what and when children learned.

The family's changing circumstances had an effect on the younger sons. Once Atsutane became an official member of the Akita retainer band, Kaneya began horseback riding and Kanesaburō started spear practice, both before their respective coming-of-age ceremonies. When Kanetane left for Akita in 1843, he took Kaneya with him. To the boy's delight, he rode out of Edo on horseback. In the meantime Kanesaburō stepped in to act as messenger while his older brother Nobutane took over dealing with publishing issues, getting the house cleaned, and doing the shopping.

The two younger daughters receive scant attention in the diary. In part this is because they did not accompany their parents or grandparents on formal occasions; they went out only when visiting a shrine or temple or going on pleasure excursions. Starting when she was six years old Mika went to stay with relatives for days at a time, perhaps to entertain those without children of their own or perhaps to become acquainted with the ways of other households in preparation for the day when she would leave her natal family in marriage. Suzu followed suit, going with either her mother or maternal grandmother to visit her other grandmother, Kanetane's mother. The grandparents bought dolls for the doll festival two days before it is held, but the diary makes no mention of the festival itself. The girls went shopping with relatives; they attended a *koto* concert; they enjoyed going to kabuki with their mother and older brothers. Mika even went to Ueno with her mother and the two younger sons to watch the arrival of a Ryukyuan emissary. It is recorded that she once received a box of sweets from her uncle, Kanetane's brother, in a suggestion that who was important was not the recipient, but the giver and what mattered were the continuing ties between the two families.

The diary notes children's activities largely in relation to those performed by adults; only when children get sick do they become visible on their own. We have already seen how Atsutane responded when Fuki died of smallpox. Her cry of pain—"Scary things have come, they've come again, oh, go away"—constitutes the sole instance when the diary records a child's voice (Watanabe 1942: 1060).

The other children too suffered from a variety of diseases. Although they all caught smallpox, none of the rest of them died. Instead they went on to suffer from measles, chickenpox, fevers, influenza, dysentery, and mumps. Parasites made them sick as well. In one of Atsutane's letters from Akita, he writes: "I am delighted to hear that the four children have been wormed. I prayed a long time, and let me tell you about worms. Watanabe Zenzō's granddaughter, at least eight years old, became peevish, cried burning tears constantly, and ate all sorts of things, ashes, dirt, incense, a difficult situation. It was too much to bear so I had her take some of that worm-expelling medicine. The next day she voided six big worms, and by the following day, she was all right" (Watanabe 1942: 547).

In an age when childhood diseases could easily prove fatal, it is not surprising that they so often appear in the Hirata family diary. When disease attacked the heir, it threatened the family's social and economic survival. Fuki's case shows how it also threatened the fabric of the family as an affective unit. Children were at their most vulnerable when they embodied disease; that is, when they brought to the surface concerns for their welfare that otherwise went unrecorded.

The Hirata family diary does not provide a thorough accounting of children's lives. Both Mika and Suzu learned to read and write, but there is no mention of when they started to study. No ceremonies marked their entry into adulthood. The only person to garner even less attention is the youngest brother, Taneo, born just a couple of months before Atsutane died in Akita. Without his famous grandfather to take him on excursions, he easily escapes notice. But because his next older brother, Kanesaburō, also receives less mention than the two older boys, it is clear that birth order as well as gender played an important role in determining the amount of recordkeeping expended on children that the family deemed necessary for its identity.

Gender and birth order inequality also permeated treatises on childhood. In contrast to texts written for girls—for example, *A Treasure House of Greater Learning for Women* (Onna Daigaku takara bako)—those addressed to men took the generic term "child" to mean boys. In his essay on household management, the village headman and Hirata disciple Miyaoi Sadao discussed how to raise a good child, one who could achieve success in this world, and he praised the virtues of loyalty and filial piety above all others (Hirano 1983: 93). In addition to Atsutane and Chinese philosophers, he quoted the eighteenth-century author Hayashi Shihei, who wrote a set of instructions for fathers and older brothers. Hayashi's aim was to help fathers achieve their goal of raising intelligent and good children (boys), a goal to be achieved by having the child internalize the four literary virtues—filial piety, obedience, loyalty, sincerity—and the four martial virtues—bravery, righteousness, honor, integrity. Although women might aspire to these virtues in an emergency, such attributes were usually gendered male. The role of the elder brother was to love and educate his younger brothers, treat them with compassion and kindness, and live in harmony with them (Yamazumi and Nakae 1983: 65–66). Neither Miyaoi nor Hayashi discussed a father's or an elder brother's role in raising girls.

FOR THE LOVE OF CHILDREN

Aside from its depiction of Fuki's death, the Hirata family diary reveals nothing about the emotional communication between parent and child. For a different perspective, let us turn to the letters written by Atsutane and his wife, Orise, when the shogunate exiled him in 1841 for unspecified reasons likely having to do with his criticism of Confucian studies. The couple went to Akita, where Atsutane had been born, and where he eventually gained warrior status and a small stipend. Addressed to the family back in Edo, the letters speak to the strong bonds between grandparents and grandchildren: the affect at play in the family game.

In his letters Atsutane often harped on themes of longing for the grandchildren. "Oh, I want to see the children. It's all the two of us talk about," Atsutane wrote in his first letter dated 1841.1.7. In a postscript he lamented, "In my dream last night I was delighted that you and [servant] Ichitarō brought Kaneya to me, but alas, it was only a dream" (Watanabe 1942: 533). This was a dream he had more than once. "On the night of the twenty-seventh of last month, one by one Suzu and the others came flying through the sky. I sat them on my lap and pressed my cheek against theirs . . . . You and Chō came afterwards and saying that it was getting late, snatched them away. I woke, asked my wife if she had seen them, and realized it was a dream" (Watanabe 1942: 588). While still on his journey, he wrote a poem describing how thoughts of his grandchildren unmanned him (Watanabe 1942: 542):

masurao to	Even I,
takebishi ware mo	a manly man
ie ni aru	when I remember
marashi omoeba	the grandchildren at home
namida gumashi mo	cannot hold back my tears.

Whether or not Atsutane actually cried, here he used tears as a textual representation of grief. As Gary Ebersole has pointed out, poems "present evidence of what was considered to be the appropriate affective (and verbal) display for a sensitive and cultivated person" (Ebersole 2008: 76). It is also important to pay due attention to the context. Atsutane never recorded having shed tears at the thought of separation from his daughter. Instead his tears were always for his grandchildren, the appropriate object of longing for an old man.

Although the bulk of Atsutane's letters concerned his own affairs, he regularly commented on his grandsons. He wanted reports on how they were doing with their studies, and he exclaimed: "Nothing makes me happier than that Nobutane and Kaneya like books" (Watanabe 1942: 620). As he pointed out: "I've heard that there is inevitably a test before employment whereby officials appear at the domain school to have the [candidate] read from the Four Books [of Chinese classics]. It's not a question of reading them all, but of opening pages here and there to be read. You need to make careful inquiries of Hirayama Keisuke so that Nobutane does not embarrass himself" (Watanabe 1942: 661–62). Since Nobutane lived in Edo, he did not attend the domain school. Nonetheless, Atsutane worried that he might face some kind of test, even in Edo, and sent this warning that the family should be prepared. He also urged Nobutane and Kaneya to be diligent in the martial arts. On the other hand, it appeared that Kanesaburō did not like to read. Atsutane suggested drawing him in by starting with a picture book about warriors. "He needs to be able to do the literary and martial arts, and I want him to like being useful in all things" (Watanabe 1942: 693).

Atsutane's letters also display attitudes toward childhood that fly in the face of conclusions reached by European students of family strategy. These scholars argue that the less children contributed to the household economy, because schooling had become increasingly important, the more they became "emotionally priceless" (Cunningham 1998: 1203). In the Hirata family of scholars, the male children were carefully schooled, letters demonstrate that they were loved, but they also participated in household enterprises. They made copies of texts for Atsutane (for example, five volumes about the domain's local customs) and copied Atsutane's texts that could then be sold to disciples or presented to patrons (Watanabe 1942: 646, 692). While still a student, Moribe's son too helped annotate manuscripts for publication and taught memorization of Chinese texts to pupils from the countryside (Takai 1991: 211, 219). As was typical for most children before modern times, they earned their keep, but in ways that contributed to their education.

Atsutane's letters show that he loved all of his grandchildren, but his chief concern was that his grandsons grow up well. He made scant mention of his granddaughters except for the baby Suzu. Instead, like the men who wrote solely about issues related to boys when they addressed the subject of childrearing, he focused his attention on the serious side of childhood—the studies and training required of a samurai/scholar boy.

Although Orise too wanted her grandsons to excel in their studies, in her letters she commented on a greater range of their activities and discussed issues pertinent to her granddaughters and the children she got to know in Akita. She lamented her separation from the grandchildren; for her nothing was more painful than the thought of not being able to see them for the next year or so, and she claimed to dream about them every night. If Atsutane could not return to Edo, then the best thing would be for Kaneya, no, the entire family, to join them. She was often ill during exile, but both she and Atsutane thought that if she had the grandchildren around her, she would quickly recover.

Like Atsutane, Orise emphasized the importance of having the children learn to take responsibility for contributing to the family enterprise, but for her "the children" meant girls as well as boys. "Ichitarō told us in detail about how Nobutane and Kaneya help out when you serve the gods, and that affected us very much. We're delighted that the two of them are such a help to you" (Yokoyama 2012: 19). Being of help was expected of children; Orise remarked at one point that "even though it's too bad that Nobutane is kept busy helping you, it's important to have him put up with it a little now so that he can become a fine young heir of use to his grandfather" (Yokoyama 2012: 47). Orise also praised O-Chō's childrearing skills: "I'm impressed that you're putting the children to work by having them compete with each other. If you do like this and send them on errands, none of them will end up lazy. Your disciplining of them is excellent" (Yokoyama 2012: 42). Orise was gratified to learn that the older granddaughter Mika had done a fine job of sewing cotton underwear, and that even at the age of seven, she had become such a help to her mother. Perhaps next year she could make underwear for Orise and Atsutane (Yokoyama 2012: 77).

The only child who had no responsibilities and the freedom to do as she pleased was baby Suzu. For her first doll's day, her mother dressed her in a loose robe and made a doll for her. Orise thought she must have looked really cute. Three months later Suzu got a long-sleeved kimono, and Orise mentioned that Atsutane was delighted that her complexion was whiter than that of Mika's friends in the neighborhood. As she got older, Suzu became increasingly mobile: "It's early for Suzu to be crawling around with her rump in the air, standing by holding onto furniture, and pulling candy out of the drawer on the hibachi to eat all by herself. How adorable" (Yokoyama 2012: 22, 46, 54).

The lack of restraints on Suzu's freedom probably did not last long. Just a few months later, on 1841.10.21, Orise warned O-Chō: "Suzu will soon become three *sai* [by Western count, she was barely over a year old], and what happens to her hereafter will be very important. You must be mindful to take good care of her because [character] will inevitably come out later. Even though you have a nursemaid, because she's your child, you must be the one to raise her" (Yokoyama 2012: 76).

At the age of six by the Western calendar, Mika was already learning how to act and dress like the daughter of a samurai/scholar. Along with her older brothers, she wrote letters to her grandparents and copied texts. Orise was delighted at her clear handwriting. At the New Year, Mika made decorated string balls and shuttlecocks to entertain her siblings. According to the family diary, she had a *koto* teacher; Orise's letters indicate that she also learned singing and *samisen,* a popular instrument that was sometimes considered more suitable to members of the commoner classes than the *koto.* Orise commented on Mika's clothes; she obsessed over the procurement of a hairpin. At the beginning of 1842, Orise wrote a New Year's greeting addressed to the women of the family—O-Chō, Mika, and Suzu. In the same envelope was a letter addressed to Mika alone:

> I've read your charming and detailed letter over and over, more times than I can count . . . . I'd like to send you some sort of toys to play with, but here I'm not allowed to go out shopping . . . . I've thought of a few things that are really boring and sent them to you just for the sake of having something to send. I've heard that you'd taken them out any number of times to play with. The next time I'll send you lots of much better things, so please be patient.
>
> You must have looked adorable at New Year's in your striped crepe kimono tied with a black obi and obi tie with cute hairpins in your hair.
>
> Your white face powder must have been skillfully applied for the New Year. Your grandfather and I have been talking about it.
>
> I've put your letter in the drawer to my sewing kit, I read it numerous times every day, and I cry tears of joy.

As usual Orise could not resist a few words of admonishment:

> Please treat your older brothers well and be charming to everyone as you get older . . . .
>
> Please be careful when you play not to fall in the pond and not to injure yourself. Please get along with everyone when you play. Your mother must be busy, but please do not take a break from practicing *samisen* and singing. I'll want to hear what you've done when we meet again. (Yamaguchi 2014: 109–10)

This missive displays the strong affective bonds between grandmother and granddaughter and how each strove to maintain them. In the private, domestic sphere that constituted Orise's chief venue, women typically took the lead in maintaining relations, performing what has been called kin work. Orise and Mika probably wrote directly to each other on other occasions as well, but this is the only missive to have survived. Mika must have written a letter describing her New Year's activities, with whom she played, and her musical studies. In return Orise sent her presents and promised better ones, offered advice on how to behave around other people, and conveyed her love for her granddaughter by recounting how she treasured her letter.

Orise often spoke for Atsutane in expressing his love for his grandchildren. While they were on the road to Akita, they became acquainted with an Akita domain retainer and his eleven-year-old son, Sutematsu, who was just the same age as Kaneya, which made him particularly attractive to Atsutane. Sutematsu diverted the couple with his antics, helped Orise pick edible plants in the mountains, and escorted them to a house party just before their departure. That night Atsutane announced that he wanted to sleep with Sutematsu in his arms. The boy replied, "Alright," and went to sleep. "He really is a cute kid," was Atsutane's comment (Yokoyama 2012: 28). This anecdote reminds us of the custom for elders to have a young person share their bed; in fact Orise mentioned that she longed for the day when they would all be together and Kanesaburō would quietly creep up to her back and take care of her (Yokoyama 2012: 11). Children warmed the bedding; they provided close and intimate companionship.

Orise's letters also give glimpses of the relations at play between children. On the one hand, she warned the brothers not to quarrel or fight with each other; on the other, in a statement addressed directly to the four older children, she instructed them to get along and praised them for doing so: "Your grandfather, Ichita[rō], and I talk daily about how the four of you are in good health and get along so well when you play. Be sure to be well behaved and I'll bring you lots of good presents next year. Wait for us, don't cause trouble for your father and mother, and don't get injured. You must treat Mika with affection and get along well together. You must also treat Suzu with affection. Once you get older, please come here" (Yokoyama 2012: 3). And what games did they play? Flying kites and spinning tops, at least for the boys. As for getting along, Orise warned: "Please tell Kaneya not to drop Suzu in the pond when he is carrying her on his back. I'm really worried about that" (Yokoyama 2012: 55).

It is well known that until recent times, children took care of other children to free their parents for productive work. Indeed, children often spent more time overseen by their siblings than by adults. In the Meiji period, taking care of infants became a strictly female occupation, as illustrated in figure 2, a carefully posed postcard from 1912 (Tamanoi 1991: 800). Orise's caution to Kaneya suggests that in the 1840s, gender mattered less than birth order and age, a finding that replicates Kathleen Uno's study of Tokugawa-period childcare (Uno 1987: 31). Kaneya was ten years Suzu's senior, whereas the age gap between Mika and Suzu was only five years, too narrow for Mika to have been able to carry her around as the girl in this postcard is doing. In fact Mika had a nursemaid herself, one who came from outside the family. Nobutane was even older, but he was taking on adult responsibilities. That left Kaneya, who did not, apparently, relish this chore.

FIGURE 2. Young girl feeding a rice cracker to her infant charge, 1912.
Courtesy of the author.

Many years later, when Nobutane found himself in the position of trying to raise a child, a different affect came into play. There were two complications: First, the boy, Shin'ichirō, was one Nobutane was trying to decide whether to adopt. Second, Shin'ichirō spent months living with Kanetane in Kyoto before Nobutane was settled enough in Tokyo to have the boy live with him.

Thanks to the system of attendance on the shogun in the Tokugawa period that took samurai men away from home for months or years at a time, raising a child at a distance had happened frequently. What mattered to Nobutane, however, was the difficulty of establishing an affective bond between Shin'ichirō and himself. As he wrote to his sister in 1870, "I want somehow to get Shin'ichirō under my own roof. This is because if I don't do so, I don't think I'll be able to consider him to be my child" (Shokan 15-38-12-1). Or again in a letter to his parents: "If I don't raise him myself, I'll not be able to think of him as my son" (Miyachi 2006: 471). To his parents he acknowledged that for them to have grandchildren with them provided consolation in difficult times. "If I summon all of the children, you'll be lonely, but if I don't bring them here, I can't raise them myself." Even if the other children stayed in Kyoto, he wanted to put Shin'ichirō on trial to see if he could be of use (Miyachi 2005: 99, 102, 103).

Once Nobutane had Shin'ichirō under his roof, he discovered that the boy resisted playing by the rules of the game. On the journey from Kyoto, Shin'ichirō had thrown his books in the river, peed in public in Odawara, stopped studying, and generally tried his tutor's patience (Shokan 15-38-14-3). Once in Edo, he played all sorts of tricks; he bit the steward; he threw stones at a servant. He took money from Nobutane's desk and went to buy candy at the teashop outside the gate; worse, he did not wear his sword when he did so. Nobutane had received sweets for his work as the emperor's tutor; Shin'ichirō rudely helped himself to them. The servants were supposed to watch him, but one day he took advantage of their inattention, removed his *hakama,* and with just a dagger went several blocks away to a bookstore all by himself. "From one day to the next, someone drags out the struggling Shin'ichirō, each short of breath, to make a complaint." Nobutane discussed his problems with an old friend who just knit his brow and sighed. "He said that sort of thing goes on all the time at his house and at Hashizume's with their sons and in other households as well. Scolding does no good" (Miyachi 2006: 484, 485, 492).

In contrast to the good children praised in the letters from Atsutane and Orise, Shin'ichirō played the bad boy, much like the boys deplored by monks in chapter 1. Not only did he act like a common thief, he also violated the norms of samurai dress and behavior, at least according to Nobutane's ideas regarding appropriate conduct. His tutor admitted that while Shin'ichirō had an open-hearted disposition, he was wild and often resorted to violence (Shokan 15-38-16). Since the tutor was responsible for Shin'ichirō's conduct as well as his studies, this was mortifying.

Shin'ichirō's actions remind us that not all children were paragons of virtue; some centered their attention on themselves. Moribe lamented that when Ito, his Kiryū disciple's daughter, came to stay with him, "because she's been raised too much as she pleases, she does what she wishes, and she's stubborn and obstinate." "The other day when we showed her the roll of cloth for a summer robe that you'd sent, she replied, 'Am I supposed to wear that?' and flung it away." What shocked

Moribe's household was not just her display of ingratitude and ill temper, but also her use of "*ore*," a man's term, for "I" (Takahashi 1991: 383). Despite her display of selfishness, Moribe remained fond of her and treated her as one of the family.

Just as the Hirata family diary contains information related to children only incidentally, the same is true for the letters written by Atsutane, Orise, and Nobutane. Nonetheless, Orise and Atsutane spared a few words for the grandchildren in almost every message, and so too did Nobutane regarding his potential adopted son. In some cases, these words repeat normative expressions of feeling, but they sometimes provide a glimpse of what the children had been doing. To the extent that they refer to concrete, singular actions, they convey a sense of the bonds of affection that held families together and point to the emotional as well as economic value children brought to the family game, what Frühstück calls emotional capital (see chapter 9).

Affection for children constitutes a powerful if overlooked motif in early nineteenth-century nativist writings. This can be seen as arising from the determination to privilege the emotions as the basis for relations between people in contrast to the suspicious rationality of Chinese thought. As the eighteenth progenitor of nativist studies, Motoori Norinaga (1730–1801), famously declared, Japanese values were superior to Chinese because they were based on the spontaneity of human feeling (Nakamura 1991: 39). Thus Moribe claimed that nothing was more important for the family than the love between husband and wife. He also stated that "filial piety should come from within the child in response to the parents' love; it should not be coerced by outside dictates [as in China]" (Takai 1991: 262, 266).

SUBJECTIVE VISIONS OF CHILDHOOD

It is difficult to know what children thought of their upbringing. Even when people look back on their childhood, they do so from an adult perspective that abridges and distorts their past. In the case of Atsutane, we have various accounts of his early years in Akita. They contradict each other and remind us that the staging of an authentic experience is contingent on a host of factors not always knowable to the individual himself. Nobutane also wrote a short statement reflecting on his upbringing; it too must be read within the context of the larger argument he was trying to make.

Atsutane's official biography, composed by his adopted son Kanetane, takes a positive approach to his early years. Born on 1776.8.24 to a middle-ranking samurai family, Atsutane was the fourth of five boys. He also had three sisters. One month after his birth, his family shaved off his birth hair and preserved it, an indication that it performed the ceremonies for him that marked a child's early years. When he was eight *sai*, the appropriate age to begin education, his father sent him to study with the domain's Confucian instructor. He also trained in the martial arts, learning how to use the bow, spear, and sword. Right before he went through his coming-of-age ceremony, his father said to him, "If Confucius had been born in this country, he would not have studied Chinese things but rather those of this country. I have not yet studied them, but I really want to have the things of this country known." Atsutane later absconded from the domain at age nineteen because he did not get along with his stepmother (Ueda 1978: 1115).

In this version of Atsutane's life, he had the conventional childhood of a samurai boy. His family made sure that he got an education, and he learned both the literary and martial arts. His father even encouraged him to excel in his chosen field. Truncated though this account is, it still allows us to see a social construction of childhood that puts the child's development first.

Atsutane recorded other accounts of his childhood that conflict with the official version. In a letter he wrote to Kanetane on 1842.11.2, he stated: "When I look back on my childhood, I remember that I was raised neither by my mother nor my father from the day I was born." In a longer fragment that may have once been attached to this letter, he described how he had been denied the warmth of family affection from birth, symbolized by his distance from the heat of the hearth:

> I was treated as a foster child and raised in misery to the age of six in the house of a poor foot soldier. I had gotten accustomed to the place when my wet nurse's husband died, and I was sent back home. There my parents and siblings maltreated me and always spoke to me in the cruelest, most outrageous fashion. From age eight to eleven, I was given over to a wealthy acupuncturist named Sakurai Shūkyū. Just when I realized that I did not want to become a crummy doctor, a child was born in my adoptive family, and I was sent back home. Thereafter I cooked the rice, did the cleaning, yanked weeds, and minced along like a messenger carrying shit. While saying we can live in harmony as siblings, my brothers treated me hatefully. They struck me, and they beat me. I never ceased having a bruised head . . . I was further disliked because I have a birthmark on my face that was said to be a sign that I would kill my brothers and take the house by force. Once when I was suffering from an acute illness for at least a year in that cold country, my oldest brother gave me a meager set of nightclothes for the first time. After he died I never received any nightclothes. By selling some handicrafts I got a little money, and with that I bought beggar's rags to wrap myself in at night. In that way I endured the extreme cold of winter, and I never tried to approach the heat of the fire even once. Even though I feared my parents and tried to avoid them, I never felt that I hated them (Itō 1973: 19–20).

According to this account, which may suffer from exaggeration, his parents did not even bother to have a coming-of-age ceremony performed for him. Having been treated so harshly and as proof that he had no intention of killing his brothers, he ran away to Edo.

Atsutane's parents had an unusually large number of children, and it is possible that his was one more birth than they could afford. In Europe as well, families would seek outside help in caring for excess children at "pressure points in the family life cycle" (Cunningham 1998: 1204). Sometimes the intent was to reclaim the child when conditions improved; sometimes the child was abandoned. That Atsutane was never reclaimed nor completely jettisoned suggests that the emotional value assigned to him by his parents fluctuated at a fairly low level.

Atsutane left a number of accounts of his childhood that emphasized how coldly his family had treated him. One scholar has even declared that Atsutane's upbringing warped his personality and contributed to the excesses in his later writings (Kamata 2000). While it is likely that he was more emotionally deprived than his grandchildren, it is also possible that his recollections, put on paper during his exile, contained a tinge of bitterness at being forced back to the town he had thought never to see again. He may also have wanted to heighten the contrast between a good childhood—living with loving parents and receiving an education—with his own in order to emphasize the obstacles he had overcome in making a name for himself.

Having experienced what was to all appearances a nurturing childhood environment, Nobutane's subjective recollections of his upbringing took a different perspective. In a letter to his mother, he wrote: "When I look at the person I have become now, I have to say that all the hardships I went through a long time ago have proved their worth. For that reason, I want you to please, please force hardships on Shin'ichirō so that he becomes a splendid person" (Miyachi 2005: 110). Forgotten are the games Nobutane played as a child, his excursions with his grandparents to view the cherry blossoms, and the celebrations for boys' day. Instead he remembers that he suffered, and that the suffering made him a better person.

CONCLUSION

Any discussion of childrearing practices, attitudes toward children, and childhood experiences in early modern Japan has to take their diversity into account. Samurai and scholars such as Hirata Atsutane, Miyaoi Sadao, and Tachibana Moribe placed great emphasis on book learning, even for girls. They articulated a vision of childhood development that would lead to the creation of a productive adult—someone of use not only to the family but also to the larger society and, in the case of Miyaoi, the imperial realm. It is easy to assume that most parents would have agreed with this goal, even if they stated it differently or employed different means.

And what about the impact of affect on the family game? One justification for sending children away from home to live and work was that tenderhearted parents spoiled their children, as Moribe hinted in his letter commenting on Ito's self-centered behavior.[3] Judging from Nobutane's recollections, indulging children was not a problem in the Hirata house. On this point as well, historians need to account for a diversity of attitudes and behavior. In his analysis of the practice of infanticide, Fabian Drixler demonstrates that it occurred more frequently in certain regions than in others and traces this variation to differences in religious belief. In a

similar fashion, I have posited the existence of various "emotional communities"—
"social groups that adhere to the same valuation of emotions and how they should
be expressed" (Plamper 2010: 253; the term was coined by Barbara Rosenwein).
The community at issue here was centered on the teachings first exemplified by
Motoori Norinaga and then expanded and complicated by later nativist scholars
such as Atsutane, Moribe, Miyaoi, and others. In valorizing Japanese sensibility
over Chinese inflected rationality, this community encouraged written displays of
familial affection. Children were important not just because they ensured the family's continuity but because as a concrete representation of the parents' love and
affection, they tied the family together.

NOTES

1. Isoda 2013: 178, 190, 193. Isoda bases his conclusions on an analysis of Utsunomiya domain
records.
2. Isoda 2013: 79; Takahashi 1991: 387. One of Orise's letters from Akita asks that O-Chō send a
secondhand child's summer *hakama*, because Atsutane's great-nephew, Ōwada Shōji's five-*sai* son, did
not have one, the Ōwada being really poor (Yokoyama 2012: 47, 58).
3. For similar sentiments, see Walthall 1991: 45.

BIBLIOGRAPHY

Note: Unless noted otherwise the place of publication for Japanese books is Tokyo.

Cunningham, Hugh. 1998. "Review Essay: Histories of Childhood." *American Historical
Review* 103(4): 1195–1208.
Drixler, Fabian F. 2013. *Mabiki: Infanticide and Population Growth in Eastern Japan, 1660–
1950*. Berkeley: University of California Press.
Ebersole, Gary L. 2008. "Japanese Religions." In *The Oxford Handbook of Religion and
Emotion*, edited by John Corrigan, 73–94. Oxford: Oxford University Press.
Hirano Mitsuru, ed. 1983. *Kanai hōshin shū* [Collection on concerns within the household].
Yasaka Shobō.
Isoda Michifumi. 2013. *Kinsei daimyo kashindan no shakai kōzō* (The social structure of
early modern daimyo retainer bands). Bungei Shunjū. First published by Tōkyō Daigaku
Shuppankai, 2003.
Itō Hiroshi. 1973. *Taigaku Hirata Atsutane den* [Biography of the great teacher Hirata
Atsutane]. Kinshōsha.
Kamata Tōji. 2000. "The Disfiguring of Nativism: Hirata Atsutane and Orikuchi Shinobu."
In *Shinto in History: Ways of the kami*, edited by John Breen and Mark Teeuwen, 295–315.
Richmond Surry: Curzon Press.
Kitahara-ke monjo. Uncataloged. Kitahara house Zakōji, Iida-shi. Nagano-ken.
Kenuki [Tweezers]. 2012. Kokuritsu gekijo kabuki kanshō kyōshitsu jōen daihon [Perfor-
mance script from the National theater kabuki appreciation department]. Kokuritsu
Gekijo.

Miyachi Masato, ed. 2005. "Hirata kokugaku no saikentō" [A Reexamination of Hirata national studies] (Part 1), *Kokuritsu rekishi minzoku hakubutsukan kenkyū hōkoku*, no. 122.

———., ed. 2006. "Hirata kokugaku no saikentō" [A Reexamination of Hirata national studies] (Part 2), *Kokuritsu rekishi minzoku hakubutsukan kenkyū hōkoku*, no. 128.

Nakagawa Kazuaki. 2014. "Hirata Atsutane shokan (Kanetane, O-Chō ate) Tenpō 13.3.14" [Letter from Hirata Atsutane to Kanetane and O-Chō, 1842.3.14]. *Suzunoya Gakkai-hō*, no. 31: 63–72.

Nakamura, Sey. 1991. "The Way of the Gods: Motoori Norinaga's Naobi no Mitama," *Monumenta Nipponica* 46(1): 27–41.

Plamper, Jan. 2010. "The History of Emotions: An Interview with William Reddy, Barbara Rosenwein, and Peter Stearns." *History and Theory* 49 (May): 237–65.

Rosenwein, Barbara H. 2002. "Worrying about Emotions in History." *The American Historical Review* 107(3): 821–45.

Shibata Jun. 2013. *Nihon yōjishi: Kodomo e no manazashi* [A history of the young in Japan: Perspectives on children]. Yoshikawa Kōbunkan.

Shokan (correspondence). Hirata kokugaku kankei shiryō [Archive of materials related to Hirata national studies]. Sakura-shi, National Museum of Japanese History.

Takahashi Satoshi. 1991. "Jūkyū seiki zaigyō machi Kiryū no kazoku to kodomo" [Family and children in the rural town of Kiryū during the nineteenth century]. Explanatory essay in *Tenpō-ki, shonen shōjo no kyōiku keisei katei no kenkyū* [Research on the process of educational formation for a young boy and a young girl during the Tenpō era, 1830–1844], by Takai Hiroshi, 371–98. Kawade Shobō Shinsha.

Takai Hiroshi. 1991. *Tenpō-ki, shonen shōjo no kyōiku keisei katei no kenkyū* [Research on the process of educational formation for a young boy and a young girl during the Tenpō era, 1830–1844]. Kawade Shobō Shinsha.

Tamanoi, Mariko Asano. 1991. "Songs as Weapons: The Culture and History of Komori (Nursemaids) in Modern Japan." *Journal of Asian Studies* 50(4): 793–817.

Ueda Mannen. 1978. *Kokugakusha denki shūsei* [Collective biography of scholars of national studies]. Vol. 2. Meichō Shukkō Kai.

Uno, Kathleen S. 1987. "Day Care and Family Life in Industrializing Japan, 1868–1926." PhD diss., University of California, Berkeley.

Walthall, Anne. 1991. "The Life Cycle of Farm Women in Tokugawa Japan." In *Recreating Japanese Women, 1600–1945*, edited by Gail Lee Bernstein, 42–70. Berkeley: University of California Press.

Watanabe Kinzō. 1942. *Hirata Atsutane kenkyū* [Research on Hirata Atsutane]. Rokkō Shobō.

Yamaguchi Setsuko. 2014. *Mairase soro: Edo-ki, tegami wo nokoshita onnatachi* [Women who left correspondence from the Edo period using polite forms of speech]. Asahi Kurie.

Yamazumi Masami and Nakae Kazue. 1983. *Kosodate no sho* [Books on childraising], no. 2, vol. 176. Heibonsha.

Yokoyama Suzuko, ed. 2012. *Hirata Atsutane gosai Orise no Akita kara no tegami shiryōshū* [A collection of letters written by Hirata Atsutane's second wife Orise from Akita]. Sakura-shi: printed by editor.

PART TWO

Early Twentieth Century

4

Consumer Consumption for Children

Conceptions of Childhood in the Work of Taishō-Period Designers

Jinnō Yuki
Translated and adapted by Emily B. Simpson

Amid the flourishing of a new culture of consumption in urban areas in modern Japan, children too came to be seen as objects of expenditure.[1] With the development of the capitalist market came information about children and products for them that spread through the populace, particularly the urban middle class, via expositions, magazines, and department stores. In my publications to date, I have demonstrated that the interaction between the disparate trends of collecting toys as an individual hobby on the one hand, and the academic study of children on the other, both drawing from the various networks of knowledge about children characteristic of the Meiji period, created fertile ground for research on and the development of goods for children that exceeded demand (Jinnō 1999, 2005). This concern for items made for and used by children was accompanied by the general expansion of domestic production including toys and stationery for children's use, mainly for export, but also in part for domestic circulation. Within this domestic market, goods for children were not only for children to use, but became the desired objects of the urban middle class, which had discovered modernity in the world of children. From then on, designs suitable to children came to be incorporated into various products.

In this paper, I trace the genesis of a view of childhood as marked by an innocence believed to be inherent, a perspective that was prominent during the Taishō period (1912–1926) and that continued thereafter, as we see in chapters 6 and 9. In particular, I examine how designs aimed at children were incorporated into products. Rather than toys and picture books geared toward children, my object of inquiry lies in the domain of furniture and interior design, where the differentiation between children and adults is precise, and wherein I analyze the process that generated the concept of designing for children.

CHILD-BASED THOUGHT AND CHILDREN'S CULTURE IN THE TAISHŌ ERA

Following the rise of children's studies at the end of the Meiji period, consideration of the theme of "children" and the "family" became all the greater in the Taishō period. Information on this subject was transmitted to people via expositions, magazines, and the like. Aiming to free people from what was deemed the traditional feudal household, those who advocated Western-style democracy, such as socialist historian Sakai Toshihiko and journalist and historian Tokutomi Sohō, came to consciously use the term *katei,* or family (Sakai 1904; Tokutomi 1891–98). The debut of this concept of family created the foundation for a transformation from children as subjects who must be educated by the state to children as members of a democratic family who should be cared for while being granted their freedom. (Of course, this exceedingly democratic and idealized image of family was only in the limelight for the brief period of Taishō; once the Shōwa period [1927–1989] began and Japan turned toward war, the family was once again reconceptualized as the foundation of the nation-state system.) Interest in this sort of family grew gradually stronger at the end of the Meiji period, with family and women's magazines appearing in quick succession. In addition to *The Japanese Family* (Nihon no katei), which ran from 1895 to 1900 and *Women's World* (Fujin sekai; 1906 to 1933), several women's magazines that began at the beginning of the twentieth century continue today: *The Housewife's Friend* (Shufu no tomo), originally *The Family's Friend* (1903); *Women's Pictorial* (Fujin gahō, 1905); and *Women's Opinion* (Fujin kōron; 1916). Women occupied a central role in the newly defined family, and among their familial duties, child rearing held an important position.

Not only magazines but also expositions emphasized children's education at home as much as their school education, presented in a fashion easy to understand. Exhibitions on the subject of children began with the 1906 *Children's Exhibition,* sponsored by the Dobunkan publishing house, and came to be held frequently from the end of Meiji onward, even at department stores. As is clear from the fact that this *Children's Exhibition* was mainly organized by the magazine *The Japanese Family,* many child-themed events gave primary place to family culture rather than school education. This focus on family lifestyle and children drew much from the growing movement during Taishō to improve the Japanese people's lifestyle.

A representative example of the expositions related to family at this time was the *Family Exposition* of 1915, sponsored by the Citizen Newspaper Company.[2] At this exposition, organizers showcased concrete exhibits and items on the subject "What is the ideal family?" It placed children at the center of the family, and along with the concept of child-centric families, the exposition presented goods suitable for giving to children. The majority of children and women's expositions at the time shared this characteristic, and the display of items pertinent to children continued in later years.

In 1917, Abe Isoo (1865–1949) published *A Child-Based Family* (Kodomo hon'i no katei). After graduating from Dōshisha University, Abe quickly became a professor at Waseda University. He participated actively in the early feminist movement and joined wholeheartedly in various activities from the standpoint of Christian humanism. As a pioneer in Japan's socialist movement, Abe called for democratization from a socialist viewpoint, connected affairs of the home with affairs of state, and advocated for the importance of family, believing that the democratization of the country would start with the democratization of the home. In *A Child-Based Family*, he suggests that building a child-based family was the best way to democratize the family, and he also emphasized home education, focusing attention on women and children. Starting at this time, the use of the phrase "child-based" or "childlike" (Jones 2001) became conspicuous within the dissemination of the modern concept of family.

Another example of the trend toward a child-based approach can be found in children's literature. Rather than the fairy tales *(otogi-banashi)* that reflected the Meiji educational outlook, at the beginning of the Taishō period, children's literature created from a child's point of view emerged. Starting with *Child's Friend* (Kodomo no tomo) in 1914, *Red Bird* (Akai tori) in 1918, and *Children's Country* (Kodomo no kuni) in 1922, children's magazines, which differed from their Meiji counterparts, appeared one after the other. In place of the mainstream view up to that point, which had seen children as the object of education, an outlook that respected children's unique world and childlike innocence spread. Out of it grew not only children's literature, but also children's songs and pictures. This movement of successive crusades for lifestyle improvements attached importance to the lifestyle of children, in accordance with the so-called "child-based" school of thought. However, later criticism of this principle of childlike innocence suggested that it glorified the innocent and pure existence of children and was no more than a view of childhood idealized by adults (Kawahara 1998).

At the same time, designers became conscious of this child-based trend of thought, and began to create designs for children. While researching this topic, I have been in charge of furniture design and decoration in the Wooden Arts Division of the Tokyo High School of Industrial Arts. My work there has brought me into contact with Taishō-period dwellings and lifestyles. In particular, I have investigated the design approaches launched by Kogure Joichi and Moritani Nobuo.

The historian of modern design Kashiwagi Hiroshi states that Kogure and Moritani put children in a central place in the household, and from there attempted to reform the family. For example, he points out that establishing a separate room for children in order to respect their individualism and privacy resulted in a demand for living rooms. The existence of families who took children seriously brought the philosophy of functional modernism into family relations. During the Shōwa period, this functional view of the household was absorbed by the movement toward a new way of organizing the family for the nation (Kashiwagi 1987). In short, a major characteristic of Japanese modernization was the incorporation of children in such efforts. For that reason, therefore, the view of childhood held by these two designers relied on an extremely modern framework, as I will discuss below. However, a closer examination of their concern for children reveals many other dimensions quite different from the principles of modernism. These dimensions gave rise to a subtle discrepancy in the practical expression of design for children.

KOGURE JOICHI'S DESIGNS AND VIEW OF CHILDHOOD

Kogure Joichi provides an excellent example of a designer and writer whose views on childhood had both a child-centered dimension and a concern for industrial production. In designing houses and furnishings, he took a decidedly modernist approach typical of the Taishō period emphasis on democracy and the individual. In his designs for toys, however, Kogure both looked back to the Edo period and tried to create products that would sell in the international market.

Although Kogure advocated various housing reforms in the Lifestyle Improvement Alliance (Seikatsu kaizen dōmeikai), it is thought that he did not personally adopt his central proposal, the "rational" Western custom of sitting in chairs, until forty to fifty years later, when his children were already adults. For this very reason, he believed that Japan should move forward with improvements in children's quality of life, and it would be most effective if people grew used to the custom of sitting in chairs from childhood. In his representative works, such as *The New House and Furniture Decoration* (Atarashii ie to kagu sōshoku, 1927), *Housing and Architecture* (Jūtaku to kenchiku, 1928) and *Improving One's Home* (Wagaya o kairyō shite, 1930), we see many illustrations of new housing, in accordance with the proposals made by members of the Lifestyle Improvement Alliance. The books also include numerous descriptions relating to children.

Kogure criticized the contemporary norm of entrusting children's education solely to schools and repeatedly put forward the importance of education at home, which had tended to be belittled. In *The New House and Furniture Decoration,* he says this about the importance of giving children their own room(s): "At this time, when children's minds and bodies are most full of vim and vigor, pay special attention to this point, and respect their individuality; guiding them to openly display their [personality] holds great significance in terms of family education" (Kogure 1927: 399). As this quotation suggests, Kogure's ideal for children's education was one that fully demonstrated the child's individuality more than anything else. As to how this individuality was to be acquired, in his pet theory, Kogure linked it with a child's creative activities: "As a rule, either in home education or together with school education, if we start with children's natural productivity—to put it differently, freely inventing and freely producing a so-called crafting lifestyle—then we can cause the individuality of children's minds and bodies to fully develop in the most natural way" (Kogure 1927: 401–2). As this shows, Kogure believed that children have an innate disposition toward creating things, and that children's handicrafts were the foundation for a gifted education and the cultivation of aesthetic sensibility. Therefore, a lifestyle full of crafts, not only at school but also at home—in other words, an environment in which children need not care about their surroundings and can make things freely—advanced children's mental and physical individuality. In addition, he felt that a space for children—the child's room—made these creative activities possible. Setting aside an individual room was an important part of encouraging the independence of every room's occupant.

Kogure's proposals contained many functional considerations for children's rooms, such as the use of desk and chairs to advance lifestyle improvements, paying attention to ventilation and lighting, and planning installation of home heaters, furniture, and the like with an emphasis on safety. However, among these proposals, we also find suggestions relating to how one should decorate a child's room and what sorts of designs are suitable for children (see also Sand 2005: 90). Under "Housing and Ornamentation," he states that "decoration is the domain of the child" (Kogure 1928: 248). Having children's walls covered with crayon drawings, maps, and cutouts for shadow puppets and the rooms decorated with flowers, goldfish bowls, and bird cages, was a part of creating the most enjoyable lifestyle for children, and he advocated essentially letting children decorate with their own hands.

Pointing out that something an adult favors may not necessarily please a child, he suggested limiting the adult's hand to the absolute minimum and repudiated the method of fitting children into adult molds. On allowing adults to participate only in making simple decorations, leaving as much room as possible for children to express themselves, he noted that "decorations which truly fascinate children are difficult to envision with good results without returning to childhood again ourselves. It would certainly be ideal to go back to thinking like a child, but once one has become an adult, it becomes rather difficult" (Kogure 1928: 245). Here, the "going back to thinking like a child" that Kogure endorsed was nothing other than the child-based philosophy of truly thinking from the standpoint of a child. We could say that he communicated precisely the principle of childlike innocence that infused the contemporary Taishō view of childhood.

Yet from his standpoint as a designer, Kogure insisted that designs for children had to meet the need to educate children in what was true, good, and beautiful, and that it had to be possible to improve their taste. This reveals his viewpoint that desirable designs were those that tamed children's minds and nurtured a spirit of creativity. If people considered that getting children acquainted with beautiful forms and colors from a young age was more important than schooling, then

FIGURE 3. A children's room that resembles a Western-style room by Okamoto Kiichi.

the role of design for children would not be denied. In his works, Kogure repeatedly emphasized that furniture design, in addition to being safe and sized to fit children's bodies, should express "a soft, childlike feeling" (Kogure 1927: 410). For example, even if an older child of eleven or twelve is the same size as an adult, he or she still requires a youthful design attractive to children. This is the other side of Kogure's philosophy: the consideration of how one expresses a "childlike" quality as a maker of items for children.

How was Kogure's thinking, which conformed to the child-based philosophy characteristic of the Taishō period, reflected in his designs? The effective link between his words and his designs are the illustrations employed in his series of books, in the sections on children's rooms. Some of the illustrations have apparently been taken from overseas literature, but even so, they introduce materially rich and dream-like children's rooms. The sort of child's room that appears in these illustrations resembles the Western-style rooms for children, overflowing with toys, being drawn by children's illustrators of the period, such as Okamoto Kiichi (see figures 3 and 4).[3]

It is worthy of note that Kogure's own expression of childlike design, shown in these illustrations by Okamoto, differed fundamentally from a child-based design that stressed possibilities, which he had otherwise emphasized. An exception appears in *Improving One's Home,* where he proposes how a children's room might be created in a regular, already-existing house through the example of the children's room at his own residence. In this room, which includes a desk and bed

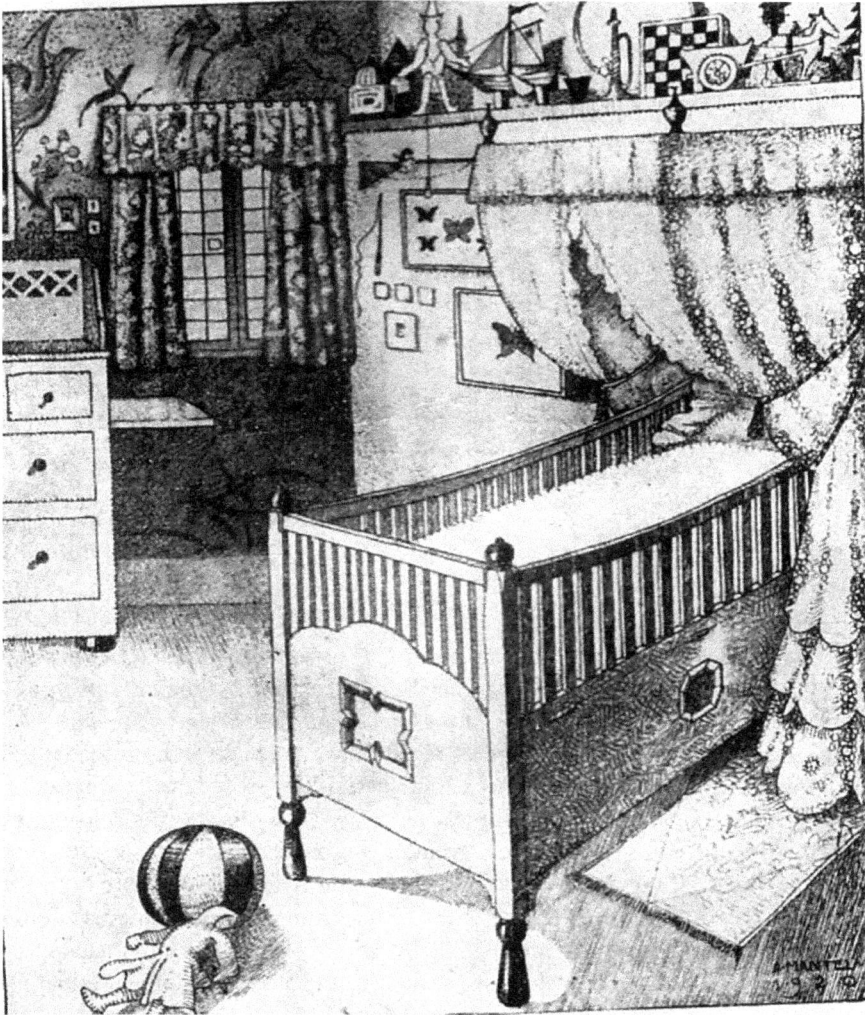

FIGURE 4. An illustration of a children's room by Kogure Joichi that originally appeared in *Wagaya o kaizen shite* (Improving one's home) in 1930.

over tatami floors, he allows for the adoption of a more practical modern design to encourage possibilities (figure 5). But this possibility is limited to this volume alone. Even though he accepted the child-based philosophy, perhaps Kogure had not quite attained a concrete image of how the idea should be expressed in design form. Was it for this reason that he published foreign photographs of children's rooms without qualm?[4]

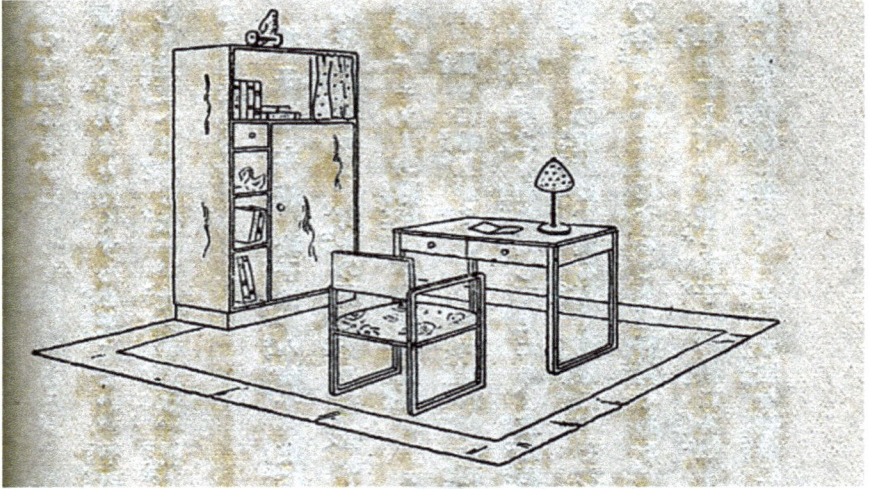

FIGURE 5. Another children's room with desk and bed over tatami floors in Kogure Joichi's residence.

If we widen our scope to encompass Kogure's view of childhood beyond the works pertaining to his profession in furniture decoration, a different dimension surfaces. In *Excerpts from My Life in the Industrial Arts* (Watashi no kōgei sei- katsu shōshi, 1942), a series of Kogure's recollections, he makes it clear that at the beginning of the Taishō period, he held a special interest in toys and began to collect international toys as a pastime. The catalyst for this was the Mitsukoshi Dry Goods Store Items for Children event, in which he participated in 1917–1918 as an employee of the Tokyo Prefectural Industrial Arts School: "Mingling with Iwaya Sazanami, Takashima Beihō and other illustrious figures, I took part in the research on children's toys as one member of the team. This event also included an examination of many toys in stock at Mitsukoshi and a competition in evaluating them, thus promoting the creation of toys" (Kogure 1942: 117).

Aiming to develop a new domestic market, the Mitsukoshi Dry Goods Store, which became a department store at that time, threw much effort into handling children's items. At the same time, a wave of development in domestic industry also enveloped children's goods such as toys, and their export value quickly increased. Nevertheless, the toy factories of the time were tiny and unable to expand their stock of goods. Mass production of inferior goods became rampant, inviting unfa- vorable criticism from abroad. Large retail stores with capital like Mitsukoshi took up the burden of product development, a position they had held since the Chil- dren's Goods Research Group (Jidō yōhin kenkyūkai) was organized in 1909 (see also Jones 2001: 101ff). An advisory organization aimed at improving the quality of goods for children, starting with toys, and disseminating them domestically, this research association attracted many celebrity members, sponsored periodic meetings, and was generally quite active.

In addition to the goals of sharing its views with merchants and capitalizing on goods, the association also had an academic nature that promoted research on children by specialists for its own sake. Moreover, in addition to scholars who worked on product research related to children, many connoisseurs who collected regional toys, following in the footsteps of Edo-period hobbyists, also participated. Having become a member of an organization that encompassed so many diverse interests, Kogure must have been strongly influenced by the hobbyists he met there.

Edo-period hobbies, some of which prospered in the Meiji period, implicitly offered criticism of the system that had developed under the Meiji state. As Yamaguchi Masao (1995) has pointed out, Kogure had played an active role in the Lifestyle Improvement Alliance under the Ministry of Education, making him a person of inconsistent views given his proposals for improvement on the side of the system and government. Considering this contrasting sense of values, we might assume that temporarily experiencing the world of individual hobbies through the collection of toys made Kogure alter his view of childhood. However, in reality, his seemingly contradictory views of childhood did not lead him in either direction, but rather coexisted. This perspective is supported by the contents of Kogure's private library, currently under the custodianship of Matsudo City Hall. Aside from materials on architecture, furniture decoration, and survey results related to his profession, his library included a great number of books on the regional toys collected by Edo enthusiasts, particularly those by Arisaka Yotarō.[5]

Rather than treating toys as objects for children, these books presented collections of objects to enthusiasts through beautiful formats and illustrations. In addition, this library contains evidence of Kogure's aim to rationalize lifestyles. We must also pay attention to the period in which these books were so vigorously published and purchased. In other words, the library reveals that not only did Kogure absorb the modern view of childhood, but he also had a personal interest in children's culture. Partially through the influence of Mitsukoshi's Children's Goods Research Group, Kogure did not stop at furniture decoration. Instead, in looking toward the development of a new market for timber crafts, he struggled ambitiously for a period of time to improve the quality of wooden toys in the toy industry (Kogure 1942: 118–21).

During World War I, when European countries such as Germany could not produce and export toys, America, the largest importer of toys at the time, sought goods from Japan. However, Japan drew criticism from the United States because it had no system of mass production in place and either could not fulfill orders for large quantities, or overproduced unsafe goods of poor quality. To ameliorate the situation, in 1914, two toy goods merchants in Tokyo, Kuramochi Chōkichi and Kojima Hyakuzō, established the Wooden Toy Production Stock Company, which aimed at creating a system to enable modern industrial production. Kogure was working at the Tokyo Prefectural Industrial Arts School at the time. He took an active role in the management of this factory, undertaking all the plans for its construction as well as the provision of equipment and machines for production. At the factory, built in Tokyo's Mikawajima district, the company actively strove to improve the quality of toy production through such means as employing students from industrial schools all over the country. Unfortunately, as soon as the factory itself was on track, America, the chief importing country, prohibited the importation of toys. It then became difficult to continue production, and in 1918 the company dissolved and the factory closed. However, during those years, Kogure certainly exhibited an interest in bringing about the industrial production of toys.

These activities, undertaken from an economics-based philosophy, preceded Kogure's later child-based emphasis. In other words, these activities clearly show another side to Kogure, as a person with economic interests in addition to his democratic view of the family, for which he was later remembered. The earlier Kogure understood that children's items must be mass produced, and his later interest in mass production that would be striking even in the West may have started then. Yet at this time, mass production was driven more by department stores' profit than children's desires. It was more concerned with production, capital, and the market, and so was decidedly based on industry.

MORITANI NOBUO'S DESIGN AND VIEW OF CHILDHOOD

Moritani Nobuo, who was in charge of furniture decoration at Tokyo Prefectural Industrial Arts School at the same time as Kogure, was like him a Taishō-period designer greatly interested in the world of children. Even as a higher-school student, he had been fascinated by toys. During the first part of his career as a professional furniture decorator, he focused on lifestyle improvement in the home, which of necessity centered on children. Nonetheless, his work differed from that of Kogure in its willingness to incorporate elements of a fantasy world. Rather than try to rationalize the production of toys, which would have taken him far afield from his profession, he enjoyed them for their own sake as an expression of a romantic view of childhood innocence.

In a short note entitled "Lifestyle Improvement and the Betterment of Furniture" (Seikatsu kaizen to kagu no kaizen), Moritani, like Kogure, pointed to the importance of children in making progress toward improvements in the Japanese lifestyle. As for the custom of children sitting in chairs, he stated that it could not be achieved without the parents' full understanding (Moritani 1928a). In other words, he thought that beyond having a modern household and understanding lifestyle customs, giving children a well-conceived room was linked to lifestyle improvement.

In *Interior Decorating from Now On* (Korekara no shitsunai sōshoku), Moritani expounded on the necessity of a child's room: "For our children, the most important people in our lives, this has been too often forgotten until now. Making unreflective assumptions about what children are has been decisively consigned to history" (Moritani 1927: 356).

Moritani also stressed the importance of thinking with a child's heart, in other words, of child-based design. In particular, Moritani drew attention to the different characteristics of children versus adults and emphasized the gap between children's reality and what adults think of as "childlike." For example, he argues that wallpaper with a pattern of dogs, cats, or other things that children would seem to like, as seen in Western nurseries, were adult conceptions and would soon be forgotten by children. To substantiate this claim, Moritani gave an example showcasing children's characteristic interests. "Even if you take a child beneath the bronze statue of Commander Hirose, he will not come to want to see it.[6] Yet it is likely that he will rejoice at seeing the train, which runs under it. Even if you bring him in front of something like the Great Buddha, it is a fact that he will take joy in the adorable puffing of the pigeons." Moreover, even if adults hang a child's favorite picture on the wall, the child does not only admire it, but touches it and finally scrawls across it with crayon. Seeing these actions, "adults, let us be of a mind that looks on with satisfaction." In this way, he classified children as completely different from adults (Moritani 1927: 357–58). Taking into account that children's essential nature differed from that of adults, he concluded that designs that were not overly finessed were good for children. This view of design was not far from Kogure's.

Moritani gave concrete examples of his child-based design through the illustrations in his books. For example, in the frontispiece entitled "An Unlikable Children's Room in America," he introduced a Western-style children's room. With checkered curtains and all furniture—chair, chest, mirror stand, toy box, and bed—uniformly white, it was a typical children's room, "from corner to corner carefully conceived for the children," as Moritani said. Nonetheless, he criticized it later in the book as "it somehow having a feeling of 'high-pressure salesmanship,' because it was a children's room favored by adults" (Moritani 1927: 359). It was clearly the children's room in an affluent family with a great many pieces of furniture to arrange. But the design did not stand out as excessive to others: the children's magazine *The Sun* (Ohisama), issued by Shiseidō, published a diagram of this same room. Far from criticizing it, the magazine endorsed it as a design recommended for a child's room (*Ohisama*, no. 7, October 1922). Moritani's second frontispiece, "An English Children's Room," shows a simpler design than the first frontispiece. Though it included a "childlike" animal-pattern frieze of the sort that Moritani had earlier repudiated, he did not criticize it.

Perhaps one might expect that Moritani disdained commercially designed children's rooms that were complete with every possible product. In his other illustrations, however, he introduced a great number of children's rooms that abounded in material objects and celebrated "childlike" design. It is therefore impossible to deny that there is some inconsistency between Moritani's assertions and his tangible designs. Having appraised the children's room in the first frontispiece as "lacking a feeling of comfort, and needing more and more 'breathing space,'" Moritani was himself unable to give an answer regarding what a design suitable for children, complete with "breathing space," should look like (Moritani 1927: 359).

Unlike the above message directed toward citizens on behalf of lifestyle improvement, Moritani's actual view of childhood was individualistic and lyrical. His exhibit in the 1925 Eleventh Annual National Arts Exhibition, three varieties of interior decoration titled "Furniture as Primary in the Dining Room, Study, and Bedroom," demonstrates this vividly. Published the following year as *Small Indoor Art* (Chiisaki shitsunai bijutsu, 1926), these three rooms, which constitute Moritani's most representative work, contained an indoor space of strong workmanship, each accompanied by a particular motif and dependent on a world of fantasy. We may observe that these rooms share a number of features, but the main ones might be "the importance of feeling," "adopting Japanese elements in detail," and "a childlike expression." This work symbolically expresses Moritani's view of childhood and design for it in its "childlike" quality.

The bedroom titled "Sleeping Beauty's Bedroom," from the Sleeping Beauty of *Grimm's Fairy Tales,* which appeared in the National Arts Exhibition, features the bedroom of a sleeping princess. So, too, in *Small Indoor Art,* Moritani wrote: "Quietly hoping for a charming princess to appear, stepping into a country of folktales, a royal palace from our native poetry." It follows that we Japanese are not limited to taking Western folktales into our own expressive work; instead we may seek direction by immersing ourselves in our own fantasy world. In this room, Moritani arranged a bed for the charming princess to sleep in. Particularly on the footboard of the wooden frame, which is replete with ornamental designs, we can recognize symbolic expressions of childhood such as moon and stars, a small castle, and a single heart (see figure 6). A similar sort of delicate outline can also be seen, for example, in the relief above the entrance to Kyoto University's Philharmonic Hall.

Moritani's "Study with a Window Reflecting the Shadow of a Bird" (Torikage no utsuru mado no shosai) was inspired by a line from *The Picture of Dorian Gray* by Oscar Wilde: "The fantastic shadows of birds in flight flitted across the long tussore-silk curtains that were stretched in front of the huge window, producing a kind of momentary Japanese effect" (Wilde 1891: 3). This was a design fully conscious of *japonisme* in the West, and here too, Moritani has added detailed childlike elements. For example, the front of the desk's tabletop features a human figure wearing a hat. A similar figure appears on the small box affixed to the side of the desk near the wall, and this "small box with a red background and a human figure," more than simply a box for putting things in, takes on the symbolic meaning of representing the child's world.

FIGURE 6. Children's bed footboard design by Moritani Nobuo, first printed in an essay on lifestyle improvement in 1928.

"Dining Room with Crimson-Painted Furniture," known for its scarlet chair, conveyed an Eastern liking for things foreign through overlapping eighteenth-century English-style furniture with China's red-painted furniture. Moritani explained: "In a spirit of playfulness, wondering 'If I took a meal on the red stand used to hold the nuptial cups of sake, how on earth would I feel?'[7] I started to want to make a dining room with the feeling of a little poem" (Moritani 1926: 5). With a degree of childlike intuition, he conceived this eclectic design. Here, too, we can observe expressions of the childlike at every turn, such as the human figure placed in a small box underneath the shelf on the sideboard, the pattern of small gold hearts, and the birds among the shelves. Since the feeling of "a small poem describing a young child taking a meal with red all around" is ultimately expressed in his creation, the image at the heart of the work was the scene of a child innocently having a meal.

Moritani did not chose children as simply an apt motif for his work in these three examples of interior decorating. Their design points to his association with Western art and decoration, renewed again and again through time spent studying abroad in Europe.[8] Yet the belief in childlike innocence, a worldview that was spreading widely among the Japanese intelligentsia of the time, is also strongly reflected in his work. Moritani had children himself, and it is clear that he was habitually concerned with children and the philosophy of their childlike innocence: we can understand these three rooms as dedicated to his own children. But

as we shall see in what follows, I suspect that Moritani's own childlike and innocent aim must have long predated having children of his own.

There is a lot of evidence which supports the supposition that from an early
period Moritani greatly admired the world of children. For example, *The Posthumous Manuscripts of Moritani Nobuo* (Moritani Nobuo ikō) features an essay called
"Achieving a Mantelpiece Lined with Toys" (Omocha wo narabeta mantorupi-su o
ete). The mantelpiece, installed in the second-floor study of his newly constructed
house, was built at his express demand, and to top it off, he lined it with the toys
he liked so much. "Every day a great number of toys above the mantle, painted in
tea-blessing [an old color close to walnut], greets me and sends me off to work.
How much better I feel turning my face to these toys than speaking with friends
who only string out pointless arguments, I do not know" (Moritani 1928d: 22–23).
We can read between the lines of this essay and find that Moritani's liking for toys,
beyond its link to his true understanding of children, was steeped in the world of
childlike innocence. Moritani was himself attached to the bedroom of the sleeping
princess. He commented that "with a child's heart and liking both toys and tales, I
wanted to make this princess's room." In other words, it was a question not only of
making it for kids, but also of pursuing his own hobby.

While one might entertain the notion that his personal fondness for toys began
either in his time in Europe or when he had his own children, we can actually trace
its roots a little further back. His lecture "Concerning the Construction of Wooden
Toys" supports this interpretation. Before embarking on explanations regarding
toy construction and facts about toys abroad, he stated that "there is in truth a
close connection between these things called toys and my actual hobbies." And he
went on to say, "Since I was small I have had a great interest in toys, and I had some
understanding of the toys favored by adults. Then later, during my school days,
every time someone took a trip to any region, I would receive as my number one
souvenir a toy made out of wood, and I always gave thanks for this gift" (Moritani
1928e: 93).

From this story, we can understand that the interest Moritani showed toward
toys from his earliest childhood became ever deeper during his time as a student
when he began collecting them. In addition, as expressed in the phrase "I had some
understanding of the toys favored by adults," Moritani, like Kogure, was acquainted
with the contemporary collections of regional toys. If he started collecting as a student at the beginning of the Taishō era, that would coincide with the period in
which research on toy development undertaken by department stores was flourishing, and expositions and other events related to toys began to be held everywhere.

We can discover many of the sources for Moritani's "becoming childlike"
designs in the children's illustrations of the same period. If we compare the childlike design found in the details in *Small Indoor Art*—and indeed in the images
and direction in all of his folktale-inspired work—to children's illustrations at
the time, we easily perceive their commonality. For example, the designs on the

FIGURE 7. A children's book illustration by Takei Takeo, originally published in *Children's Friend* (Kodomo no tomo), May 1926. Courtesy of Burando Suishin-shitsu.

"Sleeping Beauty" wooden bed frame closely resemble the style of contemporary children's illustrator Takei Takeo (see figure 7).[9] Moritani had also managed the venue design for the Imperial Grandchild's Birthday Children's Exhibition in 1926, and that design likewise bore an evident resemblance to another children's book illustration by Takei Takeo.

Furthermore, we can trace this relationship between Moritani and these types of children's illustrations to a particularly early period. In his diary entry of January 7, 1915, he recorded: "I think I will make a copy of the first issue, about Momotarō, in *A Long, Long Time Ago* (Mukashi mukashi), a young children's magazine to be published at the end of this month.[10] Publishing House: Marukiya. Price: Five Sen" (Moritani 1928f: 140).

Around the time he graduated from Tokyo Higher School of Industrial Arts, he was already handling products intended for children. At that point (1915), *Red Bird* and other children's magazines had not yet been published, and it was just before literature based on the principle of childlike innocence, stripped of fairy tales, genuinely began to blossom. Moritani's other work also includes a piece called "Momotarō," which takes the Japanese folktale as its theme. His work as an illustrator for children thus provides an important clue concerning his interest in magazines of the childlike innocence school that he later incorporated into his profession in furniture decoration.

CONCLUSION

Influenced by the lifestyle design of the Taishō period and as a result of select-ing the private domain of family life as their area of activity, these two furniture designers came of necessity to focus on children within the family. Plans for the lifestyle environment of children were bound to adopt the essential functional-ity and low price of modern design thanks to the possibility of mass production. Given the diffusion of Western-style furniture and the increasing rationalization of lifestyle, we see a tendency in both Kogure Joichi and Moritani Nobuo towards more practical proposals and modern design from the start of the Shōwa period. In relation to children's design, however, their work was limited to one part of the populace. In reality, at that time only very wealthy families were able to actually create the children's rooms that Kogure and Moritani recommended, and it was difficult to find a basis for the application of modern design. Nevertheless, behind their adherence to the world of children, we can see the influence of the culture of consumption, which began during the Meiji era.

One source of the early twentieth-century child-based philosophies, as repre-sented by the principle of childlike innocence, was a romantic view of childhood, originally idealized by adults. The "child-based" designers themselves had a view of childhood that tended toward the vague. This led them in a direction somewhat different from a modern design approach, which considered children's lifestyles from a practical perspective (as seen in chapter 12 on child welfare institutions in contemporary Japan). At the root of the expression of the "childlike" in the two designers' most active periods was its perceived contradiction with the interests and concerns of adults, seen also in the same period's view of children as pure and innocent. As a result, the commercial world picked up this contradiction and linked it to a materially rich and dream-filled image of children. In other words, Kogure and Moritani's emphasis on child-based designs and their ambiguity of expression facilitated the expansion of commercial designs for children in the Taishō period and helped to build the foundation for today's highly developed market for children's items.

NOTES

1. The research for this article was funded by a 2004–6 Ministry of Education Science Research Grant for Foundational Research on "Historical Research on Items for Children in Modern Japan: The Background and Establishment of Design for Children." This article has been translated and adapted for this volume from the author's 2007 article "Kodomo o meguru shōhi to dezain: Taishō-ki dezainaa no kodomo-kan to sono hyōgen o rei ni," *Dezain riron* [Theories of design], no. 50: 31–46.

2. *Kokumin shinbun* [Citizen newspaper], March 10, 1915, March 15, 1915, March 16, 1915, and oth-ers; Tokutomi Iichirō (Sohō), *Risō no katei* [The ideal family] (Kokumin shinbunsha, 1915).

3. After studying Western painting at the Hakubakai Aobashi Research Center, Okamoto Kiichi (1888–1930) deepened his association with kindred spirits of the White Horse Society (Hakuba-kai) and participated in the Fusain Kai (Charcoal Sketch Society. Later, his experience with children's

illustrations in *The Golden Boat* [Kin no fune] and *Children's Country* [Kodomo no kuni] led to his energetic contributions to children's illustrated magazines.

4. We see some deviation from this sort of rational emphasis and images of longing for the West in the magazine *Housing* [Jūtaku], which featured articles on children's rooms during the same period. For details, see Jinnō 1998.

5. Kogure's library included six works by Arisaka Yotarō: *A Collection of Japanese Toys: Pacifiers, Tōhoku Compilation* (Nihon omocha shū Oshaburi Tōhoku-hen, 1926); *Pacifiers, Ancient Times Compilation* (Oshaburi Kodai-hen, 1926); *A Collection of Japanese Toys: Pacifiers, Tokyo Compilation* (Nihon omocha shū Oshaburi Tōkyō-hen, 1927); *Picture Books of Toys*, vol. 1 (Omocha ehon sono ichi, 1927–28); *Picture Books of Toys*, vol. 4, *Puppy Dogs* (Omocha ehon sono yon chinkoro, 1927–28); and *Picture Books of Toys*, vol. 6, *Making Horses* (Omocha ehon sono roku umazukuri, 1927–28). It also included two other works on toys, Yamada Tokubē's *Battledore* (Hagoita 1937) and *Old Toys* (Kogan, author unknown).

6. Hirose Takeo was an officer in the Imperial Navy whose heroic death in the Russo-Japanese War resulted in his deification as a war god. His statue was erected at the Manseibashi Railway Station in Tokyo, where it remained until removed in 1947.

7. In traditional wedding ceremonies, a practice called *sansankudo* (three-three-nine-times) involves the bride and groom drinking three cups of sake each three times.

8. In a record of his experiences during his stay in Europe, Moritani frequently alluded to the influence of expressionism on industrial design. Moritani's interest in expressionism did not lay in the expressionist style of using geometric shapes or sharp zigzag lines, but rather was based on a deep understanding from the creator's perspective of how to transcend naturalism and turn toward an abstract world. Moritani himself mainly observed design museums rather than mass production factories, and these experiences stimulated his artistic sensibility. In addition, though fully aware of the necessity of popularizing in Japan the high-quality industrial design of Germany and other countries, he considered the possibility of Japan simply copying the techniques of the Secession art movement, which separated itself from official and academic art institutions. He stated that Japan must not superficially imitate the expressionism rooted in German popular history but must come to understand the spirit of expressionism and create an original Japanese style (Moritani 1928b, 1928c).

9. After studying Western-style painting at the Tokyo Art School (now Tokyo University of the Arts), Takei Takeo (1894–1993) began to produce children's illustrations for *Children's Friend* [Kodomo no tomo] and *Children's Country* [Kodomo no kuni]. Emulating the terms *dōwa* (children's stories) and *dōyō* (children's songs), he coined the term *dōga* (children's pictures) for his illustrations for "new" children. In 1927 he formed the Society for Japanese Children's Illustrators and played a leading role in the world of illustration for children.

10. Momotarō, often translated as Peach Boy, is one of the most popular Japanese folktales. It concerns a young boy born from a peach who goes on a successful quest to defeat a group of vicious demons with the aid of various talking animals he meets on the way.

BIBLIOGRAPHY

Note: Unless noted otherwise the place of publication for Japanese books is Tokyo.

Abe Isoo. 1917. *Kodomo hon'i no katei* [A child-based family]. Jitsugyō no Nihonsha.
Jinnō Yuki. 1998. "Kindai Nihon ni okeru kodomobeya no tanjō" [The birth of children's rooms in modern Japan]. *Dezaingaku kenkyū* [Academic Research on Design] 45(1): 65–74.
———. 1999. "Hyakkaten no kodomo yōhin kaihatsu" [The development of goods for children by department stores]. In *Hyakkaten no bunkashi: Nihon no shōhi kakumei* [A

cultural history of department stores: Japan's consumption revolution], edited by Yamamoto Taketoshi and Nishizawa Tamotsu. Kyoto: Sekai Shisōsha.

———. 2005. "Kindai Nihon ni okeru shōhin dezain no tenkai: Meiji-Shōwa shoki no kodomo-yō shōhin o rei ni" [The development of product design in modern Japan: Using the example of products for children's use from Meiji to the beginning of Shōwa]. *Dezain riron* [Design theory], no. 46: 67–81.

Jones, Mark. 2001. *Children as Treasures: Childhood and the Middle Class in Early Twentieth Century Japan.* Cambridge, MA: Harvard East Asia Center.

Kashiwagi Hiroshi. 1987. "Kindai Nihon dezain o yomu 3. Kodomo no hakken: Seikatsu kaizen undō" [Readings on modern Japanese design 3. The discovery of childhood: The movement to improve daily life]. *Kikanshi WACOA* [WACOA quarterly] 7.

———. 2000. "On Rationalizing the National Lifestyle: Japanese Design of the 1920s and 1930s." In *Being Modern in Japanese Culture and Society from the 1920s to the 1920s,* edited by Elise K. Tipton and John Clark. Honolulu: University of Hawai'i Press.

Kawahara Kazue. 1998. *Kodomokan no kindai: "Akai tori" to "dōshin" no risō* [The Modern View of Children: The Ideal of "Red Bird" and "Childlike Innocence"]. Chūō Shinsha.

Kogure Joichi. 1927. *Atarashii ie to kagu sōshoku* [The new house and furniture decoration]. Hakubunkan.

———. 1928. *Jūtaku to kenchiku* [Housing and architecture]. Seibunkan.

———. 1930. *Wagaya wo kaizen shite* [Improving one's home]. Hakubunkan.

———. 1942. *Watashi no kōgei seikatsu shōshi* [Excerpts from my life in the industrial arts]. In *Kogure sensei kanreki shukugakai* [Professor Kogure's sixtieth birthday celebration], edited and published by Kogure Sensei Kanreki Shukuga Jikkōkai.

Moritani Nobuo. 1926. *Chiisaki shitsunai bijutsu* [Small indoor art]. Kōyōsha.

———. 1927. *Korekara no shitsunai sōshoku* [Interior decorating from now on]. Taiyōdō Shoten.

———. 1928a. "Seikatsu kaizen to kagu no kaizen" [Lifestyle improvement and the betterment of furniture]. In *Moritani Nobuo ikō* [The posthumous manuscripts of Moritani Nobuo], edited by Moritani Isao and Moritani Nobuo ikō kankōkai. Moritani Isao.

———. 1928b. "Hyōgenha no eikyō wo ukeru kagu shitsunai sōshoku wo chūshin ni" [Focus on furniture interior decoration influenced by the expressionist school]. In *Moritani Nobuo ikō* [The posthumous manuscripts of Moritani Nobuo], edited by Moritani Isao and Moritani Nobuo ikō kankōkai. Moritani Isao.

———. 1928c. "Doitsu ni okeru kōgeikai no jijyō to hyōgenha no eikyō ni tsuite" [Concerning the circumstances of the world of industrial arts in Germany and the influence of the expressionist school]. In *Moritani Nobuo ikō* [The posthumous manuscripts of Moritani Nobuo], edited by Moritani Isao and Moritani Nobuo ikō kankōkai. Moritani Isao.

———. 1928d. "Omocha wo narabeta mantorupi-su wo ete" [Achieving a mantlepiece lined with toys]. In *Moritani Nobuo ikō* [The posthumous manuscripts of Moritani Nobuo], edited by Moritani Isao and Moritani Nobuo ikō kankōkai. Moritani Isao.

———. 1928e. "Mokkō omocha no kōsaku ni tsuite" [Concerning the construction of wooden toys]. In *Moritani Nobuo ikō* [The posthumous manuscripts of Moritani Nobuo], edited by Moritani Isao and Moritani Nobuo ikō kankōkai. Moritani Isao.

———. 1928f. "Moritani Nobuo nikki" [The diary of Moritani Nobuo]. January 17, 1915. In *Moritani Nobuo ikō* [The posthumous manuscripts of Moritani Nobuo], edited by Moritani Isao and Moritani Nobuo ikō kankōkai. Moritani Isao.

Sakai Toshihiko. 1904. *Katei no shin fūmi* [The new flavor of family]. Naigai shuppan kyōkai.

Sand, Jordan. 2005. *House and Home in Modern Japan: Architecture, Domestic Space, and Bourgeois Culture, 1880–1930.* Cambridge, MA: Harvard East Asia Center.

Tokutomi Iichirō Sohō, ed. 1891–98. *Katei zasshi* [Family magazine]. Katei Zasshisha.

———. 1915. *Risō no katei* [The ideal family]. Kokumin Shinbunsha.

Wilde, Oscar. 1891. *The Picture of Dorian Gray.* London: Ward, Lock and Company.

Yamaguchi Masao. 1995. *"Haisha" no seishinshi* [A spiritual history of "the vanquished"]. Iwanami Shoten.

5

"Children in the Wind"

Reexamining the Golden Age of Childhood Film in Wartime Japan

Harald Salomon

During the late 1930s and early 1940s, Japanese critics noted a boom of excellent "children's films." The annual top ten movies compiled by the journal *Cinema Bulletin* [Kinema junpō] confirmed their observation. Thus, in 1937, the Shōchiku production *Children in the Wind* [Kaze no naka no kodomo] ranked number four in a list of strong competitors. In the years that followed, numerous films continued to evoke the younger generation's experiences. Some of these works were based on novels that are now considered classics of Japanese children's and youth literature, such as *A Pebble by the Wayside* (Robō no ishi, number two in 1938) or *Composition Class* (Tsuzurikata kyōshitsu, number five in 1938). Other movies had less well-known sources—among them *The Story of Jirō* (Jirō monogatari, number six in 1941)—but were successfully released well into the "dark valley" of the war years.

The blossoming of the genre coincided with societal and legal debates that questioned the suitability of regular cinema programs for children and youth. These discussions informed the preparation of the film law that was adopted in April 1939 and enacted in October of the same year. Based on this law, the Ministry of Education began to screen entertainment programs for unsuitable films. Thereafter, girls and boys under the age of fourteen were no longer admitted to a significant share of domestic and foreign productions that featured "romance," "gambling," "sword wielding," or had a "bad influence on the juvenile mind" ("Officials will taboo" 1939).

Given the commercial importance of young audiences, it seems plausible to assume that these developments encouraged the production of suitable motion pictures and thus ensured the success of children's films. However, contemporary reviews held that *Children in the Wind* and similar works were not specifically targeted towards young spectators. The frequently used term "children's film" *(jidō eiga)*, they explained, referred instead to motion pictures that featured young protagonists and treated the topic of childhood for a predominantly adult audience (see Kon 1941: 18).

The question then arises as to why adult audiences should take such an interest in stories about the life of the young. Writing several decades later, film historians identified the outbreak of military conflict following the "incident at the Marco Polo Bridge" in July 1937 as a major cause. Since government institutions intensified censorship in its wake, argues Keiko I. McDonald, the "search for marketable forms of innocence" was on. Therefore, she concluded, censors in the Home Ministry have to be credited for "a little golden age of films about children" (McDonald 2000: 31). Satō Tadao equally noted a "golden age" of such movies in his influential *History of Japanese Film,* but offered a different explanation. According to him, the sudden popularity of the genre was related to easing societal tensions. After long years of internal conflicts—first caused by left-extremist and then by right-extremist terrorism—the war contributed to a new feeling of stability. The cinema programs reflected this, he contends, by the appearance of a great number of childhood and romance movies (Satō 1995: 10).

Even a cursory screening of the relevant films suggests that these explanations are wanting in several respects. As has been noted above, most of the movies were adaptations of literary works. These works were published months or in some cases even years before the outbreak of open war against China. Moreover, reducing the obvious societal interest in the life of the young to a form of censorship evasion or escapism instead of exploring its nature seems inadequate and leaves a number of intriguing questions unaddressed.[1] Did these childhood films really only "market" innocence? Were there other reasons for the genre's blossoming? Which social functions did these works fulfill? How were the narratives really related to the unfolding war?

The following examination of the golden age of Japanese childhood film contributes to answering these questions from the perspectives of the history of childhood and the history of emotions. It draws particular inspiration from the approach that Ute Frevert and her colleagues have employed in *Learning How to Feel* (2014). The contributions to this volume explore "emotional socialization" via children's fiction and advice manuals and emphasize the relevance of these processes for shaping the "emotional repertoire" of modern societies (Eitler, Olsen, Jensen 2014: 2–3).

After a short excursion into the rich history of children's representations in Japanese cinema that introduces an early work by Ozu Yasujirō, the first section turns to the "childhood boom" that evolved in 1930s Japan and intersected with print media, radio, and theater as well as cinema. This rediscovery of the early phase in life elaborated upon the authentic psychological experience of the young and thus differentiated itself from earlier popular notions of childhood that had idealized the innocence of "children's hearts" (Morimoto 2009: 57). The following part examines more closely three film projects that arguably drove this media boom. Finally, I will analyze the representation of the young generation's emotional life in these and other works of the golden age of childhood film.

HISTORICAL EXCURSION: *I WAS BORN, BUT...*

Children in the Wind and other above-mentioned childhood films were not the first successful motion pictures that featured juvenile protagonists and their "innocence." A good source is also the movies about the urban middle classes—commonly known as "films on the petit bourgeoisie" *(shō shimin eiga)*—produced by Shōchiku Studios. Managed by production director Kido Shirō, Shōchiku attempted to repeat the financial success of Hollywood studios in Japan. According to Kido, a focus on the everyday life of middle-class families guaranteed the interest of wide audience segments (Richie 1994: 8–9). As a result, children became an obvious topic, and many examples of this genre took a surprisingly complex perspective on the experiences of young urban dwellers of the 1920s and early 1930s.

A fine example is *Kinema junpō*'s number one production for the year 1932, the well-known silent film *I Was Born, But...* (Umarete wa mita keredo) by Ozu Yasujirō. Also titled *Picture Book for Adults*, this motion picture introduces the family of the ambitious employee Yoshii who moves to a new home in the suburbs, not far from the residence of his employer. For the two sons of the family, at first life in the new neighborhood reinforces their middle-class identity, based on the belief that ability and effort ensure advancement in society for everyone—and they do not appear as passive child-like beings living in a fairytale world. Rather, they are competent social actors who voluntarily enlist in their parents' project of getting ahead in the world. Thus, they feel reassured when they manage to defeat the local bully and gradually rise in the suburban gang. However, it is trust in the justice of the social order that proves to be the "innocent" element in their perspective on life. This trust is powerfully questioned when they discover that their father—contrary to their belief—lowers himself to a degree that disappoints them, in order to win the favor of his employer, Iwasaki.

In the climactic scene, the local boys attend a private movie exhibition in the home of the employer, who prides himself as an amateur filmmaker. To the surprise of the juvenile protagonists, the main attraction of the movie night turns out to be their father, who plays the fool for Iwasaki's camera. What ensues is a combined school and hunger strike that the two boys engage in against all displays of paternal authority. Finally, their mother's persuasive power and a bout of hunger bring about a solution to the conflict. In the scenes that follow, she convinces her boys to rejoin the project of getting ahead, by assuring them that they will become more successful than their father, if they only invest more effort.

EXPLORING THE AUTHENTIC EMOTIONAL EXPERIENCE OF CHILDHOOD

When *I Was Born, But . . .* was released in June of 1932, contemporary film critics did not perceive its exploration of young psychology as part of a larger trend (see, for instance, "Shin eiga hyō" 1932: 3). However, a societal interest in rediscovering childhood in terms of its emotional experience apparently developed in the following years. A piece of evidence for this development is a series of articles by Tsubota Jōji, then an established author of children's literature, which was published in July 1935 in the *Tōkyō Asahi* newspaper (Tsubota 1935).

In these articles Tsubota explored the portrayal of children in well-known examples of world literature and autobiographical writing including works by Chekhov, Dostoyevsky, Gide, Wedekind, and many others. While he noted that the emotional attachment of adults to their children, and in particular the love for a lost child, was a pervasive theme, he emphasized that the "inner world," the "character," and the "psychology" of the young themselves rarely came to the fore. The few works that did turn to the subjective experiences of children, he argued, tended to idealize their protagonists as "pure and innocent," as was popular for a time "among the families of Japanese intellectuals." According to Tsubota, this tendency—and he clearly referred to the "focus on children's [innocent] hearts" *(dōshin shugi)* mentioned above—seemed sentimental and outdated (Tsubota 1935, part 1: 9). In contrast, he singled out the Japanese authors Suzuki Miekichi and Kitahara Hakushū among an impressive selection of writers, for giving boys and girls a voice in the highbrow children's magazine *Red Bird* (Akai tori) during the two preceding decades. Since 1918, this journal had been a pioneer in emancipating Japanese children and youth literature from the strong didacticism that was prevalent until then. In Tsubota's opinion, the efforts of Suzuki and Kitahara to publish texts by children in the sections entitled "composition" and "free verse," moreover, went beyond the focus on innocence and contributed significantly to a psychologically more realistic portrayal of the younger generations. He contended that a selection of short works by girls and boys from *Red Bird* would make a fine contribution to world literature in terms of representing children (Tsubota 1935, part 2: 9).

In the last article of the series, Tsubota noted recent changes. With the translation of foreign works such as Jules Renard's *Poil de carotte* (1894, translated by Kishida Kunio as *Carrot* [Ninjin], published by Hakusui Sha in August 1933) or André Gide's *Les Faux-Monnayeurs* (1925, translated by Yamanouchi Yoshio as *The Counterfeiters* [Nisegane tsukuri], published by Hakusui Sha in 1935) along with the appearance of new Japanese works such as *A Japanese* (Ichi Nihonjin) by Sugiyama Heisuke (1925), *A Crybaby Apprentice* (Nakimushi kozō) by Hayashi Fumiko (1934), and *Towards the Truth* (Shinjitsu ichiro) by Yamamoto Yūzō (1935), qualitatively new images took shape. In Jules Renard's *Poil de carotte*, for example, an autobiographical novel about the trials of a redheaded boy who grows up in a cruelly unloving and indifferent family, children and youth were portrayed without a trace of sentimentality or "clemency" *(onjō)*. Instead, they appeared as beings possessing an emotional life that was even more intricate and fragile than that of adults (Tsubota 1935, part 3: 11).

Judging from contemporary reviews, this new perspective on the experience of life by children and youth was particularly well received. In writing about the translation of *Poil de carotte*, the writer Osaragi Jirō praised it by arguing that it enabled readers to perceive the young generation in a new light (Osaragi 1933: 6). The significant attention that foreign and Japanese adaptations of the work attracted underlines this impression. In April 1934, the Tsukiji theater produced a successful stage production, and the following year, it was aired as a radio play. The release of the film version by director Julien Duvivier (Les Films Marcel Vandal et Charles Delac, 1932) in April 1934 was a major event. When Kawakita Nagamasa, leading importer of European productions at the time, returned from a tour of Berlin, Paris, London, Vienna, and Prague where he had seen about two hundred films, his account of the meeting with Robert Lynen, the young star of *Poil de carotte*, was covered in a national news report ("Meiga 'Ninjin' no Rinan shōnen ni au." 1934: 9).

At the same time, the publication of Japanese works that assumed the perspective of children toward their environment and attempted to represent their emotional life gained momentum. Early cases in point are the above-mentioned *Towards the Truth* by Yamamoto Yūzō and *A Crybaby Apprentice* by Hayashi Fumiko. According to Baba Tsuneo, writing for the *Yomiuri* newspaper, the serial publication of *Towards the Truth* starting in January 1935 not only captured the attention of mothers, but also reminded fathers of their own childhood (Baba 1936: 5). This novel detailed the trials of Yoshio, whose mother left the family when he was a small child. Keikichi, on the other hand, the principal character in *A Cry Baby Apprentice,* had lost his father. When his mother finds a new partner, the unwanted child is sent away and passed from one aunt to another.

Film studios competed for the rights to produce screen versions. While Nikkatsu acquired the right to adapt *Towards the Truth,* Tōkyō Hassei produced *A Crybaby Apprentice.* Known for the quality of his adaptations of literary works, director Toyoda Shirō presented a much acclaimed film version of the latter work in March of 1938. A review by redoubtable critic Tsumura Hideo went so far as to speak of "the most realistic portrayal of a child in Japanese cinema to date." This referred to the performance by Hayashi Fumio, the young amateur actor chosen for the role of the protagonist (Tsumura 1938: 4).

Several autobiographically inspired works followed. Considering their enthusiastic reception across the repertoire of media, it seems justified to speak of a 'childhood boom' in 1930s Japan. Let us look more closely at *Children in the Wind, A Pebble by the Wayside,* and *Composition Class.* Their prominence within this boom is confirmed by standard works on the history of Japanese children's literature (see, for instance, Kan 1983: 258–59).

Children in the Wind by Tsubota Jōji

The novella *Children in the Wind* was serially published in the *Tōkyō Asahi* newspaper between September and November 1936. It drew heavily on challenging events in Tsubota Jōji's family history as son of the manager of a weaving factory in rural Okayama. In announcing the publication, Tsubota explained his particular angle on the emotional life of his young protagonists: "I have two children in mind. They are Zenta and Sanpei. I will place these two into the harsh and cold wind of our times. I wonder how they will protect themselves and their parents against this wind. They will rely on their innate cheerfulness and their pure character. The question of whether this cheerfulness will let them gain the upper hand [in the fight] against the darkness of the world is the topic of this work" ("Seisai o hanatsu shōsetsu jin" 1938: 11).

In fact, the two brothers in *Children in the Wind* are confronted with seriously adverse circumstances. They have loving parents, but their apparent economic security is afforded only by their father who manages the local factory. When he is suddenly arrested and charged with embezzlement, their mother is forced to find employment to make ends meet. While Zenta stays with her, the younger Sanpei is sent to live with the family of his well-meaning uncle. However, suffering from the separation, Sanpei causes so much mischief that he is returned to his family. The boys are happy to be reunited and attempt to take care of the household and cooking, which results in heart-warming calamitous scenes. Their mother's desperation grows, but then she surprisingly finds a piece of evidence that proves her husband's innocence.

Children in the Wind was read with great enthusiasm, not only by adults, but also by primary school students, as Tsubota, who received numerous student essays from a teacher in Iwate prefecture, related in the *Asahi* newspaper (Tsubota 1937: 8). A stage version by the Tokyo Children's Theater Company (Gekidan Tōdō) was well received, and Shōchiku Studios acquired the rights to produce a feature film. The task was assigned to Shimizu Hiroshi, who emphasized the need to use child-oriented directing techniques to foster natural performances ("Eigaka junbi taidan kiroku" 1937: 8). When it was finally released in November 1937, the movie did indeed gain general recognition. A review in the *Tōkyō Asahi* newspaper praised, among other points, that the common tendency of child actors to overact and to mimic adults—citing recent films with Shirley Temple—had been avoided. Instead, this work offered a pure image of the world of the young "as if painted with light watercolors" (Tsumura 1937: 10).

After the film *Children in the Wind* received an award from the Minister of Education in the following year, a sequel to the novel, titled *Four Seasons of Childhood* (Kodomo no shiki) was published in the *Miyako* newspaper from January to June 1938. It was equally well received in the world of literature for its entertainment value (see, for example, Moriyama 1938: 4) and a successful screen adaptation in two parts by Shōchiku Studios followed in 1939 (also directed by Shimizu Hiroshi, *Kinema junpō* rank number six in 1939).

A Pebble by the Wayside by Yamamoto Yūzō

A Pebble by the Wayside was serially published from January to June 1937. The fact that it appeared in both the Tokyo and the Osaka editions of the *Asahi* newspaper suggests that general interest in fictional works on the young generation became even more pronounced.

Set in the Meiji period, Yamamoto Yūzō's novel introduces the talented Goichi, who lives in a family of samurai descent. The boy desperately wishes to advance to middle school in order to get ahead in life. However, his family's poverty frustrates his one and only wish. His father, a former samurai, is involved in a ruinous lawsuit. His mother has to support the family by folding envelopes in their home, day and night, although her health suffers. Fortunately, Goichi is encouraged not only by his teacher Tsugino, but also by the owner of the local bookshop. When the latter decides to pay for his middle school tuition fees, a lucky turn of events seems imminent. However, his proud father opposes the plan and relegates his son to an apprenticeship in a kimono fabric store. While Goichi suffers from mistreatment by the family of shop owners and their employees, his mother becomes desperate and her health declines further. After she dies, Goichi runs off to Tokyo in search of his father. After many twists and turns he becomes a typesetter, attends evening courses, and finally succeeds in life by entering the publication business.

This story was also autobiographically inspired. Yamamoto's father came from a lower samurai background in Tochigi prefecture, but turned businessman and operated a small fabric store. While he supported his son's education, he did not grant his wish to attend middle school and sent him to Asakusa to serve as an apprentice in a small business. Only after many struggles and the death of his father did Yūzō gain acceptance to attend the First Higher School in Tokyo, where he became acquainted with Konoe Fumimaro (later prime minister) and writers such as Kikuchi Kan and Akutagawa Ryūnosuke. Eventually, he went on to the German Literature Department of Tokyo Imperial University and enjoyed an early success as playwright. By the 1930s, he was also firmly established as a novelist and frequently contributed to the *Asahi* newspaper. He was known for his liberal views and openly criticized the Home Ministry's censorship policies (Nagano 1986).

The authorship and publication of *A Pebble by the Wayside* is a fascinating story in itself. Yamamoto confidently announced a "family or domestic novel" *(katei shōsetsu)* for all ages revolving around the hardships and the maturation of the young protagonist, Goichi, described as follows: "He is thrown away like a pebble by the wayside. He is kicked like a pebble by the wayside. He is covered in dust like a pebble by the wayside. But sometimes, it may be that a small stone from the countryside finally arrives in the center of a big city, by being kicked again and again. Even a small stone that was stepped on all the time may end up on a roof, before one knows it, and look down on the people who pass by" ("Gantan yori rensai" 1936: 7). This tale of hardship may seem conventional, and the key to its success was, again, its novel perspective. *A Pebble by the Wayside* assumed the viewpoint of the boy Goichi, and attempted to represent his emotional experience, while simultaneously celebrating the individual, driven to fulfill his potential.

Yamamoto's agreement with the *Asahi* newspaper stated that the next part of *A Pebble by the Wayside* would appear in the second half of 1937. However, early in July, open military conflict with China broke out, and publication of the novel ceased. Reportedly, the general suspicion entertained by military institutions towards the newspaper influenced the decision. Soon thereafter, Yamamoto was approached by editors of the women's magazine *The Housewife's Companion* (Shufu no tomo), who were interested in continuing the publication. Instead of moving on to the second part, Yamamoto followed the suggestion of the editors and rewrote the novel from the beginning. However, confronted with the demands of censorship officers, he abandoned writing the second part (Yonemura 2004: 136–37).

Nevertheless, within weeks of its publication *A Pebble by the Wayside* became popular among Japanese readers. Their reactions suggest that Goichi's story was perceived as typical of Japan in the late 1930s, although it was set in the Meiji period. This is evidenced, for example, by a meeting of educators and businessmen in western Japan to discuss the "case of Goichi" in the Osaka Asahi Building in March 1937. During the ensuing discussion the owner of a large fabric wholesaler estimated that tens if not hundreds of thousands of young Japanese were in Goichi's situation. Moreover, he attested that abuses such as receiving a new name, or having to do work for the children of the family were not uncommon. The participants further raised issues such as how to deal with the educational zeal of apprentices or the benefits of night schools ("Goichi no baai" 1937: 4).

In December 1937, newspapers reported that the Ministry of Education had concluded an agreement with Nikkatsu. In an unprecedented move, it decided to coproduce a film adaptation. The ministry explicitly initiated the project as a contribution to the "Movement for the Spiritual Mobilization of the Nation" (Kokumin Seishin Sōdōin Undō), which supported the government's war effort.[2] It was planned that this first "Ministry of Education Film" would not only be released in commercial cinemas, but also be shown in nationwide public meetings organized by the National Film Education Association and especially in schools ("Monbushō eiga ni" 1937: 11).

To support the ministry's goals, Nikkatsu mobilized significant resources. Director Tasaka Tomotaka assumed the responsibility for the project, choosing a characteristic approach to representing children on screen. "I am confident that I have portrayed the children well," he noted during a roundtable discussion, "although I do not have any myself. I did not treat Goichi as a child, but as a young human being" ("Eiga 'Robō no ishi' zadankai" 1938: 3). He was joined by internationally known star actor Kosugi Isamu as teacher Tsugino. Young Goichi was played by Katayama Akihiko—the son of director Shima Kōji, a childhood film enthusiast as well—who convinced observers and critics alike. If anything, *A Pebble by the Wayside* was received even more enthusiastically than the preceding childhood films had been. Critic Tsumura Hideo reported that Japanese cinema was elevated by this "epic masterpiece." During the above-mentioned roundtable discussion joined by filmmakers and writers—including Hayashi Fumiko and Tsubota Jōji—the representation of children as social actors in the world of adults was praised ("Eiga 'Robō no ishi' zadankai" 1938: 3).

Composition Class by Toyoda Masako

A literary sensation led to another film on childhood, which ended up among *Kinema junpō*'s top ten (number five in 1938). In the summer of 1937, the publisher Chūō Kōron released a volume with autobiographical sketches by Toyoda Masako, then the fifteen-year-old daughter of a day-laboring tinsmith in the Katsushika district of Tokyo. Soon an English version followed (Toyoda and Iwadō 1938). The descriptions of everyday life by the young inhabitant of this poor area of Shitamachi were written when she attended a local primary school between the age of nine and eleven. Masako's composition teacher, Ōki Ken'ichirō, had taught her "to see things for herself, to judge them for herself, and to express her true thoughts in her own words" (Toyoda and Iwadō 1938). Realizing the quality of her short texts, Ōki sent them to the children's journal *Red Bird* for publication. While the efforts of its editor Suzuki Miekichi and the literary education movement had led to many publications by young authors from rural Japan, Toyoda's essays differed because they allowed contemporary readers rare glimpses into the authentic experience of life among the urban poor ("Tsukiji no butai ni" 1938: 11).[3] As the translator of the English version noted: "The young author pictures not a world peopled with fairies or goblins, as might be expected, but a nook of the community where men and women are not well dressed but real, and children, far from good mannered, play and scrap as they do in real life" (Toyoda and Iwadō 1938: 12).

Toyoda Masako's stories do not revolve around fictional events, and her descriptions outline adverse living circumstances. Her family lives in a tiny house near factories in "the slums of Tokyo": mother, father, and the three children socialize, eat, study, work, rest, and sleep in a six-mat room. The family lacks the most essential items such as clothing; the father is among the laborers who gather every morning in front of the city employment office. Frequently, the Toyodas subsist on only a handful of rice each day, carefully trying to conceal their poverty from their neighbors. "If I had not had my lunch at school," writes Masako, "I should have had nothing to eat." Even on New Year's Day, she has to attend the school ceremony in old clothes—much to her embarrassment (Toyoda and Iwadō 1938: 88).

Masako's "unpretentious child-like innocence" attracted interest beyond the realm of publishing. She was invited to read her stories on national radio, and the theater company Tsukiji Shōgekijō prepared a stage version that scored "one of the recent dramatic 'hits'" (Toyoda and Iwadō 1938: 11; "Japanese Modern Drama" 1938: 8). In the following year, Tōhō Studios decided to produce a screen version. Veteran director Yamamoto Kajirō chose a documentary approach to the adaptation, which featured the young actress Takamine Hideko in one of her first major roles, and this scored a hit as well. However, despite all of the media attention attracted by this sincere daughter of a day laborer from Shitamachi, Toyoda Masako went on to work in a factory after graduating from primary school. Her teacher received the royalties for the first edition of *Composition Class* because the book had been published in his name. Only later did Toyoda start a career as a writer, and in 1942, she was sent to China to report on the local situation for "the women at the home front" (Toyoda 1942: 4). In any case, her much publicized meeting with her onscreen impersonator Takamine Hideko, who was "brought up as a spoiled child" by wealthy restaurant owners in Hakodate, demonstrated the radically different courses that childhood and youth could take in wartime and early Shōwa Japan.[4]

INNOCENCE AS RESILIENCE

As we have seen, these three influential childhood projects—the literary works and their screen adaptations—received significant societal attention for their authentic representation of children's emotional experiences. Considering this fact, it is striking that most of the young protagonists are confronted with seriously adverse living circumstances. More often than not, their families are defunct, and they are burdened with having to bring about an improvement in their situations themselves. Here I examine the portrayal of children's challenges and the way they deal with them in more detail. In particular I want to highlight the characteristic nature of their innocence, which seems to be relevant for contemporary adults' everyday life as well.

Many other works that are associated with the golden age of childhood film in wartime Japan equally featured scenes of emotional hardship. An example is *The Story of Jirō* (Jirō monogari), authored by Shimomura Kojin, an educator who, among other positions, served as director of the Japanese High School in Taipei and later joined the Greater Japanese Youth Association (Dai Nippon Seinendan).

Although Nikkatsu Studios released a movie version by Shima Kōji only in 1941, the first installments of the story had already been published in the journal *New Climate* (Shin fūdo) in 1937. As the title suggests, the story revolves around Jirō, who is the second born of an established family living in a farm village in Saga prefecture, Kyushu. Shortly after his birth, Jirō is given to a foster home because his mother is sickly. There he is raised by Ohama, previously his older brother Kyōichi's caregiver. At first, Ohama is not pleased with the prospect of having to give up Kyōichi and even feels antipathy towards the "little monkey." Nevertheless, after agreeing to the "exchange" of children, in part for economic reasons, she soon builds a strong emotional relationship with her new foster child. Jirō's happy days come to an end, however, when he must return to his birth home. The story focuses on his experience of isolation and alienation thereafter.

In all of the examples mentioned above, adults cause the prevailing adverse living circumstances. In examining the psychological effects of such circumstances on children, authors and directors created impressive scenes. Thus, when Goichi in *A Pebble by the Wayside* understands that he will not be able to attend middle school, while some of his less talented but better-off friends will, he loses trust and the will to live.

His desperation culminates in agreeing to a highly dangerous test of courage upon being challenged by his friends. Goichi climbs onto a railway bridge and tries to hang on to one of the timbers, while a train is approaching. Before the train reaches him, he faints. Fortunately, the driver saves him at the last minute. Several days later, Goichi is approached by his teacher, who attempts to rebuild his confidence. Referring to the meaning of Goichi's personal name, he explains: "Your name, Goichi, means, 'I am unique' or, 'There is only one like me in this world.' I do not know how many millions of people live in this world, but you, Aikawa—are you listening?—Aikawa Goichi exists only once in this world!" Then he goes on to emphasize the preciousness of life and successfully instills renewed determination in Goichi to strive to fulfill his "potential."

The Story of Jirō contains a scene that shows how much the young protagonist suffered psychologically through his parents' decision to give him up to a foster home, only to take him back in after a few years. One summer night, Jirō is put to bed in the room next to his ailing mother. Both stare into the dark with an unfulfilled need for closeness, but neither one of them is able to overcome the emotional distance. It is the son who finally begins to roll playfully from his room towards his mother's. Reaching her side, he sees tears rolling down her cheeks and realizes that she shares his need for intimacy (see also McDonald 2000: 35).

Similar descriptions of the emotional experience of hardship and coping with it are pervasive in the stories and films discussed above, just as they are in the wartime memoirs analyzed by Piel in chapter 8. Yet the "children in the wind" delineate their own sphere of existence, which is distinct from the world of adults. The young may be affected again and again by events of the other world, like a pebble by the wayside, but the space situated between family, school, and possibly work is occu-pied by them alone. As most of the stories are set in villages or provincial cities, these spaces are wide and offer room for play without supervision. In representing this sphere, idyllic landscape images express the "wholesome" psychological con-dition of the young, that is, their "natural" innocence. The pleasure and strength they draw from play in nature is most beautifully depicted in *Children in the Wind, Four Seasons of Childhood,* and another film, *Matasaburō, the Wind Child* (Kaze no Matasaburō).[5] In these films, large groups of children celebrate summer by swim-ming in rivers and lakes; they climb enormous trees and forage in the woods for wild grapes and other food. Animals are a constant source of joy. Insects or lizards are caught and displayed to friends. Nothing is more exciting than riding horses, but children also gladly occupy themselves with taking care of goats, cows, or a calf that can be taken for a walk.

Set in an impoverished neighborhood of the capital, *Composition Class* intro-duces a somewhat different picture. Children as well as adults gather around the hydrant on which the whole neighborhood depends for water. This public meeting place is not only used for washing and for discussing the local issues of the day. It is also frequented by street vendors who perform entertaining spectacles to sell their goods, such as sweet rice dumplings. Even when the children swarm out during summer holidays, the chimneys of Tokyo's industrial areas stay within sight.

In rural as well as in urban settings, play structures or toys rarely take on impor-tance. One exception is *Four Season of Childhood,* where Sanpei's and Zenta's grandfather has a swing and other attractions built on his estate for his long-lost grandsons and neighborhood children. Needless to say, the rails of bridges and other objects can be used just as well for balancing and all sorts of entertaining activities. Thus, radio broadcasts of sports events are reenacted on tatami and medals are won by swimming through futons in *Children of the Wind.* In *Four Seasons of Childhood,* strenuous endurance tests are created by heaping thick blan-kets on the contestants during a hot summer day. In this film, isolated efforts to show off one's toys are short-lived, even when the host is handicapped by an injury.

It is noticeable that boys occupy this "wholesome" young sphere in most of the films. This conveys the impression that the source of future masculine virtues is defined. Boys usually appear in groups and are most happy in groups (as they are in the gangs described by Roberts in chapter 2). They run relentlessly to overcome distances, no matter how long or short they may be, regardless of whether they are injured. They communicate by shouting, whistling, or making Tarzan calls. They regularly wait for each other at meeting places or pick each other up, one after another.

Sometimes boys remain alone, because they are bullied or otherwise separated from the group and these boys play all the more imaginatively. In exploring the minds of the young, *Children in the Wind* and *Four Seasons of Childhood* carefully depict such scenes of idle, solitary play. In the latter, for example, Sanpei decides to stay away from school. He ends up spending time at a pond where he "makes friends" with the fish and shares his lunch and many stories with them. Even his grandfather, who eventually finds Sanpei, is impressed with how trusting the animals have become.

In accordance with contemporary regulations administered by the Ministry of Education, school classes are shown separated by gender. Girls and boys meet on the way to school, and sometimes without the supervision of peers or parents. Thus in *A Pebble by the Wayside*, Goichi spends precious moments with a girl who is his friend, sharing their ambitions for future life. However, the separation of gender spheres usually persists outside of school. In *Children in the Wind*, spending time playing with girls even takes on the meaning of a punishment. Sanpei, who was misbehaving terribly at the home of his uncle, is put under the charge of his cousin and "forced" to play dolls.

Also in *Composition Class*, which is based on an original story by a young female author and features the only female protagonist among the films discussed here, girls are confined to the larger domestic sphere. On a sunny summer day when the local boys set out with long lime-tipped poles to catch dragonflies along the banks of the river, Masako and her friends remain on a blanket in the shade to read and talk within earshot of their mothers. In fact, Masako has two younger brothers and many duties around the house. She is not only one of the few girls who do not have a school uniform, she often seems to observe the jolly life in the childhood sphere from outside.

Although the "idyllic sphere" of childhood is represented as a separate social space, numerous interactions between the world of the young and that of adults are apparent. In rural regions children's groups clearly fulfill an important social function that may be referred to—in the sense of ethnographer Yanagita Kunio— as the preservation of regional identity.[6] In other words, they play an active role in transmitting local customs from one generation to the next. The New Year's hut made from pine branches and other festive decorations where the local young socialize in *A Pebble by the Wayside* serves as an example. Equally instructive in this respect is *Matasaburō, the Wind Child*. Recommended by the Ministry of Education for its promotion of fantasy and creativity, it illustrates how an intrusive element—the "strange" urban middle-class boy Saburō suddenly appearing in their school—is integrated into rural life by drawing on the folklore of the region, that is, the legends that surround the annually appearing deity of the wind and his offspring Matasaburō. The village children are able to identify with Saburō by relating his alien appearance, behavior, and language to his descent from the wind deity.

Considering the time of their production, it comes as a surprise that neither war nor the military are featured explicitly in these films. Nevertheless, both have left traces in the commonsensical background of the narratives. Even in the earliest example—Ozu's *I Was Born, But . . .*—a careful observer will notice that the classroom is embellished with a martial calligraphy. It refers to the three army pioneers *(nikudan san yūshi)* who allegedly sacrificed their lives during the attack on Shanghai in 1932 (see also High 2003: 166). The rabbits that young Masako is so happy to take care of are closely related to the "armament expansion movement." Their fur is in demand for "military winter gear" (Toyoda and Iwadō 1938: 40).

More importantly, however, the emotional qualities that enable individuals to endure times of crisis are molded. This is why the works discussed here devote significant attention to exploring children's perception of the world of adults and their ability to act independently in it, an issue explored from another perspective in chapter 7. *I Was Born, But . . .* presented two boys who are innocent, but acute in their observations. Their rational analysis of how social injustice prevents advancement based on ability results in a major family conflict that drives the father, more than the boys, to desperation. Nonetheless, the film ends on a positive note, as the boys seem to accept the basics of social order and their (temporary) position in life.

Some of the later childhood films present a more complicated picture. Innocence continues to feature prominently, but brings about differing results. On the one hand, it is a source of misunderstanding. Thus, in *Children in the Wind,* young Sanpei visits his father at his company, only to find out that he has been forced to quit his position as manager. While his father is devastated and unable to speak, Sanpei very slowly realizes that there has been a serious conflict. Nevertheless, he is unable to understand how this event will affect his family. Innocent and implicitly trusting, he imagines how his father will found a new and better company. Later, he accidentally meets the policeman who is about to arrest his father and unknowingly takes him to the family home.

On the other hand, innocence and cheerfulness arm the children with a significant resilience to conflicts in the adult world. Even though such conflicts are present within the groups of boys and their course informs the way boys choose their leaders and change them, the fierceness characteristic of the way that grownups fight is lacking. This is evidenced, for example, in *Four Seasons of Childhood.* In the sequels to *Children in the Wind* the power struggle between the families of Sanpei and Kintarō resurges. The conflict is all the more threatening after Sanpei's father dies, leaving behind debts that endanger the livelihood of the larger family. As collateral, the villain, Rōkai, Kintarō's father, seizes factory and estate, including the above-mentioned play structures for the local children. Nonetheless, the boys continue their selfless friendship and thus show that reconciliation is possible. In order to restore harmony to the group, Kintarō literally endangers his life when he climbs a huge tree in search of sweet acorns. He falls and injures his leg, whereupon the group loyally takes care of him for weeks.

Finally, the young protagonists' sincere and innocent trust in themselves and the world is presented as a great source of strength. It allows them to persevere in the face of adversity and enables them to engage in the social world as veritable actors. As has been noted above, these "children in the wind" are frequently left to their own devices. In fact, they rely on themselves to bring about an improvement in their situation. The experiences of Goichi in *A Pebble by the Wayside* are most remarkable in this respect, but also in the *Children in the Wind* a lucky turn of events is brought about by the efforts of Sanpei and Zenta to prove their father's innocence.

CONCLUSION

By way of conclusion, I would like to come back to some of the questions raised in the beginning. Why were these films on childhood so successful? Which social functions did the works fulfill, and how were they related to the unfolding war? My reexamination of the golden age of childhood films in wartime Japan demonstrates that the success of many autobiographically inspired literary works and feature film adaptations interacted with a significant societal interest in the living circumstances of the young generation. Rather than an exercise in escapism, this interest was a "rediscovery of childhood" that emphasized the emotional experience of the early phase in life.

The enthusiastic reception of many of these feature films on childhood suggests that these particular representations of the young were productive on a number of levels. Firstly, contemporary reactions illustrate that they corresponded to the experience of a significant share of the audience—that is, male and female spectators whose living circumstances during childhood had been challenging and whose desire for education had been frustrated.

At the same time, the film projects discussed above allowed spectators to develop a new understanding of the early phase of life. Thus, they invested significant energy in defining childhood as a separate sphere and stage of life that is of particular psychological relevance for personal development. In doing so, they engaged in promoting middle-class ideals—such as innocent, "childlike" children, loving relationships among the members of a nuclear family, the need to develop individuality, and the striving for success—to broader segments of society.[7]

This is not to say that the outbreak of open military conflict with China did not exert influence on the development of childhood films. However, the relationship with the war situation is more complicated than has previously been suggested. As the example of *A Pebble by the Wayside* shows, some productions were explicitly related to propaganda campaigns and educational policies of the Ministry of Education. In commenting on later works that have received little attention here, reviewers emphasized the need to create "wholesome" circumstances for the growth of the "next generation of the nation" *(jidai no kokumin)*, especially in families (Tsumura 1941: 259). Most importantly, in my view, these childhood films engaged in shaping the "emotional repertoire" of wartime society. The pervasive positive reception of the focus on the inner life of the young generation suggests that they provided valuable emotional resources—"wholesome" feelings that audiences could apply to their everyday life and that authorities intended to mobilize in order to achieve political objectives.

In a society in which the socioeconomic transformations of modernity and war threatened personal and national existence, the "children in the wind's" approach to life provided not only comfort and refuge. Their cheerfulness, their sincerity, their devotion to family, their sympathy toward their friends, their refusal to adopt material values, and their strength in the face of adversity offered the means to endure—in Tsubota Jōji's words—"the cold and harsh wind" of their time.

FILMOGRAPHY

Jirō monogatari [The Story of Jirō]. 1941. Directed by Shima Kōji. Nikkatsu.
Kaze no Matasaburō [Matasaburō, the Wind Child]. 1940. Directed by Shima Kōji. Nikkatsu.
Kaze no naka no kodomo [Children in the Wind]. 1937. Directed by Shimizu Hiroshi. Shōchiku.
Kodomo no shiki [Four Seasons of Childhood] 1939. Directed by Shimizu Hiroshi. Shōchiku.
Nakimushi kozō [A Crybaby Apprentice]. 1938. Directed by Toyoda Shirō. Tōkyō Hassei.
Robō no ishi [A Pebble by the Wayside]. 1938. Directed by Tasaka Tomotaka. Nikkatsu.
Tsuzurikata kyōshitsu [Composition Class]. 1938. Directed by Yamamoto Kajirō. Tōhō.
Umarete wa mita keredo [I Was Born, But . . .]. 1932. Directed by Ozu Yasujirō. Shōchiku.

NOTES

1. Nevertheless, it should be noted that Keiko I. McDonald has offered interesting readings of childhood films, in particular those by director Shimizu Hiroshi. See McDonald 2000 and 2001.

2. On the Movement for the Spiritual Mobilization of the Nation, see Havens 1978.

3. The literary education movement peaked in the mid-1930s. Owing to it, no less than 112 collections of texts by juvenile writers were circulating in 1936. See Buchholz 2000: 37–59.

4. When the Takamine business eventually failed, the family moved to Tokyo where Hideko was introduced to the film studio Shōchiku. In a short time, she became the most popular Japanese child actress of the period ("Many Young Movie Actresses in Japan's Film Industry" 1939).

5. The 1940 Nikkatsu production is based on a story of the same title discovered in an unfinished state among the papers of Miyazawa Kenji after his untimely death in 1933. A revised version was published as early as 1934, and further editions followed during the war years. Although Miyazawa would become one of the most popular Japanese writers in the postwar period, his fame was far less developed in the late 1930s. In fact, the director Shima Kōji's interest was sparked by only a stage version that Tsukiji Shō Gekijō performed in February 1939. See Shima 1958: 109.

6. Yanagita elaborated on children's "ritual function" in his "Regional Customs of Children" (Kodomo fudoki), which was first published serially in the *Asahi* newspaper while childhood films remained popular (from 1 April to 16 May 1941).

7. Note that Momota Sōji, writing for the *Tōkyō Asahi* in 1941, described the important social function of excellent children's literature as correcting adults' "views on childhood" (*jidō kan*); Momota 1941: 5.

BIBLIOGRAPHY

Note: Unless noted otherwise the place of publication for Japanese books is Tokyo.

Baba Tsuneo. 1936. "Yamamoto Yūzō shi no 'Shinjitsu ichiro'" ["Towards the Truth" by Yamamoto Yūzō]. *Yomiuri shinbun*, 25 November, morning ed.: 5.

Buchholz, Petra. 2000. "Seikatsu tsuzurikata undō: Die japanische Bewegung, 'das Leben in Worte zu fassen'" [The essays on everyday life movement: The Japanese movement to express one's life]. *Mitteilungen und Materialien: Zeitschrift für Museum und Bildung* 53: 37–59.

"Eigaka junbi taidan kiroku: 'Kaze no naka no kodomo'" [Notes of a conversation on the screen adaptation of *Children in the Wind*]. 1937. *Kinema junpō*, 1 September: 8.

"Eiga 'Robō no ishi' zadankai 1" [Roundtable discussion on the film *A Pebble by the Wayside*]. 1938. *Tōkyō Asahi shinbun*, 1 September, evening ed.: 3.

Eitler, Pascal, Stephanie Olsen, and Uffa Jensen. 2014. "Introduction." In *Learning How to Feel: Children's Literature and Emotional Socialization, 1870–1970*, edited by Ute Frevert et al., 1–20. Oxford: Oxford University Press.

Frevert, Ute, et al., eds. 2014. *Learning How to Feel: Children's Literature and Emotional Socialization, 1870–1970*. Oxford: Oxford University Press.

"Gantan yori rensai: Chōhen shōsetsu 'Robō no ishi'" [Serial publication starts on New Year's Day: The novel *A Pebble by the Wayside*]. 1936. *Tōkyō Asahi shinbun*, 30 December, morning ed.: 7.

"'Goichi no baai': Yamamoto shi no shōsetsu o toriagete shōnen shidō no zadankai" ["The case of Goichi": Roundtable discussion on youth guidance taking up the novel by Mr. Yamamoto]. 1937. *Tōkyō Asahi shinbun*, 21 March, evening ed.: 4.

Havens, Thomas R. H. 1978. *Valley of Darkness: The Japanese People and World War II*. New York: Norton.

High, Peter B. 2003. *The Imperial Screen: Japanese Film Culture in the Fifteen Years' War, 1931–1945*. Madison: University of Wisconsin Press.

"Japanese Modern Drama." 1938. *Japan Times and Mail*, 3 July: 8.

Kan Tadamichi. 1983. *Nihon jidō bungaku* [Japanese children's literature]. Ayumi Shuppan.

Kon Hidemi. 1941. "Jidō eiga ni tsuite. Eiga jihō" [On children's films. Film times]. *Nippon eiga*, 18 January.

Lewinsky, Marianne, and Peter Delpeut, eds. 1994. *Producer of Directors: Kido Shiro. In Celebration of Shochiku Centennial*. Amsterdam: Nederlands Filmmuseum, 1994.

"Many young movie actresses in Japan's film industry." 1939. *Japan Times and Mail*, 26 May: 4.

McDonald, Keiko I. 2000. *From Book to Screen: Modern Japanese Literature in Film*. Armonk, NY: M. E. Sharpe.

———. 2001. "Saving the Children: Films by the Most 'Casual' of Directors, Shimizu Hiroshi." In *Word and Image in Japanese Cinema*, edited by Dennis Washburn and Carole Cavanaugh, 174–201. Cambridge, United Kingdom: Cambridge University Press.

"Meiga 'Ninjin' no Rinan shōnen ni au: Eiga no tabi kara kichō shita Kawakita shi no kyōmi bukaki miyage banashi" [A meeting with young [Robert] Lynen acting in the noted movie *Poil de carotte*: The highly interesting account of Kawakita who returned to Japan from his film travels]. 1934. *Tōkyō Asahi shinbun*, 31 August, morning ed.: 9.

Momota Sōji. 1941. "Jidō shū no ranshutsu: saikin no jidō bungaku" [The increased publication of children's works: Recent children's literature]. *Tōkyō Asahi shinbun*, 18 May, morning ed.: 5.

"Monbushō eiga ni: Honshi rensai 'Robō no ishi'. Zenkoku sho gakkō ni teikyō" [*A Pebble by the Wayside*, serially published in this newspaper, will become a Ministry of Education film: It will be offered nationwide to schools]. 1937. *Tōkyō Asahi shinbun*, 25 December, morning ed.: 11.

Moriyama Kei. 1938. "Kodomo no shiki" [Four Seasons of Childhood]. *Tōkyō Asahi shinbun*, 19 September, morning ed.: 4.

Motomori Eriko. 2009. *'Kodomo' katari no shakaigaku: Kingendai Nihon ni okeru kyōiku gensetsu no rekishi* [The sociology of 'child' narratives: A history of educational discourse in modern and contemporary Japan]. Keisō Shobō.

Nagano Masaru (Hg.). 1986. *Yamamoto Yūzō*. Shinchō Nihon bungaku arubamu, vol. 33. Shinchō Sha .

"Officials will taboo showing of 'hot' reels to under-age patrons." 1939. *Japan Times and Mail*, 6 April: 2.

Osaragi Jirō. 1933. "Ninjin" [Poil de carotte]. *Tōkyō Asahi shinbun*, 10 November, morning ed.: 6.

Richie, Donald. 1994. "Kido Shiro." In *Producer of Directors: Kido Shiro. In Celebration of Shochiku Centennial*, edited by Marianne Lewinsky and Peter Delpeut, 8–11. Amsterdam: Nederlands Filmmuseum.

Satō Tadao. 1995. *Nihon eiga shi* [History of Japanese film]. Iwanami Shoten.

"Seisai o hanatsu shōsetsu jin: Chikaku hanagata sanshi no rikisaku rensai" [The vibrant world of literature: Shortly fine works by three star authors will be published serially]. 1938. *Tōkyō Asahi shinbun*, 18 August, morning ed.: 11.

Shima Kōji. 1958. "Inshō ni nokoru kodomo tachi" [Children that left an impression on me]. In *Nihon eiga daihyō shinario zenshū* [Collected exemplary Japanese film scenarios], vol. 4, p. 109. Kinema Junpō Sha.

"Shin eiga hyō: Nikkatsu Shōchiku yūshū nihen" [Reviews of new films: Two excellent works from Nikkatsu and Shōchiku. 1932. *Yomiuri shinbun*, 10 June, evening edition: 3.

Toyoda Masako. 1942. "Jihen go shūnen o mukaete: Chūshi o meguru 1" [Traveling in Central China on the occasion of the fifth anniversary of the "incident"]. *Tōkyō Asahi shinbun*, 4 July, morning ed.: 4

Toyoda Masako. 1938. *The Composition Class: Japanese Life as Seen by a Schoolgirl.* Translated by Z. Tamotsu Iwadō. Herald of Asia.

Tsubota Jōji. 1935. "Bungaku no naka no kodomo" [Children in literature]. 3 parts. *Tōkyō Asahi shinbun*, 19–21 July, morning editions.

———. 1937. "'Kaze no naka no kodomo' to shōgakusei" [*Children in the Wind* and primary school students]. *Tōkyō Asahi shinbun*, 18 June, morning ed.: 8.

"Tsukiji no butai ni 11 shōjo no meisaku. Dōshin hikaru 'Tsuzurikata kyōshitsu'" [The masterpiece of an eleven-year-old girl is brought to stage in Tsukiji. *Composition Class* radiates childlike emotions]. 1938. *Tōkyō Asahi shinbun*, 12 February, morning ed.: 11.

Tsumura Hideo. 1937. "Shin eiga hyō: Kaze no naka no kodomo" [Reviews of new films: *Children in the Wind*]. *Tōkyō Asahi shinbun*, 8 November, morning ed.: 10.

———. 1938. "Shin eiga hyō: Nakimushi kozō" [Reviews of new films: *A Crybaby Apprentice*]. *Tōkyō Asahi shinbun*, 19 March, evening ed.: 4.

———. 1941. "Kokumin eiga to shite no 'Ai no ikka' ni tsuite" [On *A Family of Love* as a Film for the Nation]. *Nippon hyōron* [Japan Review] 16, no. 8 (August): 259.

Yanagita Kunio. 1941. "Kodomo fudoki" [Regional customs of children]. *Tokyo Asahi shinbun*, 1 April–16 May.

Yonemura Miyuki. 2004. "'Robō no ishi' to Monbushō kyōka eiga" [*A Pebble by the Wayside* and the educational films of the Ministry of Education]. In *Nihon eiga to nashonarizumu* [Japanese film and nationalism, 1931–1945], edited by Iwamoto Kenji, 133–55. Shinwa Sha.

6

Children and the Founding of Manchukuo

The Young Girl Ambassadors as Promoters of Friendship

Koresawa Hiroaki
Translated and adapted by Emily B. Simpson

It took decades for the modern view of childhood to take root in Japan. The school system established in 1872 systematically conceived of children as the modern objects of education, but the populace did not internalize this view until around 1897 (Koresawa 2009)[1]. From the early twentieth century through the 1920s, children as literary subjects, by contrast, served as the antithesis of modernization. Starting with Ogawa Mimei (1882–1961) and his notion of children "as the poetry, dream, and regressive fantasy of the adult writer," a romantic view of children in which childhood is seen as a pure and unsullied existence appeared (Karatani 2004: 159; see also chapter 4), and children were almost excessively praised. Centered on the children's magazine *Red Bird* (Akai Tori), published from 1918 onward, the children's literature movement also created the concept that people who understood children (and childlike innocence) and adults whom children liked were themselves good people. Ultimately, both notions came to overlap with concepts such as peace and friendship in the 1920s and 1930s and were put to use in international relations.

After the Russo-Japanese War (1904–5), a great number of "international friendship groups with the aim of maintaining worldwide peace and friendly relations with foreign countries at the popular level" were created in Japan (Matsumura 1996: 214). Only during the 1920s, however, did women and children enter the stage as the protagonists of international cultural exchange and foreign propaganda. In 1927, for example, there was a doll exchange between Japan and the United States (Koresawa 2010). Initiated by Sidney Gulick, a former missionary to Japan, through the Committee on World Friendship among Children, almost thirteen thousand blue-eyed dolls arrived in Japan in time for the Doll Festival on March 3. The entrepreneur Eiichi Shibusawa then responded with fifty-eight dolls splendidly attired in kimono sent to museums and libraries across the United States.[2] In 1930, as an expression of gratitude for U.S. aid at the time of the Great Kantō Earthquake of 1923, five young Japanese women were dispatched as "ambassadors returning thanks to America," sponsored by news corporations of the day. In addition, there was the work of Japan's Junior Red Cross, which touted international harmony and promoted the ideal of international understanding. After the Manchurian Incident of 1931, manufactured by the Japanese army as an excuse for taking over northeastern China and turning it into ostensibly independent state called Manchukuo, this organization changed its activities to showcasing Japan and providing foreign publicity (Iimori 2009). This incident caused a considerable change in the tenor of the newspapers and national consciousness while Japan plunged into the so-called Fifteen Years War (1931–45).

As the pillar of an image strategy aimed at purifying an adult society engaged in an international bloodbath, children (notably, preteen girls) and young, unmarried women began to be actively embraced as messengers of peace and appeared as protagonists in a continuously moving tale. Their principal stage was northeastern China, and their activities began with the planning of consolation visits by elementary school children to the Kwantung Army, the Japanese continental troops stationed there. In order to promote the establishment of Manchukuo, the state dispatched embassies of young girls from Manchukuo, plus Japanese schoolchildren and representatives with Manchukuo dolls to celebrate the first full year of the state's existence. Through a so-called "child diplomacy" of children and young women, the state tried to advance mutual understanding between Japan and Manchuria. What follows is the first scholarly description of these child ambassadors and their activities between the Manchurian Incident that began on September 18, 1931, and the founding of Manchukuo on February 18, 1932 (Koresawa 2010).

In its initial response to the founding of Manchukuo, its recognition by Japan, and the report by the Lytton Commission appointed by the League of Nations that declared Japan the aggressor in Manchuria, Japan launched the Manchukuo Young Girls Embassy, a component of its external publicity regarding Manchukuo (Koresawa 2013). These girls were entrusted with an emotional message about the "harmony of peoples," pairing specific images of children with the rhetoric of peace and friendship. This rhetoric, which featured "small citizens who will create the world of the next generation" with hands "clasped tightly" asking for "the path to peace not only in East Asia, but throughout the world," was modeled on the 1927 Japan-U.S. doll exchange, which first gave rise to the idea of deliberately using children and young women to project images of Japan for both domestic and foreign consumption. This chapter aims to examine the process by which government officials and mass media came to use such tools and methods in an effort both to deliberately shape domestic public opinion on politics and war, and to expand newspaper circulation.

Let us examine the circumstances under which girls (together with young, unmarried women) were used to create a domestic Japanese image of the founding of the new nation Manchukuo. I explore this topic through newspaper accounts and the reception of two groups which came to Japan but, in line with the theme of this volume, I will focus on the Manchukuo Young Girls Embassy rather than the two young women ambassadors dispatched concurrently by the Manchukuo Concordia Society (hereafter, Concordia Society Women Ambassadors) in order to argue for the politico-emotional importance that both the state and the media ascribed to the role of the then-popular image of children as pure and innocent creatures.

THE MANCHURIAN INCIDENT AND THE MAJOR NEWSPAPERS

The growth of popular culture characterized the interwar period. Due to the full-blown development of the manufacturing industry following World War I, urbanization and population growth continued to expand, and the majority of the increased population was absorbed into manufacturing and service, the second- and third-tier industries of large cities. The attendance rate for compulsory education surpassed 99 percent, the size of the intellectual class drastically increased due to the expansion of secondary school facilities, and along with the spread of moveable type and a new print culture, journalism also expanded. Radio broadcasting began in 1925, and popular magazines sold hundreds of thousands of copies per month. The popular and mass-producing Kōdansha Publishing House's launch of *Boys' Club* (Shōnen kurabu) in 1914, *Girls' Club* (Shōjo kurabu) in 1923, and *Young Children's Club* (Yōnen kurabu) in 1924 helped popularize so-called "child and youth cultural property."

The growth of popular culture is also implicated in the modern wars waged by nation-states, which depend on popular support. Wildly enthusiastic citizens and their vocal support for war helped accomplish the Manchurian Incident, but the problem of how to shape public opinion—and who would shape it—remained. With mass production and mass consumption, the people's way of life became increasingly standardized while also becoming increasingly information-driven through the growth of mass media. A relatively small number of producers came to influence an overwhelming majority of consumers. Through coverage of the First World War, the great Kantō earthquake, and the Manchurian Incident, the five big newspapers —the *Osaka Daily Newspaper* (Osaka mainichi shinbun), hereafter *Osaka Daily;* the *Tokyo Daily Newspaper* (Tokyo hibi shinbun), hereafter *Tokyo Daily;* the *Osaka Asahi Newspaper* (Osaka asahi shinbun) hereafter *Osaka Asahi;* the *Yomiuri Newspaper* (Yomiuri shinbun); *and* the *Tokyo Asahi Newspaper* (Tokyo asahi shinbun), hereafter *Tokyo Asahi*—all rapidly expanded their circulation. Printing a combined total of around a million copies per day, they played a large role in shaping public opinion.

When the Kwangtung Army instigated the Manchurian Incident on September 18, 1931, it did not make the public aware of this fact. In Japan, the story was that China had "unlawfully and cruelly destroyed the South Manchurian Railway, the foundation of Japan's lifeline," thus twisting the legitimate defensive response of the Chinese forces to Japan's attack into the fantasy of the Manchurian Incident. Furthermore, when the League of Nations' board of directors adopted a resolution on October 24 recommending the withdrawal of Japanese troops from Manchuria by a November 16 deadline, the news media inflamed public opinion by suggesting that "the intentions of the victims were manipulated by the aggressors," meaning that China had cleverly brought international opinion to its side. This misapprehension came to permeate domestic opinion, leading to "an eruption of wild sympathy and support for the army's actions" (Eguchi 1975: 162).

The mass media built on and contributed to popular opinion. According to the Newspaper Commission of 1932, the *Osaka Asahi* sent "3,785 telegrams, 75 correspondents (not including permanent on-location staff), 20 liaison personnel, and 177 flights" to Manchuria and also filmed movies in 1,501 locations, held assemblies featuring reports from special correspondents in 77 locations, and published 130 extra editions for an audience of six hundred thousand people. At the same time, the *Osaka Asahi* and the *Tokyo Asahi* called for "letters of support from all elementary school students across the country" to "provide solace to the officers and soldiers of the occupation forces, and to boost their morale all the more" (*Tokyo Asahi,* October 28, 1931, morning ed.: 7; for more on how children were to provide solace to soldiers, see chapter 9).

While these attempts to shape public opinion were geared toward children, they also constituted one link in a campaign on the Manchurian Incident focusing on adults and aimed at expanding newspaper circulation. Popular opinion had already favorably received the image of children—the very young as well as older girls and boys who must be protected as innocents in order to shoulder the burdens of tomorrow—providing encouragement for the soldiers occupying Manchuria for Japan's benefit. Arising from competition among mass media, one new effective strategy was the linking of children (notably preteen girls) to a war fought for peace and in defense of Japan's interests (see Koresawa 2015). Thereafter, when Manchukuo next expected aid from its neighbor Japan and asked for cooperation, understanding, and recognition as a nation, two groups of girls and young, unmarried women entered the stage in the leading role of ambassadors.

THE TWO EMBASSIES AND THE MAJOR NEWSPAPERS

The Manchukuo Young Girls Embassy of June 17 to July 11, 1932 publicized the nation-founding spirit of Manchukuo to Japanese boys and girls. The embassy was sent to Japan in order to promote "Japanese-Manchurian friendship and harmony" and reinforce the idea that Manchukuo was a country that had rejected the tyranny of Chinese nationality. It had become an independent, new country full of ideals, touting national concord, and asking for peace in East Asia and in the world. As if in concert with this ideal, the state recruited young Japanese, Korean, and Manchurian girls of twelve and older living in Manchuria—specifically in Mukden (now Shenyang), Changchun, and Andong—picking two each based on the recommendation of the Manchuria Railway School Affairs Division. In promoting peaceful exchange through the children who would one day bear the next generation, these young girl ambassadors mimicked the form of the earlier doll exchange.

Around the same time, from June 19 to July 7, 1932, as part of its activities on behalf of harmony between the many ethnic groups throughout Manchuria and in order to "publicize the recognition and progress of the new country and the founding spirit of Manchukuo," the Manchurian Concordia Society sent fifteen ambassadors (six Japanese and eight Manchurians), two of whom were unmarried women around twenty years old, in three groups to Japan. Elsewhere I have written about the origin and goals of young female ambassadors (Koresawa 2013); here I would like to narrow my focus and discuss the Japanese news coverage of the young girl ambassadors.

The major newspapers extensively covered the daily movements of both the Young Girls Embassy, which visited Japan for twenty days, and the Concordia Society Embassy, which was in Japan for fifteen days. In addition to articles, often illustrated with inset photography, two papers published the message brought by the Young Girls Embassy: the *Tokyo Daily* (June 2, morning ed.: 11) and the *Osaka Asahi* (June 21, morning ed.: 11). Both the *Tokyo Asahi* and the *Osaka Asahi* held welcome receptions centered on children's organizations, while the *Tokyo Daily* and *Osaka Asahi* primarily sponsored symposia and published articles on both groups of young female ambassadors. Yet the frequency of reporting on the Young Girls Embassy was greater, and the papers in Osaka more enthusiastic than those in Tokyo.

In Tokyo, government and newspapers worked together in promoting the embassies. Records of the Ministry of Foreign Affairs for June and July 1932 contain reports on the movements of both embassies and their activities, sent to the Home Minister and Minister of Foreign Affairs from the local administrative chiefs of the various regions where the embassy groups stayed. Both embassies first went to Tokyo, paid ceremonial respects to the Imperial Palace, and visited both the Meiji Shrine, where the Meiji emperor is enshrined, and the Yasukuni Shrine, where the souls of the war dead are enshrined. Then the Young Girls Embassy visited various government ministries, including the Prime Minister's Office, the Home Ministry, the Education Ministry, the Army and Navy Ministries, the Ministry of Colonial Affairs, and the Railway Ministry, as well as the five major newspapers. It also attended a reception sponsored by the *Tokyo Asahi,* a symposium sponsored by the *Tokyo Daily,* and various other welcome receptions centered on children.

The Concordia Society Embassy similarly attended a welcome reception sponsored by the *Tokyo Asahi* and a symposium sponsored by the *Tokyo Daily*. Then the women in the group visited the wife of Kwantung Army commander Honjō Shigeru while the men visited government ministries. In this way, the men engaged with the practicalities of government, while the two women shouldered the role of poster-girls for mass communication. It is clear that the schedules of both embassies were founded on the close cooperation of the major newspapers and the administration of the Manchurian and Japanese governments.

Judging only by the number of items about these embassies in newspapers, children were the more likely subjects of articles than young, unmarried women. Moreover, the places where the Young Girls Embassy went, from observations at various elementary schools, interactions with educators, and trips to famous places to radio appearances, were out in public, and thus they were easier to cover. Yet, as is apparent from the amount of journalism on both embassies, this prolonged coverage, accompanied by sensationalist titles and fervent public enthusiasm, leaves the impression that it was also sustained by a craze of welcome throughout the nation following the Manchurian Incident.

For example, *People's Newspaper* (Kokumin shinbun) reported on the situation in the following manner. The people who gathered at Tokyo Station at night an order to greet the young girl ambassadors and their party were "in addition to the officials concerned, a crowd of three thousand average citizens, waving five-color Manchurian flags and Japanese flags." Furthermore:

> A sudden, unexpected chorus of banzai! Into a throng so thick it was impossible to move, the six ambassadors looked out on this congested welcome from the rear of a second-class sleeper car, before they stepped onto the platform wearing charming smiles. In that instant, a whirlpool of excited people surrounded these adorable, rare guests, and Miss Ishida shouted, happily at first, "Please don't push the poor children!" as the cameraman's flashes rained down . . . . today, with bouquets of flowers from the Japanese girls, a significant social interaction between Japanese and Manchurian girls occurred. Caught in the wave of a manic welcome, the adorable young girls were sent off with shouts of acclaim as they went through the exit and entered the Imperial Hotel." (*Citizen Newspaper*, June 24, 1932)

When asked about her impression of Tokyo during her stay, one young girl ambassador said "we were told that we would receive a big welcome, but we didn't expect it to be this wildly enthusiastic, almost like a storm. Yu [a young girl representing Korea] and the others were worn paper-thin" (*Tokyo Daily*, June 28, morning ed.: 8).

Why were both embassies sent to Japan at the same time? After the Manchurian Incident, military affairs and diplomacy as well as the real power behind domestic administration for territory in northeastern China occupied by the Japanese army lay in the hands of Japanese officials. On March 1, 1932, Manchukuo was established as a state, its independence achieved at the voluntary behest of those living in Manchuria, with the last Qing emperor, Puyi, as administrator. In the meantime, the

Chinese government appealed to the League of Nations that the Manchurian Incident constituted an invasion by the Japanese military. In April of that same year, the Lytton Commission entered Manchuria to investigate the situation on the ground. In order to make Japanese control over Manchuria a *fait accompli* before the Commission arrived, Manchukuo was born. The Lytton Commission officially announced its report in October; directly beforehand, on September 15, Japan gave a strong push to military and domestic public opinion by sealing the Japan-Manchuria Agreement, formally recognizing Manchukuo. The Young Girls Embassy and the Concordia Society Embassy were both sent from Manchuria between these events, at the end of June through the beginning of July, and served as an opportunity to build up the recognition of Manchukuo with the Japanese public.

The two embassies represented and received sponsorship from different sets of organizations then feuding over how to develop and administer Manchuria. The Concordia Society had a bigger role in the government of Manchuria than might appear at first glance. It spread the spirit of nation-formation and touted anticommunism, the anti-San Min Doctrine (the three principles of Sun Yat-sen), and pro-monarchy sentiments. Officially recognized by the Kwantung Army and the government of Manchukuo, it became an agency for distributing funds, allocating expenses, and dispensing military subsidiary aid. In contrast, the Young Girls Embassy bore a message from the Home Minister as an official embassy of Manchukuo, and they were supported by the Resource Management Bureau (soon to be abolished). The Southern Manchuria Railway and elements in the government of Manchukuo were also involved whereas the Manchurian Youth League sent the Concordia Society Embassy. As a result of the antagonism between the two groups during this period, the two embassies' schedules for visiting Japan were not coordinated and indeed overlapped.

Consequently, as far as we can tell from the records of the Ministry of Foreign Affairs, both embassies were treated roughly equally in Japan. The same is true for their treatment by the Kwantung Army. According to the official diary kept by Honjō Shigeru, the army's commanding officer, the Concordia Society Embassy came on June 18, 1932 at 2:20 p.m. and the Young Girls Embassy at 2:30 p.m., both to give their farewell addresses (Honjō 2005). Once he realized that the two embassies were coming to Mukden on the same day, he staggered the times of their visits and provided each with encouragement. Although their parent organizations could not—or would not—coordinate the schedules for the two embassies' visits to Japan, the embassies essayed, in their individual ways, to achieve national unity, a goal which the Japanese government also honored.

THE YOUNG GIRL AMBASSADORS IN JAPAN

The Young Girls Ambassadors from Mukden (Shenyang), Changchun (Hsinking), and Andong (Dandong) consisted of two Japanese, two Koreans, and two Manchurians:

Tsuda Sumi, a sixth grader in the regular course at Mukden Kamo Elementary School; Izumi Miyuki, a sixth grader in the regular course at Changchun Nishi-Hiroba Elementary School; Kim Kunhi, a fifth grader in the regular course at Andong Normal School; Yu Fukujun, a fifth grader in the regular course at Mukden Normal School; Yang Yun, a first-year student at the Changchun Public School Higher Division, and Lei Jingshu, a first-year student at the Mukden Public School Higher Division. These girls were all twelve to thirteen years old. They were led by Ishida Toyoko, principal of the Dairen (Dalian) Manchurian Railways North Park Kindergarten.

The two girls recommended to represent Mukden were Tsuda Sumi, whose father worked at the Mukden branch of the Korean Bank, and Yu Fukujun, whose father had lived in Mukden for six years and was engaged in the business of buying and selling land. Along with Lei Jingshu, these three girls were all athletes with excellent grades and could be considered children who excelled in the samurai educational identity of "both the literary and military arts." It is noteworthy that Lei's father, a military man, enrolled her in Mukden Public School because he wanted her to receive a Japanese education (*Osaka Asahi,* June 15, morning ed.: 7). Lei's mother was said to have graduated from Tokyo Higher Normal School for Women, now Ochanomizu Women's University, so she must have been a teacher who had experienced studying abroad in Japan. Also, the father of Kim Kunhi from Andong was known "as a leader of the Koreans, willing to risk his life for his brethren, who made great efforts" on their behalf (Ibid.).

The *Tokyo Daily,* which published fewer articles on the assembly than did the other major newspapers, covered the assembly with headlines such as "Young Girl Ambassadors from Manchuria: With Childlike Innocence, without National Borders" (*Tokyo Daily,* May 28, morning ed.: 11); "The Cornerstone of Human Paradise: A Handshake of Childlike Innocence between Japan and Manchuria: "Little Angels" with a Mission to Bring about World Peace (*Tokyo Daily,* June 2, morning ed.: 11): and accounts of the initial decision to send the embassy, its arrival at Moji Bay (Fukuoka prefecture), the car ride up to Tokyo (*Tokyo Daily,* June 2, morning ed.: 8), and a detailed schedule of their time in Tokyo (*Tokyo Daily,* June 24, morning ed., p. 11). All of the major newspapers repeatedly reported the movements of the young girl ambassadors, revealing that the attention shown to them by the major newspapers was greater than that shown to the Concordia Society ambassadors. In particular, *Osaka Asahi* introduced the six girls in detail and with pictures on the seventh page of the morning edition on June 15, before the Young Girl Ambassadors came to Japan, "as a work offered to this newspaper by the Young Girl Ambassadors of Japanese-Manchurian Friendship, chosen by the bright ambassadors to convey their joy."

"Childlike innocence transcends national boundaries! . . . six young girls depart from Dairen on the twentieth and come to Japan at last." Before printing this, the *Osaka Asahi* had solicited compositions by the girls in which they highlighted the fluttering of their hearts at being chosen as ambassadors. These were published as

"Please Look at the Feelings of These Young Girls, Pure of Heart." Consider, for instance, Manchurian Representative Yang Yun (Changshun Public School First Year): "It makes me very anxious that someone like me, who speaks no Japanese, has so easily earned this role. I'm especially nervous about speaking Japanese to everyone in Japan. (I've studied Japanese since the second year of elementary school, but in three years I haven't used Japanese much, and most of my family doesn't speak it either, so I have not become fluent). Almost every day, instructor Kawada asks me questions like 'Why was Manchukuo created?' and 'How should Japan and Manchuria move forward?'"

Japanese representative Izumi Miyuki, a sixth grader at Changshun Nishi-Hiroba Elementary School, had this to say: "What should I talk about when I make friends in mainland Japan, in places like Tokyo, Osaka, and Kyoto? What does the mainland think about us Manchurians? They don't imagine a scary Manchuria full of war and bandits, do they? This Manchukuo is born from the honest appeals of many people. And those of us who live within it are happy and get along well! If I can talk about this, I will succeed in my work [as an ambassador]."

Manchurian representative Yang Yun, the oldest daughter of a general store owner and the oldest ambassador at the age of fourteen, did not understand much Japanese, but says that her teachers talked about Manchukuo every day at school. Lei Jingshu, a first-year student at Mukden Public School Higher Division appeared keen on engaging in her mission: "I'd already learned that the scenery of Japan is extraordinarily beautiful, the transportation convenient, and men and women both work a lot; about Tokyo, Osaka, and Kyoto, and about the beauty of Mount Fuji and Nikko. But now, for the first time, I can go to the country I've been longing for; I've never been so happy."

At the time of the Japanese-American Doll Exchange in 1927, the young girl selected for first prize at the welcome poetry competition sponsored by the *Osaka Asahi* was featured in similar headlines: "Miss Chou, Wide-Eyed as if in the Country of Her Dreams" and "Like a Young Girl Who Has Come to a Fairytale Land, Surprised and Full of Happiness." By reporting her shock at Osaka's illumination and the rushing back and forth of cars and trains that signified Japan's modernity, the newspaper created the image of a bewildered young Korean girl (Koresawa 2010: 169–70). This was the same as in the case of Lei coming from Manchuria.

Yu Fukujun, who represented Korea, provided a different response. She said that after traveling for four weeks, she was "away from home for a long time. I wanted to see my mother, younger brother, and friends so badly I couldn't stand it . . . . I really wanted to go home, and in the evenings Ms. Kim and I cried together" (*Osaka Daily*, July 1, evening ed.: 2).

The young ambassadors departed from Changchun on June 18, and after paying homage to the Shinto shrine in Dairen, they attended a welcome reception at the South Manchurian Railway Club before setting out for Tokyo. They arrived in Moji Bay on June 22 and took the sea route to Kobe, where they transferred to a train to go to the capital. The head official in each place they stopped sent detailed reports of their movements to the government. For example, although Nakayama Sanosuke, the prefectural governor of Fukuoka, surely already knew the daily schedule of the young girl ambassadors from having met with Morimoto and Saitō of the Resource Management Bureau, he reported the circumstances at Moji Bay in the following manner:[3] "On the decks of the ship stood (in order of precedence) the mayor of Moji-Gotō City and his wife, Kubota, head of the School Affairs Division, the leading sixth-year student at Nishiki Elementary School, Senda Tsuchiko, and eleven others. In addition, nineteen representatives of the Kanmon Ladies Alliance visited the ship, carrying out the first exchange between Japanese and Manchurian girls. They set sail for Kobe without mishap" (34). As his account shows, from city mayors and down through those connected to the schools, the ambassadors received a big welcome wherever they went.

The welcome reception in Tokyo was even more clearly designed as a media event. The young girl ambassadors arrived at Tokyo Station at 8:25 p.m. on June 23, where they received a magnificent welcome. In order to cover the event, reporters from the *Tokyo Asahi* and *Tokyo Daily* had boarded the train at stations such as Kōzu and Namazu along the route. The *Tokyo Daily* featured a record of these midroute visits in the women's column on June 24 (morning ed.: 8), and reported that as the group approached Tokyo Station, the girls changed into Manchurian and Korean traditional costumes at the instruction of their leader, Ishida Toyoko. Although Ishida herself wore a traditional Japanese outfit, the two Japanese girls wore Western clothing, blouses, and skirts, and held their caps in their hands, most likely in an effort to emphasize Japan's modernity. Everything from the photographs taken at Tokyo Station and other official events to the ushering of news reporters through stations along the route was arranged with its media propaganda value in mind. Consider this article from the third page of the June 14 morning edition of the *Tokyo Asahi*, published beneath the editorial and accompanied by a photograph:

> [As the reporter who met the young girl ambassadors at Kōzu entered the car,] the girls all charmingly called out together with delight and came to shake hands. While looking at him with friendly eyes, they conducted themselves with a brightness like the clear skies of Japan. When one thinks of how these dear young girls with their innocent, childlike hearts must have trembled at the oppression of the old army faction and the rampant bandits and local rebels, one can only feel fury . . . unable to bear forcing the great innocence of these young girls to remember the calamity of war again, the reporter firmly rejected talk of the Manchurian Incident. At Yokohama Station, an employee of this company's Yokohama branch greeted them with the company flag in hand and shouted, "Banzai for the young ladies!" Then, all together the girls broke out singing the Manchukuo national anthem . . . a sight to make one overflow with tears. Their welcome at Tokyo Station was full of deep emotion from start to finish. Voices shouting "Banzai! Banzai! Banzai!" swirled up like a storm as a crowd of three thousand enveloped the ambassadors.

Images of innocent preteen girls helped adults avert their eyes from the truth of the invasion. Suggesting that children lived a pure and unsullied existence, disconnected from the schemes and crafty speculations of the adult world, the reporter quoted above conveniently abandoned the topic of the calamities of war. I wonder, however, whether the *Asahi* newspapers' reporters did not avert their eyes from that reality themselves, in that they continued to write articles in support of military actions. In so doing, they projected their irresponsible ideals onto the young girl ambassadors in the name of "peace," "innocence," and a "pure heart."

Given that these were elementary school students, the daily schedule for the young ambassadors in Tokyo was grueling, and this did not change in Osaka. As we know from the quantity of newspaper reports, the battle over news coverage unfolded even more fiercely there, where the major newspapers had their headquarters, than it had in Tokyo. For example, in order to convey that the girls of Osaka could not wait for the young girl ambassadors to arrive, the *Osaka Asahi* put together news features before they even came: "This Beautiful Childlike Innocence, the Adorable Ambassadors Entering Osaka Tomorrow, the Excitement of the Japanese Girls Who Come Near Them" (*Osaka Asahi,* June 25, morning ed.: 5).

The media frenzy increased as the girls neared Osaka. "Traveling across the long sea route from afar, visiting Japan from Manchuria, the first young girl ambassadors have finally taken their first step toward entering our Osaka on the 30th. On that day, sponsored by Osaka City, and on the 1st, sponsored by our headquarters, they will clasp hands with the young girls of Osaka." In addition, the major newspapers published several compositions by Japanese girls, filled with impatience to meet the ambassadors. In an essay titled "Older Sister," by a fourth grader at Ritsuhan'ai Elementary School in Osaka, the student wrote: "Ah, I think that Manchuria and Japan should always be friends and help each other. Also, I think it is important for us to get to know each other . . . whether looking at your pictures in the newspaper or reading your writing, you seem charming and kind . . . . I feel exactly as if I've been waiting for an older sister to emerge like this from among my relations."

The selection of compositions included this poem, "Holding Hands," by a fourth grader at Aijitsu Elementary School in Osaka:

> Friends from Manchukuo
> You have come; welcome!
> Please be our friends
> Let us join hands and play
> Good friends, side by side
> Matching step and holding hands
> Let us walk together happily
> Come soon, won't you, to Osaka?
> I am eagerly, eagerly waiting to meet you.

As far as we can tell from the overbooked schedule and news coverage, the young girl ambassadors' welcome in Osaka was far greater than they had expected. They had left Tokyo on the 9:25 p.m. overnight train and arrived in Osaka the next day. Still exhausted from their journey, they floated into the day's news coverage:

> As the 8:56 a.m. train arrived at Osaka, Ms. Lei and Ms. Kim, shaken awake with the words "It's Osaka," sleepily rubbed their eyes and suddenly spoke with great joy: "Oh my, many friends in Osaka have kindly come to meet us!" When they stepped onto the platform holding beautiful bouquets, they were suddenly surrounded by greeting parties, starting with 150 female students of Nezaki Elementary School, and then the National Ladies Alliance, the National People's party, and employees of our headquarters. The young ambassadors were almost buried in the waving five-colored flags of Manchuria, and their faces looked as if they had had their feet trampled and were trying not to cry. Everything came to a standstill for a short while. (*Osaka Daily,* July 1, evening ed., p. 2)

On June 30, the Young Girls Embassy was supposed to attend a welcome reception with Osaka City schoolchildren at 3 p.m. then a symposium on the swift recognition of Manchukuo at 6 p.m. (overlapping with the Concordia Society Embassy). At the same time, the Manchukuo Special Envoy and Secretary-General of Communication—as well as Manchukuo's first ambassador representing its citizens and entrusted with promoting the recognition of Manchukuo—Ding Jianxiu, stopped in Osaka for one hour on his way to Tokyo.

When Ding and his staff arrived at Osaka Station at 8:48 p.m., the young girl ambassadors were there to greet him. Since the first day of the "welcome schedule for the Young Girls Embassy" in Osaka records only visits to newspaper companies, the military, and the government offices in the morning and a social meeting in the afternoon (38), this performance seems to have been prepared in a hurry. The *Osaka Asahi* prominently reported it on the center of the front page on July 1 (evening ed.) as "a beautiful spectacle at Osaka Station." The image of the young girl ambassadors exchanging words with Ding Jianxiu was of "a dramatic audience filled with emotion between an important person of the nation and charming young girls. . . . Again the great jubilations of excited people [shouting] 'Banzai!' echoed through Osaka Station. Then Ding Jianxiu said to the girls, 'Thank you, thank you for working so hard. We will also carry out our mission tirelessly so that we rival all of your efforts.' As he kindly stroked their faces, a scene dramatic beyond measure unfolded" (*Osaka Daily,* July 1, morning ed.: 11).

The July 2 evening edition of *Osaka Daily* reported the arrival of Ding Jianxiu's Manchukuo Special Envoy group at Tokyo Station on July 1 around 8 a.m. on the front page with photos. However, this event did not receive all that much treatment. Instead, on that day, the movements of the Lytton Commission in Manchuria took center stage. The next day, while Ding's meeting with Army Minister Araki Sadao was reported on the second page of the evening edition under the society column, it was a far cry from the sensationalist treatment that the Young Girls Embassy received. Rather, Ding and his party's coming to Japan became a topical issue only because it overlapped with the embassy of young girls. To borrow a headline from *Osaka Asahi* (July 1, morning ed.: 1), the young girl ambassadors were "charming diplomats with whom adults cannot compare."

On July 1, over two thousand residents of Osaka gathered in spite of torrential rain for a national symposium on "welcoming the ambassadors from Manchukuo and on the swift recognition of Manchukuo," sponsored jointly by three organizations based in Osaka, namely the National People's Party, the Association for National Defense, and the National Women's Alliance. They held a welcome reception for both groups of ambassadors at the Osaka Central Public Meeting Hall (39) where the audience heard "a fervent speech by an adorable young girl ambassador's representative on the theme of 'Please Recognize Our Manchukuo Quickly'" (*Osaka Daily*, July 2, morning ed.: 11), greetings from a representative of the Concordia Society Embassy, and then the appearance on stage of five young girl ambassadors (one was sick and, thus absent). Speaking for all of them, Tsuda Sumi addressed the crowd: "Please recognize our Manchukuo as quickly as possible," while Ma Shijie, one of the Concordia Society female ambassadors, explained the current situation in Manchuria in flawless Japanese. She pleaded for the assistance and leadership of Japanese citizens, concluding with "Please love us as if we citizens of Manchukuo were your younger brothers and sisters."

To compete with *Osaka Daily*, which sponsored the symposium with both the Young Girls Embassy and the Concordia Society Embassy, advertised in the feature article quoted above, its rival *Osaka Asahi* sponsored a welcome reception, also advertised in an article. On July 1, the young girl ambassadors spent the morning visiting Sumiyoshi Shrine and the afternoon at a Children's Convention Welcoming the Young Girls Embassy sponsored by the Asahi Corporation. Of course, *Osaka Asahi* focused on this event rather than the citizens' symposium. After a preliminary announcement, "Tied to Children's Heaven: An Artless Spectacle of Friendship" (*Osaka Asahi*, July 2, evening ed.: 2), it reported on the great success of both meetings, which assembled roughly fifteen hundred people: "Everyone, we are now relatives who get along, suddenly united in childlike innocence through experiencing the deep emotion of General Muro's address," (*Osaka Morning*, July 2, morning ed.: 11). Along these lines, three hundred copies of a phonograph record entitled "Welcoming the Young Girls of Manchuria" were produced.

In the competition to stage events centered on the Young Girl Ambassadors' visit, the *Osaka Daily* was not about to lose the fight. It reported the movements of the girls practically every day, a total of twenty-five times, more than did *Osaka Asahi*. The newspaper companies promoted social gatherings centered on children, expecting that they would garner people's attention and expand circulation. In a later "Japan Children's Embassy," fifteen children were chosen from among the elementary students of every region in the whole country and sent to Manchukuo.

The *Osaka Daily* July 3 morning edition featured an article on the "Welcome Symposium for the Young Girls Embassy of Manchukuo" (7). At this symposium with Osaka elementary school student representatives, the two groups exchanged trifling pleasantries about Manchuria and about their lives at school. The paper published large photographs of all of the girls attending (the six from Manchuria and ten from Japan). At the beginning, in a conversation about their movements prior to arriving in Japan, Izumi Miyuki said, "On the 17th, we met Yu-san, Lei-san and Yang-san at Changchun, and that afternoon we went to pay our respects to Minister of State Affairs Ding and the Consulate. On the 18th we left Changchun for Mukden and arrived at Mukden at lunchtime." To this, their leader Ishida promptly interjected, "We met the army commander at Mukden, didn't we?" Izumi replied, "Oh, I forgot an important thing! Yes, yes, we met the army commander." As this dialogue shows, even here the Kwantung Army constituted a weighty portion of the subject matter.

Following the meeting with Japanese elementary school students at Nara City Public Hall on July 3, the girls went on a field trip to the Takarazuka Revue. After the curtain fell at Takarazuka, the top actress in the Snow Troupe called the young girl ambassadors on stage before the audience, and a storm of clapping shook the venue. Then, "the young women of the troupe all took Manchukuo's flag in hand and sang the national anthem of the newly established Manchukuo from the stage, and so unfolded an unexpected and dramatic scene" (*Osaka Daily,* July 4, morning ed.: 7). According to the report from Hyōgo Prefectural Governor Shirana Takesuke to Home Minister Yamamoto Tatsuo and Minister of Foreign Affairs Saitō Makoto, who was concurrently prime minister up to July 1932: "Those in the Takarazuka Revue at the time were the definition of welcoming. They introduced the young girl ambassadors from Manchuria in the audience and together with the Takarazuka school students, sang the founding anthem of Manchukuo. The group of young girl ambassadors, though sitting, joined them in song, and the scene left a deep impression."

On July 4, the ambassadors went sightseeing at the mint, and at noon attended a luncheon party, to which they were invited by the Osaka Women's Alliance. Then they visited city hall, the Asahi Newspaper Corporation and the Mainichi Newspaper Corporation. They headed to Kyoto the following day. The July 9 radio program *Children's Hour* featured "Goodbye, Everyone: Farewell Party for the Manchukuo Young Girls Embassy." The program included: "The Manchukuo Commemorative Song; Greetings from the Young Girl Ambassadors; reading aloud of a message from Prime Minister Zheng, translated; Manchurian Song (first in Manchurian, then in Japanese); Farewell Words; Parting Words; the founding anthem of Manchukuo; the Japanese national anthem" (*Osaka Asahi,* July 9, morning ed.: 14). Through the radio, this program appealed to all citizens. Then, "with distinguished service in the diplomacy of childlike innocence as a souvenir," the young girl ambassadors moved from Kyoto to Kobe, paid their respects at Minatogawa

Shrine, an important shrine in prewar Japan that commemorates the death in battle of Kusunoki Masashige in 1336, and began their journey home.

In short, the government, the organs of mass communication, and educators
throughout Japan gave the young girl ambassadors, who had come to express the
nation-building spirit of Manchukuo, a huge welcome.

CONCLUSIONS

Girls and young, unmarried women first began to appear on the stage of international relations and foreign publicity in earnest in the late 1920s. In the five short
months between the Manchurian Incident and the founding of Manchukuo, they
started to be deliberately and assertively utilized. In other words, with the Manchurian Incident as a catalyst for the journalism battles of the major newspapers,
delicate young girls as well as young women were mobilized in the name of peace
and protection—the protection of national interests—as a subject that could easily
earn the support of the public for the war.

In order to appeal to the Japanese public regarding the necessity of Japan's
leadership of and support for Manchukuo in a visible manner, girls and young,
unmarried women appeared as the protagonists of two embassies: the Manchukuo
Young Girls Embassy and the Concordia Society Embassy. The younger children
in particular had even more topical appeal and attracted more attention than the
youthful and unmarried women. The enthusiasm directed towards these child
ambassadors was enormous; along with sensational headlines, the persistent and
prolonged coverage sustained the citizens' news craze.

Newspapers covering the Young Girls Embassy promoted an image of Manchurian and Korean girls surprised and bewildered by Japan's modernity. The Young
Girls Embassy's trip to Japan also fulfilled the role of transmitting the image of
Japan as modern nation-state, first to Japan and Manchukuo and later to the whole
world. What's more, the image of young girls, under the aegis of "purity," "innocence," and "peace," masked the reality of the invasion. Having Manchukuo Special
Envoy Ding Jianxiu, secretary of communications, meet the young girl ambassadors at Osaka Station also served to show the envoy to advantage, demonstrating
the children's "charming diplomacy," impossible for adults (*Osaka Asahi,* July 1,
morning ed.: 3).

At the same time, for the newspaper corporations holding events centered on
children, this was an enterprise aimed at garnering societal attention and enlarg-
ing their circulation. Afterward, under the primary sponsorship of the *Osaka
Daily* and *Tokyo Daily* newspaper corporations, the Japan Children's Embassy,
comprised of elementary school students chosen from each region of the country
to be sent to Manchuria, emerged in response to the Young Girls Embassy. It is
significant that the overlapping Young Girls Embassy and the Concordia Society
Embassy each in its own way created an image of foreign publicity for the founding

of Manchukuo that was centered on girls and young, unmarried women, no doubt confirming that preteen girls easily captured the people's interest and compassion. The basis for this initiative was not only military might, but also contrasting lifestyles and societal systems; in every way, Japan had an overreaching consciousness of itself as an equal to the major powers of Europe and America. It is easy to see the correlation with the idea of Japan protecting the Manchurian people from the tyranny of Republican China and leading Manchukuo toward becoming a modern nation-state. What is significant is how successfully children were employed as a means to communicate this vision of Japan to the public. Their prominence in the news reports of the day provides evidence that the modern view of childhood had become fully popularized in the Japan of this time.

NOTES

1. For more on the transformation of the modern view of childhood in Japan, see Honda 2000, and Koresawa and Koresawa 2012. Translator's note: In English, see Jones 2001.

2. Translator's note: See Taylor 1985.

3. It is impossible to confirm the pronunciation of the characters in many of the Chinese, Japanese and Korean people's names mentioned here. The romanizations provided are based on the author's judgment.

BIBLIOGRAPHY

Note: Unless noted otherwise the place of publication for Japanese books is Tokyo.

Asahi Shinbunsha. 1995. *Asahi shinbun shashi* [History of the Asahi Newspaper Company]. Documents. Tokyo: Asahi Shinbunsha.

Assorted Matters from Foreigners' Stays, vol. 20. Ajia rekishi shiryō Sentā [Asian history document center].

The Concordia Society Edition 1994. *Eizō no shōgen: Manshū no kiroku* [The testimony of tilm: A record of Manchuria], vol. 21. TenSharp.

Dornetti, Filippo. 2013. "'Manshū kyōwakai' no seika to kadai" [The achievements and challenges of research on the Manchurian Concordia Society]. *Mita gakkai zasshi* 105, no 4: 693–717.

Eguchi Keiichi. 1975. *Nihon teikoku shūgi shiron* [Historical treatise on Japanese imperialism]. Aoki Shoten.

Honda Masako. 2000. *Kodomo hyakunen no epokku* [The hundred-year epoch of children]. Furēberukan.

Honjō Shigeru. 1967 (2005). *Honjō nikki* [Honjō's diary]. Hara Shobō.

Iimori Akiko. 2009. "Shōnen sekijūji to tōyō chihō shōnen sekijūji kaigi no shōchi" [The Junior Red Cross and the invitation of the East Asian Junior Red Cross Council: Concerning international understanding]. In *Ningen kagaku no keishō to hatten* [The history and development of human science]. Mito: Kami Kōji Sensei Tsuitō Ronbunshū Henshū Iinkai.

Jones, Mark. 2001. *Children as Treasures: Childhood and the Middle Class in Early Twentieth-Century Japan*. Cambridge, MA: Harvard University Press.

Karatani Kōjin. 2004. *Teihon Karatani Kōjin shū: 1, Nihon kindai bungaku no kigen* [Collected manuscripts of Karatani Kōjin: Volume 1, the origins of modern Japanese literature). Iwanami Shoten.

Kawahara Kazue. 1997. *Kodomokan no kindai* [The modern view of childhood]. Chūō Kōron Shinsha.

Kishi Toshihiko. 2010. *Manshūkoku no bijjuaru media: posutā, ehagaki, kitte* [Manchukuo's visual media: Posters, picture postcards, and stamps]. Yoshikawa Kōbunkan.

Koresawa Hiroaki. 2009. *Kyōiku gangu no kindai: Kyōiku taishō toshite no kodomo tanjō* [Educational toys of modern times: The birth of children as the objects of education]. Yokohama: Seori Shobō.

———. 2010. *Aoi me no ningyō to kindai Nihon: Shibusawa Eiichi to L. Gyūrikku no yume no yukue* [Blue-eyed dolls and modern Japan: The course of Shibusawa Eiichi and L. Gulick's dream]. Yokohama: Seori Shobō.

———. 2013. "Nichibei ningyō kōryū kara Manshūkoku shōjo shisetsu e: kokusai kōryū ni okeru kodomo no katsuyō" [From the Japan-U.S. Doll Exchange to the Manchukuo Young Girl Embassy: The use of children in international exchange]. *Rekishi hyōron* [Historical critique] 756: 70–86.

———. 2015. "Manshū jihen to kodomo: 'Ōsaka asahi shinbun' no hōdō wo chūshin ni shite" [The Manchurian Incident and children, centering on the coverage of *Osaka Asahi*]. Ōtsuma *joshi daigaku kiyō kaseigakubu* [Otsuma Women's University Bulletin, Home Economic Department] 51: 73–82.

Koresawa Hiroaki and Koresawa Yūko. 2012. *Kodomozo no tankyū: Otona to kodomo no kyōkai* [The search for figures of children: Boundaries between adults and children]. Yokohama: Seori Shobō.

Mainichi Shinbun hyakunenshi kankō iinkai. 1972. *Mainichi shinbun hyakunen shi: 1872–1972.* [Hundred Year History of the Mainichi Newspaper: 1872–1972]. Mainichi Shinbunsha.

"Manchukuo Concordia Society's Embassy sent to Japan." In *Assorted Matters from Foreigners' Stays* 14 (H.7.2). JACAR, "Asian History Document Center," Ref. B05016212200, "From 103–4 Image."

Matsumura Masayoshi. 1996. *Kokusai kōryūshi: Kingendai no Nihon* [The history of international exchange: Modern and contemporary Japan]. Chijinkan.

Sasaki Takashi. 1999. *Nihon no kindai: 14, media to kenryoku* [Japan's modernization: vol. 14, media and authority]. Chūō Kōron Shinsha.

Taylor, Sandra C. 1985. *Advocate of Understanding: Sidney Gulick and the Search for Peace with Japan*. Kent, OH: Kent State University Press.

Yamamuro Shin'ichi. 1993. *Kimera: Manshūkoku no shōzō* [Chimera: A portrait of manchukuo]. Chūō Kōronsha.

PART THREE

Asia-Pacific War

7

Reversing the Gaze

The Construction of "Adulthood" in the Wartime Diaries of Japanese Children and Youth

Aaron William Moore

On 25 April 1944, seventeen-year-old girls' high school student Horibe Chieko was being trained to join her classmates in a factory near Nagoya; they had been mobilized by order of the authorities, removed from their homes, taken out of school, and put into a dormitory. The singular preoccupation among the girls was who was going to get leave to go home, and when. When they were told by a teacher, Mrs. Okayo, that they could not go home to see their families, Chieko wrote in her diary that "everyone's face got dark, and we thought of our teacher." At that point, the girls began moaning about staff members who, in addition to their teaching responsibilities, had been tasked with abetting student mobilization on behalf of the state. "That Okayo! She's without any pity or mercy," wrote Chieko in her diary, "We went to bed [in the dormitory] and everyone started complaining. Nobody could sleep . . . . She doesn't understand a thing" (Horibe 1989: 25 April 1944). Chieko was hardly the first teenager to say "no one understands me;" the gulf between young people and adults was a real one then, just as it is today. Chieko and her classmates viewed adult authorities as an arbitrary and often ignorant external force, completely at odds with the youthful society in which they forged independent hierarchies, values, and rules.

From a structuralist perspective, analyzing the concept of "childhood" should require a simultaneous investigation of "adulthood," particularly from the perspective of the youth for whom adults were the Other, but this is rarely a part of the historiography. Instead, the "new sociology of childhood" has influenced historians to look at the fluctuating, artificial categories that we have applied to age cohorts, mirroring prior and ongoing theoretical interventions in the history of race, gender, and sexuality (James, Jenks, and Prout 1998; Waites 2005; Stearns

FIGURE 8. Drawing by evacuee Noma Seizō, entitled "The Thief," 1944, apparently depicting a child watching an adult stealing from a drawer. The drawing is preserved at the (Kyoto) State School Museum (Kokumin Gakkō Hakubutsukan).

2011; Cunningham 1998). The historical research focuses almost exclusively on deconstructing the ponderous writings of Foucauldian "specialists" like educators, social reformers, legal experts, and psychologists. Meanwhile, Mary Jo Maynes has argued that historians' treatment of young people has mirrored their past treatment of other disempowered social groups (Maynes 2008: 116), which puts us at risk of conflating the cultural history of "childhood" with narrating children's history (although these are inseparable subjects). To make matters worse, children tend to be heavily focused on their peers rather than adults, keeping their descriptions of the latter comparatively brief.[1]

Nevertheless, adult society was a source of texts, films, images, and speech from which children drew inspiration, and young people universally recognized the power that grownups possessed over them (Rohlen 1989). Historians of education and youth have shown how adults intervened directly into the process by which Japanese children learned life writing, including the *tzuzurikata undō*, or life writing movement, that had become ubiquitous by the period of total war. Critical analysis of adult views will continue to be methodologically necessary, but young people's views of adulthood are also crucial for the deconstruction of concepts such as "childhood" and "adulthood."

Further, the degree to which young people were influenced by adults is dependent on how they viewed adult authority figures, so understanding the construction of adulthood among children and youth is part of revealing the mechanisms of social-ization that have affected us all. Rather than dwell on whether there is an "authentic" voice for children (or adults), this essay will simply "reverse the gaze" and see how young people, like Horibe Chieko, described grownups in their personal documents. In particular, I wish to focus on the transition from "childhood" (six to twelve years old, *kodomo / jidō / gakudō*) to "teenager" (thirteen to eighteen years old, *shōnen / shōjo*), and how descriptions of adults and their world changed. In wartime Japan, this transition coincided with leaving primary school and, increasingly, entering the workforce, which meant taking on more adult roles. Expectations related to gender, class, and age intersected at a time when young people's language skills developed at rapid pace and they became more self-reflective. As the famous French teenage diarist Marie Bashkirtseff put it: "While shooting I am a man; in the water a fish; on horseback a jockey; in a carriage a young girl; at an evening entertainment a charming woman; at a ball a dancer; at a concert a nightingale with notes extra low and high like a violin . . . . Seeing me with the gun, no one would imagine I could be indolent and languishing at home" (Bashkirtseff 1912: 5 October 1873).

This chapter will examine how young people wrote, in their personal diaries, about the social leaders, state officials, and family members who exercised power over them. The transition to adolescence brought great changes to juvenile sub-jectivity, namely: the awareness of larger, abstract social structures dominated by grownups, the identification of adults as eventual peers, and the transformation of the family from a source of security to an object of affection.

THE DEVILS YOU KNOW: INTERACTING WITH SOLDIERS, TEACHERS, AND OTHER AUTHORITIES

By 1937, the Japanese government was heavily involved in the management of society and the economy, resembling what Theda Skocpol considered a social revolutionary force, even if the values it espoused are today considered "conser-vative" regarding gender, sexuality, and class (Skocpol 1979; Ambaras 2006: 168). Whenever representatives of the state attempted to influence children and youth, they experienced mixed success. First, children had a weak concept of the state apparatus, discussing only the individuals with whom they had direct, personal contact, and they largely tried to obey representatives of the state as they would adult relatives. Second, while teenagers had a much stronger ability to perceive adults operating on behalf of the state as part of a network of abstract, largely unseen structures, teens also felt that these authorities were legitimately subject to personal scrutiny; in other words, teenagers embraced, endured, or sometimes challenged adults who represented the Japanese government as they sought to dis-cover their place in society.

Evacuated schoolchildren were bombarded by Japan's complex social networks as they became wards of local governments and groups. Kids from the city were looked after by village leaders, barracks commanders, youth clubs, school head-masters, dormitory mothers, teachers, Women's Society (Fujinkai) members, local veterans, and ordinary village residents; the argosy of adult authority figures was intimidating, and children made an effort to get to know them, including learning local dialects.[2] Adults who tried to make the children laugh, or showed a little bit of kindness, were noted with greater fondness than teachers who looked after them every day. One evacuee described the delight that a particularly self-deprecating local, with a thick country accent, gave the children during a short lecture: "Itō Taisaku's talk was a lot of fun. It was all just about how great his village is. So funny. He said, 'I be Itō Taisaku, who Mister Teacher Shionoiri just introduced. I'm big and fat, just like my name says.' (太作) When he spoke like this, it was so funny, and he made all of us laugh" (Nakamura 1971: 122 [30 September 1944]).

By contrast, teenagers mobilized by authorities for war production (gakuto dōin) were more likely to complain about the conditions that adults inflicted on them. Even in letters home that were subject to prying eyes, teens subtly criticized the factory managers who cut their rations, writing, "When you're starving, you're willing to eat just about anything" (Takahashi 1992: 114 [1944]; also regarding the focus on food, see Kotoku 1992: 106–7 [1945]). Still, most teens embraced their role as laborers for the war effort even more aggressively than adult workers did. Girls pulled into factory work could incite each other to increase production, despite the fact that their diaries revealed they were losing weight due to the strict ration-ing system (Ōhayashi 1995: 95 [26 April 1945]). For these girls, the adults who man-aged the factory system for teenagers were judged strictly on their ability to live according to values they espoused among the young, and avoid overt hypocrisy. Consequently, some teenagers, like Sonematsu Kazuko, wanted to challenge their contradictions directly: "As a girl, I should be taking home economics, but from here on out Japanese girls cannot just busy themselves with girls' things. No, girls will have to be able to do what boys do as well. Boys must go to the battlefield. We want to go, too, but currently the state won't give us that freedom. But now the time will come when they *must* give it to us" (Sonematsu 1978: 807 [6 January 1945]). Simultaneously, however, wartime social demands, including giving up school for war work, could be disappointing for teenagers who had only recently been told to forgo their personal ambitions in favor of public service (Ōhayashi 1995: 88 [19 April 1945]). While children simply observed whether a grownup was likely to be supportive or abusive, teenagers tried to grasp the extent to which adult systems served their individual expectations regarding how the world should work.

In wartime Japan, soldiers were perhaps the most important symbols of author-ity; paper plays (kamishibai) regularly depicted idealized interactions between children and soldiers, conflating the innocence of childhood with the purity of service (Matsunaga 1939; McCowan 2015: 16–17; Kushner 2009: 243–64; Orbaugh 2015; see also chapter 9).[3] Children wrote consolation letters (imonbun) to (unre-lated, unknown) soldiers; in personal diaries, some children apparently viewed this as an enjoyable moral obligation: "When I got home [from school] I wrote letters to the sailors in the Navy. As always, I worked hard to make the soldiers happy" (Nakane 1965: 30–31 [8 May 1945]). Some evacuated children were billeted next to servicemen, and thus had ample opportunity to reflect on the relationship they shared with these men. Other representatives of the state (e.g., teachers, evacuation officials, and barracks commanders) encouraged them to interact with soldiers as part of the latter's rehabilitation, "consolation," or "rest and relaxation." Evacuated children wrote home describing how they "played" with soldiers and "got along well with them" (Andō 1990: 247 [5 January 1945]). When children spent considerable time with soldiers, they sometimes enjoyed the privileged access to rationed foods that these men enjoyed, including beef; in return, the children entertained the men:

> After eating dinner with the soldiers, we had a talent show *(engeikai)*. First, we sang "When I Go to Sea" (Ume yukaba), "My Song of Youth" (Waka washi no uta), "Commander Hirose" (Hirose chūsa), "Wibble Wobble" (Tekkuri tekkuri), "Jump, Jump, Jump Up" (Tobe tobe tonbi) and other games, my counting song, and the girls all sang "In the Next World" (Tsugi no yo). Then the soldiers got on stage, too, and painted their faces, and the school headmaster got up as well. We asked the soldiers to do something, so they sang, did sword dances, and performed magic tricks. Mr. Kumatani sang some songs from Isumi and Akita, then we sang the school anthem and it was over. (Asano 1984a: 249 [21 March 1945])

Interaction between servicemen and children was normalized in wartime Japan, from photos soldiers took with children (both at home and abroad) to media representations such as film, comics, novels, and paper plays. At least in Japan, where soldiering was publicly celebrated, children viewed time spent among servicemen as exciting, fun, and especially pleasurable whenever food was involved. Nakamura Naohiko described a visit to the barracks involving the consumption of biscuits, potatoes, miso soup, chestnut rice, beef, grilled tofu, spring onion soup, beans, fish, and sashimi—an incredible feast for a child in the war's leaner years (Nakamura 1971: 126 [24 November 1944]). Nevertheless, unlike with teachers, the names and personalities of individual servicemen rarely shine through, so children wrote about them with about as much affection as a parent's business associate bearing gifts or a distant cousin's amusing pet dog.

By contrast, teenagers' descriptions of encounters with the military authorities were influenced by how they perceived both their position within the broader society and the future course of their lives. Boys who entered military life early, such as teenaged flight cadets *(yokaren)*, saw their superiors as tough but fair guides to a secretive world that they were eager to join. Drillmasters and instructors rapped the beds of cadets with bamboo batons, shouting, "Get up you lazy bastards," but students like Nishimoto Masaharu listened to their explanations closely during induction, writing in their diaries, "At last, my time has come."

These attitudes could change with greater experience in the ranks: as the end of the war approached, Masaharu began to see capricious military commanders as irrational and abusive (Nishimoto 2007: 12–16 [13–15 December 1944], 222 [30 June 1945]). , while other teenage students were eager to assimilate to military culture (Nakamura 1986: 22). In vocational *(senmon gakkō)* and higher schools as well, teenage boys composed "letters of resolve" in which they declared their desire to "give my body to the empire," reflecting an attempt to meet the expectations of instructors who were part of an increasingly militarized education system (Akai 1968: 9). Although teenage girls were never conscripted, some found their "resolve" *(kakugo)* through interactions with male siblings or cousins in the armed forces, while others, like Yoshida Fusako, articulated sympathy for fighting men she did not personally know: "I learned of the sad fate of the [soldiers] who died on Attu. Tears fell down my face" (Yoshida 1987: 118 [31 May 1943]). Girls also looked on the technological might of the armed forces with awe as they became part of the military labor force: "On our way to Yokosuka, we were excited to see the largest aircraft carrier in the world, but it didn't come out. They say ordinary people don't get to see the Navy factory, but we could get a good look. It really demonstrated the majesty of our great Navy. The Yokosuka Navy Hospital was splendid. Whenever they used X-rays, an alarm would sound. The contrails from the aircraft were beautiful" (Kaneda 2007: 36 [6 November 1944]; also see Ōhayashi 1995: 86 [17 April 1945]).

It is well known now, however, that teenagers drafted at all levels of elite universities, middle, and high schools had wide-ranging responses to giving up education for service (Wadatsumi-kai 1988; Seraphim 2006). As the conflict in China was heating up in August 1937, sixteen-year-old Nakano Takashi's friend Masuda Ei'ichi sent him an antiwar poem:

> War is bad
> I do not want to die, therefore
> I oppose the killing of men
> Those who wish to be killed
> Or would enjoy killing what they love
> Only those kinds of people could celebrate war
> All other people will oppose it
> I hope that you will agree with me, and forgive the foolish words of
>   an idiot writing on a hot summer day
> (Nakano 1989: 148–149 [4 August 1937]).

While few doubted the importance of military authority in wartime, teenagers were far more likely than children to perceive the adults within the armed forces as flawed, arbitrarily abusive, and open to interrogation. This was particularly so if they felt that their life trajectory was being thwarted by conscription, but even those who embraced the call to arms wanted the imperial forces to be more rational than they actually were (Nakamura 1986; analysis in Moore 2013: 188–89).

Unsurprisingly, teachers enter into children's records frequently as authority figures, and primary schoolers carefully discriminated "fun" staff from the disciplinarians. Younger children wished to win the approval of adults, and these figures oversaw the practice of life writing itself, including the *tsuzurikata undō*, as nine-year-old evacuee Nakane Mihoko's diary reveals: "During Japanese class we read everyone's composition exercises *(tsuzurikata)*. Most people wrote on swimming. I also wrote about "Having fun swimming." Everyone did such a good job. In my evaluation [the teacher] wrote 'well done', but there were some corrections. I thought, *I will pay attention to fixing my errors and doing even better in areas of praise*" (Nakane 1965: 90 [25 August 1945, postwar]).Some teachers came across as stern and unlikeable, sending children on personal errands, having them labor on behalf of the school or state, or simply scolding students for simple infractions. For many first-year primary school students, however, (particularly female) staff members made a special effort to make the institution less threatening by playing games, telling tales, and refraining from scolding the children. "Today I went with mama to school," wrote Shimura Takeyo in his *katakana* diary, "When I got there everyone was already there. Teacher told us a funny story and made everyone laugh" (Shimura 2010: 30 [1 April 1940]). Teachers were seen by children as sources of amusement whenever the grownups decided to show films, invite outside speakers, or belittle themselves to get a quick laugh. Many of these events were militaristic in content, but children described such entertainments in their diaries as "fun" or "good." Primary school students recorded the names of many films, usually accompanied by *Nippon nyūsu* newsreels, with subjects including kamikaze, "unsinkable battleships," and struggles over Pacific Islands, which were sometimes the subjects of mimetic play (Iida: 3 December 1944; Nakamura 1971: 125 [7 November 1944]; Tsujii 2009: 18 November 1944; Shino 1990: 7 [28 November 1944]; Kan 1990: 41 [10 March 1945]; on *Nippon nyūsu,* see Nornes 2003). Apart from patriotic movies, schoolchildren also fondly described games that the teachers played. Card games, skiing, fishing, and other outdoor activities supervised by teachers could be the highlight of a child's term time.[4] Schoolboy Watanabe Haruhiro, in his entry for the class *yosegaki,* wrote: "I've never had so much fun as when I played dodgeball with the dorm ladies in front of the old school" (Tsutamoto gakuryō 1945: "Dai-2-han"). Children took great delight whenever adults relaxed and joined them for snowball fights, comedy performances during student talent exhibitions, and sporting events. These were, it must be said, rare occasions, as wartime Japanese adults seemed to put a greater than usual emphasis on sternness and fortitude; nevertheless, these messages peddled by teachers were much less likely to find fertile ground in the minds of children, who were more interested in playing and being entertained.

For evacuated children, their relationships with powerful, nonfamilial adults were even more important, as siblings, old playmates, and loving parents were far away. Sometimes adults appeared as stern authority figures—elder men and women who lectured children from the city on discipline and exhorted them to work hard: "Mr. Okumura came to see us sixth graders from Osaka's Shinpō School," Fuji Shōhei wrote, "He told us not to complain about material shortages and learn to discipline our hearts" (*kokoro wo migaku;* Fuji 1996: 4 November 1944). Some of the evacuated children formed close relationships with the adults who looked after them in the countryside. This was true even for teachers, who gave the children a sense of continuity with home, as Shōhei's diary shows: "Today when I was on my way back from school, the kids [billeted] in Shinshūji Temple were gathered in the main hall of Honkakuji Temple to discuss [my teacher] Mr. Takegami. Thinking, I wonder what this is about, I listened carefully—it was a surprising announcement that he will be leaving! It was like I was stuck in a bad dream, as I had learned from him for five years and like him, but it can't be helped. That night we had a goodbye ceremony for Mr. Takegami" (Fuji 1996: 5 October 1944). Evacuees also had a "dormitory mother" *(ryōbo)* who was responsible for their security, health, and happiness outside their classroom activities and, later, their labor on behalf of the state. Newly evacuated students sometimes slept on the same futon as the dormitory mother until they became accustomed to their new lives; memoir literature is full of fond reminisces and hagiographies regarding these women. Sometimes students, like the schoolboy Asano Takahiro, became so attached to their dorm mothers that, when these parental surrogates left, the children would cry (Asano 1984b: 269 [20 June 1945]). These relationships were utterly dependent on the children's willingness to form bonds with adults who gave them some measure of consolation during a time of great difficulty.

Unsurprisingly, perhaps, teenagers could take a different view of school authorities, particularly when they struggled to understand the rhyme and reason of the systems adults created. For those who were fortunate enough to enjoy middle and girls' high school education, teachers still fulfilled an important role in determining a teenager's future, so girls like Yoshida Fusako watched nervously as classrooms and groups were assigned faculty at the beginning of the year (Yoshida 1987: 116 [5 April 1942]). As Japanese teenagers began to select their own reading materials from newspapers to novels, however, the parameters of public education could feel confining. Fifteen year old Kojima Yoshitaka had little interest in what his schoolmasters in Nagoya were trying to teach him: "Actually, these days I never study and am just caught up in writing my diary. Today when I got home from school I took off my [military style] boots, ate a sweet potato, read the morning edition [of the news], did some sketching, and then read some more of Sōseki's *Botchan*—that was my day. I just did a little bit of English homework and that dispatched my obligation for the day. I'm in trouble!" Inspired perhaps by *Botchan's* irreverent satire of the teaching profession, the next day Yoshitaka was overjoyed to discover that his mandatory archery practice had been cancelled, so he ducked out of extracurricular activities right away—only to be "caught" by his teacher outside the toilets. "I made him wait outside the work shed for up to an hour when he decided I'd forgotten [about my jobs] and went home. I'm going to get it tomorrow, what a worry." For Yoshitaka, there was a far more interesting world of literature and learning outside of the schoolhouse (Kojima 1995: 96 [19 January 1944]).

For those who were being pulled out of school and into the state's mandatory labor system, experiencing the arbitrary nature with which adults wielded power over them triggered frustration rather than playful rebellion. When sixteen-year-old Inohara Mitsuko's youth labor factory decided to distribute winter coats based on a lottery instead of need, it triggered an uncharacteristically strident anger:

> Sensei read the winning numbers. I listened as hard as I could, straining. Out of the four girls in my room, I was the only one not called. I went back to my room and cried bitterly. Why, in this world, does nothing turn out the way I want it? I don't even want the coat anymore—I'd just give it to a girl who doesn't even have one. But no one thinks this way except me. People only think of themselves, and I just rolled up in my futon and cried. I was overwhelmed with emotion, and wrote my mom a letter. People who won a coat are now chattering about buying tickets to visit home. I became enraged. I tried to console myself by going to bed early, but my eyes were wide open and I couldn't sleep at all—even when I told myself that this is fate. (Inohara 1991: 15 January 1945)

Nakano Takashi, who at sixteen years old saw his teacher conscripted for service in China, looked on the older man with contempt. The teacher was, according to Takashi, probably sacked during the 1920s "military reduction" (gunshuku) period and forced to become a physical education instructor. Referring to the teacher's personal philosophy as a "mess" (mecha-kucha), Takashi's description of his teacher suggests that he saw the older man's absurdities as a synecdoche of the stupidity of the adult world around him. In the style of Botchan's protagonist, who gave staff members in his school nicknames like "Mountain Storm" and "Red Shirt," Takashi had taken to calling the newly-commissioned officer "Kiln Head" (Jagama) after seeing him in a large, ridiculous white helmet. Watching the older man ride away in a train, waving with his dress-uniform white gloves, Takashi wrote: "The train whistle blew, and it rocked back and forth while moving forward. People were shouting 'Banzai! Banzai!' I screamed angrily: 'Banzai, Jagama! BANZAI!' Moving along with the train, Mr. Jagama saluted with a gloved fist, and at the entrance to the train car he stood starkly in the middle of his messed up ideology" (Nakano 1989: 154 [24 August 1937]). Thus, while young children tried to situate adults into categories such as "fun" and "strict," teenagers were able to express a greater range of views when describing their putative superiors, including derision, which reflected their struggle to find their place in a social world controlled by such people.

For the most part, adult authorities in the personal records of evacuated schoolchildren were inscrutable supporting actors. Nevertheless, children did value the views of their elders, and little girls like Nakane Mihoko often worried, "I wonder if I've been a good girl this month? Next month I'll be even better, and make mother and father happy" (Nakane 1965: 76 [31 July 1945]). By contrast, teenagers felt freer in directly criticizing their superiors while seeking to understand them as individuals, sometimes seeing these authorities as irrational, unfair, and stupid. The concept of "adulthood" changed significantly as children matured into teenagers, diversifying in representation depending on how the young adolescent diarist understood his or her position within larger, abstract social structures.

RULING IN THE HOME: PARENTS AND OTHER FAMILY AUTHORITIES

For young children, whether they were evacuated or forced to become refugees, separation from the home was a source of anxiety and trauma; the diaries make it very clear that, regardless of adult efforts to construct a more resilient childhood for evacuees, little children's constant desire to go home was difficult to overcome. Evacuated schoolboy Nakamura Naohiko wrote excitedly about his father's impending visit: "Finally dad is coming to visiting hours. If only tomorrow would come a little more quickly!" (Nakamura 1971: 126 [20 November 1944]). Fifth-grader Umano Yōko, who was removed from Tokyo's Shinagawa Ward to rural Shizuoka Prefecture, described her reunion with her father in an evacuation diary: "I began running, saying aloud, 'Daddy.' I was so happy, so happy, I couldn't help myself. I had not seen my dad's face in a month. I was crying. [On the next day, her class went to collect chestnuts.] I followed my dad and the others. Dad collected so many for me, so our group got the most. [After feasting on the chestnuts and other foods, her father had to leave the next day.] I was sad, but not everyone's mom or dad could come, so I had to be strong" (Umano 1988: 10–12 October 1944). In some cases, children did not admit to missing their parents, or feeling disappointment when reunions were thwarted, particularly if they had already taken pains to construct a heroic persona for themselves in their personal records. Sixth-grade schoolboy Fuji Shōhei worked hard to cultivate such a stance: "Today we were meant to sleep in till 8 a.m., but we were woken up at 5:30. Then, mom said to come to Fukui station because she would be there as part of a comfort service *(imontai)*, so I went to see her. But orders were changed, so nine different people were sent. My mom wasn't there, but Ueda's uncle was there, and he gave us all kinds of things to eat and took us to Fujishima Shrine for a memorial photo. I was happy." Nevertheless, Fuji's longing still appeared subtly in his diary. After declaring he had "resolved to obey my teacher's lessons," Fuji wistfully recalled a day out with his father, writing "the weather in Osaka's Uranama Park was so nice last autumn. It leaves in me a feeling of disappointment and loneliness. We plan to put on a happy face for the people of Fukui during our sports day" (Fuji 1996: 9 October and 5 November 1944). Authorities worked diligently to generate resilient evacuees, but children's emotional attachments to adult relatives could not be so easily managed, even when the kids were trying to play along.

It would be wrong, however, to see the family solely as a social structure in opposition to militarism or mobilization programs. According to Fuji, adult relatives in Osaka sent military-themed toys to children evacuated to Fukui Prefecture (Fuji 1996: 24 September 1944), and other children recorded visits by cousins, uncles, and elder brothers in the service who passed on heroic war stories. The toys, clothes, and tales from family tied into the rituals organized by schools, social clubs, and evacuation authorities, becoming a part of the shared culture of children and youth:

> On 6 January [1945], we prayed hard for victory, marching to Yamagata Shrine [in Yamanashi Prefecture]. We purposefully took the long route there. I also put three books in my rucksack as well as tying a headband (hachimaki). I used the headband dad gave me, the kamikaze one . . . The Yamanashi Youth Corps (sei-shōnendan) came and gave each evacuated child a lump of coal so we wrote thank-you cards for them. This week I'm the weekly head (shūbanchō) for our group. I'm already done being a trainee (kyūchō) and am now a unit commander (butaichō)—I lead the 2nd Unit. (Asano 1984a: 248 [8 January 1945])

Because younger children could not apparently grasp abstract concepts such as economies, governments, and war, they largely accepted what trusted adults told them about these things. That being said, the fervor with which adults supported the war could be frightening as well, even if children did not record these feelings at the time (Shimura 2010: 42).

Meanwhile, authorities may have considered teenagers adults for the purposes of labor mobilization, but their hearts appeared tied to home life as strongly as ever. Even a working-class girl like Mikawa Michiko loathed compulsory labor and wanted to go home. The arrival at her factory dormitory of a woman who had worked for years with Michiko's family was a source of considerable excitement. "When the train arrived and I saw her happy, smiling face," she wrote in her diary, "I was hit by happiness beyond words and tears came streaming down my face." The presence of a beloved friend of the family, whom the children all called "auntie," inspired Michiko to write that she could "overcome any adversity" in her life away from home (Mikawa 2002: 12 [20 May 1945]). Despite authorities' redefinition of adulthood, teenagers rebelled, and not simply because they were elites and thought they deserved better. As Saitō Tsutomu showed, Tokyo teenagers of various backgrounds organized strike actions, sabotage, and even walked away from the factory, saying "the teachers on the floor said we could go," when they wanted to return home as materials and rations ran out in the dormitories. Sometimes adults won the admiration of students when they protested working conditions, with students gathering outside factory management offices shouting "Go, sensei, go!" as a teacher shouted at a foreman (Saitō 1999: 340–48). Cultures of labor resistance in the home exacerbated these tensions: Morizaki Azuma recalled his elder brother saying, "[Prime Minister Tōjō Hideki] murders fourteen- and fifteen-year-old boys" and "If this was a factory where the management cared more about paying deference to royals than injuries suffered by their workers, we'd smash them with a strike action" (Morizaki 1971: introduction). The reverse was also true, however: girls raised in patriotic households could bring fire to the dragging feet of unenthusiastic faculty. Girls in Osaka critiqued teachers in their high school group diary for failing to turn up to work and meal time—"I felt like the teacher should've been there, because even one absence will reduce war production"—and encouraging each other to carry on in the face of adversity (Fumimaro: 16 June 1945). Such dedication must have secretly terrified some staff members.

Nevertheless, teenagers' forcible entry into the working world changed their view of the home: newfound independence inspired teenagers to see family primarily as an object of love, no longer merely a necessary source of security. In many cases, this was the direct result of experiencing independence: "Our mobilization order has come at last. The headmaster told us. I was still anxious about it when I went home. When I got home, I resolved to accept it. I will go, absolutely . . . . Visiting Miura's house, her mum said, 'When you go, you'll only have yourself to rely on.' This hit me like a ton of bricks" (Shinozuka 2007: 21 [21 September 1944]).

Some teenagers, including sixteen-year-old Suwa Kanenori, initially embraced the new experiences that work and dormitory life afforded. Unlike the evacuees, Kanenori was excited to be on his own, working alongside his school friends in a dormitory. Once the war brought bombers to his native Kagoshima, however, Kanenori wrote at length about family back home, including the adults who had once exercised authority over him: "Today Ōzawa came for the first time, and we really got the job going. Ah, going to work is great fun. [Iwo Jima has fallen, so] I'm really worried about Kagoshima. They're going to get it for sure. I sent dad a letter asking if everything is fine. Oh, please get through this—mom, dad, my brothers, my friends" (Suwa 1997: 58 [20 March 1945]). As for many adults, desiring independence did not mean that teens wanted to be miles away from their families. Just a few days after she was drafted and sent to the factory dorms, Inohara Mitsuko wrote in her diary, "Tomorrow at last I can go home. I am so happy. I miss my mom so much. Please, please let me go home early." Mitsuko, who felt unready to leave home when mobilized, was no longer simply pining for the security of being in her parents' house. After all, once Osaka was devastated by air raids, her home would hardly have been a safe haven, as she was well aware: "I bet Osaka is in a sea of flame. I began to worry about my parents at home. Then, it started to rain. Was it a blessing from heaven, coming to suppress these fires? . . . The next day we learned that Osaka's Tenōji and Nishinari Wards were utterly destroyed. After breakfast, I went back to bed, but I couldn't sleep. I have no energy, not until I know my family is safe" (Inohara 1991: 12 January and 14 March 1945). Kanenori's diary went further: labor mobilization and the bombing war not only redefined his relationship with his parents, it exposed an entire network of known and unknown adults who were negatively influencing his life.

> During this world war, I have for the first time seen how things really are at school, and everything else. Up until now, things have been really easy going to school far away. Instead of coming all this way to Handa, though, I would rather be doing my best closer to home. When the decisive battle comes to the home islands this autumn, I think I'm better off at Kagoshima . . . . I haven't had any letters in ten days. They've probably all been burned in an air raid. Just the thought of all of those letters burned up in my old hometown. And, I've not written any postcards or letters lately. There's no paper so we're all cutting back, but without any messages from home, in this far off town, it's really hard, so you lose all spirit. (Suwa 1997: 59 [26 March 1945])

As these accounts show, teenagers reacted differently to labor mobilization depending on many factors, but most important were their expectations for the future, which were significantly influenced by gender and class. Nevertheless, the experience of work and dormitory life birthed different views of adult relatives than those articulated by evacuated children: teenagers began to express love and concern for their family that did not involve a fear of being left to their own devices.

With the arrival of aerial bombing of the main islands, however, children and teenagers had to confront the fact that relatives could not protect them from large organizations run by hostile adults—otherwise known as "the enemy." As children transitioned into adolescence, they wrote with greater clarity on abstract, unseen structures that victimized not only young people, but also their parents, uncles, and other affiliated adults. Children struggled to understand networks of unknown (and hostile) adult actors, sometimes viewing them through the lens of religious, supernatural, or magical thinking, as nine-year-old Nakane Mihoko's diary reveals:

> At about 1 a.m. there was an air raid warning. We all woke up and went into the shelter. It was dark and I couldn't figure out what was going on, but once I calmed down I got in OK. Then after a bit the enemy planes came making an awful noise. Father looked out a little bit at the sky and it lit up. He said, "Oh! Oh! They're close." Mother said, "It's OK, they're not that close." Then "boom, boom, boom" went the bombs, making a terrible noise, but it didn't seem like they fell in our neighborhood. Every time I heard those noises, I prayed to the gods. Then we heard the all clear. I was so happy. I believe our house was saved by the gods, so I thanked them from the bottom of my heart. Afterward everyone laughed about how father said "Oh! Oh!" every time the bombs fell. (Nakane: 12 [4 April 1945])

Older teens saw more clearly how the bombing war was a process determined by organized adults at home and abroad. In May 1945, fifteen-year-old Kojima Yoshitaka, who had been loaded with many children onto a train, was warned of the impending arrival of Allied planes in an air raid over his hometown of Nagoya. As the train stopped, he quickly grabbed his younger brother, ran for an air raid shelter just outside the city, and watched Nagoya being systematically destroyed. Yoshitaka's understanding of how adult systems functioned, and that the enemy targeted them, makes his diary read very differently from Mihoko's.

> Nagoya is shrouded in black smoke. They say four hundred enemy planes attacked us. I pray for the safety of my father and sister. The north and east wards, as well as the suburbs of Nagoya, are under heavy bombardment . . . . Looking from Tenjin-bashi, I could see smoke coming from the direction of our house, and my heart shivered with fear [kokoro ga ononoku]. Fortunately, in the north ward, our neighborhood was spared. I heard Mitsubishi Aircraft Manufacturing at Kami-Iida, the Mitsubishi plant at Ōzone, and other factories were totally destroyed. Rumors are growing that the prefectural and municipal government buildings, as well as the castle, were all wiped out in Nagoya . . . . Fires dance in the evening sky; rumbling of the B-29 engines; firing antiaircraft; between life and death, air raids at night.[5]

The discovery, particularly in the teenage years, of a larger social environment that was beyond the control of parents and familiar adults could be an unsettling one, especially at a time of total war. An integral part of the transition from childhood to adolescence seems to have been teenagers' realization that, ultimately, they would have to navigate a world replete with complex and unseen structures and engage with adults who had no reason to treat them kindly.

CONCLUSION: POWER, HIERARCHIES, AND THE CONSTRUCTION OF ADULTHOOD

Adults directly influenced the way young people wrote about themselves, and in the historiography of childhood and youth this discussion takes the form of the production of children's media, the work of education systems, or the transmission of social values. Adults also deeply affected young people, however, through directly damaging means such as psychological abuse, neglect, and physical violence. Yamada Kikue, a housewife and mother of four children, reflected on the enormous impact that adults had on young people during the war years. When the firebombing of Hachiōji began, local authorities blocked her children's entry into air raid shelters, Allied forces dropped incendiary bombs that severely injured the hand of her school-aged son, and Japanese doctors refused to treat her son's wounds at hospitals, causing the hand to be later severed in an emergency operation. "He kept rubbing and waving the stump around," she wrote, "saying, 'Fix my hand, fix my hand!' He'd ask me, 'Mama, when will a hand come out? When will I grow fingers?' . . . It was excruciating for me." At the end of the war, rationing authorities would not issue her extra cloth to fashion longer sleeves so that she could hide his scars. Teachers declined to protect her son from bullying and turned a blind eye when he was ostracized (Yamada 1975: 84–85). Adults had nearly all of the power, and one of the most important lessons of wartime youth was that grownups were often dangerous and untrustworthy, despite what social lessons about "adulthood" may have tried to teach them.

Adulthood was an important concept for children and youth, and they formed opinions of it that were divorced from the discourse that adults generated about themselves. Furthermore, views of the adult Other went through considerable change as children matured into teenagers, encountered shifting social expectations, and discussed these issues with other young people around them—what we might consider a form of scaffolding for socialization. "Childhood" and "adulthood" were thus not merely fixed as an equally dependent binary; they were rather defined by the imbalance of power between adult authorities and the young people whom they sought to nurture. Unlike colonialism, patriarchy, institutionalized racism, or other cases where linguistically reinforced divisions were used to support "violent hierarchies," to use Derrida's phrase, childhood was always seen as a transient state in which the ruled would inevitably become rulers within a single lifetime. Sixteen-year-old Lena Mukhina, in wartime Leningrad, captured the vicissitudes of this process in her diary:

> Sometimes mama wants me to kiss her, or embrace, and I become depressed because of the sad thoughts in my head. I shout to myself: Go on then, cry! But I must restrain myself, and in my heart I feel helpless. I always feel like something is missing. When mama isn't home, I want her to come back, and when she is at home, I don't want to see or hear her. To me, [she is so] boring. . . . I want to meet new people, see new faces, everything new. Something new. . . . I would love to run away somewhere far, far away . . . I want to go to a new best friend, who loves me, and tell her my sorrows. . . . But I have no one, I'm lonely. And none of this can be said. Silly mama, she doesn't understand much. Not very much at all. (Mukhina 2011: 23 May 1941)

Thus, when teenagers grappled with the irrationality of adult social structures or redefined the home as an object of affection, they were not just reinventing their subjectivity, they were also involved in a power struggle.

Meanwhile, children had a weak grasp of the abstract concepts and structures that adults invested so much energy in creating, maintaining, and re-producing; consequently, and in their search for security in wartime, they were firstly attentive to discriminating adults as kind, helpful, and "fun." Teenagers, at least in part due to a presentiment of their future roles in the labor force, were far more capable of, and interested in, understanding the social, political, and economic structures that adults constructed, and finding a place within them—although not every teen arrived at this point at exactly the same time. Adults' ability to establish a rapport with young people was determined, first and foremost, by the willingness of children and teenagers to engage on their own terms; because adults wielded almost all of the power, the only weapon young people had in response was to ignore them and, in the passage of time, let the formerly powerful pass away into obscurity. As adults, parents, and teachers, we should be careful not to mistake compliance for influence, because our power to construct them as "children" passes with time, but their power to construct us as "adults" will come to define our experience of old age.

ACKNOWLEDGMENTS

Travel expenses, photograph equipment, and research time for this project were funded by the UK Arts and Humanities Research Council ("Remembering and Recording Education, Childhood, and Youth in Imperial Japan"). I wish to thank Sabine Frühstück, Anne Walthall, L. Halliday Piel, and Peter Cave for feedback on my work, and especially Elise Edwards for suggesting an important change in the main argument of this chapter.

NOTES

1. For example, in Kan Yoshiko's otherwise articulate diary, her entries on adults were short: she described Ms. Kanemaru as "very nice," feared the strict gym teacher who screamed "idiot" *(baka)*, and was so upset, along with the other girls in her group, at potentially being stuck with a teacher named Yoshino that they all broke out in tears. Kan 1990: 38, 40, 42 [20 September 1944, 9 October 1944, 7 March 1945].

2. Nakamura 1971: 128 [4 January 1945] and 135 [26 February 1945]. Asano 1984b: 268 [17 June 1945]. Although he mentions only the local village *fujinkai,* by 1945 this was probably a National Women's Defense Society branch (Kokubō fujinkai). For dialects, see Nakamura 1971: 124–27 [20 October to 24 December 1944]. Also see Umano's teacher's warning that they should endeavor to get the locals to "like you." Umano 1988: 12 September 1944.

3. "Paper plays" (*kamishibai*) were put on by itinerant narrators who displayed drawings of scenes while telling a story. Although attendance was free, children who bought candy from the narrator were allowed to sit in the front of the audience. This was a popular form of mass entertainment in the first half of the twentieth century.

4. Asano Yukio recorded many games played with adults, including four squares, *hyakunin isshu,* and rock-paper-scissors for biscuits (Asano 1984b: 263–64 [2 January 1945]).

5. The Shōnai River runs across north Nagoya, and into the sea directly west of the city. Tenjin-bashi, Kami-Iida, and Ōzone, were all parts of northern Nagoya or its suburbs during the war. Kojima is commenting on well-known areas around his home, and the urban systems that supported them (Kojima 1995: 14 [17 May 1945]).

BIBLIOGRAPHY

Note: Unless noted otherwise the place of publication for Japanese books is Tokyo.

Abbreviations

HmPM: Himeji Peace Museum (Himeji heiwa kinenkan)
KaPM: (Yohohama) Kanagawa Peace Museum (Chikyū shimin Kanagawa puraza, Heiwa tenji-shitsu)
NWHM: (Tokyo) Nakano Ward Local History Museum (Nakano-ku kyōdo shiryōkan)
OIPM: Osaka International Peace Museum (Ōsaka kokusai heiwa kinenkan)

PA: (Nagoya) Peace Aichi (Aichi-ken kokusai heiwa kinenkan)
SSM: (Kyoto) State School Museum (Kyoto-shi gakkō rekishi hakubutsukan)
TWHM: (Tokyo) Toshima Ward History Museum (Toshima-ku kyōdo shiryōkan)

Akai Teruaki. 1968. "Nyūgaku no ketsui" [Induction day resolutions]. In *Dōin gakuto shi* [Mobilized students journal], edited by Hiroshima-ken dōin gakuto shi henshū iinkai, 9. Hiroshima: Self-published.

Ambaras, David R. 2006. *Bad Youth: Juvenile Delinquency and the Politics of Everyday Life in Modern Japan.* Berkeley: University of California Press.

Andō Sadahide. 1984 (1960). "Correspondence with mother and sister." In *Gakudō sokai no kiroku* [Record of student evacuation], edited by Gekkōhara shōgakkō, 247–48. Miraisha.

Asano Yukio. 1984a (1960). "Letter to father." In *Gakudō sokai no kiroku* [Record of student evacuation], edited by Gekkōhara shōgakkō, 249. Miraisha.

———. 1984b (1960). "Diary." In *Gakudō sokai no kiroku* [Record of student evacuation], edited by Gekkōhara shōgakkō, 263–70. Miraisha.

Bashkirtseff, Marie. 1912. *From Childhood to Girlhood.* New York: Dodd, Mead, and Company.

Cunningham, Hugh. 1998. "Review Essay: Histories of Childhood." *American Historical Review* 103(4): 1195–1208.

Fuji Shōhei. 1996. "Diary." In *Ōsaka no gakudō sokai* (Osaka's student evacuation), edited by Akatsuka Yasuo, 582–601. Kurieitibu.

Fumimaro Rie. 1945. "Diary entry." In *Ōsaka Seikei kōtō jogakkō: Gakkyū nisshi* [Osaka Seikei higher girls' school: Class diary], edited by Ōsaka Seikei kōtō jogakkō. OIPM 88–50/319.

Horibe Chieko. 1989. *Gakuto dōin to Toyokawa kaigun kōshō* [Student mobilization and the Toyokawa navy factory]. Nagoya: Self-published. PA.

Iida Eizō. "Sokai nikki" [Evacuation diary]. KaPM.

Inohara Mitsuko. 1991. "Dōin nikki" [Mobilization diary]. In *Tojōryō no shojotachi* [The girls of Tojō dormitory], edited by Morikawa (nee Inohara) Mitsuko, 5–37. Ikagura, Nara: Self-Published. OIPM.

James, Allison, Chris Jenks, and Alan Prout, eds. 1998. *Theorizing Childhood.* Cambridge, UK: Polity Press.

Kan Yoshiko. 1990. "Diary." In *Toshima no shūdan gakudō sokai shiryōshū: Nikki / shokan-hen* [Records of Toshima's mass student evacuation: Diaries and correspondence], edited by Toshima kuritsu kyōdo shiryōkan, vol. 1, 37–46. Tokyo: Self-published.TWHM.

Kaneda Toyoko. 2007. "Diary [November 1944]." In *Uminari no hibiki wa tōku: Miyagki-ken dai-1-kōjo gakuto kinrō dōin no kiroku* [The far-off echoes of the sea: Records of the No. 1 Miyagi Prefecture Girls' Higher School military labor conscripts], edited by Nakajima Kaoru, 36. Sōshisha.

Kojima Yoshitaka. 1995. *Guriko nikki: Boku no mita Taiheiyō sensō* [Glico diary: The Pacific War as I saw it]. Nagoya: Gakuseisha.

Kotoku Tadao. 1992. "Shōwa 20-nen gantan no nikki" [Diary: Dawn of the New Year 1945]. In *Zero no seishun: Taiheiyō sensōka no chūgakusei no kiroku* [Zero youth: Records of middle school students during the Pacific War], edited by Akita kenritsu Yokote chūgakkō dai-43-kisei, 106–7. Akita: Self-published.

Kushner, Barak. 2009. "Planes, Trains and Games: Selling Japan's War in Asia." In *Looking Modern: Taisho Japan and the Modern Era,* edited by Jennifer Purtle and Hans Bjarne Thomsen, 243–64. Chicago: University of Chicago Press.

Matsunaga Kenya. 1939. "Harappa no kodomotachi" [Children of the fields]. Kyōiku kamishibai kyōkai. Kitakami heiwa kinenkan [Kitakami Peace Memorial Museum].

Maynes, Mary Jo. 2008. "Age as a Category of Historical Analysis: History, Agency, and Narratives of Childhood." *Journal of the History of Childhood and Youth* 1(1): 114–24.

McCowan, Tara. 2015. *Performing Kamishibai: An Emerging New Literacy for a Global Audience.* London: Routledge Research in Education.

Mikawa Michiko. 2002. *Jikyōbo: Enko sokai no jogakusei nikki* [A record of self-strengthening: A schoolgirl's record of private evacuation]. Yasendai, Chiba: Sōeisha.

Moore, Aaron William. 2013. *Writing War: Soldiers Record the Japanese Empire.* Cambridge, MA: Harvard University Press.

Morizaki Azuma. 1971. "Introduction." In *Isho* [Final testament]. Tosho Shuppansha.

Mukhina, Lena. 2011. *Blokadnii dnevnik* [Blockade diary]. St. Petersburg: Azbuka.

Nakamura Naohiko. 1971. "Diary." In *Gakudō sokai no kiroku* [A record of student evacuation], edited by Shionoiri Mansaku, 122–40. Aoi ori-sha.

Nakamura Tokurō. 1986. "Diary." In *Tennō heika no tame nari* [For his imperial majesty], edited by Wadatsumi-kai. Komichi Shobō.

Nakane Mihoko. 1965. *Sokai gakudō no nikki: 9-sai no shōjo ga toraeta shūsen zengo* [Diary of an evacuated child: Before and after the end of the war from a 9 year old girl's perspective]. Chūkō Shinsho.

Nakano Takashi. 1989. *Chūgakusei no mita Shōwa 10-nendai* [1935 to 1945, as a middle schooler saw it]. Shin'yōsha.

Nishimoto Masaharu. 2007. *Yokaren nikki* [Flight cadet diary]. Kumamoto: Kuma-shin shuppan.

Nornes, Abe Markus. 2003. *Japanese Documentary Film: The Meiji Era through Hiroshima.* Minneapolis: University of Minnesota Press.

Ōhayashi Toshiko. 1995. "Diary." In *Saigo no jogakusei: Watashitachi no Shōwa* [The last schoolgirls: Our Shōwa era], edited by Toyohashi Girls High School 45th Class, 85–146. Toyohashi: Self-published.

Orbaugh, Sharalyn. 2015. *Propaganda Performed: Kamishibai in Japan's Fifteen-Year War.* Leiden: Brill.

Rohlen, Thomas P. 1989. "Order in Japanese Society: Attachment, Authority, and Routine." *Journal of Japanese Studies* 15(1): 5–40.

Saitō Tsutomu. 1999. *Tōkyō-to gakuto kinrō dōin no kenkyū* [Research on Tokyo student labor mobilization]. Hachiōji: Nonburusha.

Seraphim, Franziska. 2006. *War Memory and Social Politics in Japan, 1945–2005.* Cambridge, MA: Harvard University Asia Center.

Shimura Takeyo. 2010. *Shōkokumin-tachi no sensō: Nikki de tadoru senchū / sengo* [The little citizens' war: Exploring wartime and the postwar through diaries]. Shakai hyōronsha.

Shino Chizuko. 1990. "Diary." In *Toshima no shūdan gakudō sokai shiryōshū* [Records of Toshima's mass student evacuation: Diaries and correspondence], edited by Toshima kuritsu kyōdo shiryōkan, vol. 2, 5–34. Tokyo: Self-published. TWHM.

Shinozuka. 2007. "Diary fragment" [November 1944]. In *Uminari no hibiki wa tōku: Miyagi-ken dai-1-kōjo gakuto kinrō dōin no kiroku* [The far-off echoes of the sea: Records of the No. 1 Miyagi Prefecture Girls' Higher School military labor conscripts], edited by Nakajima Kaoru, 21. Sōshisha.

Skocpol, Theda. 1979. *States and Social Revolutions: A Comparative Analysis of France, Russia, and China.* Cambridge: Cambridge University Press.

Sonematsu Kazuko. 1974. "Diary." In *Kawasaki-shi kūshū/sensai no kiroku* [A record of the Kawasaki air raids]. Kawasaki: Self-published.

Stearns, Peter N. 2011. *Childhood in World History.* New York: Routledge.

Suwa Kanenori. 1997. "Gakuto dōin nikki" [Student mobilization diary]. In *Handa kūshū to sensō* [Handa air raids and the war], edited by Handa kūshū to sensō wo kiroku suru kai, no. 14, 55–68. Handa: Self-published. PA.Takahashi Yoshio. 1992. "Haha e no tegami" [A letter to mother]. In *Zero no seishun: Taiheiyō sensōka no chūgakusei no kiroku* [Zero youth: Records of middle school students during the Pacific War], edited by Akita kenritsu Yokote chūgakkō dai-43-kisei, 114. Akita: Self-published.

Tsujii Hideko. 2009. "Gakudō sokai nikki" [Student evacuation diary]. Hiroshima: Self-published. HmPM.

Tsutamoto gakuryō. 1944–45. *Omoide no Yumoto* [Memories of Yumoto]. NWHM.

Umano Yōko. 1988. "Diary." In *Shinagawa no gakudō shūdan sokai shiryōshū* [A documentary collection of the Shinagawa Ward mass student evacuations], edited by Shinagawa kuritsu rekishikan. Shinagawa Ward Government.

Wadatsumi-kai, ed. 1988. *Kike, wadatsumi no koe* [Listen to the voices of the sea]. Iwanami shoten.

Waites, Matthew. 2005. *The Age of Consent: Young People, Sexuality, and Citizenship.* London: Palgrave Macmillan.

Yamada Kikue. 1975. "Itsu ni nattara te ga dete kuru no" [When will my hand grow back?] In *Hachiōji no kūshū to sensai no kiroku: Shimin no kiroku-hen* [A record of Hachiōji's air raids and war damage: civilian records edition], edited by Hachiōji kyōdo shiryōkan, 84–85. Hachiōji: Self-published.

Yoshida Fusako. 1987. "Diary." In *Senjika no shomin nikki* (*Wartime diaries by ordinary people*), edited by Aoki Masami, 111–31. Nihon tosho sentā.

8

Outdoor Play in Wartime Japan

L. Halliday Piel

Rarely does the Second World War evoke a mental picture of children at play; instead what grabs our attention is their suffering and sacrifice. In Japan, war meant hunger (and inadequate food rationing), the fire-bombings of major cities by the Americans, child labor for the war effort, child soldiers in the form of volunteer brigades, evacuation of school children from cities into camps, and homeless orphans begging in train stations, not to mention Japanese children abandoned in China during Japan's retreat. In face of the overwhelming narrative of suffering, a discussion of childhood play may seem frivolous and disrespectful.

However, not all children were in the line of fire, and many found moments for play. The interview subjects contacted for this paper invariably apologized for not being among those who suffered, and initially doubted whether their memories of daily life, including play, had much value for an oral history project concerning the war years.[1] But wartime play matters to historians, partly because wartime leaders sought to indoctrinate the masses in ultra-nationalism through formal education, as well as through informal channels, such as toys, games, and picture-story shows (*kamishibai*). As it is not possible to observe children in the past, this paper turns to indirect evidence, namely, adult memories of their own childhoods, corroborated by their childhood drawings, when such documents have survived (which is rare). The sample size (nineteen persons) is too small to be treated as statistically significant; rather, the testimony is suggestive of a collective attitude towards child play, supported by depictions of play in wartime children's magazines, a 1943 survey of children's play, and ethnologist Yanagita Kunio's 1941 essay, *The Regional Customs of Children* (Kodomo fūdoki).

How is it that interviewees have happy memories of self-directed, unsupervised play, when the wartime cultural atmosphere in which they grew up expected them to shoulder responsibilities alongside their elders? Textbooks and propaganda tracts issued by the Ministry of Education recast children as productive "little nationals" (shōkokumin), while their parents, the imperial national subjects (kōkokumin) or citizens (shimin), were "children" of the emperor father figure. In the words of Norma Field, "the notion of the state as family with all the people as the children" symbolizes "an obliteration of childhood through its universalization" (Field 1995: 66).

Nevertheless, the nineteen interviewees (ten male, nine female), widely dispersed from Hokkaidō to Kyūshū, consistently remember playing "freely" without adult supervision, sometimes alone but more often in groups, even outdoors in the streets or in the backwoods, places that today would be considered dangerous for unaccompanied children (but not for those in Edo Japan; see chapter 2). They report more free time and less homework than their grandchildren, and consider it normal for parents and teachers to stay out of children's games. They insist that this was not parental neglect. They were middle class, the children of small business owners or land-owning farmers; although three identify themselves as elites.[2] Follow-up interviews were conducted with the most articulate informants.

Was there a cultural space in the wartime mentality that recognized self-directed play as a legitimate part of the "little national" persona? Or was it merely a question of children in the rural hinterland being less affected by the war than urban children? I argue that it was a combination of both: Certain forms of self-directed child play were acceptable so long as they supported what is sometimes called "conservative culturalism" (de Bary et al. 2006: 535) underlying Japanese ultranationalism. At the same time, Japanese children were not all equally affected by the war.

THE PERIODIZATION

The Second Sino-Japanese War, or Fifteen Years War, is usually defined by historians as beginning with Japan's invasion of Manchuria in 1931. This paper concerns play towards the end of Japan's fifteen-year war, rather than at the beginning. This is because civilian life, including childhood, was reshaped by "total war" policies implemented in the years 1937–41, a watershed moment in the middle of the war. The preceding years are perhaps better understood as an interwar period leading up to Japan's formal declaration of war against Chiang Kai-shek's Republic of China in 1937. In this period, the military gained political power in the Japanese government, and there was a surge of militarism and support for imperialism in popular culture.[3]

The second stage of the war was marked by a full-scale Japanese invasion of China from July 1937 onwards. On the Japanese home front, Prime Minister Konoe implemented total war policies through his National Mobilization Act and National Spiritual Mobilization Campaign in order to better control the civilian economy for the war effort and to drum up support for the war using what Gregory Kasza (1995) has called "administered mass organizations." Life for school-aged children changed. They were sent to work on farms during school vacations as part of their "patriotic work service." The type, amount, and duration of work increased as the war went on.

Children were also affected by the rationing system, which became more severe as resources were depleted by a protracted war in China and the opening of a second front in the Pacific after the Japanese attack on Pearl Harbor on 7 December 1941. According to interviews, war shortages reduced access to commercial toys and games, so even middle-class children had to make do with hand-me-down toys from older siblings or to craft their own.

This change is apparent when we take the age of the interviewees into account. Nakajima Shigeru (b. 1932), the son of a small-town business owner in Ibaraki prefecture, spent his allowance on penny candies and cheap cards, available in the *dagashiya,* a type of sundries store originating in the Meiji period that was popular with children.[4] The son of a schoolteacher in rural Aomori prefecture, Kubota Haruyoshi (b. 1925) traded store-bought sweets for fruits and nuts gathered in the mountains by impoverished farmers' sons.[5] But ten years later, a temple priest's daughter in Shiga prefecture, Shingū Mitsue (the youngest of the cohort, born 1937), points out that when she entered elementary school there were no toys or sweets for sale (sugar being severely rationed). As the sixth of eight children, she inherited her sibling's toys and books. She often felt hungry, and her outdoor play partly consisted of foraging for chestnuts or freshwater clams.[6]

Ikeda Giichi (b. 1936), son of a postmaster in a mining town in Kyūshū, made candles out of old wax droppings, and kites and birdcages out of bamboo slivers, which he then sold or bartered. Ikeda showed initiative at a time when consumer goods were scarce and the military commandeered household items made of metal, along with temple bells. Finances were tight in his family of eleven, so Ikeda's play was productive.[7] This comparison illustrates why it is necessary to differentiate between wartime childhood as experienced before and after 1940.

Because economic hardship continued into the American Occupation period, wartime play patterns persisted into the early postwar period, as observed by Peter Grilli, a son of the American Occupation, who grew up in Tokyo from age five in 1947. "Everything we had to make ourselves, or someone else made them in front of our eyes," he recalls of his own play with neighborhood Japanese children in the streets.[8] Similar observations by anthropologists in the 1950s, such as Beardsley, Hall, and Ward's *Village Japan* (1959), are still relevant to play in the 1940s.

THE WARTIME CHILD AS PRODUCTIVE "LITTLE NATIONAL"

In February 1941, the journal *Education* announced that the Japanese Diet's special task force on education had launched a planning committee, the future Japan Children's Culture Association (Nihon Jidō Bunka Kyōkai), in December 1940 to "take absolute lead in creating a new child culture," a euphemism for censoring children's literature ("Jidō bunka no shin-taisei" 1941: 13, 15). Serving on the committee was child psychologist Hatano Kanji (1905–2001). Four months earlier, Hatano had argued in the same journal that "child's mind-ism" *(dōshin shugi)* was mere infantilization and impeded children's maturation.[9] He warned that, "This view of the child is based on individualism and liberalism, and does not match reality. So we cannot support it" (Hatano 1940: 245). Hatano advocated the term already in use, *shōkokumin* or "little nationals." In March 1941, the Japan Children's Culture Association renamed itself the Japan Little Nationals Culture Association (Nihon Shōkokumin Bunka Kyōkai). The term *shōkokumin,* instead of *jidō* or *kodomo* (child), enabled policymakers to envisage child labor for the war effort.

Hatano believed that it was developmentally natural for children to want "to be included in the productive life of adults." He concluded, "Children do not know the hardships involved, so although we should guide them properly, there is no reason for us to suppress their desire to be included." The little national would undergo "training" *(rensei)* in the newly reformed and renamed "national school." "It means training children for good development, not leaving them freely as they are," Hatano explained. "Training does not mean sharp-tongued scolding. Rather it is about helping them build character and be independent. The childlike child mindset is unable to do this. By spoiling and mollycoddling children, it cannot build character" (Hatano 1940: 246, 247, 249).

Under the National School Ordinance (Kokumin gakkō rei), school children would participate alongside adult mass organizations in prayers at imperial shrines and sendoffs for soldiers. They would perform public service tasks, such as writing letters to the front and working on farms. The schools were to train children and youth to "uphold society, and promote the cult of the emperor, service to the nation, community assistance, respect for rules and the work ethic" (Nihon Seishōnen Kyōiku Kenkyūsho 1983, afterword: 3). "I would like to see a culture that makes children positively participate and work, not one that treats children as precious," Hatano declared. Consumer products for children are extravagant and wasteful, he thought. Instead, children's recreation should be based on production, not on consumption, and on "a children's culture that is truly Japanese" (Hatano 1940: 243). In Hatano's language, there seems to be no room for free and idle childish play. The emphasis is on work for the nation.

PLAY ACCORDING TO INTERVIEWS AND MAGAZINES

With the increased emphasis on children's responsibilities for the war effort, we would expect less child play in the media, which was now highly censored. Nevertheless, the "little national" image did not preclude play, even while magazines published more images of children doing patriotic work service from 1938 onwards. After all, child's play, like school education, could be employed to disseminate propaganda messages to children and adults. Sabine Frühstück argues that militaristic propaganda used the trope of the "innocent child," in the form of children playing soldier or interacting with soldiers, to humanize the war (see chapter 9). Toy makers produced military-themed toys. Children's literature and picture-story shows were coopted to shape children's understanding of Japan's imperial war. In the words of Barak Kushner, "a less easily quantifiable arena of propaganda was after school, on the playground, or on the streets" (Kushner 2009: 245).

A detailed comparison of pre- and post-1937 children's magazine images is not possible here, so I draw on Yamanaka Hisashi's selection of children's magazine illustrations in his *Illustrated Children in the War* (1989) to represent the wartime ideals of appropriate child play for the little national. There are similarities and differences between the illustrations and the interviews. For instance, pictures show children playing with war-themed board games and commercial toys. Some interview subjects recall *sugoroku*, the snakes-and-ladders type board game typically associated with New Years festivities. Most, however, recall playing with toys that were either very cheap or made at home. Girls sewed and juggled beanbags called *o-tedama* (also known as *o-jammi*). Boys mostly played with cheap cards called *menko* (also known as *patchi* or *bida,* or *marui menko* in the case of round cards). Players would take turns throwing down a card to flip over an opponent's card with air pressure. A player could claim an opponent's card if it flipped over. The four interviewees who were sons of farmers in Ibaraki prefecture report that they had no commercial toys other than flip cards. Eizawa Kōtarō (b. 1935) made his own stilts (*takeuma,* or "bamboo horse") and swings. Itakura Nobuo (b. 1931) said that, like all the boys in his village, he made stilts and a flying toy, *taketombo* ("bamboo dragonfly").[10] Nakajima made spinning tops. Shingū folded origami dolls.

In the interviews he has conducted to date, Peter Cave has likewise noticed that beanbags and flip cards are by far the most commonly mentioned games. He surmises that most children "were making their own entertainment," because families before 1945 spent on average about half of their expenditure on food, and only 7–8 percent on "education, recreation, and miscellaneous," according to government data.[11] On the other hand, schools supplied materials to make toy warplanes. Ueda Hiroaki (b. 1933), the son of a high-ranking Army general, says that his woodworking textbook included patterns for gliders, and that he entered a children's contest for propeller planes. "All boys during the war were airplane maniacs to a greater or lesser degree, absorbed in model making," he recalls later in his childhood memoir, based on his personal diary, which he kept from March 1944, when he was ten, until August 1945 (Ueda 2003: 69–72).

Magazine images represent outdoor play in gendered terms. It is girls who play house on the street in an illustration by Kurosaki Yoshisuke in *The Good Child's Play* (Yoi ko no asobi), published by Kodansha in 1941. The scene is identifiable as a wartime image by the *monpe* trousers imposed on women during the war. In a 1938 *Kinder Book* (Kindā bukku) picture, girls watch from a distance as boys play soldier with toy sabers, helmets, and flags. Interview subjects agree that play was segregated at school. Eizawa claims that gender segregation started after the second grade. Male interviewees in this sample recalled playing with male friends, and did not mention playing with girls. When asked, Ueda replies that he never played with girls. Gender segregation, he insists, arises from intrinsic differences: "We male brats quickly form groups, organize ranks, bully or get bullied, swagger and boast, flatter and kiss ass, and try to figure out how to get away with breaking rules."[12]

Female interviewees on the other hand sometimes recall a male playmate. Before she was evacuated with her school, an Army doctor's daughter, Maeda Tokuko (b. 1934), played at home after school with her older brother and his model airplanes. Shingū Mitsue's recollections of outdoor play indicate that boys' groups and girls' groups played in proximity, and occasionally interacted. Shōji Kakuko (b. 1935) in Hokkaidō and Yamagishi Sachiko (b. 1934) in Toyono, Nagano prefecture, state that they regularly enjoyed rough-and-tumble play with boys. Shōji's school diary shows a picture of a snowball fight with boys on the roof of her house.[13] Yamagishi says that she climbed trees and played soldier with neighborhood boys. (Climbing trees was considered a boy's activity, according to Maeda Tokuko, who avoided it). Nakai Kiyotoshi (b. 1932) describes his childhood friend Yamagishi as a tomboy and leader. He jokes that Yamagishi should have been the boy, and he the girl, because he was shy, preferring to stay at home and study.[14]

The above examples suggest that children's play was mostly gendered according to the norms shown in children's magazines, but that gender segregation was not as strict as magazine illustrations might lead us to believe. Play outside of school appears to have been largely free of adult supervision, which means that there was leeway for gender mixing. There may have been unwritten rules among children for how boys and girls were to interact when playing together. For example, according to *Village Japan*, in early postwar Japan, "Most boys would not be caught dead playing the games that are popular among girls," but some girls could cross the border into boys' games, such as flip cards (Beardsley, Hall, and Ward 1959: 310).

The shrine festival and the schoolyard were common places for children to play, and appear in illustrations in *Children's Asahi* (Kodomo asahi), published by the Asahi newspaper in 1940. This is no doubt because city alleyways were too narrow for games requiring space, such as hide-and-seek and tag games such as *oni gokko* ("play demon"), while country fields might be flooded for rice paddies. Yamagishi's play territory, for instance, was the local shrine (of which her father, a farmer and carpenter, was an important patron). But some children ranged far and wide. They climbed hills to forage for food in the shared village woodland, as in the case of Shōji, who was living in Hokkaidō. In her third-grade school diary, written when she was living in the town of Hakodate, Shōji relates taking a train with friends to the outskirts of town to gather lily of the valley, or play hide-and-seek around the moat of an old fortress. They made up new games, such as biting down on the bean pods of *azuki* plants to make them pop.

In the fourth grade, after she and her family had moved to Otaru, Shōji roamed the woods with her small team of friends led by a sixth-grade boy. Once, while they were climbing a hill, it began to pour, and the children made a temporary shelter to wait in until the rain stopped. By the time she returned home it was dark, but her mother was not particularly concerned, just glad to see her safe and sound. "We were really as free as that," Shōji recalls. "Our parents didn't obsess about our safety." Two years later (by which point the war was over), Shōji's mother scolded her for wanting to learn modern dance. It was a "trauma" she never forgot. What stands in remarkable contrast to today's standards is that her mother considered unsupervised outdoor play normal for children, but was alarmed by the "vulgarity" of modern dance.

An illustration in a 1938 *Kinder Book* shows two girls and a toddler, all dressed in *yukata* (summer-weight kimono), sitting on the veranda of a bucolic farmhouse, stringing beads of pearly white seeds called Job's tears *(jezudama)*, which were also used in Buddhist rosaries or brewed as tea. In the background, an older boy is helping a younger girl pick the seeds on a riverbank. Maeda Tokuko says that she was aware that girls made beads from *jezudama*, which grew in her parents' backyard, but that nobody taught her how to do it.[15] This kind of rural tradition interested Yanagita Kunio (1875–1962), "Japan's most influential folk scholar" both during and after the war, according to Melek Ortobasi (Ortobasi 2014: 2).

Yanagita collected descriptions of children's games related to Shinto festivals or natural objects that were formerly sacred. For instance, in his 1941 *Regional Customs of Children* (Kodomo fūdoki), originally published serially in the *Asahi* newspaper from April to May 1941, he writes, "There are many people today who know hook pulling *(kagihiki)* as a children's game." However, what most do not know is that "from the northern part of Mie prefecture to the Kōga area of Shiga prefecture there is a ritual called *kagihiki* to welcome the mountain gods into the village in early spring." He believes that the two were related, because both shared the same name and involved pulling hooks. In another homologous game, which Shōji says she played using violets and plantain weeds, a pair of children would pull at two interlocking plant stems. The child whose stem broke would lose. "I do not think that *kagihiki* and stem pulling, although they are separate games, have separate origins," Yanagita writes. The origin is the hook used in the spring ritual, symbolizing the "hooked branch" that was used as a plow "in the days before iron." Yanagita believes that "people of old recognized from experience the power of the tree branch." "Children's games," Yanagita concludes, "reveal traces of serious rituals from an ancient time when adults were more childlike" (Yanagita 1941: 29–30).

Yet, interview subjects rarely mentioned such indigenous games. Aside from beanbags and flip cards, they describe games they played with their school groups. Some of these games point to cross-cultural diffusion during Japan's modernization in the Meiji period. Ueda drew a picture of playing "kick horse" (*uma keri*, see figure 9), in the school gym. He no longer remembers whether it was part of

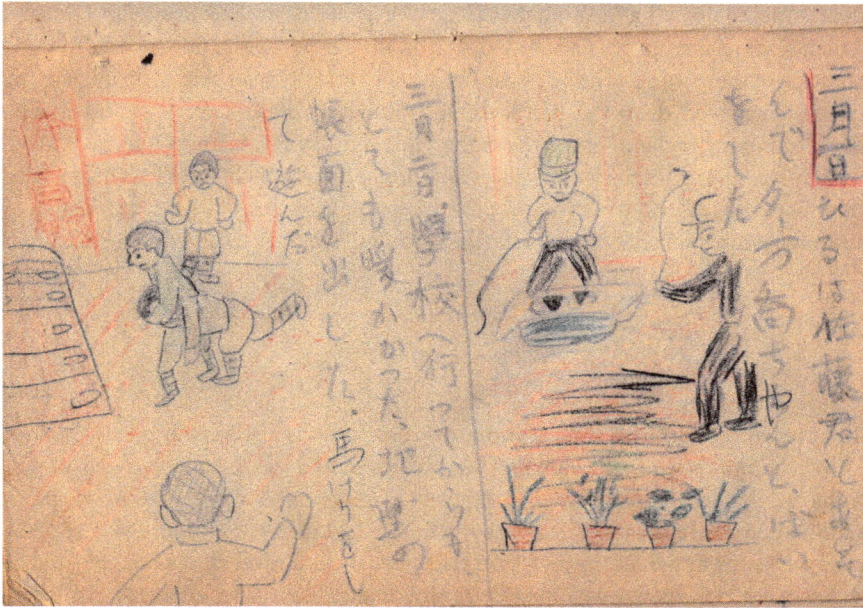

FIGURE 9. *Uma keri* (kick horse), drawing by Ueda Hiroaki, 1945. Courtesy of Ueda Hiroaki.

physical education, but the game is possibly a variation of *uma tobi* ("jump horse"), played by Kinoshita Masako (b. 1933) in Osaka. Both games involve one or more children forming a "horse." In the case of "kick horse," the "horse" tries to rear-kick an opponent. In "jump horse," the opponents hop onto the "horse" one after another until it caves under their weight. Yanagita sees a tenuous link between "jump horse" and "Deer, deer, how many horns?" (*Shika, shika, nannpon*), in itself a variation of "How many horns has the buck?" once played widely in Europe. An elderly woman in Niigata prefecture told Yanagita that she remembered learning "deer deer" from an American teacher at her girls' school in the early Meiji period (Yanagita 1941: 88). Thus it is possible that a foreign game initially introduced by Western educators evolved over time into a version transmitted by Japanese teachers at school (perhaps "kick horse") and a variant played by boys in the street ("jump horse").

Can kicking *(kan keri)*, recalled by Maeda, is clearly the game known as tin can tommy in England and by various names, including kick the can in the United States, which "seems to have been well known in city streets before the First World War," according to Iona and Peter Opie. It elaborates the basic hide-and-seek pattern, with a can to mark territory where the seeker will hold captive hiders until they are rescued by fellow hiders (Opie and Opie 1969: 165, 167). Variations on this theme include play battleship *(senkan)*, a war game described to me by Ueda, in which a minelayer must "sink" either one battleship or several destroyers. The orientation of the visors on the boys' caps indicates which type of ship they are playing.

Maeda played drop the handkerchief *(hankachi otoshi)*, an "old and much-loved game in England" since the eighteenth century (Opie and Opie 1969: 168). To stay warm in winter, she played *oshikura manjū*, in which children cluster with their backs together, trying to shove each other out of a ring.[16] This is suggestive of sumo wrestling, a version of which (*oshidashi* or "frontal push out") Maeda did in her physical education class.

THREE CONCEPTS OF PLAY ACCEPTABLE FOR "LITTLE NATIONALS"

The preceding narrative indicates that wartime children were still playing games known before the war, unaware that some of them had Western roots. Adults seem to have tolerated games played in the street, while actively encouraging some at school. Wartime educators clearly saw value in the latter. Here I propose three reasons why prewar games might retain relevance to a cultural climate of censorship that was unfriendly to consumerism, individualism, frivolity, idleness, and Westernization. By no means does this scheme constitute a complete picture of play as variously theorized by educators, psychologists, and anthropologists, or even as a complete picture of play during war.

The first reason is that play can be a form of learning adult roles, even if it involves some fantasy or make-believe. Ueda was still "playing" when he made model airplanes in 1944, but in that same year, many middle-school students were mobilized to aircraft and munitions companies where they made airplane parts for real. Thus, Ueda's play can be seen as preparing him for a possible role in the war. The line between "play" and "work" is blurred. Although it is appropriate play for the little nationals, it carries some risk when it is self-directed. For instance, in a private diary entry of 5 June 1944, the eleven-year-old Ueda praises the enemy planes: "The B-29 has a really good shape," and the P-51 Mustang "is the world's coolest airplane." Such statements would have been unacceptable in the classroom.

A second reason is that play can transmit state-sanctioned culture. In the conservative cultural climate of the war there was value in games handed down through the ages, such as those associated with festivals and holidays reinforcing community traditions. Because conflict between nations intensifies national consciousness, any game seen to reflect Japanese identity would be appropriate for the little nationals. Yet, when self-directed, traditions can be distorted or mocked by using taboo words as well as scatological or sexual jokes, at which point, play may become, in the words of anthropologist Allison James, "as much about social disorder as order" (Montgomery 2006: 145, 147).

No such cases have been brought to my attention, but Ueda has heard of war-time schools banning top spinning *(begoma)*, flip cards, and marbles *(biidama)* for their presumed association with "gambling."[17] Ironically, top spinning and a game similar to flip cards, flipping chess pieces *(jōgi taoshi)*, appear in a woodblock print by Utagawa Hiroshige, depicting boys' games around 1830. The girls' game *hajiki,* also played like flip cards but with flat marbles, is described in Ōta Sajirō's three-volume compilation of children's games by region *(Nihon zenkoku jidō yūgihō)*, published by Hakubunkan in 1901. Thus, merely being old does not necessarily qualify a game as "traditional" (or ancestral) in the formulation of the wartime Japanese spirit.

A third reason is that play may be seen to have physical or spiritual benefits. Play in nature, which includes hunting, fishing, netting insects, gathering fruits and nuts, as well as chase games requiring space, may contribute to physical strength, health, and nutrition. Interviewees often mentioned climbing trees and swimming in rivers. However, when unsupervised, such play carries the risk of serious injury.

Free outdoor play has been associated with progressive education for imagina-tive, self-expressive individualism since Jean-Jacques Rousseau penned his *Émile, or On Education* (1762). In Japan, progressive educators in the interwar era experi-mented with new concepts like the Seaside School, founded in 1921 in Nagasaki, and the Roofless Kindergarten in Osaka prefecture. The leading kindergarten expert Kurahashi Sōzō prescribed the types of games permissible under the rubric of free play, which, of course, is not the same thing as letting children do as they please. His choice of games would be familiar to wartime children: playing tag, playing house, and playing war, along with stringing paper flowers, and playing "rolling ball" *(tama korogashi)*, a variant of marbles or pinball on a wooden track (Suwa 1992: 146).

Certain child-centered developments of the interwar period may have been as much about adult efforts to control the development of children towards an ideal as they were about giving children more freedom. In Mark Jones's words, educated elites in the Taishō period (1912–1926) envisioned play as "child's work" and "acci-dental education," and they "folded the child's play world into a search for authen-tic experience and a solution to the deficiencies of civilization," namely a more humanistic and "cultured living" *(bunka seikatsu)* (Jones 2010: 251, 262, 263, 288). David Ambaras (2006) sees a less benevolent, more coercive, attempt to socialize "delinquent youth" in the seemingly altruistic efforts to protect juveniles made by government officials, concerned mothers, welfare reformers and religious groups. Such findings suggest that caution is necessary when examining the "progressive" and "child-centered" rhetoric of interwar "Taishō liberalism." There are underlying continuities between one era and the next. What changes between 1921 and 1941 is not so much the type of game, or the extent of children's freedom, but rather the ideal to which adults hoped to shape the child's development.

Why were there not injunctions against free play in *Education (Kyōiku,* a jour-nal produced by the publisher Iwanami Shoten between April 1933 and March

1944) during the war comparable to warnings against progressive children's literature? One possibility is that adult authorities did not take play among children as seriously as they took the messages that adults might disseminate to children through education, leisure reading, and consumer products.

Play was not a prominent theme in Ministry of Education documents, unlike children's literature, which had its own wartime committee starting in 1938. However, the Japan Youth Education Research Office sought to make the case for the importance of play in its 1943 survey of six schools (two rural and four urban), conducted the previous year. This research institute was founded in 1941 in conjunction with the formation of the Great Japan Youth Association. It produced two publications about "training youth for social life" before releasing the 1943 study on play. "Social life" *(shakai seikatsu)* meant the cooperative performance of duties expected of neighborhood associations mobilized for the war effort (Nihon Seishōnen Kyōiku Kenkyūsho 1943, 3–5). The survey on play must therefore be seen in the context of the greater agenda of civilian mobilization for total war.

In the preface, the author explains that child play "on the one hand has meaning as training *(shūren)*, and on the other hand can be seen as a child's form of public affairs *(kōji)*." In the classroom, the author continues, the child's relationship is with the teacher. "So the child's interaction with other children naturally occurs through play. In our eyes it follows that for children, play is actual life and constitutes social life *(shakōtekina seikatsu)*. A child who does not play is cast out of children's society." Here we see that the author respects children's self-organized interactions with peers, free of teacher influence, as a form of training in social intelligence for group cohesiveness. In the context of civilian mobilization, teamwork and team spirit were essential learning outcomes. "If we are to guide play" (presumably towards this ideal), the report states, "we first must understand how children play" (Nihon Seishōnen Kyōiku Kenkyūsho 1943: 88–90).

The survey finds that 53 percent, mostly girls, of 1,385 children play "athletic games" (e.g., tag and hide-and-seek), 10.5 percent do imitative role play (e.g. playing house and playing soldier), while 8.1 percent, mostly boys, forage in nature. The remaining five categories (involving activities such as making things, luck-based games, watching films or listening to records) were "extremely few" (Nihon Seishōnen Kyōiku Kenkyûsho 1943: 90, 93–95). Although there are differences from my interview sample (in which luck-based games—flip cards and beanbags for example—are the most commonly remembered), the report supports the interviews by indicating that outdoor play among peer groups was the norm.

YANAGITA KUNIO: THE VOICE OF FREE PLAY IN THE WARTIME CULTURAL CLIMATE

Yanagita Kunio is not mentioned in the 1943 report, but his discussion of traditional games provides a key to understanding why autonomous peer groups could be seen as beneficial to society. His *Regional Customs of Children* was not about contemporary play. Rather it concerned the memories of grandparents in rural farm communities. "Parents in the olden days almost never thought up games for children," he writes. "And children were not unhappy about it, but grew up playing to their hearts' content. This is a significant difference with the children's culture of today" (Yanagita 1941: 39). Here, Yanagita waxes nostalgic for an imagined loss of autonomy, even though the 1943 report suggests otherwise. This is probably because Yanagita's real interest was not children but Japanese indigenous culture, which he believed could be found in games of the past. He had read the work of British anthropologist Edward Burnett Tylor (1832–1917), who in 1879 proposed tracking cultural evolution through the transmission of children's games (Montgomery 2009: 142). One contributor to *Folklore* (Minkan denshō), a journal founded by disciples in Yanagita's Thursday Club, writes that the games in *Regional Customs* demonstrate Hans Naumann's (1886–1951) theory of *gesunkenes Kulturgut* ("sunken culture," or *chinka bunka* in Japanese) according to which the primitive rituals of an elite trickle down to ordinary people and become folk culture. The key to tracking this process in children's games is to look for patterns in game vocabulary across regions (Kuchida 2012 [1941]: 146).

Although his methodology drew on Western scholarship, Yanagita differs from his Western counterparts, according to Mori Kōichi, in viewing human culture not as discreet "stages as development" but as the "coexistence" of primitive and modern "spiritual structures" (Mori 1980: 90). In the rituals of folk religion, Yanagita hoped to uncover the still living essence of the Japanese spirit. In that sense, he can be viewed as one of the "Return to Japan" intellectuals who sought to define what it meant to be Japanese in the context of global modernity and competing nation-states. The Kyoto School philosophers of "Japanese spirit" or "Japanism," for example, studied Western thinking to rediscover Japanese identity by comparison.[18]

Yanagita's vision of premodern childhood required children's autonomy and agency in order to transmit the primitive traces of indigenous spiritual life. His chapter on playing house is not about playing house with toy utensils as shown in the children's magazine mentioned earlier. Rather, it harkens back to the living memory of grandparents in rural areas, when village girls gathered on beaches or uncultivated fields together to cook "spirit food" *(seirei meshi)* during the Obon (All Souls) festival using a small portable stove without the help of their mothers. In some regions, Yanagita explains, younger girls cooked under the supervision of an older one. In others, only girls of "marriageable age" (sixteen or older) prepared the food. Yanagita sees in this cooking ritual a rite of passage, qualifying girls for marriage (Yanagita 1941: 61–62). The custom began dying out in the 1920s (Moriyama and Nakae 2002: 237–38).

Similarly, boys had their own self-governing groups (*kodomo gumi,* not to be confused with *wakamono gumi,* associations of young men). Boys' groups dating back to the Edo period (1600–1868) carried portable shrines in Shinto festivals, and exorcized ghosts during the New Year's and Obon celebrations. In the Sagichō festival, during the New Year, boys in some regions would gather under the leadership of a fifteen-year-old "czar" *(oyadama)* or "general" *(taishō)*, and build huts, spending several nights together before torching the huts in an act of exorcism. Yanagita claims that this custom ended around the time of the Manchurian Incident (1931), when a boy sleeping in one of the huts was inadvertently burned to death (Yanagita 1941: 58).

In one Obon custom, boys in outlying villages near Osaka were allowed to steal dumplings specially made for the occasion. They would slide a sharpened stick through a hole in the neighbor's fence in order to lift a dumpling from the strategically placed pile. Some towns sanctioned pranks, such as blocking off roads with mud-coated ropes, badgering passersby for spare change, or intruding in a family's attempt to make dinner. Adults tolerated the pranks because they believed that children (like Shinto priests) represented the gods during Obon season. Yanagita points out that such mischief is no longer tolerated "today" (in 1941).

Shōji remembers making a clay oven for the Obon festival, while Nakajima recalls a "midwinter" game called *natto* thief *(natto dorobō)*, in which children would "steal" *natto* (fermented bean paste) from a neighbor's kitchen, not unlike Yanagita's dumpling stealing. However, he also says that New Year's was not as important as it is today. His wife Kimiko, a salesman's daughter in Ibaraki prefecture, likewise says that the doll festival was not the big affair it is today. Shingū remembers that her town's Hachiman and Sagichō festivals were canceled during the war. Most of Shingū's nature-related play involved foraging for food in the hills and swamps of Ōmi Hachiman, either alone or with neighborhood children. Ironically, the war may have temporarily undermined the connection between children's games and ritual festivals that fascinated Yanagita.

In sum, Yanagita's view of play included the concepts of play as learning, play as transmission of culture, and play in nature. He accepted self-directed free play because traditionally it took place in peer groups, socializing children for village life. "His conception of the individual was not that of an autonomous subject guided by his own will," Mori Kōichi explains, "but one whose daily life has its foundation in the group" (Mori 1980: 104). The absence of individualism in Yanagita's vision of play could be construed as compatible with the aforementioned 1943 report, which had been produced in the context of the Ministry of Education's attempt to control children's culture.

Yet, to complicate matters, Yanagita was an intellectual maverick, and his relationship with wartime ideology continues to be debated by historians. In an essay, "About our Ancestors" of April-May 1945, according to Mori, Yanagita "insists that his idea of ancestor worship does not harmonize with that of 'the state as family' *(kazoku kokka)*, the official ideology of the Meiji and Shōwa wartime governments," and thus he "opposed facile universalization" (Mori 1980: 96, 99). For him, the "group" meant the household and the small community, and he favored the small tutelary village god over State Shinto. Perhaps for that reason he did not use the word little nationals when referring to children. He criticized the Imperial Rescript on Education for being based on Confucian obligations, preferring to view loyalty to the emperor as an authentically "religious feeling" (Mori 1980: 105, 107).

In *Regional Customs*, Yanagita indirectly takes aim at the school system, writing that, "compared to the system of separating children by age in elementary school," children in the olden days enjoyed the responsibility of passing on their games to younger ones, while being conscious of growing up. "There was nothing more fun than figuring out by themselves the ways to play, the names of things, the words of songs and the movements" accompanying games" (Yanagita 1941: 39). Here, Yanagita implies that by separating age groups, the school system was interrupting the transmission of folklore, the root of Japan's cultural identity. Ortabasi explains that Yanagita went against the grain of centralized education because he opposed modern language reform in the late Meiji and Taishō periods. A Tokyo dialect had been chosen as a common language to help nationalize the masses. Yanagita wanted the common language to evolve organically from the bottom up, on the basis of local dialects, instead of being imposed from the top down. Only in this way would a national language be the result, not the cause, of Japanese identity (Ortobasi 2014: 17–18).

"Games and children's made-up words, like song and dance, are flip sides of the same coin," Yanagita writes in *Regional Customs*, before gently taking aim at the games that educators compose for children: "Even in the new games of elementary school, educators try as much as possible to add modern songs *(shōka)*, but maybe because of the way the lyrics are mixed in, children put too much effort into the words and treat the movements lightly, or become so absorbed in the game that they play it silently" (Yanagita 1941: 16). He turns to "bird in a cage" *(kagome kagome)* to illustrate how children in the past found their own perfect combination of rhythmic words and movements. Chanting children dance in a circle around a seated child, who must guess which dancer stands behind him or her when the dancing abruptly stops. Yanagita takes particular interest in guessing games, but never describes war games, not even sword play *(chanbara)*, which surely has a long history.

Ueda dismisses Yanagita's guessing games as the sort of thing only girls would play. Indeed, it is a woman, Shingū, who recalls a similar game, one *monme* of flowers *(hana ichi monme)*, in which two opposing groups of girls skip back and forth chanting a song that begins, "Bridal trousseau chest—which child do you want?" *(Tansu nagamochi dono ko ga hoshii).*[19] Taking turns, one girl from each side summons a child from the other side to come over, while performing a challenging task, such as hopping on one leg. Shingū recalls a girl bursting into tears when she could not do a somersault on command. Shingū learned this game from her neighborhood peers. Her mother and older sisters were too busy working for the war effort to play with her. Her story provides one indication of how the war both impeded and furthered Yanagita's ideal of play by shutting down shrine festivals while weakening the influence of parents.

GEOGRAPHIC AND OTHER CONSTRAINTS

Although all interview subjects claim that their games were self-directed, it must be acknowledged that the degree of freedom relative to adult intervention varies. No interviewee self-identifies as a child of the working poor (tenant farmers and menial laborers), so the focus here is not on socioeconomic differences, but on whether the child lived at home or was evacuated during the American fire bombings of 1944 and 1945. Evacuation altered the types of play experiences taken as normal in the aforementioned 1943 report.

It is no accident that Shōji, whose play was most "wild and free," was living in Hokkaidō, surrounded by nature and insulated from American bombing raids. Maeda, on the other hand, was evacuated with her elementary school, first to a farm in Kumegawa, a suburb of Tokyo, and then to the town of Fukumitsu in the alpine region of Toyama prefecture. Her school diary before evacuation contains many more pictures of play than after the evacuation, when she began recording communal dormitory life. The school now planned her day from breakfast to bedtime, leaving less time for free play.

A chronology of events compiled in 1989 by twenty members of Maeda's alumni circle from their wartime picture diaries shows that chores increased for the older students. For instance, in Kumegawa in September 1944, fifth-grade pupils cut grass, pulled weeds, and gathered firewood, in addition to the chores they shared with the third and the fourth graders, namely, picking beans and preparing the communal bath. Only the youngest cohort, the third graders, "played with rabbits" (Ochanomizu gakudō sokai no kaihen 1989: 12). The class timetables of fourth-grade girls and sixth-grade boys show that both groups had five hours of classroom education from Monday to Saturday, but that the sixth graders had an additional hour of "work" (sagyō) (Ochanomizu gakudō sokai no kaihen 1989: 38). Maeda, who was in fifth grade, reports that her chores in Kumegawa included peeling potatoes, cutting grass, hauling well water, gathering sticks to use as fuel to heat the bathtub, and washing towels. In Fukumitsu, she transported food and took turns with her classmates taking charge of a bath at the house of the sake brewer who lodged them. At 8 p.m., there was an hour of free time before bed, which she chose to spend writing her diary and postcards home.[20] Being a member of the elite (as a doctor's daughter), Maeda had grown up with maid service and was unaccustomed to doing chores. So, naturally, before evacuation her afterschool time had been spent on play.

When the evacuees moved to Fukumitsu, the amount of classroom time fell to three to four hours per day, which restored time for play that had been lost in Kumegawa. Yet, it was not free. Teachers kept an eye on the schoolyard, and supervised children swimming in summer. They prohibited mixing with local children. Maeda's contact with children outside the group was limited to the son of the sake brewer in whose house she lodged. Obviously this situation reduced the transmission of culture among children. Maeda was surprised to learn later in life that evacuees at a different school ate the roasted beans inside their beanbags. "I didn't have the wisdom to figure that out," she says. "I doubt the sixth graders knew either. If they had, they would have told us how."[21] Maeda learned to juggle beanbags by watching a teacher demonstrate. Another teacher taught her to knit. However, she learned to play cards by watching the older girls.

Even children who were evacuated individually, not in groups, faced disadvantages in terms of free play. Oota Masami (b. 1936), the son of a salesman in Osaka, was sent to live with his aunt and uncle in a family of nine in Kumihama, outside Kyoto. Oota was left out when his classmates went swimming in the river or foraging in the woods for mushrooms, because he did not know how to do either.[22] Ueda likewise believes that he was discriminated against as an outsider when he and his mother moved three times to escape the Tokyo firebombings. According to Ueda, veterans of school evacuation mistakenly believe that children evacuated individually had an easier time just because they lived with relatives. But being evacuated individually, instead of together with school companions, placed Ueda and Oota at a disadvantage when it came to playgroups.[23]

Local farm children were in a better position than evacuated children to be "wild and free" in nature, but with the caveat that they could be put to work at a young age. Oota believes that fifth-grade and sixth-grade pupils in Kumihama did not have much time for play because the commute to school took one hour each way on foot, and then there was farm work to do at home for family survival. When Ueda entered the Kamisato school in Toyono, Nagano prefecture, he was put to work on a farm with his sixth-grade class starting in March 1945. As a result, pictures of his agricultural work dominate his personal diary from March onwards. Gone is the variety of games he used to play. Instead, his leisure activities are limited to aiming at sparrows with slingshot, or looking at pictures of airplanes in magazines and playing Japanese chess (shōgi), usually while sick in bed, after getting a fever from the festering of cuts and blisters suffered during farm labor. Maeda escaped farm work, possibly due to her elementary school's high status, being affiliated with the Tokyo Women's Higher Normal School (now Ochanomizu University). However, as explained above, evacuation curtailed free play in other ways.

POSSIBLE DIALOGUE WITH THE POSTWAR "EDUCATION CRISIS"

Memories of free play notwithstanding, these anecdotes illustrate how the worsening of the war affected play by making demands on children's time and by disrupting daily lives, especially in the case of children over ten or those who were evacuated. Still, there is little way to verify the memories of interview subjects. One interviewee has no memories of play during her school evacuation (she was in the same school as Maeda), even through her school diary contains a handful of pictures of play.[24]

Because most interview subjects nevertheless report freedom relative to their grandchildren, it is necessary to consider the possibility that their memories are shaped by an unconscious dialog with contemporary issues, which is a phenomenon observed by scholars in the context of war trauma memory.[25] Being adults, not children, the interview subjects remember their childhoods through the lens of seeing their own children and grandchildren grow up under different circumstances. Their memories may have also been shaped by the barrage of media concern in the 1980s about school bullying, school refusal, and "adult diseases," blamed by child experts on the stress of "education as endless labor" (Field 1995: 53). Experts at the time attributed children's bad behavior to a lack of social skills, caused in part because "children were spending less time in experiences of play, daily life, and nature." Such concerns drove the education reforms of the 1990s (Cave 2007: 18).

In addition to having less time, children today have less space. As Howard Chudacoff points out in the context of American history, "between the colonial era and today, natural play sites have diminished, thus reducing the ability of children to go 'roving' and 'roaming'" (Chudacoff 2012: 215). Meanwhile, the new virtual play spaces online are poorly understood in terms of their impact on children's development of social skills. Anxieties about change may thus lead interview subjects to privilege in memory what they perceive is missing in contemporary childhood. Another possibility is that remembering "freedom" is overcompensation for the embarrassment of wartime "deindividuation," to borrow a term from social psychology. In Keiko Matsuki's words, "The narrative is not a simple reflection of experience, but . . . reconstitutes our identity." In the act of remembering and narrating life experiences, the narrator invests old memories with new meanings to explain how past behavior is still consistent with current self-image. Matsuki theorizes that people born between 1926 and 1934 try to negotiate the 180-degree flip in their identities caused by Japan's surrender by recalling "rebellious" thoughts towards symbols of pre-defeat authority, such as teachers and policemen (Matsuki 2000: 536, 538). Perhaps free play falls into the category of rebellious memory.

However, a likely explanation in my view is that what may be called a "return to free play" is actually a "transwar" concept, to borrow a term from Andrew Gordon, allowing interview subjects to take comfort in a particular continuity between past and present thinking about childhood. According to anthropologist Joy Hendry, postwar Japanese educators appear to take the idea of socialization through peer groups as self-evident, and even manipulate peer pressure to control children's behavior in the classroom (Montgomery 2006: 129). Yanagita's privileging of children's self-directed play over games designed by adults may be echoed in the Ministry of Education's decision in the 1990s to increase school holidays, supposedly so that children would have more free time "to learn freely through experience and exploration outside of school" (Cave 2007: 19). Some games that Yanagita loved and upheld as manifestations of Japanese spirit, such as bird in a cage, continue to be taught in elementary schools and kindergartens by teachers aware of the nation's cultural heritage (Peak 1993: 48, 82).

CONCLUSION

Japanese children between 1941 and 1945 enjoyed self-organized free play according to interviews, even though the wartime concept of the little national emphasized duty and work ethic, rather than choice and leisure. Despite wartime shortages of consumer toys, there was a rich and varied culture of children's games that children learned at school, or more informally from each other after school in neighborhood green spaces, such as the village shrine or communal woodland. Some of these games were rural traditions, romanticized by Yanagita Kunio as important to Japanese identity.

Using interviews, and magazine illustrations, a wartime survey, and Yanagita's *Regional Customs of Children* as a barometer for the wartime cultural climate, I conclude that child play was acceptable as a form of learning, physical exercise, and transmission of Japanese identity. Unsupervised play was tolerated because adults like Yanagita believed that autonomous play in groups promoted socialization for harmonious cooperation, not selfish individualism. Rather, it was the interwar-era proponents of the "childlike child" who could be accused of interfering in children's natural play with their foreign educational games and playground equipment.

Yanagita's thought was not identical to nationalistic statism. His suspicion of top-down education and his preference for grassroots initiative enabled his ideas to survive into the democratic postwar era. The notion that free play is both desirable and endangered still resonates strongly with adults today, enabling the wartime generation to remember free play without shame, if not with pride. In practice, however, there may not have been quite as much freedom as remembered. From late 1944, children evacuated in school groups experienced a more regimented lifestyle, organized and monitored by teachers. In that sense, they may have been more like the cram-school generations after the war than like their rural peers, whose lives were not (yet) turned upside down by the war.

NOTES

1. This research is supported by the project "Remembering and Recording Childhood, Education and Youth in Imperial Japan, 1925–1945," directed by Peter Cave, University of Manchester (UK), funded by the UK Arts and Humanities Research Council.

2. Interview subjects do not use this term. In postwar Japan, class differences tend to be down-played, or indicated indirectly through one's place of residence. Here, "middle class" is used according to Andrew Gordon's designation of a "mainstream" *(chūryū)* that emerged between the 1920s and the 1960s and engaged in consumption and leisure (2007).

3. See, for example, what Louise Young calls the "cultural deluge" of popular media support for Manchukuo, the "puppet state" under construction by the Japanese Kwantung (Guandong) Army (Young 1998: 69).

4. Nakajima Shigeru, interview, Tsukuba, Ibaraki-ken, 8 January 2014.

5. Kubota Haruyoshi, interview, Tokyo, 10 August 2010.

6. Shingū Mitsue, interview, Ōtsu, Shiga-ken, 10 August 2010.

7. Ikeda Giichi, interview, Kumamoto, Kumamoto-ken, 2 January 2014.

8. Peter Grilli, interview, Auburndale, MA (USA), 12 June 2013.

9. This term refers to child-centered romanticism in the progressive children's literature of the previous Taishō era (see chapters 4 and 5).

10. Eizawa Kōtarō, interview, Ishiku, Ibaraki-ken, 7 January 2014.

11. Personal communication, 7 February 2015.

12. Email correspondence, 16 January 2015.

13. Shōji Kakuko, interview, Honolulu (USA), 29 December 2013.

14. Takatsu Yoneko, Yamagishi Sachiko, and Nakai Kiyotoshi interview, Toyono, Nagano-ken, 12 June 2015.

15. Maeda Tokuko, interview, Kawasaki, Kanagawa-ken, 9 June 2015.

16. Maeda Tokuko, interview, Kawasaki, Kanagawa-ken, 15 January 2014.

17. Personal correspondence, 10 February 2015.

18. Takeshi Morisato, "What does it mean for 'Japanese philosophy' to be 'Japanese'? A Kyoto School discussion on the peculiar character of Japanese Thought," presented for the British Association for Japanese Studies Annual Conference 2015, School of Oriental and African Studies, University of London, 11 September 2015.

19. A *monme* is a unit of coinage used in the Edo period (1600–1868)

20. Email correspondence, 7 January 2015.

21. Maeda, interview, 9 June 2015.

22. Oota Masami, interview, Tokyo, 9 January 2014.

23. Aaron Moore has suggested in personal conversation that school evacuees formed their own cultural identities, not just during the war, but years later through class reunions.

24. Mikawa Sueko, interview, Kawasaki-shi, Kanagawa prefecture, 17 June 2015.

25. For instance, some atomic bomb survivors decided to tell their stories "out of a sense of urgency and with a great deal of self-awareness about the act of telling the past" because they oppose recent government efforts to remilitarize or revive patriotic education (Yoneyama 1999: 86).

BIBLIOGRAPHY

Note: Unless noted otherwise the place of publication for Japanese books is Tokyo.

Ambaras, David R. 2006. *Bad Youth: Juvenile Delinquency and the Politics of Everyday Life in Modern Japan.* Berkeley: University of California Press.

Beardsley, Richard K., John H. Hall, and Robert E. Ward. 1959. *Village Japan.* Chicago: University of Chicago Press.

Cave, Peter. 2007. *Primary School in Japan: Self, Individuality, and Learning in Elementary Education.* London: Routledge.

Chudacoff, Howard. 2012. "Play and Childhood in the American Past: An Interview with Howard Chudacoff." *American Journal of Play* 4 (Spring): 395–406.

de Bary, William Theodore et al., eds. 2006. *Sources of Japanese Tradition 1600 to 2000,* abridged edition. New York: Columbia University Press.

Field, Norma. 1995. "The Child as Laborer and Consumer: The Disappearance of Childhood in Contemporary Japan." In *Children and the Politics of Culture,* edited by S. Stephens, 51–79. Princeton, NJ: Princeton University Press.

Gordon, Andrew. 2007. "Consumption, Leisure and the Middle Class in Transwar Japan." *Social Science Japan* 10(1): 1–21.

Hatano Kanji. (1940) 2012. "Jidō bunka no taisei" [The child culture system]. In *Jidō bunka to gakkō kyōiku no senchū sengo* [Wartime and postwar child culture and extracurricular education], edited by Katō Osamu, Kawakatsu Taisuke, and Asaoka Yasuō, 236–252. Kanagawa: Yūgen Kaisha Minato no Hito.

"Jidō bunka no shin-taisei" [A new order for children's culture]. 1941. *Kyōiku* [Education] 9(2): 12–18.

Jones, Mark. 2010. *Children as Treasures: Childhood and the Middle Class in Early Twentieth Century Japan.* Cambridge, MA: Harvard University Asia Center.

Kasza, Gregory J. 1995. *The Conscription Society: Administered Mass Organizations.* New Haven, CT: Yale University Press.

Kuchida Ichirō. 2012 (1941). "Jidō bunka to minzoku gaku" [Children's culture and folklore studies]. In *Jidō bunka to gakkō kyōiku no senchū sengo* [Wartime and postwar child culture and extracurricular education], edited by Katō Osamu, Kawakatsu Taisuke, and Asaoka Yasuō, 144–47. Kanagawa: Yūgen Kaisha Minato no Hito.

Kushner, Barak. 2009. "Planes, Trains and Games: Selling Japan's War in Asia." In *Looking Modern, Taisho Japan and the Modern Era,* edited by Jennifer Purtle and Hans Bjarne Thomsen, 243–64. Chicago: University of Chicago Press.

Matsuki, Keiko. 2000. "Negotiation of Memory and Agency in Japanese Oral Narrative Accounts of Wartime Experiences." *Ethos* 28(4): 534–50.

Montgomery, Heather. 2006. *An Introduction to Childhood: Anthropological Perspectives on Children's Lives.* Chichester: Wiley-Blackwell.

Mori, Kōichi. 1980. "Yanagita Kunio: An Interpretive Study." *Japanese Journal of Religious Studies* 7(2/3): 83–115.

Moriyama Shigeki and Nakae Kazue. 2002. *Nihon kodomo shi* [History of Japanese children]. Heibonsha.

Nihon Seishōnen Kyōiku Kenkyūsho. (1943) 1983. "Jidō seikatsu no jittai" [The actual state of childhood]. In *Nihon jidō mondai bunken senshū* [Selected documents on Japanese childhood issues], vol. 12, edited by Jidō Mondai Shi Kenkyūkai. Nihon Tosho Sentâ.

Ochanomizu gakudō sokai no kaihen, ed. 1989. *Dainiji sekai taisen gakudō sokai kirokushū* [Second World War school evacuation compilation]. 11 vols. Tōkyō joshi kōtō shihan gakkō fuzoku kokumin gakkō [Tokyo Women's Higher Normal School affiliated national school].

Opie, Iona, and Peter Opie. 1967. *Children's Games in Street and Playground.* Oxford: Oxford University Press.

Ortabasi, Melek. 2014. *The Undiscovered Country: Text, Translation, and Modernity in the Work of Yanagita Kunio.* Cambridge, MA: Harvard University Asia Center.

Peak, Lois. 1993. *Learning to Go to School in Japan: The Transition from Home to Preschool.* Berkeley: University of California Press.

Suwa Yoshihide. 1992. *Nihon no yōji kyōiku shisō to Kurahashi Sōzō* [Kurahashi Sōzō and the discourse of Japanese early childhood education]. Shin Dokushosha.

Ueda Hiroaki. 2003. *Sokai enikki: Gakudō sokai dosamawari* [My evacuation picture diary: Child evacuation wanderings]. Bungeisha.

Yamanaka Hisashi. 1989. *Zūsetsu Sensō no naka no kodomotachi: Shōwa shōkokumin bunko korekushon* [Illustrated children in the war: Shōwa Little Nationals library collection]. Kawade.

Yanagita Kunio. (1941) 1990. "Kodomo fūdoki" [*Regional Customs of Children*]. In *Yanagita Kunio zenshū* [Collected works of Yanagita Kunio], vol. 23, 9–91. Chikuma Shobō.

Yoneyama, Lisa. 1999. *Hiroshima Traces: Time, Space and the Dialectics of Memory.* Berkeley: University of California Press.

Young, Louise. 1998. *Japan's Total Empire: Manchuria and the Culture of Wartime Imperialism.* Berkeley: University of California Press.

9

" . . . And my heart screams"

Children and the War of Emotions

Sabine Frühstück

In 1937, an eleven-year-old girl named Omiya Setsuko wrote a poem for her free-writing class entitled, "Older Brother Is Strong and Healthy, Isn't He?"

> Mother who until now had diligently affixed sliding doors suddenly
>   looks at the newspaper.
> "What is it, mother?"
> In the newspaper is a photograph of IJA soldiers shouting, "Long
>   live His Majesty!"
> Mother's eyes brim with tears.
> Mother remains silent while lighting a candle at the shrine.
> I too recall older brother on the battlefield and my heart screams
> (Tomonaga, Tanaka, and Ienaga 1993: 339).

In previous histories, the culture of the Asia-Pacific War has been primarily discussed in terms of propaganda and indoctrination, major forces "steering children's minds toward militarism," effective tools "in every aspect of war bond drives," and "important in morale boosting" (Earhart 2008: 186–91; Kushner 2007, 2009; Dower 1987, 2010; Cave 2016). Children were encouraged to role-play as soldiers, young teenagers were drafted to work in munitions factories, and children of all ages were taught that death in military service was honorable and probable (Manabe 2013: 105). Indeed, after World War I, the leaders of most modern and modernizing nation-states ascribed to the promotional tactic of symbolically fusing childhood and war—a tactic most succinctly conceived by Adolf Hitler in *Mein Kampf*: "The tactical objective of the fight was the winning over of the child, and it was to the child that the first rallying cry was addressed: "German youth, do not forget that you are German," and "Remember, little girl, that one day you must be a German mother." Those who know something of the juvenile spirit can understand how youth will always lend a glad ear to such a rallying cry" (Hitler (2010 [1925]: 19).

Like their German counterparts, Japanese propaganda professionals, educators, writers, artists, and publishers who engaged in familiarizing and inducing children to see themselves as either soldiers or "wombs of the empire" (Shigematsu 2012: ix) knew to aim for a balance between discipline and fun, rules and play. In the following analysis of Japanese children's roles in wartime culture, I propose that children were implicated in a much more complex and ambiguous emotional regime than the language of suppression and control, propaganda and indoctrination suggests. In this essay I will describe how children's early socialization into a military-centric culture went hand in hand with campaigns for both the suppression and incitement of emotion on the part of adults and children alike. The political, educational, and cultural production elites did not just attempt to control and manage children's emotions—they also saw children as mediators of and chief manipulators of adult emotions. As such, the emotions evoked in representations of children depicted in wartime child publications could not be farther from the raw pain that Setsuko expressed in her poem.

But the ideological dynamics of the Asia-Pacific War went far beyond the suppression of children's individual emotions about the war and its consequences. Yes, wartime publications, which narrated for child readers both the war and children's roles in it, worked to suppress certain emotions in both children and adults; but they also forcefully incited and nurtured other, equally powerful sentiments: gratitude, friendship, pity, empathy, and pride. The key media that conveyed and incited these feelings in children were children's books and magazines, which also romanticized children, evoked pity and sympathy, and manipulated the context and consequences of war—especially for the adults who read and explained those texts and images to preliterate or early-reader children. Because though the politico-sentimental lessons were often, in essence, directed explicitly to the Japanese *child* readers, books and magazines were nonetheless delivered and read to children through the filter of *adults,* particularly parents. Not surprisingly, publishers capitalized on this dual readership in the course of crafting and packaging their messages. In this chapter, I examine the various ways children—and the sentiments that have been attributed to them—were manipulated in order to shape the emotions of both children and adults.

What I call "emotional capital"—akin to Pierre Bourdieu's economic, cultural, and social capital—constituted a prime "use value" (Hutnyk 2004) of children. Bourdieu proposed that capital can take on three guises: namely as "economic capital," which is immediately and directly convertible into money and often institutionalized as property rights; "cultural capital," which can be convertible into economic capital and institutionalized as educational qualifications; and "social capital," which comprises social obligations, can be convertible into economic capital, and can be institutionalized, as in a title of nobility. I propose a fourth such category: "emotional capital." In this discussion, I consider the "emotional capital" of children as comprising the emotions attributed to children as well as the emotions adults are expected to have in response to both children and representations of children. (These representations could include pictures of children and objects associated with children and childhood sensibilities.) In such instances, children's "emotional capital" signifies two things: the assumption that children were politically innocent, morally pure, and endowed with authentic feelings; and the expectation that adults would respond to the sight of children as vulnerable and innocent creatures with a specific, predictable set of emotions. (In principle, "emotional capital" could also be applicable to emotions tying an adult to another, but that exceeds the scope of this discussion.)

Along these lines, anthropologist Liisa Malkki (2010) observed, in the context of humanitarian engagements at the margins of war, that "children occupy a key place in dominant imaginations of the human" and of the "world community." She finds that today's humanitarianism utilizes "special, observably standardized, representational uses of children" in five registers that have "affective and ritual efficacy." These include children as embodiments of basic human goodness and symbols of world harmony, children as sufferers, children as seers of truth, children as ambassadors of peace, and children as the embodiment of the future (Malkki 2010: 60). These registers function in contemporary humanitarian work under the rubric of the "infantilization of peace." Under this rubric, the word "peace" cannot be uttered without the representational presence of a child. And, precisely because of the mediating role of the child, "peace" is no longer a serious option—the concept of peace is made infantile, a utopian ideal that has no place in modern society. Viewed through the lens of "emotional capital," the representational uses of children that Malkki identifies as essential to the iconography of humanitarianism at the beginning of the twenty-first century share a lot of similarities with the iconography of the child culture of war at the beginning of the twentieth (for another example of a child's role in the iconography of humanitarianism, see chapter 13).

In around 1900, when Japan waged war first against China (1894–1895) and then against Russia (1904–1905), children's relationship with war was one of mere casualties. But by the early 1930s, when the Japanese took control of Manchuria, children (and infancy) had become utilized as the figures that make war appear inevitable, natural, and intrinsically human. These articulations are particularly prominent in writings, drawings, and photographs in children's books and magazines, which juxtapose and link children with soldiers in order to create and perpetuate this message. In these publications, children are employed to portray the humanity, the inherent necessity, and the inevitability of war. A range of pictures and stories of children with soldiers worked to transmute war into an aesthetic and rhetoric: not of destruction but rescue, not of battle but peace, not of chaos but comforting order. These representations aimed at steering the emotions of children and adults by monitoring, molding, training, and honing them—even as they suppressed emotions by prohibiting their expression. Images and rhetoric were at once repressive and productive, restrictive and liberating. More than any other configuration, representations of children interacting with soldiers blended the two normatively distinct worlds of childhood and war. They have thus been open to an infinite number of political maneuvers and legitimating efforts across periods of war and, as we shall see, times of peace. In fact, throughout the first half of the twentieth century, visual and narrative articulations about the precise relationship between childhood and war proliferated. Children were increasingly represented as vulnerable and in touch with their feelings, and childhood was envisioned as a time of molding and disciplining that moved children away from a state of nature and innocence. Children were therefore capable of lending moral authority to war. War, on the other hand, was rendered as "uncivilized," especially when conducted by other nation states, and yet inevitable and inherent to human nature.

VULNERABILITY AND THE EMERGENCE OF MODERN CHILDHOOD

Before turning to the complex field of children and emotional capital, let us first examine the changing constructions of conceptions of childhood. From early on in the Meiji era, views of the child and childhood were central to public debates on a range of issues. The new Meiji government, the education establishment, the military, and the fledgling modern print media all sought to disassociate the samurai class from its image as warmongers and to link children to the welfare and power of the nation. These efforts manifested themselves in earnest in 1872, when the Meiji government implemented two laws that had revolutionary, modernizing, and democratizing effects. One was the universal and mandatory Conscription Act. This act subjected all twenty-year-old males to a conscription exam, followed by the potential of military service; at the same time, widespread dismissive references were made about the samurai class as men who, according to some commentators, "led an easy life, were arrogant and shameless, and murdered innocent people with impunity" (Lone 2010: 15). The second law was the Fundamental Code of Education, which mandated elementary education for both boys and girls. The Conscription Act established new bounds for male maturity (the age of twenty as the age of eligibility for military service) and rewrote what exactly such male adulthood signified (in principle at least, the will of all able-bodied males to kill and die in the name of the emperor).

Likewise, the Fundamental Code of Education together with a modern education system in the making introduced new names, parameters, distinctions, and to some extent identities among the young, primarily by level of schooling. The Education Law of 1879, which replaced the Fundamental Code of Education classified all "children of elementary school age" as *jidō*; "student" *(seitō)* was universally applied to children between elementary school and university. The Kindergarten Ordinance of 1927 distinguished kindergarteners as yōji; later, the post-Asia-Pacific War education laws distinguished between kindergarteners *(yōji)*, elementary school children *(jidō)*, middle school and high school children *(seitō)*, and university students *(gakusei)* (Moriyama and Nakae 2002: 18–21). As the universal school system developed, age gradually replaced class status as a significant social marker during childhood. In rural areas, it should be noted, children and youth groups had long been considered more important communities than were schools, and they remained so for a time—but eventually new identities gradually replaced the older ones there as well. Eventually, terms such as the "child that was young enough to still nurse" *(chigo)*, the child that had "messy hair and laughed a lot" *(warawa)*, and a multitude of other older expressions that signified children of one kind and age or another disappeared from use (Moriyama and Nakae 2002: 8–19; see also Kinski 2015; for more on age-specific naming practices, see chapter 1).

Such stratification of childhood prompted some of the earliest debates about children's rights. In the fall of 1886, Ueki Emori (1857–1892), a prominent member of the Freedom and People's Rights Movement, asserted that individuals, not families, should be seen as the basic units of a society; further, he declared that children should also be considered individuals, not simply entities that benefit their parents (Sotozaki 1956). Of course, many "progressive" ideas can take some time to take hold, and, indeed, family rights continued to be prioritized over individual rights for several decades thereafter. All the same, this radically modern conception of childhood gradually gained acceptance, ultimately becoming codified in a long-term process in which political, legal, and cultural institutions came to declare children, young children in particular, as vulnerable, innocent, and in need of adult influence—the latter regarding protection and care as well as discipline and control. From the Fundamental Code of Education to the Imperial Rescript on Education of 1890 and beyond, modern education legislation conceptualized children as yet-to-be-formed individuals who would one day realize adult goals for the nation (Okano and Motonori 1999: 15–19; Ienaga and Inagaki 1994: 79).

In the process of childhood coming to be recognized as a time separate from adulthood, the concept of just what childhood was varied a great deal. As a construct, "childhood" could encompass only a few years or it could be extensive, all depending on conceptions of maturity, expectations of independence, and legal measures and practices related to education, welfare, labor, and criminality. But, despite such variations, children generally were viewed not just as part of the nation but also as a prototype of the people—people who should be educated, conquered, and seduced, in order to bring them from a place of weakness to one of strength, all in service to nation and empire.

Children were also seen as embodying a number of binaries: as both loveable and horrible, vulnerable and demonic, valuable and burdensome. Policy makers, military strategists, educators, social welfare engineers, and ordinary men and women alike believed that, though children were "worthy" of rights, they had little agency; in addition, though these parties considered children to be vulnerable, they were also seen as a potential threat to social order. Essentially, notions of childhood abounded; the only factor they shared was the concept of childhood as being distinct from adulthood.

In addition to the Fundamental Code of Education and the Conscription Act, other legislation also institutionalized the separation of childhood from adulthood, including the Foundling Law of 1871, as well as subsequent legislation designed to ensure basic livelihood to the most unfortunate children (Namaye 1919). In 1874, for example, poverty legislation prescribed support for children younger than thirteen. At the time, 10 percent of children between the ages of eleven and fourteen were employed, as were about 90 percent of children fifteen and older (Fujino 2009: 889–90, Ambaras 2006: 41). A decades-long debate about children's labor and exploitation, and especially the exploitation of girls, resulted in a 1916 law prohibiting children under the age of thirteen from working more than twelve hours a day in a seven-day week.

The effects of such child labor legislation were widespread. For one, there was a phenomenal increase in school attendance rates; I return to this topic below. In addition, medical practitioners established a separate field of pediatrics, whose representatives aggressively promoted the notion that childhood ought to be a realm separate from adulthood. They insisted that children were particularly vulnerable and worthy of study, special care, and protection—concepts that were framed primarily in terms of social order and control, and only secondarily in terms of scientific and sociopolitical concerns.

In 1909, prominent pediatrician Takashima Heisaburō claimed that only "in countries where civilization has not progressed, ignorant people abuse children, deny them education, and view them as their personal possession. In civilized countries, child protection activities are flourishing" (Ambaras 2006: 86–87). Similar ideas were fashionable in modern and modernizing nation-states around the world and were often attributed to the Swedish feminist Ellen Key, who claimed the new century to be the "century of the child"; indeed, such was the title of the 1909 English translation of her 1900 publication *Barnets århundrade*. Alerted to these new concerns about childhood, anxious parents in Japan and elsewhere increasingly turned to pediatric experts for advice.

As these experts' work gained traction, growing numbers of people outside the academy began to think of the infant years as educationally productive (Koresawa 2009: 6–8). This conversation spread across several intellectual and academic fields, infiltrating popular science journals and parents' self-help guides and finding its way into households far beyond the middle class. Pedagogues, physicians, politicians, and others concerned with the future of the Japanese empire began to promote programs to improve children's physical exercise and cleanliness in schools. They sought to balance scholastic training—which had come to dominate school education—with physical modes of training. In addition, welfare institutions for children were developed, and child protection laws were implemented (Frühstück 2003).

After several instances of severe child abuse scandalized the nation—resulting in popular calls for legislation to protect "innocent children from crimes"—the legislature enacted the Child Abuse Prevention Act in 1933 (Mishima 2005: 31–36). This law was yet another piece of legislation that codified children's vulnerability, innocence, and need of protection—sometimes even from their own parents.

At the same time, women were naturalized as children's primary caretakers and educators of children in the home; over time, women became educators in grade schools as well. The twentieth century ushered in cultural expectations regarding the proper way for parents—especially mothers—to love their children. As a result, maternal love became obligatory and was increasingly declared natural, instinctual, and normative. In turn, public intellectuals interested in creating a "child-centered society" that would produce healthy, happy, and well-loved children capable of becoming "ideal students" targeted their advice toward mothers (Jones 2010).

Mostly male experts advised mothers on nutrition, home medical remedies for minor ailments, children's reading and educational materials, and the benefits of proper play (Frühstück 2003: 50–52). They encouraged mothers to "carefully monitor and channel their children's potentially evil instincts and turbulent passions until they evolved into mature, well-adjusted people" (Ambaras 2006: 95). Guidebooks for home use, such as *The Health Reader for Daughters, Wives, and Mothers* (Musume to tsuma to haha no eisei dokuhon), and *Methods of Pregnancy, Safe Birth, and Child Rearing* (Ninshin to ansan to ikujihō), described how good mothers guided their offspring toward adulthood, leaving nothing to chance—least of all the training of children's emotions.[1]

RESCUING THE CHILD AT WAR

Most woodblock prints featuring battles from the Sino-Japanese and Russo-Japanese wars depicted dramatic militaristic tableaux: disciplined soldiers looking down from above; officers striking dramatic poses, swords held high; troops advancing, military flags fluttering, foes retreating (Dower 2008: 8–9). Such scenes do not cry out to have the image of a child added within their frames. And yet, beginning in 1894, representations of children occasionally entered visual and narrative representations of Japan's modern wars, through a number of different channels. In some instances, members of the Imperial Japanese Army are depicted "clutching a Chinese child found abandoned in the battlefield." In such images, the child takes the place of the inanimate object of symbolic value: the flag or the sword the charging officer would have otherwise held aloft. But the emphasis is always on the courageously charging man, not the presumably frightened child. The child's face is invisible, its emotional state impalpable. After all, these prints were designed as propagandistic "war reportage"; as such they depicted what artists envisaged as beautiful and heroic in modern war (Dower 2008: 4, 15). Accordingly, children appear in soldiers' arms in order to enhance the hero's righteous cause, not his humanity.

In addition to such products of the era's emerging propaganda machine, the Sino-Japanese War and its successor, the Russo-Japanese War (1904–1905), also saw a boom in portrait photography of men in uniform, sometimes with family members, including children, personalizing the generic warrior. During that same period, children also became subjects of hobby photography in their own right, often featured singly or with other children. In these portraits, national affairs had no place; it was the stages of childhood that inspired typical amateur photographer fathers, who captured such rituals as the "first eating" *(okuizome)*, first-hundred-days celebrations, and Shichi-Go-San, the annual November festival for three- and seven-year-old girls and three- and five-year-old boys. They collected images of these important days in their children's lives in family albums. Then, beginning in the early 1930s, alongside those younger-days photos were added photographs of boys playing soldier in remnants of uniforms, holding toy rifles or bayonets, stern-faced, at attention, or concentrated at an all-boys' "rifle practice."

This pattern was heightened when photo magazines encouraged hobby and professional photographers to submit commemorative family photographs and portraits to photography competitions. Winning photographs were printed in the publications, their exposure thus expanding to a wide audience. For these photographs, parents often dressed their children in military garb and posed them with toy weapons. The 15 June 1932 issue of the photo magazine *Tainichi Gurafu* printed an entire page of baby pictures sent in by readers. Central to the array is a photograph with the title "Children's Heaven" of a little boy in a tank-shaped stroller pushed by a girl of about five. The caption reads: "Baby in tank—he is going to Manchuria but the tank won't move. So his sister pushes from behind" (*Tainichi Gurafu* vol. 4, no. 6). Similarly, the elegant magazine *Home Life* (Hōmu raifu, October 1938) printed a shot by photographer Yamagami Entarō of a boy in underwear and a helmet waving a flag that read, "This is a soldier's home" (Tsuganezawa 2006: 152). The photograph was captioned "The Commander of Our House."

Adults were likely the primary consumers of this type of photography, but illustrations with similar motives and settings also adorned children's books and magazines, which proliferated as the print media market rapidly expanded. Within the pages of such publications could be found visual representations of soldiers with children, as well as of children embodying and playing soldiers. As print media progressed in the 1930s, these representations appeared in text as well as image. The products specifically manufactured for elementary-school-age children—and, presumably, their mothers—intentionally depicted war through children's eyes, making the soldier appear not as a fierce warrior but as a playmate, substitute mother, savior of children, or big brother. To achieve a complementary emotional effect, roles of strength and vulnerability were also switched. In these, the soldier is featured as having a childlike need for care, indicating the interchangeability of children with soldiers. Each is reflected in the other, with the child serving as reminder of the past just as the soldier speaks to the future.

The production and publication of pictures and narratives representing children with military paraphernalia, play-acting war, or interacting with soldiers all served to exploit the feelings of tenderness associated with images of children. These representations tied notions of glory and heroism to warm sentiments of belonging to family, community, and nation. They evoked excitement about war as adventure, and constructed wartime experience as a means by which to accelerate entry into adulthood, bringing honor to the country via meaningful contributions of bona fide men rather than merely the make-believe play of boys.

By the early 1930s, textual and visual representations of children with soldiers featured regularly in military postcards and textbooks, commercial children's books, magazines, and newspapers. Unlike woodblock prints depicting soldiers as warriors, these images focused on children's sweetness and innocence. Magazines published stories about children's relationship to war, whether that took place in Japan, in the colonies, or behind the frontlines. These stories invented new ways to blend soldiers with children, war with play, and violence with care. On some occasions, the military invited children onto bases to comfort and entertain soldiers, to eat with them, and to bring them small gifts. Some of the visiting boys no doubt looked up to the soldiers around them, perhaps aspiring to someday proudly wear the boots of war. Some girls might have imagined themselves "do[ing] their part for the war effort" by becoming nurses or romancing soldiers, marrying them, and producing more soldiers; some others wished they had been born as boys and could go to battle themselves (Kameyama 1997 [1984]).

Many of these stories and pictures had one thing in common: they concealed the exact nature of the relationship between soldiers of one nation and the children of another, as well as the circumstances of their encounters. The use of little children as key messengers for adult readers became ever more commonplace in the wake of the beginning of a full-blown war with China. Less than three months after the Nanking massacre, the 2 March 1938 issue of the photo magazine *Asahi Graph* (Asahi gurafu) featured a series of photographs from the Chinese front. Next to many photographs of troops going about various activities—other than fighting—one photograph features a very young-looking Japanese soldier with two Chinese girls. The smaller girl sits on his lap. The older one stands right next to them and looks into the camera. The young man smiles. The caption states that upon the Japanese soldiers' arrival in the city, these "picture perfect, lovely bobbed-haired" girls cheerfully called out in Japanese, "Long live the Japanese Army" (16). The declared adorability of children is put to work in order to sideline, if not make invisible, the extreme mass violence that the army—of which the young man is a member—had just perpetrated. For another example of how adorable children were used to conceal violence perpetuated by the army, see chapter 6.

The cover of that issue of *Asahi Graph* features three boys dressed in military uniforms and gear at the National Foundation Day Festival. Employing the child language of both war technology and folk and fairy tales, the accompanying headline reads, "Plane or anti-aircraft gun? The midget heroes of the National Foundation Festival" (*Asahi Gurafu,* 2 March 1938, vol. 30, no. 9: cover and p. 16). Again, the chubby faces and the boys' clumsy attempts to look and strut like adult soldiers work to playfully undermine the deadly force of the military plane and anti-aircraft gun evoked in the caption text.

The sentiment and iconography of friendship with and gratitude toward Imperial Army soldiers was also widely commercialized in advertisements for a slew of products, especially foodstuffs, sweets, and tea. Ads for caramels told war stories concocted in a harmonious universe where the worlds of children and soldiers intersected through the exchange of a single, highly desirable piece of candy. A 1939 issue of the children's magazine *Children's Club* featured caramels by Meiji Seika, a confectionary company founded in 1916. Variations of the ad reappeared across a number of issues of the same magazine. One such ad depicts in the foreground an Imperial Army soldier giving a Meiji caramel to a Chinese child; in the background, a Japanese mother gives a Meiji caramel to her children. The text notes that, when the clock turned three, the Chinese child would receive a Meiji caramel from an IJA (Imperial Japanese Army) soldier just as Japanese children back home would (*Yōnen Kurabu,* vol. 14, no. 13, table of contents flap). In both scenes, the children happily accept the candy—and in that brief moment of transaction, the Japanese soldier in China slips into the role of the Japanese mother.

Candy advertisements had been couched in the terms of military conquest since the mid-1910s. Throughout the 1930s and early 1940s, a great many other products—from toothpaste to fountain pens—followed suit. In many advertisements, the soldier is stripped of his identity as combatant and instead adopts a familial role, particularly in encounters with Chinese and other colonized children. The children are represented interacting with IJA soldiers, sometimes even playing with them and marching along with them in a continuous process of slipping in and out of, imitating, even temporarily embodying the figure of the soldier. Especially for children younger than twelve or so, all things military were aestheticized, fictionalized, and familiarized in ways that focused not on the battle but on its aftermath. Whether as passive recipients of candy from soldiers or as active players in the pursuit of peace and nation building, children repeatedly appear as triggers of warm feelings.

Like many illustrated children's books, the *Kōdansha Picture Book: Japan's Army* introduced the military to beginning readers through "stories of soldiers and children behind the frontlines." One of these one-page visual narratives shows two members of the military police giving candy to Chinese children: "The Military Police play the role of police within the military. The picture is about the place where members of the Military Police divide up caramels and give them to Chinese children" (*Kōdansha no ehon: Nippon no rikugun*, October 1940, p. 41). Many such narratives represent children as the beneficiaries of Japanese soldiers' friendliness and playfully protective spirit.

In some depictions, soldiers' status vis-à-vis children is more ambivalent: they are depicted as the vulnerable ones, in need of care and attention. The book *Japan's Children* (Nippon no Kodomo 1941) promoted children's imitations of battles and encounters with soldiers in pictures spread out over several pages, all designed for the smallest, beginning readers. It also includes a scene, however, that had already appeared, ubiquitously, in many children's books and magazines. The scene features a woman accompanying a group of four children—two boys and two girls— to a military hospital. One girl gives an injured soldier a bouquet of flowers; in accompanying text she says: "How are you, Honorable Soldier? We all came and brought you flowers." One of the boys talks with a second injured patient, a smiling soldier propped up on his elbow in his hospital bed: "How is your wound, Honorable Soldier? Please accept one of my drawings" (*Nippon no Kodomo* 1941: 6). Neither the two soldiers nor the woman speak. All three adults simply smile at the children, who appear more intimidated than pleased by this response.

Similarly, *Kōdansha Picture Book: Japan's Army* (1940: 75) has three elementary school boys chat with three injured soldiers while a Red Cross nurse stands by (figure 10). They learn where in China they fought and how they got injured. In turn, they ask the soldiers what subjects they had most liked at school.

So while products specifically manufactured for elementary-school-age children depicted war in way they imagined to be suitable for young children's eyes, they frequently depicted Japanese soldiers with enemy children or Japanese children in easy-going conversations, mostly representing soldiers as children's saviors and allies, and claiming a natural affinity and interchangeability between soldiers and children. Furthermore, children in stories, cartoons, advertisements, and personal photographs are often dressed and posed as soldiers; in turn, soldiers are depicted with childlike faces and bodies that blend in with the children around them—depictions that trivialize and flatten the soldiers' varied experiences as well as the differentiated thoughts children had about soldiers and adults more generally (see chapter 7).

On 20 January 1941, Fröbel Hall, an organization devoted to children's education and play, published an issue of its popular "Children's Book" series with the title *Kinder Book: Getting Along with Neighbors* (Kindā bukku: Otonari nakayoshi 10, no. 13). On its cover are three figures: a Japanese teenage boy wears a school uniform in the colors of the Imperial Army and an upper armband with Japan's national flag; he holds the hand of a small girl in Korean traditional dress, representing Japan's colony; she in turn holds the hand of a slightly older boy in Chinese

FIGURE 10. Japanese children with injured members of the Imperial Army, 1940. From *Kōdansha no ehon: Nippon no rikugun—Jūgo dōwa heitaisan to kodomo* (Kōdansha picture book: Japan's Army—Home-front children's stories about soldiers and children), Dai Nippon Yūbenkai Kōdansha, 1940, p. 75.

dress, most likely representing Manchukuo. (Note that, in 1941, Manchukuo had been under Japanese control for almost a decade, since before either of the small children in the picture was born). Those two children, who might be about three and six years old, gaze sweetly at the Japanese youth. In turn, the Japanese boy "soldier"—soft-faced and young looking, almost like a child himself—gazes down at the children with the gentle smile of a loving older brother. Here, the connection that is visually established between child and boy soldier suppresses the would-be incompatibility between war and vulnerability, between the perpetration of acts of kindness and the horror of victimization.

Children's Book: Getting Along with Neighbors was just one of many publications promoting this message. Young readers were repeatedly reminded that, just as they might grow up to become soldiers, soldiers had once been children like them. Indeed, the depiction of children with soldiers also embodies soldiers' ties to their own, once innocent, childlike selves. These allusions seem designed to obscure the mass violence of war, and to assure young readers that brothers, fathers, and uncles fighting abroad were just as caring toward "other" children as they were toward their own.

These representations may have allowed soldiers to reconnect with their own (prewar, preadult) innocence. They also signaled to Japanese children that, though their brothers, fathers, and uncles were physically far away at war, they remained emotionally close through their caring interactions with enemy children. Providing children with a Robinson Crusoe-like idyllic image from the South Seas, Kawasaki Daiji's *Village Nursery School* (Mura no hoikusho 5–7; Kawasaki 1944) features IJA soldiers playing with brown-skinned children. The text explains that letters from children in Japan had just arrived, and the soldiers had cheerfully offered to read to them aloud.

One might be tempted to assume that the primary purpose of these representations was to satisfy individual soldiers' need for emotional redemption. Through touching children and embracing their childlike innocence, it would appear that soldiers could connect again to their own childhood. It is easy to imagine that, after battle, soldiers might turn to children—perhaps even to the children whose fathers they had just killed—"out of regret, relief that they had not destroyed everything, respect for life, or because they missed their own children" (Linhart 2010: 141–42). Though some soldiers indeed reported such sentiments, both during the war and later in memoirs, these representations were not simply unmediated depictions of soldiers' sentiments. After all, even during the severe wartime paper shortage, children's color books and magazine publications remained common in Japan, perhaps one of the strongest indications of their use value. Furthermore, postcards depicting these representations were given away or cheaply sold. In addition, veterans' memoirs, other stories from the frontlines (written by former IJA service members for a young Japanese audience), and a variety of other publications continuously reproduced such sentiments. These representations clearly had both commercial and political value. They invested the military and war with familiarity and individuality—while also redeeming the soldiers and appeasing children on both sides of the war. Illustrators and authors of children's books and magazines, soldier memoirists, artists, and authors all mobilized children's vulnerability in order to reinvent soldiers as children's protectors, saviors, and playmates—whether behind the frontlines, in occupied territories, or back at home. Ultimately, soldiers' unlikely and fleeting friendships with the young were evoked to cleanse them from the violence they had committed and suffered—at least in the eyes of the young and adult consumers and readers of such stories and pictures.

These representations communicate as much through what they leave out as through what they depict. The children shown in these images are healthy, smiling, properly clothed; children suffering from hunger, trauma, or injury are left out, as are dead children. And though these representations show IJA soldiers interacting with both Japanese and colonized children, enemy (colonized) soldiers are removed from the vicinity and rendered invisible. Children in these images appear happy. They look friendly and grateful in the course of interacting with soldiers—or even in imitating them, temporarily embodying the figure of the soldier.

The oft-repeated paired configurations of child and soldier exploited the emotional capital of children—embedded in innocence, vulnerability, malleability, and cuteness—to shape affective responses to and emotional conventions regarding the military and war.

REINVENTING VULNERABILITY

Article 9 of Japan's postwar constitution called for the dissolution of the IJA, which saw completion on 30 November 1945. At that point Japan officially and swiftly moved from the imperialist victory culture it had known for the first half of the twentieth century to the victim culture of the second half. Initially, the production of the victim culture drew primarily from both the bombings of Hiroshima and Nagasaki and the resurrection of the child as a symbol of suffering and the need for peace. Many of the same writers, illustrators, and publishers who had previously worked to militarize children's worlds now made energetic pronouncements about how to transform children into proper pacifists—and back into "true children"—by providing children with the conditions to preserve their innate innocence, vulnerability, and natural inclination toward peace.

And yet, illustrators and photographers continued to produce depictions of soldiers with children, and these still were published in a range of venues. American and British soldiers clad in the uniforms of the Allied occupation of Japan were featured in photographs, print media, and children's publications, in arrangements strikingly similar to their wartime IJA opponents. Allied soldiers were depicted as cheerful and warm-hearted as they handed chocolate and chewing gum to Japanese children. The photographs suggested that these soldiers were keen on befriending children everywhere. It is noteworthy that illustrations and photo-graphs of Japanese children with American and British soldiers also served to paint over the dramatic demonization of westerners so recently widespread in Japanese wartime propaganda.

Publically posted as appeals to consider the Americans "everybody's friends," these representations addressed anxieties regarding Japan's former enemies turned occupying armed forces. Here as before, children were enlisted as mediators. Such representations were utilized by 1946 textbooks for the first post-Asia Pacific War English-language course, titled *Come, Come, English for Everyone*—a title bor-rowed from the theme song of Hirakawa Tadaichi's English conversation radio program. The simple everyday English phrases in the textbooks accompanied illus-trations of a conversation between a Japanese boy in school uniform and a friendly American soldier. The context of the encounter of the boy with the soldier—Japan's occupation by allied armed forces—is brought into the pictures only via the sol-dier's uniform, his tall frame, and his stereotypical blond hair and blue eyes. The illustrations mirrored the wartime iconography of colonized children's encounters with Imperial Japanese Army soldiers, as well as the contemporary, occupation-era iconography of Japanese children's encounters with Allied soldiers. Yet, in all other respects, the two characters in this language course interact in a manner that differs significantly from wartime representations of soldiers and children.

Rather than embodying the cheerful and grateful recipient of caramels or chew-ing gum, the boy becomes a guide to the adult soldier-tourist in Japan. The Japanese child and the American soldier meet in a park, a distinctly nonmilitary setting. The soldier is unarmed. In contrast to the emotional weight of wartime representations of (Japanese) soldiers with Japanese or enemy children, the boy does not primarily appear sweet and helpless, neither does the soldier appear patronizingly tolerant of the boy. Instead, even though the purpose of this textbook and the associated radio lessons was to help Japanese adults and children learn English, it is the American soldier who asks questions about Japan, and who in turn is the happy recipient of information about Japanese customs that the boy provides.

In contrast to him and many other happy children interacting with American G.I.s so often depicted in photographs, magazines, books, and newspapers of the occupation era, children who had lived through the war had a more mixed reac-tion to the soldiers. Akabane Reiko, a young teenager at the time, recalled that American and British soldiers seemed "almost like the Kamikaze pilots," she had been enlisted to wave farewell to during the last months of the war. "They were almost as young and appeared even nicer because they expressed themselves more directly" (Scherer 2001: 113). She fondly remembered the chocolate they gave her, and how she had enjoyed playing cards with them at her house (113). Other chil-dren felt more apprehensive toward their occupiers. Miyazaki Hayao, today an acclaimed filmmaker, was eleven when the Allied occupation of Japan came to an end on 28 April 1952, following the signing of the San Francisco Peace Treaty between Japan and the Allied Powers. Miyazaki described himself as "the kind of kid who was too ashamed to ask the Americans for chewing gum or chocolate" (Miyazaki 2014).

As much as publishers' efforts during the Asia-Pacific War and the occupation era were directed at encouraging positive feelings of children towards the war, Japan's soldiers, the children on the other side of the frontline and, afterward, towards the occupation forces, some were not to be fooled. The relentlessly repeated cheerfulness gave way to Setsuko's pain, Reiko's fondness, and Hayao's ambivalence.

THE END OF INNOCENCE?

In 2015, Japan celebrated the seventieth anniversary of the end of the Asia-Pacific War. During that same year, Abe Shinzō's administration introduced controversial security legislation that triggered popular resistance in Japan and a great deal of anxiety among Japan's neighbors, as well as intense discussions about implications for the future of the Self-Defense Forces (SDF), which succeeded both the wartime Imperial Japanese Army and Navy. "Abe's Japan," writes Gavan McCormack (2016), the "peace state" Japan, had effectively become a "war-capable state."

In a country that had been at peace for over three generations, though the Self-Defense Forces engaged in a broad range of domestic and international missions, they did not make war. Working hard to shed their association with the Imperial Army, the Ground Self-Defense Force had little international involvement until 1992, when it was deployed on a peacekeeping mission in Mozambique. In the wake of this controversial deployment, it discovered the necessity and utility of shaping its public image, domestically and internationally, through public relations efforts that increasingly incorporated female television celebrities, cute imagery, and manga and animation elements (Frühstück 2007).

At the beginning of this century, these public relations campaigns took another turn when two separate institutions—the military and popular culture—rediscovered the appeal of representations combining children and the military. Self-Defense Forces iconography and narratives have reincorporated representations of children and childlike creatures on recruitment posters, animation available on the homepage of the Ministry of Defense, and open house festivals on individual bases. A brochure produced to explain to a wary Japanese population the Self-Defense Forces' effort to help "rebuild Iraq" features two drawings by children and two photographs of Iraqi children. In one of the photos, a child sits on the knee of a Japanese service member. The Self-Defense Forces' role in Iraq primarily concerned infrastructure, and the brochure takes great pains to convey, to both the Iraqis and the Japanese back home, that the SDF were in Iraq to rebuild, not to fight.

Similarly, a Maritime Self-Defense Forces public relations video released on 1 March 2011 declares service members' "pride" and "joy" in their "mission and duty" to secure Japan's borders. It ends with a uniformed male service member taking into his arms a female toddler dressed in soft pink while a young, smiling woman—likely his wife and the girl's mother—happily looks on.[2]

The Self-Defense Forces and mainstream mass media also collaborated on the exploitation of children's emotional capital regarding the SDF's deployment to northeastern Japan to provide relief for what is often referred to in Japan as "3/11" and known elsewhere as the "Fukushima disaster"—a 9.0 earthquake that resulted in a tsunami and the meltdown of a nuclear power plant in March 2011. One particular joint effort, the *Mainichi Illustrated Magazine of the Self-Defense Forces' Other Frontline* (Mainichi mukku Jieitai mo hitotsu no saizensen, 29 July 2011: 6–7), is visually wrapped in pink. On the cover, a small girl dressed in bright pink, with a forlorn yet determined look on her face, marches ahead of a group of Self-Defense Forces service members; she carries a big bag, itself pale pink, which appears to contain all her remaining belongings. On the back cover, two girls, both wearing shades of pink, wave at a jeep; this image is juxtaposed against a child's thank-you letter written on pink stationery.

Similarly, a photograph that first appeared in the magazine *Bessatsu Takara-jima*, on the topic of "The Self-Defense Forces vs. the Eastern Japan Great Earthquake" (23 July 2011, no. 1780: 9), features a female service member with a little girl dressed all in pink in front of a makeshift bath. Smiling, both flash the peace sign. In another photograph, a male service member lovingly smiles down at a rescued baby in his arms. Numerous other photographs featured in SDF public relations materials and mass media publications in the following years retell the story of children's privileged relationship with soldiers, highlighting laughter and play, solidarity and kinship. These images were widely circulated, as later were the thank-you notes and letters children were encouraged to write to their heroic Self-Defense Forces.

Perhaps it is unseemly to critically address commercialized representations of SDF efforts to ease suffering in the wake of a devastating disaster. Yet it is important to consider how often these images depict a specific type of child: a preschool- or elementary-age girl or girls, dressed in an inordinate quantity of pink in order to accentuate their innocence and vulnerability.

Indeed, this particular iconography echoes Japanese popular culture at the edge of the mainstream. Only very recently have magazines, manga, anime, and other media begun to feature and embrace military themes. In such publications, though female figures' looks vary considerably, their age—prepubescent—is fairly constant. But even the variations in costume falls into an interesting range. In one part of the story, the figures may wear the short dresses typical of elementary-school girls, while at another, they appear half undressed and holding machine guns, thus suddenly embodying a key figure in Japanese popular culture: the fighting girl, who ties together prepubescent sex appeal with the capacity to engage in deadly mass violence.

The main characters in *Strike Witches* (Sutoraiku Witcheezu, 2010–present), for example, all appear to be younger than ten years of age. Some have animal ears and tails that enhance their feminine yet infantile cuteness. For most of the story, the characters wear clothes that are perfectly mainstream for five- or six-year-olds. And yet, whenever they use their weapons, they appear to be wearing only panties—suggesting a confluence between two different kinds of exhilaration and excitement on the part of the reader or viewer. Similarly, in *Infinite Stratos* (Infinitto Sutoratosu, 2009–present), young girls put on high-tech suits that essentially turn them into living weapons capable of mass destruction. These girls can show a great deal of skin—quite similar to the "fierce flesh" of the "sexy schoolgirls" in *Sailor Moon* (Allison 2006: 128)—but only when they are fighting. Similarly, *Military!* (Miritari! 2009–present) and *Warship Collection* (Kantai Korekushon, 2013–present) also feature groups of heavily armed fighting girls within a continuum of sexualized and pornified settings.[3] While specialists of media and popular culture have pondered whether such figures represent girl empowerment, feminism, or only yet another version of the sexual exploitation of girls and women, I believe it is important to note that the Self-Defense Forces, newly equipped with the legal means to cause mass destruction in the context of war, have adopted such fighting girls into its public relations campaigns. In 2016, three striking female fantasy figures from a new television series titled *GATE–Thus Self-Defense Forces Fought in that [Distant] Land* (GATE–Jieitai kanochi nite kaku tatakaeri) began to appear on SDF recruitment posters, working hard to convince its audience that the SDF's core goal has remained: "to protect someone."

CONCLUSION

Long before the current global debate about child soldiers, children have been eminently useful to military establishments and militarism (Pignot 2012; Robson 2004; Macmillan 2009). Throughout the twentieth century and into the twenty-first, the military and militarism have relied on specific notions of children and childhood. During the first half of the twentieth century, children's use value laid in their presumed vulnerability, innocence, and sweetness, characteristics that could be tapped to paint a picture of war as righteous and just and of the Imperial armed forces as composed of good men out to protect Japan's children and rescue those in colonized territories and behind the frontlines across Asia. During the late twentieth century and particularly during the first decades of the twenty-first, the SDF has made increasing use of children's emotional capital in an effort to build legitimacy for its missions abroad and at home and to shape children's and adults' sentiments towards the armed forces. In publications of the SDF and the growing popular culture around it, representations of children and childlike creatures do a great deal of emotional work to endear the military to a population that had seemed to have overcome the modern habit of glorifying the military and war.

While, thus far, the SDF's missions could not be more different from those of their predecessor, their appeal to the emotional capital of children has only intensified over the last two decades. In both instances, the respective military establishments have worked hard to engage mass and popular culture in order to employ the emotional capital ascribed to children for securing the legitimacy of their missions and, indeed, their existence.

NOTES

1. Both readers were distributed as supplements to the subscribers of *The Housewife's Friend* (Shufu no tomo, vol. 21, no. 8, 8 July 1937, and vol. 21, no. 2, 8 February 1937, respectively); the issues were between 330 and 450 pages long.

2. For the video, see "Japan Maritime Self Defense Recruiting Video -2008-," YouTube video, posted by Tarō Yamamoto on 29 March 2009, https://www.youtube.com/watch?v=Ejiog3AM9do.

3. For the manga and animations mentioned in this paragraph, see http://movie.douban.com/photos/photo/2235646233/ and http://movie.douban.com/photos/photo/2220906719/ (accessed 3 May 2015). These images are widely shared by Internet users throughout Asia on video-sharing sites, including the Chinese platform Douban, for other users to comment on.

BIBLIOGRAPHY

Note: Unless noted otherwise the place of publication for Japanese books is Tokyo.

Allison, Anne. 2005. *Millennial Monsters: Japanese Toys and the Global Imagination.* Berkeley: University of California Press.

Ambaras, David R. 2006. *Bad Youth: Juvenile Delinquency and the Politics of Everyday Life in Modern Japan.* Berkeley: University of California Press.

Cave, Peter. 2016. "Story, Song, and Ceremony: Shaping Dispositions in Japanese Elementary Schools during Taisho and Early Showa." *Japan Forum* 28(1): 9–31.

Dai Nippon Yūbenkai Kōdansha. 1940. *Kōdansha no ehon: Nippon no rikugun—Jūgo dōwa heitaisan to kodomo* (Kōdansha picture book: Japan's Army—Home-front children's stories about soldiers and children). Dai Nippon Yūbenkai Kōdansha.

Dower, John W. 1987. *War without Mercy: Race and Power in the Pacific War.* New York: Pantheon Books.

———. 2008. "Throwing off Asia II: Woodblock Prints of the Sino-Japanese War (1894–95)." https://ocw.mit.edu/ans7870/21f/21f.027/throwing_off_asia_02/index.html.

———. 2010. *Culture of War: Pearl Harbor, Hiroshima, 9–11, Iraq.* New York: W. W. Norton.

———. 2008. *Certain Victory: Images of World War II in the Japanese Media.* New York: M. E. Sharpe.

Frühstück, Sabine. 2003. *Colonizing Sex: Sexology and Social Control in Modern Japan.* Berkeley: University of California Press.

———. 2007. *Uneasy Warriors: Gender, Memory and Popular Culture in the Japanese Army.* Berkeley: University of California Press.

Fujino Kakinami Atsuko. 2009. "History of Child Labor in Japan." In *The World of Child Labor,* edited by Hugh D. Hindman, 881–88. Armonk, NY: M.E. Sharpe.

Hitler, Adolf. 2010 [1925]. *Mein Kampf,* translated by James Murphy. Bottom of the Hill Publishing.

Hutnyk, John. 2004. "Photogenic Poverty: Souvenirs and Infantilism." *Journal of Visual Culture* 3(1): 77–94.

Ienaga Saburō and Inagaki Masagami. 1994. *Nihon heiwaron taikei 15: Mō hitotsu no hansenfu.* Nihon Tosho Sentā.

Jones, Mark A. 2010. *Children as Treasures: Childhood and the Middle Class in Early Twentieth-Century Japan.* Cambridge, MA: Harvard University Asia Center.

Kameyama Michiko. 1997 [1984]. *Kindai Nihon no kango-shi II: Sensō to kango* [The history of nursing in modern Japan II: War and nursing]. Domesu Shuppan.

Kawasaki, Daiji. 1944. *Mura no hoikusho 5–7* [Village nursery school, for ages 5–7]. Kokumin Tosho Kankōkai.

Kinski, Michael. 2015. "Japanische Kindheiten und Kindheitsbilder: Zur Einleitung." In *Kindheit in der japanischen Geschichte/Childhood in Japanese history,* edited by Michael Kinski, Harald Salomon, and Eike Grossman, 3–32. Wiesbaden: Harrassowitz.

Koresawa Hiroaki. 2009. *Kyōiku gangu no kindai: Kyōiku taishō toshite no kodomo no tanjō* [Modern educational toys: The birth of the child as an object of education]. Nara: Bunkyōdō.

Kushner, Barak. 2007. *The Thought War: Japanese Imperial Propaganda.* Honolulu: University of Hawai'i Press.

———. 2009. "Planes, Trains and Games: Selling Japan's War in Asia." In *Looking Modern: East Asian Visual Culture from Treaty Ports to World War II,* edited by Jennifer Purtle and Hans Bjarne Thomson, 243–64. Chicago: Center for the Art of East Asia, Art Media Resources.

Linhart, Sepp. 2010. "Die Grossasiatische Wohlstandssphäre exemplifiziert auf Ansichts-karten." In *Von der Lust an der Grenzüberschreitung und vom Reiz der Verweigerung,* edited by Ilja Steffelbauer, Bernd Hausberger, and Andrea Schnöller, 137–43. Vienna: Edition Ad Fontes Agricolae.

Lone, Stewart. 2010. *Provincial Life and the Military in Imperial Japan: The Phantom Samurai.* Vol. 58, Routledge Studies in the Modern History of Asia. London: Routledge.

Macmillan, Lorraine. 2009. "The Child Soldier in North-South Relations." *International Political Sociology* 3: 36–52.

Malkki, Liisa. 2010. "Children, Humanity, and the Infantilization of Peace." In *In the Name of Humanity: The Government of Threat and Caring,* edited by Ilana Feldman and Miriam Ticktin, 58–85. Durham, NC: Duke University Press.

Manabe Noriko. 2013. "Songs of Japanese schoolchildren during World War II." In *The Oxford Handbook of Children's Musical Cultures,* edited by Patricia Shehan Campbell and Trevor Wiggins, 96–113. Oxford: Oxford University Press.McCormack, Gavan. 2016. "Japan: Prime Minister Abe Shinzo's Agenda." *The Asia-Pacific Journal: Japan Focus,* vol. 14, issue 24, no. 1 (December 15), http://apjjf.org/2016/24/McCormack.html.

Mishima Akiko. 2005. *Jidō gyakutai to dōbutsu gyakutai* [Child abuse and animal abuse]. Seikyūsha.

Miyazaki Hayao. 2014. "Constitutional Amendment Is Out of the Question." *The Asia-Pacific Journal,* vol. 12, issue 36, no. 1 (September 6), http://apjjf.org/2014/12/36/Miyazaki-Hayao/4176/article.html.

Moriyama Shigeki and Nakae Kazue. 2002. *Nihon kodomo-shi* [A history of children in Japan]. Heibonsha.

Namaye Takayuki. 1919. "Child Welfare Work in Japan." *Extract from Standards of Child Welfare: A Report of the Children's Bureau Conferences,* May and June 1919, conference series 1, Bureau publication 60, 321–38.

Okano Kaori and Motonori Tsuchiya. 1999. *Education in Contemporary Japan: Inequality and Diversity.* Cambridge: Cambridge University Press.

Pignot, Manon. 2012. "Introduction." In *L'enfant-soldat: XIXe-XXIe siècle (Le fait guerrier),* edited by Manon Pignot, 5–16. Paris: Armand Colin.

Robson, Mark. 2004. "The Baby Bomber." *Journal of Visual Culture* 3(1): 63–76.

Scherer, Klaus. 2001. *Kamikaze: Todesbefehl für Japans Jugend: Überlebende berichten.* Munich: Iudicium.

Shigematsu, Setsu. 2012. *Screams from the Shadows: The Women's Liberation Movement in Japan.* Minneapolis: University of Minnesota Press.

Sotozaki Mitsuhiro. 1956. *Kazoku seido kara no kaihō: Katei no kōfuku to minshu shugi o mamoru tame ni* [Liberation from the family system: For the protection of the household's well-being and democracy]. Kōchi: Kōchi Shiritsu Shimin Toshokan.

Takeda Yukio and Toda Katsumi. 1941. *Nippon no kodomo* [Japan's children]. Osaka: Tanaka Tōru.

Tomonaga Sanjūrō, Tanaka Shōzō, and Ienaga Saburō, eds. 1993. *Nihon heiwaron taikei 5: Hansen heiwa bungeishū: Shōsetsu shiika bungei hyōron.* Nihon Tosho Sentā.

Tsuganezawa Toshihiro. 2006. *Shashin de yomu Shōwa modan no fūkei* [Reading the modern landscape of the Shōwa era in photographs]. Kashiwa Shobō.

PART FOUR

Contemporary Japan

10

From Grade Schooler to Great Star

Childhood Development and the "Golden Age" in the World of Japanese Soccer

Elise Edwards

The enjoyment of sports,
The enjoyment of soccer,
The joy of moving your body,
The feeling the moment you score a goal.
The experiences and things learned
During the golden age
Are great assets for the future.[1]

If you are a parent living almost anywhere in Japan with preschool-age children, you may have seen advertisements for or already participated in one of the Japan Football Association's (JFA) "soccer kids" festivals. These festivals target children six years and under and are a central component of a JFA educational initiative launched in 2003, interchangeably called the "kids' programme" and "kids' project."[2] The JFA hosts these daylong, high-energy gatherings for preschoolers along with other events, such as "ladies and girls festivals" and "family *futsal*," several times per month in prefectures from Hokkaido to Kyushu.[3] Uniqlo, Japan's globally known clothing manufacturer and retailer, sponsors the most heavily advertised and attended premier kids' events. In 2015, the JFA proudly held fifteen official "Uniqlo Soccer Kids" events, and for each provided a complete report on the day's activities, including photos, reflections from coaches and prominent attendees as well as tallies of the number of "soccer family" members—kids, parents, and other guests—in attendance. In less densely populated prefectures, such as Toyama and Fukui, attendance runs between two thousand to three thousand people, while events held in Tokyo (at prominent sports venues such as Tokyo Dome and Seibu Stadium) easily draw close to ten thousand attendees, including well over two thousand participants under the age of six.

At these events, parents often hear presentations from JFA coaches and receive pamphlets outlining the importance of physical activity for their children, and, in particular, the importance of play. These inform them that it is vital that children learn to play with a soccer ball, of course. However, the pamphlets point out that it is equally critical to provide children with environments where they can learn many other movements: to run, climb, swing, balance, throw, and so on. Parents are instructed to allow their children to play freely, and to avoid intervening even when they are having "trouble" with playmates. Some pamphlets also look ahead in children's development and inform parents that around the age of nine or ten, their son or daughter will be entering the all-important "golden age."

A concept introduced by top JFA technical staff in the mid-1990s, the golden age is the period between the ages of nine and twelve years when the opportunity for physical skill development is said to peak. Since the early 2000s, the rapid growth of JFA development programs targeting youth players and their coaches has popularized the golden age to the point that it is now ubiquitously recognized and frequently used in youth soccer coaching contexts. While "youth development" was certainly a part of soccer programming for the JFA and its associated local clubs in previous decades, the JFA's kids' program, inaugurated in 2003, constituted an unprecedented reorganization of resources and activities focused on increasing the number of children playing soccer and the quality of the training provided to them. At the organization's own admission, a great impetus for the change was the men's national team's disappointing performance at the 2002 World Cup, which Japan cohosted with South Korea. A handful of key administrators within the JFA developed the new approach, and with it, a new understanding of children's development and potential

The concept of the golden age popularizes what I will call a vision of a segmented childhood, places a new sense of primacy and gravity on a particular period within new age divisions, and reframes the relationship between youth experience, future potential, and adult performance. The golden age child sits at the center of a system of age grades and developmental stages that popularizes a reformulated vision of the early years of a child's life and figures one's potential in adulthood as intricately and indissolubly tied to experiences and learning accrued prior to the age of twelve. The JFA's kids' project also draws on more long-standing assumptions about the importance of play in child development and is positioned as a clear response to contemporary anxieties around childhood and children. JFA officials appeal to popular fears about children and their future to justify and underscore the value of their activities, yet offer up their own unique set of problems and solutions as well. JFA officials' desires for stronger national team players to help the country win a World Cup, and concerns among parents and society more broadly that children's futures are less than bright, converge in a new game plan that explicitly outlines a path of proper development and skill acquisition that may impose new kinds of pressures and educational expectations on children at exceedingly young ages. Consistent with earlier nationalist projects that have tied Japan's successful future to the proper education and training of children, the JFA locates and imagines not only future World Cup championships, but also Japan's future more broadly, in the bodies of children. (An alternative future is represented by juxtaposing images of soldiers and children; see chapter 9.)

CHILDREN AND NATION

While many JFA administrators and coaches have long extolled the societal benefits of soccer, the men's national team's disappointing results at the 2002 World Cup inspired a dramatic overhaul of the organization's mission and methods, which meant a new approach to the general population and an increased focus on a particular subset of citizens. In its own words, winning a (men's) World Cup by 2050 was going to require a "reformation" and a "reborn JFA" focused and ready to provide children with "the appropriate content at the appropriate age" (JFA 2004: 9). JFA leaders also boldly claimed that the new approach would be good not only for soccer but also for the nation. New marketing efforts promoted the JFA as interested in social welfare and the sport of soccer as a means of producing happier and healthier citizens. The organization liberally attached terms such as "grassroots" and "soccer family" to campaigns encouraging people to participate in soccer regardless of age or ability. The most pronounced shift in the JFA's approach, however, was a new focus on children. "Children are our 'fortune,' so let's get started!" begins the opening line of the JFA's Kid's Programme pamphlet (2004). Having laid out ambitious targets to grow the "soccer family" to five million strong by 2015, and to a whopping ten million by 2050, JFA officials had to increase soccer opportunities for young children, which they have done with considerable success.[4] On the ideological front, the organization also constructed a narrative about the current state of Japanese children, the societal dangers they face, and the role of soccer in curing both the children and their maleficent environment.

Despite its ambitious targets for the "soccer family," the current popularity of soccer in Japan points to the existing societal reach of the JFA and its potential influence in the future. Annually, approximately 7.5 million people—about 6 percent of Japan's total population—play soccer either competitively or recreationally. Almost one million soccer players, males and females ranging from youth to seniors, are formally registered players with the JFA. Based on survey evidence from the JFA and the Sasakawa Sports Foundation, it is reasonable to estimate that at least a quarter or more of all adolescents play soccer and are involved with soccer educators in either school or club settings at some point in their elementary and middle school years. In Japan, as in the United States, soccer is the most popular children's sport. A recurrent survey question in magazines and newspapers involves asking elementary and middle school students about future career aspirations. I have yet to see a survey in the last five years in which the top answer for boys was something other than "become a professional soccer player."

Both online and in print, the JFA's youth program coaching and promotional materials are replete with images of young children of all sizes running with abandon across manicured expanses of green grass, standing contentedly in coordinated uniforms in front of coaches and parents, and playing in large groups, grinning mouths open, their giggles and shrieks almost audible. Both boys and girls appear in the majority of images, thus visually implying that *all* children are "JFA kids."

However, the running narrative in promotional materials also presents the impetus for the kids' project as the desire to improve the men's national team and win future men's World Cups. The fact that a gender-inclusive children's development program is presented as intended to help the country win a future *men's* World Cup is just one example of the ambivalent relationship that the JFA has with female players. Japan's women's national team, popularly known as Nadeshiko Japan, won the women's World Cup in 2011. While it has been impossible for JFA leaders to ignore the team, which captured the hearts of the nation and won the prestigious National Honor Award, the women's team's achievements have never factored into the "JFA Dream" (2005a), and the JFA does not recognize the women's team's World Cup win in 2011 as *the* World Cup championship for which they have been so arduously striving. This does not mean, however, that top soccer officials are against the promotion of girls and women's soccer. Central to all JFA initiatives is a commitment to the value of soccer for promoting the physical and emotional health of all children regardless of gender. JFA coaches and administrators also now commonly acknowledge that supporting female soccer players ends up benefiting the men's side of the sport: beyond expanding the nation's soccer fan base, soccer-loving mothers are a critical means for ensuring the production of future stars. The fact that the men's national team's performances serve as *the* measure of the nation's soccer prowess is significantly shaped by the financial landscape of global soccer, in which men's competitions are the premier money-making events. In addition, persistent assumptions about inherent male superiority in almost all athletic realms set men's performances as the yardstick for calculating not only individual skill, but also the sporting skill of a nation. With regard to the JFA's kids' project, a genuine faith in the positive, child-strengthening—and thus the nation-strengthening—potential of soccer guides the "soccer for all" approach; however, the male bias in Japan and internationally also guarantees that the performance of the country's "best" team—the men's national team—will be the barometer of the quality and success of all youth development programs, and that a *men's* World Cup championship will be the ultimate goal.

Returning to the idyllic scenes of young boys and girls frolicking with soccer balls in JFA kids' project publications, one is immediately struck by the jarring counterpoint often present in the accompanying text. "Children are in danger!"

FIGURE 11. "Children are in danger!" or "Children are danger!" from a section on "changes occurring in children," JFA's Kids' Programme pamphlet, 2004.

large bold script exclaims across the bodies of preschoolers rolling with great hilarity over each other on the ground (figure 11). Due to the ambiguity of the Japanese language, the text could also read "Children are danger!" There is reason to believe the double entendre is intended. The images communicate quickly and positively that soccer is good and fun for children. However, as the reader is drawn in, the text proclaims that beyond the images, and even within the children, danger is present. The logic of the narrative is that a carefully and scientifically managed childhood *could* be idyllic—and this is the future that the JFA wants to promise. Playing both the role of doomsayer and savior, and posing children as both at great risk and of great promise, the JFA engages with some of the most popular contemporary tropes about children in Japan—as well as the national body more broadly—while also trying to make a case for its own societal importance.

Rather than focusing on soccer, as one might expect, much of the content in "Kids' Programme" publications is devoted to the perilousness of children's corporeal and psychological development. For instance, a one page of the pamphlet aimed at parents has an entire page dedicated to current statistics on the most common childhood problems, including physical ailments, school-related issues, juvenile delinquency and criminality, *and* the country's declining birthrate (JFA 2009₄). (Perhaps "kids are in danger" in part simply because there are fewer of them?) Drawing from an issue of the "Children's Physical and Mental Health

White Paper" (Kodomo no karada to kokoro 2005), which includes a compilation of preschool and elementary school teachers' reflections on students' "abnormalities in physical function," the JFA pamphlet presents a rather curious list of "top ten" issues, including bad posture, an inability to sit still in class, lack of flexibility, regular complaints about being "tired," dry skin, and abnormally low body temperature. Longitudinal data is also included, comparing recent data on "abnormalities" with top ten lists from 1990 and 1978, all to underscore the alarming fact that the most common ailments for primary schooled aged children have increased two- to three-fold (JFA 2004: 6).

The problems witnessed in children today, according to the JFA, are caused by dramatic changes in their social and physical environments. A prominent narrative in JFA coaching materials engages in a popular dyadic trope contrasting an idyllic "past" with a problematic "present" (JFA 2004: 5). Children are cast as disadvantaged by a world filled with television, computer games, and other distractions encouraging solitary play. The loss of large families means they are prone to over-scheduling and over-policing by ambitious parents and unable to benefit from the competition and socialization lessons that apparently come with numerous siblings. The "past" is figured as a time of greater discipline and social consciousness, yet also a space of greater freedom to play, to engage with friends, and to explore personal interests (for more on play in the past, see chapters 2 and 8). Teachers held higher status, parents were better disciplinarians, and there was great interaction and connection across generations. According to the JFA, the present social decline takes physical form in the bodies of children, who are increasingly obese, have poor posture due to inadequate back strength, lack dexterity with their hands, suffer from flat feet, "lay atop their desks," and are "unable to sit properly in their chairs" due to overall physical infirmity.

Echoing the JFA's ambiguous entreaty about children being "in danger" or actually "dangerous" themselves, several scholars of Japan have pointed to the rise of a discourse over the last two decades that envisions not only children at risk, but also children *as* risk (Allison 2013; Arai 2000, 2003). Repeating concerns commonly circulated in the media, the JFA alerts readers that "today's children" are potential victims of school bullying, health problems such as high blood pressure and obesity, and psychological threats such as "acute social withdrawal syndrome" *(hikikimori)*. Then again, they are also perpetrators. Since the 1990s, tabloids have regularly featured stories of children as the most pathological of criminals, attacking and sometimes killing their parents or other children. While steering clear of the most sensational stories, JFA materials point to the more commonplace problems that many fear are precursors to the most extreme behaviors: children cannot concentrate, exhibit sudden emotional outbursts, skip school, disrupt and commit violence in classrooms, and are arrested at ever-higher rates. The consistent culprit for all problems—physical, psychological, and behavioral—is a radical reduction in the time children play outside. Reversing that trend, by engaging children in soccer and other sports, will not only save children, according to JFA officials, but the Japanese nation.

Leading scholars of childhood have consistently contended that societal paranoia about dangerous children, or childhood in danger, is typically connected to broader malaise rooted in socioeconomic instability and uncertain futures (Allison 2013; Arai 2003, 2005; Frühstück 2003; Ivy 1995; Stephens 1995). Failing children become both metaphors for and physical evidence of a nation in danger. Throughout JFA materials, changing sociocultural realities, particularly in the realms of home and school, are marked as prime causes of the physical and psychological decline of children. However, the causal relationship also becomes ambiguous: Children's weak and inactive bodies are presented as both reflecting and producing social and moral decline of the nation. "It's not just the soccer world," states current JFA president, Kawabuchi, at the opening of one kids' publication, "the entire Japanese nation must sense the impending crisis and come to grips with it" (JFA 2004: 2). Similarly, pointing to the JFA's "Dream" project and the ultimate goal of winning a men's World Cup by 2050, the organization states that "this is not simply a goal of the JFA, but rather a promise exchanged with all of the people of the nation" (JFA 2011: 2). Japan's "future" depends on parents and other adults applying JFA knowledge in their "own real lives" and taking responsibility to make sure that children are healthy, happy, and in an environment where they can "strive for large dreams" (2). More than anything, however, the future depends on children; they are not only "assets for the future," but "leaders" needed in order for the promise exchanged between the JFA and the nation to become a reality (2). While children are posed as bearers of great responsibility, sport is figured as the only resource left to correct the social ills that are hurting their chances at success. "Sports possess things that are lacking in society," readers are reminded regularly, and provide the only route to restoring them (see JFA 2004: 4). The JFA's child-focused project is nothing less than a nation-saving campaign.

This is not the first time that leaders in Japan have drawn connections between the bodies of children and the health of the nation, and, additionally, trusted in outdoor play and sport for children as a means of strengthening the national body. Until the final years of the Asia-Pacific War, physical education and school sports were central components of the Japanese imperialist state's efforts to train stronger and more disciplined soldiers, and produce healthier mothers capable of reproducing greater numbers of future soldiers to populate Japan's growing empire (Narita 1988: 97). During the Occupation, administrators for the Supreme Commander of Allied Powers (SCAP) again identified children's physical education classes as critical sites for rebuilding the war-torn nation and strengthening the moral fiber of the country. Educators from the United States, for instance, proposed that democratic ideals could be effectively inculcated through activities such as baseball, basketball, badminton, and square dancing (Edwards 2003).

The nationalist rhetoric infusing the JFA's kids' program resonates with language used to justify earlier initiatives. The organization has legitimized its efforts to corral the financial backing of municipalities for new professional J-League teams by asserting that soccer promotes positive citizenship in the form of "sports volunteerism" as well as new relationships between residents, local governments, and corporations that hold the promise of a "happier country" (J-League 1993). The "JFA Academy" system, a year-round residential school and soccer training system started in the early 2000s for promising middle- and high-school-aged players supports a model of "elite education" that the JFA argues is necessary to train leaders ready to "pull up" the rest and help Japan compete on the "world level" (Tashima 2007: 34). The JFA consistently connects its projects with broader national affairs, actively shaping popular understandings of "Japan's problems" while offering up soccer as the surest path to solving them.

While the JFA has eagerly expressed interest in helping the nation-state, the state has reciprocated at times by working in the interest of soccer, and much of that support has been focused on youth. Beginning in the 1980s, government officials, notably Prime Minister Nakasone, dedicated more money to a variety of sports, including soccer, as a means of addressing perceived problems with Japan's image internationally, national pride domestically, and school children specifically. Poor performances by Japanese athletes at international competitions motivated much of the support, but for Nakasone sport was just one prong in a broader plan focused on schools and other institutions that he felt needed to do more to instill national pride, protect "national culture," and positively influence Japan's troubled youth (Seki 1997).

The issue most quickly targeted by Nakasone's advisors and consistently supported financially through the early 1990s by the Ministry of Education and the Japan Sports Association (JASA) was the education of well-trained coaches. In 1987, approximately thirteen hundred soccer coaches were licensed instructors with the JFA, and licensing courses were held at most once annually. By 1993, however, the JFA announced ambitious plans to create sixty coaching academies nationwide and to train and license ten thousand new soccer instructors within the next five years (JFA 1994: 4–11). In 2000, the JFA had exceeded its goals, reporting a total of almost twenty-two thousand licensed coaches. According to the JFA's most recent published reports, in 2015 the count reached almost seventy-five thousand, with the largest proportion (over forty thousand) holding "D" licenses, the most common license for those coaching children's teams (2015). The nationalist interests of state leaders' allowed the JFA to build the country's largest contingent of licensed coaches in any sport in Japan, and more than half of them are trained to work with the youngest of players, those under twelve years—including those in the "golden age." While the Nakasone administration was more focused on gold medals, and the JFA more on the men's World Cup, both goals justified and motivated large expenditures of money and energy and an intensified focus on training children in more programmatic and calculated ways.

The JFA's new formula, tying an elusive World Cup championship to the proper training of the country's youngest soccer players, inextricably links World Cup success, the welfare of the Japanese nation, and the health and well-being of children. It also, however, often conflates them as one and the same. In coaching and promotional materials filled with smiling children and foreboding messages about their welfare, the JFA presents coaches as knowledgeable protectors of children and green soccer fields as havens from a range of contemporary problems negatively affecting childhood. While much of JFA rhetoric engages with an existing discourse about dangerous and endangered children, the organization is also popularizing new knowledge about childhood. The JFA's kids' project is constructing new ways of conceptualizing children, their potentials, and the greatest threats to their well-being.

The ultimate concern for the JFA when it comes to Japan's children is not a general state of ill health, inactivity, or lack of outside play, but rather that children are not learning what they should when they should. According to JFA kids' program materials, many common contemporary child health issues, such as poor posture, fallen arches, inadequate dexterity, and other physical ailments are occurring because children are not learning "age-sensitive abilities" at the appropriate times in their development. "Critical periods" are being missed and a generation of children is under threat of compromising their adulthoods. While couched in images of frivolous and frolicking children's play, the JFA's kids' program is very deliberate and specific in its goals: to provide learning environments "appropriate to a child's stage of development." The JFA's kids' program is built on a model of child development that privileges age as the most reliable predictor of a child's abilities and potential, creates hierarchies of value between children, and marks the period known as the golden age as a time in human life like no other. Similar to the JFA's ambivalent messages about children as promise but also under threat, the construct of the golden age presents an analogous tension of promise and fear as it celebrates the possibilities of this magical window for learning, while simultaneously underscoring the failures that have already occurred and are yet to come if it is not approached properly.

THE CRISIS OF CRITICAL PERIODS

Takeshi Ono is credited with introducing the golden age paradigm to the Japanese soccer world. He began writing about the concept as early as 1996, and by the early 2000s it had become the centerpiece of the JFA's kids' development project. In the mid-1990s, Ono was arguably at the peak of his influence in the JFA, as a member of the coaching staff of the 1998 men's World Cup team and a JFA Technical

Committee member. Now the head manager of a second division J-League team, Ono no longer holds the sway he once did; however, his systematic and scientifically infused approach to youth soccer players has become the bedrock of the JFA Technical Committee's kids' project.[5] His central argument is that there are particular ages when it is "most advantageous" to develop particular physical abilities and skills. Ono and other coaches regularly refer to these stages of development as "critical periods" *(rinkaiki)*, a concept employed in various neurobehavioral fields of child development, such as developmental biology and psychology. Throughout JFA coaching directives, the golden age—the *most critical* of the critical periods— and the developmental periods that surround it are presented as crucial "windows of opportunity." Often in a truly alarmist tone, the publications contend that if critical periods are not approached correctly, the talents of future soccer players— and the future potential of children more generally—will be compromised.

While it is possible to find references to the golden age in conjunction with other sports in Japan and other countries, I have found no other sports league or federation that employs the concept in such a thorough and programmatic way. Also, when Japanese coaches from other sports reference the golden age, they often allude to it as a product of the JFA and its coaches. The primary author of the golden age concept, Takeshi Ono, has stated in various publications that many international football associations employ the paradigm. While it is true that you can find blogs and coaching materials in which coaches from many countries reference the "golden age of development" or the "golden age of learning," here and there, their engagements in no way compare to those of the JFA.

The JFA's reformulated strategy for building a world-champion soccer team starts with the assumption that bigger numbers beget better possibilities: statistically, a larger pool of players increases the odds of finding a superstar. And, while increasing the overall size of Japan's soccer playing population is desirable, the players of greatest interest are some of the youngest of the country's citizens: children under the age of 6 (U-6). These children constitute the base of a development system imagined as a pyramid of players and teams in graduated layers that increase in age and talent and decrease in population while nearing the peak. The full adult men and women's national teams comprise the peak. The other layers between the base and the peak are made up of discrete age groups: U-8, U-10, U-12, U-14, U-16, and U-18. The gradual narrowing of the pyramid indicates that attrition occurs—either voluntarily or via selection—as age increases; the older you get the less likely it is that you will play. The message of ultimate interest to the JFA, however, is that in this schema, a larger base promises a higher peak. Therefore, national team success is largely dependent on the broad and enthusiastic participation of children. Faith in the value of large numbers is not unusual in the world of sports, and, in fact, the logic is often used to explain the success of teams from exceedingly large countries such as the United States, China, Russia, and Brazil. What is arguably distinctive about the

JFA's formulation is the implicit understanding about the relationship between age and potential talent.

In the JFA's pyramidal system, even more crucial than the size of the population, or base, is its age. According to the organization's expositions on coaching children, the ratio of talent is *highest* in the youngest of players, a potential easily lost if not quickly identified and properly nurtured: "We have come to realize that the younger the age the more potential talent there truly is" (2005b: 5). The child's body is imagined as abundant with untapped potential—but that potential diminishes with age. Mirroring the pyramidal shape of the larger soccer playing population, the individual athlete's life-course too is shaped like a pyramid; individual potential diminishes as one grows older. This realization, of course, brings with it a weighty responsibility: "From the perspective of physical growth and development, we know that the amount and range of outside activities that preschoolers experience has an extremely large effect on their future growth" (JFA 2005b: 5). The prospects for mature adult athletes are predetermined, it would appear, on what they did or did not do as preschoolers.

The JFA kids' project engages with existing dominant tropes about childhood but also creates new delineations, complexities, and hierarchies. In contemporary fields of child development, ranging from psychology to neurobiology, it is common to see the child "figured as a more dynamic body than its adult counterpart" (Castañeda 2002: 56). In the JFA age-graded model, children are not only more dynamic and full of potential than adults, but also more so than children just a year or two older. Increasing age may bring greater maturity, but it does not hold greater promise. In contrast to this "dynamic child" paradigm, there also are competing popular and scientific portrayals of children as incomplete, or still "lacking of knowledge, abilities, competencies, morality, or other qualities seen as critical to adulthood" (Montgomery 2009: 56–58). In the JFA's kids' training system, although youth soccer players are always presented with the tacit form of a mature, ideally trained, and capable adult athlete in the background, contrasts between age-levels are foregrounded and treated as much more important. These contrasts, however, are also complicated, as age-levels are not always construed as clearly linearly connected. A fourteen-year-old, for instance, is not simply a more complete version of a twelve-year-old; the fourteen-year old may actually be clumsier and less able to acquire new skills. Age groups have their own unique characteristics and abilities, yet they are also wholly interdependent. If the physical and cognitive potentialities that emerge at one age-level window are not developed and mastered, they cannot be accomplished as successfully (or at all!) in later years; and, thus, it follows that whatever development is targeted in the following stages becomes compromised as well.

While age group divisions existed prior to the kids' program, under its new plan the JFA has segmented existing age groups into smaller units as well as created a brand-new division for preschoolers. The two-year delimited age groups created as part of the JFA's soccer education program do not map onto the age divisions that determine memberships in teams, or registration with the JFA. When the JFA counts the country's soccer-playing population it uses age groups constructed by the education system: elementary, middle school, high school, and post-high school (e.g. college teams, adult club teams, etc.). When local soccer clubs or community groups organize teams, they often use school grades rather than biological ages when composing teams (although, admittedly, these two categories are isomorphic in the Japanese school system). However, for many clubs and teams, even school age is relatively insignificant. Women's soccer clubs, for instance, commonly pool their middle- and high-school-grade players together on a "junior" team, and then have a "senior" team composed primarily of high school graduates. Put simply, the typical vagaries of team composition indicate that frequently age corresponds with ability only in the most general of ways.

The new educational components of the "JFA Dream," however, have dissected and privileged age in new ways. JFA-organized training camps for the most elite players reflect this fact as they split youths up into U-18, U-16, U-14, and U-12 cohorts. International tournaments governed by FIFA (Fédération Internationale de Football Association) impose age grades for competitions for players under twenty-three-years of age (e.g., U-23, U-20, U-17, U-15), thus requiring the JFA to identify and train players for those competitions. However, the JFA's system does not map perfectly onto the one prescribed by FIFA. Furthermore, its educational program extends the age divisions down to those under six years old, a system, to the best of my knowledge, with no counterpart in any FIFA-devised curriculum. Also, it is a system with a gravitational center—the golden age—dictating how age divisions preceding and following it (the "pre-golden age" and the "post-golden age") are understood and valued.

Paradigms of time-limited stages are not new in the sciences of child development; however, the popularization of this model of child maturation in the realm of Japanese soccer coaching, and sports in Japan more generally, is to the best of my knowledge unprecedented, and, I argue, significant. As early as the 1920s, Swiss psychologist Jean Piaget began formulating a theory of children's intellectual development as composed of distinct stages loosely associated with different ages (1970). Unlike the nineteenth-century linear models that preceded it, Piaget's system imagined a series of stages marked by transformative shifts in cognitive capacity. Mastery at one stage was required to pass to the next, and skills attained in previous stages were also thought to transform as new cognitive capacities were achieved in later ones. Analogous to the way a stairway is connected and allows ascent, but is at the same time composed of discrete steps, "Piaget's stages yield a discontinuous but also cumulative, increasingly complex cognitive system" (Castañeda 2002: 48).

In his writing on the golden age, Ono regularly calls on the authority of science to increase the legitimacy of his claims. In addition to using graphs and technical terms, he references some of the most classic—as well as sensational—examples from biology and psychology to explain the concept of "critical periods": kittens with eyesight impairment caused by light deprivation; Amala and Kamala, the "feral" Indian twins reportedly raised by wolves in the 1920s and left developmentally impaired; and, the story of Genie, a young girl confined to her room for thirteen years, leaving her severely behaviorally and developmentally harmed. Perhaps Ono includes these cases, which are far afield from the worlds of sport and soccer, to grab his readers' attention. Whether intentional or not, he links the development of present-day Japanese children with arguably fear-inspiring narratives of drastically different times and even species, underscoring the criticalness of critical periods. "Similar to those cases," he writes, a "critical period" for developing children's athletic ability also exists. The most important of those windows, the "golden age," is between the ages of nine and twelve, "when the neural circuitry of the cerebral cortex is almost complete" (Ono 2005). This period, when the outermost folded neural tissue finalizes its growth, is the "climax for development of movement" and the "optimal time for learning."

According to Ono's exposition, the golden age is not just special, but almost magical, with the human body exhibiting abilities never seen before, and never to be seen again. Ono argues that during this period, and *only* during this period, children are able to grasp and perform new movements quickly and nimbly. This capacity for "instantaneous learning" contrasts strikingly with adults, who have to intellectually comprehend every movement to become proficient. Golden age children, Ono proclaims, "immediately understand a movement when they see it," and can execute it completely and perfectly. Children at this age are cast as almost superhuman. There is nothing "regular" or "normal" about them: "They totally jump over the regular process of learning acquisition" (Ono 2005). This exceptional ability is attributable, Ono asserts, to the "plasticity" of children in this period: their brains can agilely respond to changing circumstances and movements. This plasticity, however, does not last, and the threat of squandering this "critical period" always looms. Furthermore, the stage that follows is as notably unimpressive as the previous one is spectacular. When children enter adolescence and puberty, "they become clumsy," Ono writes, and due to rapid growth in size and strength, it is difficult for them to learn new skills. Even after puberty ends, the learning abilities associated with the golden age "do not return."

Discussions of child development in Ono's works and JFA materials clearly reflect the influence of psychological paradigms traceable back to Piaget; however, when it comes to explaining the golden age, they rely on very early work in the biology of growth and development. They point to the genesis of the golden age in the "Scammon growth curve," a conceptualization of infant and childhood growth developed by biologist Richard E. Scammon in the 1930s. Dusting off old data and combining it with new, Scammon came up with a schema of child development that diverged significantly from earlier models.[6] Scammon found that different parts of a child's body—limbs, immune system, neurological system, internal organs, and so on—grew at different rates. When he graphed these varying growth rates together, they produced an image of nonsynchronous curves, a picture of syncopated growth captured in one frame.

Scammon's work has been foundational in the field of human growth and development and his schema shaped and continues to be reflected in the work of evolutionary biologists, physical anthropologists, and others studying human development. He may, however, be most alive in the hands of JFA coaches. More-over, in the work of Ono and others, the "critical periods" reflected in Scammon's plotted lines take on meaning unique from that intended by Scammon and other biologists who followed with similar research. Scammon's original graph did not factor in the presence or absence of environmental stimuli over the course of a child's development. Instead, the system was assumed to be autonomic. Children's biological development, according to Scammon's formulation, is a process not requiring any particular inputs, and certainly not external vigilance to make sure that windows of development are not missed. It is a process that occurs automati-cally, "a remarkable picture of syncopated growth that clearly represents a great deal of internal, invisible coordination" (Hall 2006: 83). Inserted in the age-based training regimens constructed by Ono and others, however, the complexities of nonsynchronous development signified by Scammon's graph present physical potentialities and learning opportunities that need to be seized and managed. It is not a chart of automatic occurrences, but rather a plotting of "windows of oppor-tunity" that if properly approached can maximize developmental potential—and, thereby increase the possibility that a "star" will appear. Less optimistically, the graph maps "windows of opportunity that nature flings open, starting before birth, and then slams shut, one by one" (Begley 1996: 56–57). Arguably, Scammon's research does not provide the best evidence in support of optimal periods or of the cornerstone of the JFA's youth development program, the golden age. One could argue, however, that Scammon's now iconic graph and the staying power of his original research provides an authority that Ono and other JFA administrators believe lends credibility to the golden age concept and its corresponding procla-mations and projects.

In the first decade of the twenty-first century, more than anything the Scam-mon curve underscored missed opportunities for Ono and other JFA Technical Committee members who were convinced of the inadequacy of Japan's youth development program: "In the case of most children, these important years for the development of movement simply pass without us capitalizing on them; and, trying to regain what has been lost is incredibly difficult" (Ono 2005). Even if training is approached correctly, according to Ono, every developmen-tal opportunity is shadowed by the looming possibility of failure. It is this con-viction that has provided much of the impetus for the JFA's new age-delineated kids' program.

THE FATE OF TWENTY-FIRST-CENTURY CHILDREN

It is too early to know the full effects of the JFA's golden age paradigm and its corresponding educational curriculum, including the new Uniqlo-sponsored kids' festivals. However, conversations I have had with current and former soccer players as well as an informal survey of players and parents of all ages make it clear that the concept of the golden age is well known and has already had palpable effects. Almost half of the people I spoke with and surveyed said that knowledge about the golden age influenced how they approached training individually and how their coaches designed practices. Several noted that they understood that during the golden age period they were "like a sponge," and "could more easily absorb things," so they made a point of trying to get in as much practice time as possible and committed significant time to repetitively training specific skills. Some also expressed concern about missed opportunities ("I wish I had started soccer earlier in life"), and questioned what the golden age paradigm meant for those beyond the age of twelve ("What are you supposed to do when the golden age is over?"). This sample of responses points to some of ways that the concept of the golden age might influence contemporary understandings of childhood and the possible effects of those new understandings. As the JFA continues to expand its kids' project, it is important to note that while JFA officials agree with many scholars and social critics about children and childhood being at risk, they hold different ideas about what the biggest risks happen to be. They also see different responses as necessary to improve the situation of Japan's children, and thereby assure Japan's future.

Since the burst of Japan's bubble economy in the final decade of the twentieth century, scholars, journalists, government officials, and other commentators have expressed a range of concerns about Japan and its future. And, as is often the case in moments of cultural discomfort, many of the concerns have been focused on children. Not surprisingly, the problems of youth have frequently been linked to the failings of Japan's education system, although ideas about what needs to be fixed and how vary widely. Regardless of political affiliation, since the 1980s Japan's reform debate has been "dominated by the language of 'crisis' and 'systemic malfunction'" (Takeyama 2010: 57). For many right-wing politicians, and most prominently, Prime Minister Abe Shinzō, a lack of "moral" and "patriotic" education has left school-age children feeling "worthless," and, in the words of famous neo-nationalist and Abe administration advisor, Watanabe Shōichi, believing that "Japan is no good" (McNeill 2013; Penney 2014). Others have criticized both "relaxed" and creative classrooms and overly competitive and rigid school environments, with some concerned that the former discriminate against already disadvantaged children, and others that the latter are introducing competition at ever-earlier ages to the detriment of children's creativity and psychological well-being (Arai 2005, Tawara and Leibowitz 2008). Many are also concerned that neoliberal logics inherent in practical classroom dynamics and nationalistic "moral" education are effectively (re)producing inequality and self-responsible subjectivities to meet the needs of a capitalist system requiring a "fine-tuned supply of elite and non-elite workers" (Field 1995: 65; also see Arai 2005, 2013). In contrast to Ono and JFA officials, whether it is concerns about insufficient patriotism, or increasing inequality, politicians and other education critics do not tend to express fears about children at particular ages, but rather make more blanket arguments about how the quality of education for all children—from elementary ages through high school—is lacking. It is not that grade levels and age-specific aptitudes are not recognized, but rather that we do not see arguments about a "golden age" for creativity or moral education. While there generally appears to be a more expansive and less segmented notion of childhood and youth in education discourse when compared to the JFA's age-graded schema, in recent decades a few critics have argued that childhood in its entirety is disappearing.

Due to birthrates consistently ranked among the lowest in the world, scholars have asked if Japan is becoming a "childless society," and Japanese government officials have tried to implement a variety of policies and campaigns to stem the tide. Others have more radically asked if "childhood" is even available to those infants who are born. In the mid-1990s, while debates ensued about appropriate education reforms, Japanese literature scholar and social critic Norma Field was one of the most vociferous critics of the "soft violence" inflicted by the Japanese education system on children (1995). She argued that the education system more than anything else was destroying childhood in Japan, and, in fact, making childhood identical to adulthood in the most negative of ways. The unremitting demands, excessive discipline, and relentless competition in contemporary schools, she argued, were causing children to have "adult diseases," such as high cholesterol, high blood pressure, and ulcers (53). Parents and teachers no longer treated children as individuals needing protection, but rather as subjects to be pushed, disciplined, and even punished in order to insure their eligibility for employment in Japan's "frantically competitive society" (60). For Field, school and work had become "increasingly continuous," and the goals of education were devoid of "a modicum of autonomy from the goals of the economy." She found proof in parents', teachers', and students' parallel experiences with chronic fatigue and stress—ailments produced by a system that made inhumane demands of children as well as the adults who supported them (62). In light of golden age logic, it worth noting that Field severely criticized a movement popular at the time that promoted the benefits of educating children when they were "age zero," or even still in utero.[7] Similar exhortations to capitalize on infants' memory capacities, or the proclivities of a child's right brain (which reportedly remains particularly receptive up through the age of seven), or the small motor skills of two year olds, were equally specious and problematic, because the goal was not to produce happier children, but rather "adults tolerant of joyless, repetitive tasks—in other words, disciplined workers" (54).

The JFA too is critical of the education system as well as parents' complicity in a structure that keeps children "over-scheduled," "over-policed," and unable to experience the psychological freedom and physical activity of the nostalgically imagined "past" (JFA 2004: 4). However, much of the training recommended as part of the JFA's new youth program involves significant repetition and discipline. From the JFA's perspective, if the activities are "age appropriate," disciplined practice, even at early ages, does not threaten childhood, but instead helps to protect it. Some might argue that this simply a different path to producing the disciplined and self-responsible subjects needed in the contemporary labor market.

CONCLUSION

Arguments about new continuities between childhood and adulthood forged by the disciplinary mechanisms of the education system are credible and intriguing, not least because it was the advent of formalized education that greatly shaped the delineation of these modern categories of personhood in the first place. It is also worth contrasting ideas about the disappearance of childhood with the vision of development figured by the JFA's "golden age." Rather than erasing the division between childhood and adulthood, it creates new and significant divisions within childhood itself, and arguably establishes discontinuities between the categories of children and adults that did not exist previously. The JFA regularly proclaims that "children are not little adults" and should not be treated as such. In the JFA schema, children are categorically different from adults and not linearly connected across a clearly evolving path of development. In addition, the space of childhood has become more complex, bestowed with internal differences and hierarchies previously unimagined. Rather than fueling anxieties about children without childhoods, the JFA's paradigm poses the conundrum of children never becoming fully formed adults, or, never becoming adults equal to the potential present within them at birth. The flexible yet stage-dependent child embodies the fear that "critical periods," and the golden age in particular, will not be adequately utilized, leaving the child—and the future adult—incomplete and possibly not even close to realizing his or her true potential. Despite all of the discontinuities between childhood and adulthood suggested by the JFA's model, it is reasonable to wonder if, in fact, childhood is not simply being tethered to adulthood in new and potentially troubling ways, since future World Cup wins are conceptualized as largely dependent on how many six year-olds are playing soccer *and* training properly.

The JFA's golden-age-centered system is just one of many contemporary engagements with children and childhood in Japan that attempt to make sense of and propose solutions to the various anxieties attached to youth. For some the answer to unstable presents and uncertain futures is a desperate effort to guarantee children's success in careers and life by drawing education and work into ever-more seamless connection. In contrast, JFA top coaches argue that childhood should be protected and children not rushed into adult tasks. "The appropriate stimuli at the appropriate age," goes the mantra. Instead of teaching children to be adults, the JFA suggests, we must help them be *better children* if there is going to be any chance of promise in their adulthoods. "We can't just wait for children to grow up," writes Tashima Kozo, the present technical director of the JFA, who has continued to develop and assiduously promote the golden age system first envisioned by his predecessor Ono almost twenty years ago (JFA 2004: 10). If not offered the right environment- and age-appropriate stimuli, he argues, critical periods will pass with nothing achieved. Scammon derived his curve from measures of growth and development understood to happen automatically; his curves chart development that is assumed to happen naturally in children in a range of environments. In noteworthy fashion, visionary JFA coaches appropriated that data and their graphic representation to advocate for a view of children as not only endangered but also victims of a society that has waited for them to grow up on their own.

The JFA now sits as not only one of Japan's most popular sports organizations, but also one of the most influential national cultural institutions. Its teams, coaches, and development programs reach all corners of the country and fans and players of all ages. In an effort to produce World Cup-winning teams, the JFA has created a system that delimits childhood in new ways, placing primacy on the acquisition of motor skills, coordination, and athletic talent. It is easy to imagine how a periodization of childhood development derived from measures of physical growth could be applied to other areas of aptitude and which begin before the age of six and end at eighteen, formulate a model of development that is much more interdependent and less forgiving. There are no second chances; windows of opportunity close permanently as age progresses. This new worldview also proposes new hierarchies of value among children, which among many other things place great importance (and, one might assume, pressure) on some children, particularly young children, and lower the expectations and potentials of others.

NOTES

1. Words featured on the inside cover of the JFA's "Kids U-10 Coaching Guidelines" (2003).

2. I will use the terms "kids' program" or "kids' project" to reference this initiative except where "Kids' Programme" is the proper title used in a JFA publication. It is noteworthy that the JFA uses the British English spelling of "programme" on the covers of pamphlets and on websites intended for coaches and parents. In Japanese-language publications, the deliberate use of the British "programme" indexes the JFA's overwhelmingly European orientation and identification.

3. *Futsal* is a variant of soccer that originated in Uruguay in the 1930s. It is typically played indoors on gym floors with five players per side.

4. The JFA has not come close to meeting these ambitious targets. In 2013, the JFA counted all individuals registered with the JFA as players, kids' instructors, *futsal* referees, and so on, and reported a total of approximately 1.5 million in the "family."

5. Ono's expositions on the golden age are featured in JFA coaching publications, on websites (see Ono 2005), and in his book *Creative Soccer Coaching for Training World-Class Players* (1998).

6. Scammon combined contemporary measurements of children's internal organs and lymphatic tissue with data collected by a French nobleman in the mid-eighteenth century, who meticulously documented the physical growth of his son from infancy through adolescence.

7. Before his death in 1997, former Sony CEO Ibuka Masaru wrote several books focused on early childhood development and education, with titles such as *Why Age Zero? Life is Decided at Age Zero* (1989), and *The Fetus Is a Genius: Education Begins before Birth* (1992). Both an education advisor to former Prime Minister Nakasone, and the head of the Organization for Child Development, Ibuka argued that attending vigilantly to early child development was critical to guaranteeing quality of human character, even more so than intelligence.

BIBLIOGRAPHY

Note: Unless noted otherwise the place of publication for Japanese books is Tokyo.

Allison, Anne. 2013. *Precarious Japan*. Durham, NC: Duke University Press.

Arai, Andrea. 2000. "The 'Wild Child' of 1990s Japan." *The South Atlantic Quarterly* 99(4): 841–63.

———. 2003. "Killing Kids: Recession and Survival in Twenty-First-Century Japan." *Postcolonial Studies* 6(3): 367–79.

———. 2005. "The Neoliberal Subject of Lack and Potential: Developing "the Frontier Within" and Creating a Reserve Army of Labor in 21st-Century Japan." *Rhizomes* 10, 1–14.

———. 2013. "Notes to the Heart: New Lessons in National Sentiment and Sacrifice from Recessionary Japan." In *Global Futures in East Asia*, edited by Ann Agnost, Andrea Arai, and Hai Ren, 175–96. Stanford, CA: Stanford University Press.

Begley, Sharon. 1996. "Your Child's Brain." *Newsweek* (February 19): 55–62.

Castañeda, Claudia. 2002. *Figurations: Child, Bodies, Worlds*. Durham, NC: Duke University Press.

Edwards, Elise. 2003. "The 'Ladies League': Gender Politics, National Identity, and Professional Sports in Japan," diss., University of Michigan.

Field, Norma. 1995. "The Child as Laborer and Consumer: The Disappearance of Childhood in Contemporary Japan." In *Children and the Politics of Culture*, edited by Sharon Stephens, 52–78. Princeton, NJ: Princeton University Press.

Frühstück, Sabine. 2003. *Colonizing Sex: Sexology and Social Control in Modern Japan*. Berkeley: University of California Press.

Hall, Stephen S. 2006. *Size Matters: How Height Affects the Health, Happiness and Success of Boys—and the Men They Become*. New York: Houghton Mifflin Harcourt.

Ivy, Marilyn. 1995. "Have You Seen Me? Recovering the Inner Child in Late Twentieth-Century America." In *Children and the Politics of Culture*, edited by Sharon Stephens, 79–104. Princeton, NJ: Princeton University Press.

Japan Football Association (JFA). 1994. *JFA News* 125.

———. 2003. *Kizzu (U-10) Shidō gaidorain* [Coaching Guidelines for Kids (U-10)]. Nihon Sakkā Kyōkai.

———. 2004. *We Start Kids' Programme*. Nihon Sakkā Kyōkai.

———. 2005a. "JFA 2005 Declaration." www.jfa.jp/about_jfa/dream/.

———. 2005b (2009). *We Start Kids' Elite Programme*. Nihon Sakkā Kyōkai.

———. 2009. *We Start Kids' Programme*. Nihon Sakkā Kyōkai.

———. 2011. *Kizzu (U-8/U-10) Handobukku* [Handbook for Kids (U-8/U-10)]. Nihon Sakkā Kyōkai, .

———. 2015. *"Dētabokkusu"* [Data box]. www.jfa.jp/about_jfa/organization/databox/, last accessed January 24, 2015.

J-League. 1993. *J-League Hyakunen kōsō* [J-League one-hundred-year plan]. www.jleague. jp/aboutj/100year.html.

Kodomo no karada to kokoro no hakusho shuppan iinkai. 2005. *Kodomo no karada to kokoro no hakusho* [Children's physical and mental health white paper]. Book House HD.

McNeill, David. 2013. "Back to the Future: Shinto, Ise and Japan's New Moral Education." *Asia-Pacific Journal* 11, issue 50, no. 1: 1–8.

Montgomery, Heather. 2009. *An Introduction to Childhood: Anthropological Perspectives on Children's Lives*. Oxford: Wiley-Blackwell.

Narita, Jūjirō. 1988. *Supōtsu to Kyōiku no Rekishi* [The history of sports and education]. Fumaidō Shuppan.

Ono, Takeshi. 1998. *Sekai in tsūyō suru purēyā ikusei no tame no kurietibu sakkā kōchingu* [Creative soccer coaching for training world-class players]. Taishūkan Shoten.

———. 2005. *Gōruden eiji no shidō* [Coaching the golden age]. http://jcollege.at.webry. info/200501/article_2.html.

Penney, Matthew. 2014. "'Why on Earth Is Something as Important as This Not in the Textbooks?': Teaching Supplements, Student Essays, and History Education in Japan." *Asia-Pacific Journal* 12(1): 1–36.

Piaget, Jean. 1970. *Structuralism*. New York: Basic Books.

Seki, Harunami. 1997. *Sengo Nihon no supōtsu seisaku: Sono kōzo to tenkai* [Sports olicy in postwar Japan: Structure and development]. Taishūkan Shoten.

Stephens, Sharon. 1995. "Children and the Politics of Culture in 'Late Capitalism.'" In *Children and the Politics of Culture,* edited by Sharon Stephens, 3–48. Princeton, NJ: Princeton University Press.

Takeyama, Keita. 2010. "Politics of Externalization in Reflexive Times: Reinventing Japanese Education Reform Discourses." *Comparative Education Review* 54(1): 51–75.

Tashima, Kōzō. 2007. *"Gengo gijutsu" ga Nihon o kaeru* [The "art of language" will change Japanese soccer]. Kobunsha.

Tawara Yoshifumi and Adam Leibowitz. 2008. "The Hearts of Children: Morality, Patriotism, and the New Curricular Guidelines." *Asia-Pacific Journal* 6(8): 1–5.

11

Treatment and Intervention for Children with Developmental Disabilities

Junko Teruyama

Autism has come to be broadly acknowledged in Japan over the past decade through the spread of the term *hattatsu shōgai*. Translated literally as "developmental disability," it is a generic term for congenital disabilities caused by brain disorders. The three major categories of disability that *hattatsu shōgai* encompasses are learning disabilities (LD), attention deficit hyperactivity disorder (ADHD), and autism spectrum disorder (ASD). The term for developmental disabilities is not a diagnostic category in itself. Rather, it is a term in general usage—used by both laypeople and psychiatrists—to refer to any of these disabilities, alone or in combination (see figure 12).

In recent years, educational and welfare policies for children with developmental disabilities in Japan have emphasized the importance of early diagnosis and intervention. The mandatory physical checkup for three year olds has provided one of the primary opportunities for screening, as has the pre-enrollment checkup for elementary school enrollment. Many children who receive diagnoses early on through these screening processes are referred to remedial education programs *(ryōiku)* for the purpose of scaffolding their development and learning, and helping them better adapt to preschool or elementary school regimens. Remedial education programs vary greatly. Since there is no institutionalized system to accredit or license these programs, it is solely up to the parent to choose among a vast range of programs administered by different organizations and based on diverse methods of instruction. Some intervention programs are run by children's hospitals or clinics, while others are run by nonprofit organizations, private corporations, or parents' organizations. Some meet weekly, while others enforce a more intensive commitment or involve overnight stays; still others are based on distance learning.

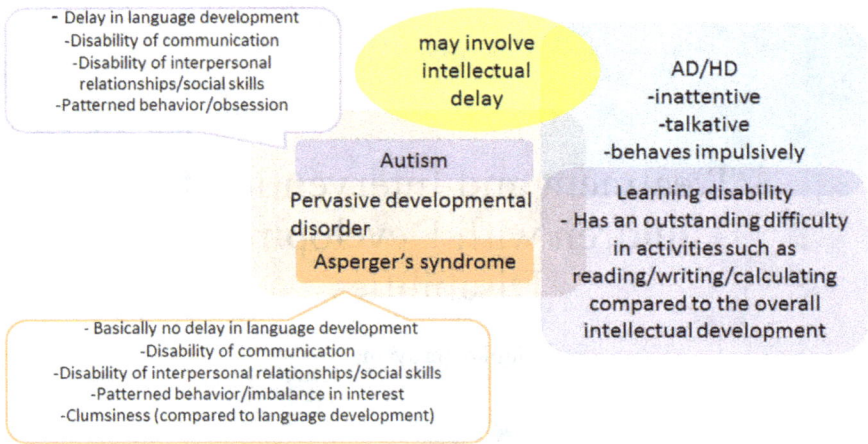

- Delay in language development
-Disability of communication
-Disability of interpersonal relationships/social skills
-Patterned behavior/obsession

may involve intellectual delay

AD/HD
-inattentive
-talkative
-behaves impulsively

Autism

Pervasive developmental disorder

Asperger's syndrome

Learning disability
- Has an outstanding difficulty in activities such as reading/writing/calculating compared to the overall intellectual development

- Basically no delay in language development
-Disability of communication
-Disability of interpersonal relationships/social skills
-Patterned behavior/imbalance in interest
-Clumsiness (compared to language development)

FIGURE 12. Conceptual diagram of developmental disabilities. Courtesy of the author.

Their approaches are similarly diverse, but the most common program consists of social activities and individualized learning exercises, implemented in ways that are informed by practices in applied behavior analysis (ABA), social skill training, TEACCH (Treatment and Education of Autistic and Related Communication Handicapped Children), and play therapy, among other clinical methods of intervention. Some parents elect to try other, less conventional methods such as art therapy or animal therapy, and some program administrators are venturing to collaborate with emerging approaches such as the applied use of robots to assist in social interaction. Apart from the vast array of remedial education programs that are available today, one can find numerous books on how to practice remedial education at home, and there also are many seminars and symposiums for professionals to share and exchange thoughts on successful methods of intervention.

The term *ryōiku* (remedial education) is short for *chiryō-kyōiku* (treatment education) and was originally introduced as the Japanese translation of the German term *Heilpädagogik*. For more than four decades, the term has been used to refer to remedial education programs for children with various disabilities, including physical as well as cognitive disabilities. Early scholars defined *ryōiku* as "a special educational scheme that incorporates findings in medicine, psychology, education, sociology, and engineering, among others, to help with the self-fulfillment of children who will not fully benefit from regular education and instruction" (Itō 1970), and as "education with the purpose of medical treatment, education that includes treatment, or a method of treatment utilizing educational means" (Kan 1969). As implied by these early definitions, the relationship between *chiryō* (medical treatment) and *kyōiku* (education), in the context of *ryōiku* practice, has been, and continues to be, interpreted in multiple and divergent ways. Today, psychiatrists rarely conduct remedial education programs for children with developmental disabilities and, in that sense, the "medical treatment" dimension to remedial education is on the wane. There exists, instead, an increasingly ambivalent sentiment towards the notion of corrective intervention. The "education" dimension, on the other hand, is incorporated in remedial education practices only in a generalized sense, in that most remedial education programs include very little academic curricula and focus more on the child's behavioral and social training and growth (for more on the emphasis placed on social training for young children, see chapter 12).

This chapter is primarily based on my ethnographic fieldwork at several remedial education programs from 2008 to 2010. A significant part of this fieldwork took place at a privately-owned program in a metropolitan setting where I worked as an intern. The program attracted thirty to forty children aged three to fifteen, each of whom belonged to a particular class grouped by age and ability that mostly met once a week. There were two full-time staff members who were responsible for the overall management, and several interns and volunteers who came on a part-time basis to support the day-to-day programs. Apart from this specific program, I also visited several other programs to conduct participant observation and interviews with staff members and parents.

The common purpose of all remedial education programs, despite their diverse methods, is to help children "fit in" at school and in the larger society. The question of what it means to "fit in" entails larger questions regarding individuality and membership in Japanese society. In other words, external factors that define the type and degree of individual "difference" that can be subsumed into the mainstream population inform the designs and practices of intervention programs. Children with developmental disabilities are considered to be incapable of adapting to the regular classroom without the extra support provided by these programs. By looking closely at how these programs function and how they engage with the ideas of *caring* for children with developmental disabilities and *curing* the disabilities, I aim to shed light on the meanings of difference and adaptation, as expressed in practice in the remedial education setting. In other words, I posit that children in this setting act as symbolic agents taking on two conflicting roles; that of the defiant and resistant rebel/delinquent who requires appropriate socialization and training, and that of the vulnerable and susceptible member of society who requires protection, support, and encouragement. I will show how those who work in the remedial education programs interact with the children, interpret their behavior and aim to elicit positive changes while working with these conflicting images of the child. I focus primarily on the environment and the interaction that takes place in this setting, but my observations and interpretations are also informed by semi-structured interviews with parents, staff members, and older children (where possible) that I conducted at a later date.

SPATIAL DISPOSITION AND STRUCTURE

On the first day of my visit to one remedial education program, a staff member welcomed me and told me to wait in the playroom until the day's program started. Several staff members were standing in the room, chatting about the activities that were to take place that day. I sat by myself in a corner of the room, by a wall filled with boxes that contained toys. The room was about seven hundred square feet, the size of an elementary school classroom, and was divided into sections by the placement of low cabinets (see figure 13).

The section that I was in was carpeted so that children could play on the floor. Another section was organized as a workshop with large tables and arts and crafts equipment. The largest section looked like a classroom, with wooden floors and several small chairs and a blackboard mounted on the wall. About fifteen minutes before the program, parents began dropping off their preschool-aged children. The children were allowed to play freely with the toys until the program began. Knowing this, they walked right into my section and started opening the boxes to look for their favorite toys. One of the boys took out a train and started dragging it across the floor. When the train bumped into my foot, the boy looked up and glanced at me without interest. A staff member who was standing nearby spoke loudly in a cheerful tone: "Wow, you're the first one to notice her! She's Junko-sensei." The boy didn't respond, but as he continued to drag the train on the floor, he avoided me.

Seeing that everyone had arrived, the staff members brought the children to the main section and sat the children in small chairs organized in a circle. There were six children, all of them in preschool, and only one of them was a girl. One of the staff members took attendance. When their names were called, children responded by saying *"hai"* (here). Some yelled and jumped up excitedly from their chairs. The girl had turned her chair sideways and sat as if turning her back to the center of the circle. When it was her turn, a staff member walked up to her and held out her hand while calling the girl's name. The girl temporarily turned around and slapped that hand in response. Another staff member standing nearby whispered to me: "That girl has selective muteness. She doesn't speak here. Her mother says she talks just fine at home, though."

After attendance was taken, a staff member placed colored magnetic stickers with illustrations of activities on the board, explaining what activities would take place that day and the order in which they were to be done, thus giving the children a general overview of the day's schedule. Visualization of the day's agenda at the beginning of the day was a crucial part of all the remedial education programs that I observed. It was explained to me that children needed to have a grasp of the larger picture of how the day was going to be organized. Throughout the day, the staff members would continue to remind children of where they were in the schedule, when the current activity was going to finish ("Look at the clock. When the long arm hits eight, you have to come back here"), and what would be coming up next.

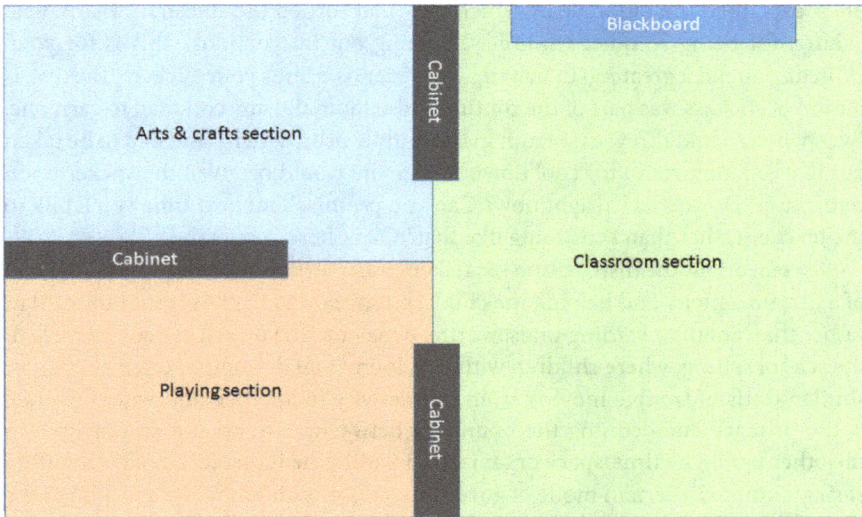

FIGURE 13. Remedial education room layout. Courtesy of the author.

Such instructions were often paired with the disposition of space: certain activities were associated with particular spaces, so that children would move to different sections of the room to read, eat, play, or study. Often children had difficulty letting go of one activity to move onto the next, even when the time was up. They would linger in the reading section, unable to give up the book that they couldn't finish, or would be caught up in the ordeal of arranging their crayons in a particular order of color long after the drawing time was over. In such cases, a staff member would stay with the child and remind him or her that the rest of the group had moved on to a different activity in a different part of the room. This seemed to be effective, because the child often glanced across the room to where everybody else was, and recognized that he or she was behind by that spatial distance from where he or she had been left alone. In some cases, the staff members pointed at the agenda on the board or to the clock, helping the child recognize that the time was over. When even that failed, they would tell the child that they would count to thirty and encourage him or her to finish up with the activity within that time frame so as to join everyone else. Activities were compartmentalized in this way through spatial and temporal allocation, and a great amount of emphasis was placed on the children's ability to perceive the rules of this structure and to regulate their behavior according to the collective schedule.

As an additional measure to enforce this rule, the staff members gave out stickers at the end of each activity; one sticker after the reading period, another after snack time, and another after the art activity. The children were told that they had to "be good" during the activities to earn these stickers, and the staff members often explained the rationale by which they had earned the stickers: "Thank you, Sakura, for being so quiet while I was giving out instructions. This is for you." "Yūichi, you did a great job in helping your friends. Here's your sticker." The distribution of stickers was part of the routine and seldom did any child fail to earn one. Even when a child threw a tantrum in the middle of an activity and had to be taken out to a different room to "cool down," he or she would be given the sticker upon returning: "Do you feel alright now? Can you promise that next time you'll talk to the teacher rather than screaming like that? Okay, here's yours then."

It seemed that the distribution of stickers was more about demarcating the end of a certain activity and helping the children move on to the next event in the day, rather than about rewarding praiseworthy behavior. The practice is comparable to the school setting, where children with developmental disabilities often encounter similar kinds of trouble moving from one activity to another, and where the bell is the primary cue defining the boundary between class, recess, and lunch. On the other hand, the time/space organization within the remedial education setting clearly enforced a certain mode of governmentality. It undoubtedly disciplined the children to follow the existing school system regimen, but it apparently left little room for the children to explore their interests, creatively engage with the activities, or to freely interact with others without the constraints of time and space (for a contrast with wartime Japan, see chapter 8).

The use of picture cards represented another salient feature of the kind of communication that took place between the staff members and the children. Not only were the day's activities depicted on large cards with colored pictures of toys (indicating play time), snacks, and books (for study time), but smaller picture cards were also used in various circumstances during the session. On one occasion, when one of the children displayed unwillingness to participate in an activity, a staff member walked up to him and showed him several cards, asking what he would like to do. He glanced through the cards and, without a word, slapped on one displaying the picture of a toy car. Seeing his response, the staff member said, "Okay, you want to play with cars. Good. The cars are in that basket. Let's go and fetch them." Holding his hand, the staff member led the boy to where the toy cars were stored.

Unlike the aforementioned girl with selective muteness, this boy was capable of expressing his opinion through words, but I learned that an open-ended question like "What do you want to do?" is often more difficult to answer for children with developmental disabilities; communication is made easier by offering them clear choices. This method worked particularly well with children who are stronger in visual input than auditory input, for they often seem to have difficulty taking in a full set of options when choices are spoken or read to them.

The physical layout of the room, visualized schedules, and clear task organization are all adopted from the Treatment and Education of Autistic and related Communication Handicapped Children (TEACCH) program. TEACCH was originally developed in 1966 by Eric Schopler, scholar and psychologist in the department of psychiatry at the University of North Carolina (UNC), as a statewide program for the treatment of autistic children in North Carolina. Sasaki Masami, a Japanese child psychiatrist and a close friend of Schopler's, made numerous visits to UNC and, from the early 1980s, was instrumental in bringing the ideas and practices of TEACCH to Japan. Today, components of TEACCH's treatment style are invariably incorporated into almost all remedial education programs, although few programs make the claim that their practices are strictly and exclusively aligned with TEACCH. In some ways, the essence of TEACCH, called "structured teaching," has become common knowledge among the professionals in the remedial education industry, wherein the "best practices" of remedial education often refer directly to Schopler's innovations: effective room layouts, schedule visualization and use of picture cards.

SOCIAL SKILLS TRAINING AND STRATEGIES OF SELF-CARE

One day, the staff members for the remedial education program that I was observing decided to have the children interview one another. While the children got into pairs and started talking about their favorite TV programs and sports, a boy wandered off to a different section of the room and began playing with toys. A staff member walked up to him and spoke to him in a soft tone. "This isn't the time to be playing. What's wrong?" The boy glanced back at the staff member but didn't answer. "If you don't want to do the interview, you need to talk to Yamada-sensei" (Yamada was in charge of the interviewing activity). With this, the staff member held out his arm, encouraging the boy to stand up and go to Yamada-sensei. The boy hesitantly stood up and went to Yamada-sensei who was watching this interaction. He spoke slowly: "I don't want to do the interview." "Why not?" "It's not fun." After a moment of silence, Yamada-sensei said, "Alright then. Thank you for telling me. You have permission to sit at the back of the room and watch, but don't play with the toys because everyone else would want to do the same, and it won't be fair if only you are allowed to play." The boy nodded with a relieved look and walked to the back of the room, where the staff member who first approached him had pulled out a chair for him to sit on. He spent the next five minutes watching the rest of the class, but became increasingly restless. He finally decided to return to the group and was warmly welcomed by Yamada-sensei.

At the meeting held later in the day, I asked what the staff members thought about this incident. Yamada-sensei replied: "Of course there are times when kids don't feel like participating. We make it a point that that's alright, so long as they speak to one of the staff members about it. We're not forcing them to do anything. But it's problematic when they just wander off like he did; it's not acceptable behavior in school or at work. You need to be able to talk about it. I'm glad you brought this up, because it took us much time and effort to make the kids understand that rule." Another staff member added: "He said the interviewing wasn't fun, and that's okay for preschool kids, but if he were a bit older we wouldn't have tolerated that. Things you do in school aren't always fun, and that's not reason enough to leave the group. Kids in our older-aged group can be exempt from an activity only if they're not feeling well, or something."

Hearing this explanation, I realized that this was a form of social skills training. Social skills training (SST) constitutes a major part of intervention practices in the remedial education setting. In fact, SST has become prevalent in various programs for individuals with developmental disabilities; it is practiced in self-help groups for adults with developmental disabilities, and there are various training courses in which schoolteachers and parents learn the basics of SST. Robert Paul Liberman, a psychiatry professor at UCLA, originally developed the SST training concept in the 1970s and 1980s as a rehabilitation program for persons with schizophrenia. His original work, however, is seldom referenced in the Japanese context. Instead, the term is used in a more generic sense to refer to a diverse range of activities and exercises aimed at enhancing children's capabilities to relate to others in socially appropriate ways. In this instance, the emphasis was not so much on making the children follow the strictly defined routine of the program as it was on helping them understand what constituted acceptable and inacceptable behavior within the context of a given circumstance.

Sometimes, social skills training was taken up in more explicit ways through activities such as role-playing. The roles were typically set up to simulate a situation where there was a clash of interests; sessions led to discussions about the appropriate course of action was to resolve the conflict. For younger children, the general purpose was to teach when to thank or apologize to others, and how to ask for favors. For older children, the scenario was often more realistic and thus complex, involving issues such as bullying, taking sides, reciprocating friendly approaches, and being sensitive to the age or social rank of others. Apart from this structured training, the staff members also gave frequent feedback on the way children spoke to one another and to the teacher. During a drawing activity, one boy asked for an extra piece of paper. Turning to a nearby staff member, he murmured, "paper," at which she handed him the paper replying, "It would've been better if you'd said, 'Please give me a piece of paper.'" In another instance, one child tripped over some Lego blocks with which another child was playing. The boy immediately apologized, "Sorry for stepping on them!" Seeing this, a staff member instantly gave him positive feedback: "That was a good way of apologizing. Well done!" It was through the accumulation of these consistent micro-level interventions that the children slowly learned the "correct" way to interact with others.

Acquisition of such social skills is considered an important component of remedial education programs, for it helps the children to get along better with their peers in school and other social occasions. Expressions of appreciation and apology do not come naturally for many children enrolled in remedial education programs. Instructions such as "try to walk in other people's shoes" and "you should reciprocate kindness" often don't register with them, especially with those with autistic tendencies. It was therefore important for children to have these typically unspoken rules of social interaction be overtly stated through specialized instruction. The staff members often joked about how children new to participating in the program would, without intending to hurt anyone, make mildly offensive comments about staff or the other children. One staff member reported, with a laugh: "When we first met, the first thing he said was 'You're too fat.' He was just being honest, you know. These kids are really honest/innocent *(sunao)* and have beautiful hearts." Not only the staff members of remedial education programs, but also many professionals and parents seem to think highly of the children's honesty. The distinction between *honne* (private self) and *tatemae* (the persona/mask) is learned early on in preschools and elementary schools; these principles constitute a critical dimension to Japanese socialization. The difficulty that the children with developmental disabilities experience in understanding and making use of this distinction in conversation is precisely what necessitates intervention in this field, but many adults, at the same time, seem to think of such honesty as an expression of "beautiful hearts," untainted by social imperatives. As one staff member confided, such honestly is representative of a candidness that fully socialized members of the society are deprived of: "We all think like that, you know, when you try to remember someone, you think, 'Oh that bald man' or 'That short woman' but you can't say that out loud, right?"

Social skills training is, therefore, a form of intervention in the broad sense of the term. But, more precisely, it is a means of having the children acquire the skills to cope in a society filled with people who interact and socialize in ways that may seem unintelligible to them. Without entailing a fundamental transformation in their worldview or personhood, SST helps them effectively "translate" between cultures, so to speak, through the acquisition of a particular mode of language. In this sense, SST is a technique of self-care; it is a survival skill that helps the children avoid unnecessary conflicts or tensions with others.

CARING FOR THE CARETAKERS: MOTHERS AS RECIPIENTS OF SUPPORT

While remedial education programs are principally designed according to the needs of children with developmental disabilities, they also serve an important function for the children's mothers. The brief visits when mothers come to drop off and pick up their children often entail chats with staff members, and casual reporting often takes place regarding how their children had been doing over the past week. The conversation naturally flows to the mothers' complaints about interactions with other family members or with the child's primary school administrators.

More than once I saw mothers shedding tears while confiding their emotional burden and the sense of helplessness and solitude they sometimes felt in raising their children. Such conversations were semi-private. With voices kept low; the content of the discussions rarely entered the weekly staff meeting. Instead I often eavesdropped on such conversations while helping the children get ready to go home. "My mother-in-law disapproves of his disability and says he's just being lazy and keeps asking herself how he ended up this way. She's talking to herself but she knows I'm listening, so it's sort of directed at me, you know . . ." "Yes, it's hard for people of that generation to understand." "Yeah I know, but . . ." "*Okāsan* (mother), you're his only mother. I know it's hard, but you've got to hang in there *(shikkari shinakya)*."

The staff members listened, encouraged, supported, and sympathized with the mothers. It was clear that many of these mothers had few other places to share their feelings. Other than remedial education, there is in fact a dearth of communities and resources directed specifically toward parents who need emotional help in raising children with disabilities. Although parents' organizations fulfill this function in some ways, these are usually run by parents of relatively older children, given the amount of time and commitment that they require. Parents' organizations are also more inclined towards political advocacy and public awareness campaigns, rather than toward peer support around issues of day-to-day care. Mothers with younger children, therefore, have limited opportunities to interact with understanding professionals and sympathetic peers.

Raising a child with developmental disabilities is different from raising a child with congenital physical or intellectual disabilities. Because a developmental disability is usually not visibly identifiable, the child's behavior and inability to comply with certain rules or directions tend to be mistaken for a sign of irresponsible child-rearing practice and lack of discipline by the parents. Mothers involved in the parents' organizations often share bitter episodes of being wrongfully accused of some kind of complicity in their child's (mis)behavior. This social stigma is historically rooted in a long genealogy of scholarship, as well as popular representation that has been instrumental in producing and perpetuating the parent-blaming (and especially *mother*-blaming) discourse. The "refrigerator mother" theory (Bettelheim 1967) blamed mothers as the primary cause for their children's autism, and in the book's Japanese counterpart, the notion of "illness caused by the mother" (Kyūtoku 1979), was used to critique industrialization as having "negatively" shifted the lifestyle of Japanese women, the argument being that modern women had become "narcissistic" and thus were lacking in the "child-rearing instinct" (Lock 1987).

Although these ideas are rarely voiced in such explicit ways today, mothers raising children with developmental disabilities continue to be the target of suspicion and criticism. As exemplified in the conversation cited above, mothers also find themselves in difficult positions within the extended family. The responses of in-laws (the father's parents) usually manifest as either mother-blaming or plain indifference. Family members all too often blame the mother for the child's condition, directly or indirectly, hinting at her inadequacy as the primary caretaker. Mothers tend to internalize this accusation to varying degrees, which consequently shakes their confidence in their own child-rearing skill. In the second type of response, that of the extended family's indifference, inlaws might mention that their children (the husband and/or his siblings) had tendencies similar to developmental disabilities when growing up, suggesting that the mother is being too sensitive, overreacting to behavior that is "normal." In such cases, mothers often have to fight against the family's passive resistance in order to enroll their children in remedial education programs and to get other professional help.[1] In either case, what further complicates family relationships is the idea of blood and heritability.

Research shows that developmental disability is to some degree genetically inherited, although it cannot be traced to a single gene and its mechanism of inheritance is as yet unclear (Bailey et al. 1995; Castles et al. 1999). Most mothers are aware of this, having gained the information through self-help books or other media. Members of the extended family, on the other hand, seem to be mostly unaware of up-to-date information, and thus their responses rely on popular beliefs and uninformed assumptions. In spite of, or precisely owing to this knowledge gap, mothers tend to take their in-laws' comments to heart, interpreting them in light of ubiquitous misinformation and confirming their legitimacy. In the typical parent-blaming scenario, the mother is blamed for introducing a problem that had not existed in the husband's family lineage. One mother I interviewed said that her mother-in-law explicitly stated, "It's not on our side, so it must be in yours. You know someone in your family like this, don't you?" Sometimes the mother herself identifies with the child, recalling that she had similar experiences during childhood, which often deepens and exacerbates her sense of inadequacy. In the typical scenario of extended family indifference, it is very often the case that the father of the child, and/or his siblings, had similar issues, triggering the suspicion of the in-laws that the mother is making a "big deal" out of the child's uniqueness. In this case, the mothers believe that there is indeed a genetic component to the child's condition and that it just went unnoticed for the earlier generations, which only reinforces the mother's urge to seek support and intervention for the child despite the lack of cooperation from her extended family members.

It is under such circumstances that mothers come to rely on remedial education staff members as supportive mentors. Remedial education staff members are not psychiatrists (if they were, they might, in fact, appear too professional—too distant—to the mothers), nor are they schoolteachers or officers in the public welfare administration (who might be threatening in another sense, as stakeholders with authority to provide or withhold resources for children). Instead, remedial education staff members are both accessible individuals with specialized knowledge and providers of the service that the parents have purchased. The relationship they provide aims to strike a balance between the personal and the professional. There is also a gender component to this relationship: a majority of the remedial education staff members are women in their late-twenties to forties, meaning that they are usually around the same age or slightly older than the mothers, making them reassuringly approachable.

Staff members know that the mothers' understanding of, and commitment to, remedial education practice—including its application at home—counts a lot towards a fruitful intervention. Given the limited time that the children spend in remedial education programs (typically around two to three hours a week), the staff members try to engage the mothers as much as possible. Such engagement also entails that the staff members be the mothers' best listeners, at times providing a shoulder to cry on. Thus remedial education programs become a place where mothers can confide their stories and release their stress and pressure, providing a short respite from their daily lives. The staff members then encourage them and help them to move forward.

AMBIVALENCE TOWARDS THE NOTION OF "CURING": REMEDIAL EDUCATION AS A LIMINAL SPACE

As I have discussed, remedial education involves the practice of *caring* in multiple dimensions. The other key component of remedial education that this chapter seeks to engage, the idea of *curing* developmental disabilities, is similarly complex. When defined as the complete elimination of symptoms, the concept of "cure" becomes a controversial issue among professionals in this field. Throughout my fieldwork, I was taught by the staff members—both explicitly and implicitly—that cure is not the goal of their program, and that it is quite inappropriate to question remedial education's efficacy in those terms. Indeed, there is a consensus within the medical community that developmental disabilities cannot be cured completely through intervention. Still, the sensitivity displayed by remedial education administrators towards the idea of curing went beyond a simple embrace of this notion, which triggered my interest in exploring this issue further. While distancing themselves from the idea of cure, the administrators usually designed their programs to help children expand the realm of their achievement in order to facilitate a positive change in their developmental trajectory. In that sense, it can be said that remedial education staff were negotiating a blurred line between *care* and *cure* in invoking an image of the optimum child as the goal of their programs while carefully distancing themselves from the idea of blindly molding the child to fit the social norm.

Part of this negotiation has to do with remedial education's close relationship with mothers. As I have pointed out, there is an long genealogy of literature of mother blaming and, not surprisingly, such discourses persist. *Sankei News,* a newspaper with nationwide circulation, did a series in 2010 on parental education

("Oyagaku Q&A" 2010). The series emphasized the importance of the parents' roles in supporting the healthy development of children, stating that developmental disabilities can be prevented if parents reclaim "traditional" Japanese childrearing ways. This article stirred a great deal of controversy within the online community of parents, not only because the claim was unsubstantiated, but also because it reads as a shameless revisiting of the idea that illness is caused by the mother. In this discursive context, the notion of curing developmental disabilities becomes a highly sensitive issue, for it evokes the supposition that it is somehow possible to undo the disability through appropriate training and discipline. This idea, then, alludes to the problematic and stigmatizing conclusion that the disability in fact results from certain parenting dynamics.

This is obviously not the only story. The informed ambivalence that the remedial education staff holds towards the notion of cure has much to do with the idea of liminality associated with the space of the program. In a way, both staff members and mothers consider the remedial education program to be an experimental space where children are trained to acquire basic social skills through trial and error. Failing to comply with social norms and expectations is not seen as a problem, so long as nonconforming behaviors are contained within the space of the program, because, in that context, they do not result in significant practical consequences such as having strained relationships with friends or being reprimanded by schoolteachers. For that reason, a staff member will gently tell the child what is wrong and lead him or her to make corrections, so that new behaviors can be practiced in real-life settings. In this sense, remedial education constitutes a liminal space, one free from the social imperatives of actual society. It is a kind of rehearsal—a "mock" society that simulates real-world events. At the same time, though, I found that many staff members shared a romanticized idea of remedial education space as being a space for metamorphosis, where children come to self-awareness and reach significant developmental milestones through their support. Staff members took meticulous notes on children's behaviors and reactions, while awaiting transformative moments with hope. Accounts of best practices, as reported in publications and conferences, are filled with glorious stories of children going through visibly identifiable changes and positive transformations in social engagement. In this sense, the space of remedial education functions as a buffer zone; the programs help bridge the gap between the personal and the social realm, home and school, and relative immaturity and age-appropriate development.

This unique characteristic is at the heart of many remedial education practices. As I have discussed, the process of trial and error is considered to be an integral part of the learning experience. The staff members quietly observe as the child makes mistakes, postponing intervention while the child finds his way on his or her own, and praising his accomplishments when he or she does so. This kind of practice, the staff explains, provides an education that cannot take place in schools with large class sizes and standardized, impersonal curricula. The rules are generally looser than those in the public schools. Staff members have room to provide and engage in alternative modes of communication, such as encouraging the girl with selective muteness to take part in roll call by slapping the hand of a staff member.

Rather than focusing solely on the children's adaptability to the existing educational system, remedial education programs place particular importance on fostering a space where children can experiment and learn in a less structured way, express themselves uniquely, and interact with others more freely. In this sense, although they prepare children for school, remedial education programs do not see themselves as an extension of the public school system, nor do they emphasize the need to mold the children's behavior to adapt to the regular classrooms. In fact, many staff and administrators that I met during the course of my fieldwork seemed to believe that adaptation to school is merely one of the short-term goals, and that remedial education should be conducted with a vision of life beyond school, so as to help the children grow up to be independent members of society, with fulfilling jobs and rich social lives. This promise was reflected in conversations during staff meetings; the staff members very rarely, if ever, spoke from a paternalistic position. They did not see themselves as representative of an institution to which a child should adapt. Rather, they tried their best to put themselves in the children's shoes and to understand how children see and experience the world.

The way in which remedial education grapples with developmental disabilities as a category of disability can be understood as a form of resistance to ableist ideology. Ableism views disability as a deviance from normalcy and thus establishes an imperative to train children to "overcome" their difference and behave as "normally" as possible (Linton 1998). In other words, although remedial education aims to scaffold the children's development, it does not embrace the corrective undertone of authoritatively disciplining the children to forcefully fit them into the mainstream society. Being a "buffer zone" or a space of in-betweenness, it is one of the few places for the children to engage in learning experiences at their own pace, to comfortably be who they are without having to worry about their deviation from the idealized norm. Remedial education staff members are well aware that the ideology of "curing" developmental disabilities would entail a more paternalistic, top-down approach that identifies pathology in the children's behavior and frames difference as a problem to be resolved. In that sense, they reject the premise that children are "afflicted" with a disability that necessarily bars them from mainstream society until they are appropriately treated and trained to conform to the norm. To be sure, the general public's understanding of remedial education is often not too far from the pathologizing model that remedial education staff seek to avoid, but those who work in the industry would see such an agenda as denying the heart of their practice. As much as it is an institutionalized program that tailors to and maintain links to external resources such as clinics, hospitals, schools, and welfare offices, it is also one of the few places where children and their mothers can feel safe and accepted without being pushed and shoved to "fit in."

CULTURAL NOTIONS OF EMBODYING ILLNESS/
DISABILITY

At the end of each day's program, there was a staff meeting to go over the day's activities. On one particular day, the seven staff members who were present sat around a small table in the meeting room and opened their notebooks to take notes. One of the senior members took the initiative and began by going over the operation of the activities: "Some of the children didn't understand the instructions in the role-playing activity and were confused during the first round. Next time we should have a visual board to explain the roles." Others added comments: "Perhaps it would be a good idea to have several staff members come up to the front and play it out, wearing paper masks for each character." "I think the confusion was caused by giving actual names to the characters. We should've just named them 'student A,' 'student B,' 'teacher,' and so on." All members actively participated in the discussion, nodding at one another's suggestions and taking notes. They often referred to ideas and practices they had heard from colleagues in other remedial education institutions that had demonstrated positive outcomes, or cited journal articles and conference presentations that they recently read or attended. In fact, remedial education for children with developmental disabilities has grown into a large industry; major bookstores invariably have sections devoted to remedial education practices, and there are conferences, journals, and funding sources available for professionals. This has entailed the professionalization of remedial education workers and enabled the creation of a forum where knowledge gained from practice is accumulated, evaluated, and disseminated as standardized practice to other remedial education settings across the nation.

The meeting continued, and the discussion began to turn attention to individual children. Each staff member reported on the child in her charge. Many of the comments made in this part of the meeting anticipated how each child was experiencing the environment around him or her: "I think the noise coming from the air conditioner was so overwhelming that he couldn't make out my voice." "He was having a hard time folding the origami, and he finally panicked because he couldn't tolerate his own clumsiness." "I didn't look closely enough, but perhaps she was doing it according to a pattern" are a few of the comments that I heard being made at these meetings, each alluding to how a particular child experienced the day's activities in ways that might be different from others, and thus not immediately apparent to the observer. Their narratives were based on the shared understanding that children with developmental disabilities experience the environment in a different way, and that the disability is manifested precisely in their unique cognition.[2] In essence, developmental disability is seen as deeply embedded in and inseparable from the individual's embodied experience, in a way that is perhaps close to a chronic or constantly present illness or innate weaknesses of the constitution as described by Ohnuki-Tierney (1984). She writes: "Written in two characters, the first one meaning 'carrying' and the second one 'illness,' *jibyō* means an illness that a person carries throughout life, and suffers at some times more acutely than at others. People very often attribute their 'down' condition to an attack by *jibyō*" (Ohnuki-Tierney 1984: 53).

Ohnuki-Tierney cites rheumatism, weak stomach, and high blood pressure among her examples of chronic illness. Innate constitutional weakness, on the other hand, is defined as inherent to the constitution with which one is born, which might be healthy, weak, or susceptible to certain illnesses, and as Ohnuki-Tierney points out, chronic illness and constitutional weakness are at times interchangeable. Although developmental disability is not listed in the repertoire of either, it could just as well be considered as either or both, in the sense that it is something that one is born with and that one has to deal with throughout life; it is inseparable from the character of the person and is also an embodied trait, which manifests itself strongly in some instances while at other times remains latent. The staff meeting can be understood as an exchange of information and ideas regarding the management of a chronic condition, over which the child himself or herself still has little control.

Ohnuki-Tierney goes on to argue that, although Japanese culture provides various means to deal with chronic illnesses, they are "aimed not at the elimination of pathogens, as in biomedicine, but at the restoration of the balance between opposing forces in the body" (Ohnuki-Tierney 1984: 73). In other words, it is essential to learn to live with a chronic condition, effectively managing it to circumvent difficult situations. The idea of "curing" developmental disabilities, on the other hand, evokes the premise of eliminating a foreign pathogen that is inhibiting the child's true individuality. The remedial education programs, in seeking to help children to embody their disability, can be seen as a practice guided by insights echoing those informing Ohnuki-Tierney's work. Remedial education staff guide children with developmental disabilities toward coping with disability in a way that fulfills their academic and social responsibilities while allowing them to feeling comfortable in the expression of their own uniqueness.

CONCLUSION

What I have attempted thus far is to organize my ethnographic data and lay out my thoughts in light of the key concepts of *care* and *cure*. The actual activities, interactions, and exchanges that take place in the programs are more complex than I have described here. The care/cure axes are experimental theoretical devices that I utilize to distill and reframe the essence of remedial education practice. My informants never explicitly referred to the dichotomy of care and cure, nor did they categorize or identify their jobs in these terms. They did, however, have a specific understanding of what intervention should and should not entail, one that seemed to be founded upon a particular understanding of developmental disability and the children who struggle with it. By theorizing this interpretive framework, I am attempting to capture and illuminate some dimensions of the culture of remedial education that are not always apparent, even to those in closely related fields such as education and child psychiatry.

On the other hand, how children are experiencing these programs, what they actually learn, and how they would reflect on their experience later in their lives remains a field to be explored in the future. During my fieldwork, I overheard conversations about how a child who was excelling in the program was experiencing difficulty in real-life social interaction involving stickier situations. I never asked to interview or observe the children outside the program, but wondered how they, in fact, applied what they learned, and whether and how it actually helped them get by. Remedial education is, for better or for worse, a safe laboratory, one that does not replicate the world outside. As a means to move beyond this limitation and to envision a kind of intervention that unfailingly prepares children for the world outside, perhaps there needs to be a stronger focus on peer interaction and on "self-learning" as a practice apart from the adult-initiated learning model that remedial education still tends to privilege. Throughout my fieldwork, I heard the word *kakawari* used numerous times by those in the remedial education industry. While the word literally means involvement or commitment in a relationship, staff members of programs used the term to refer to the ways in which they engage with the children; in that context, the term is defined and shaped through their understanding of the ideal style of intervention. "We need to change our way of involvement with him, because he's not responding well," was a comment that I heard often in meetings. However, at the same time, *kakawari* is a word that refers to interpersonal relationships in a very general sense. To ask about one's *kakawari* with another person is to inquire into how one met that person, what the two have in common, and what ties them together. The image behind this lay usage of the term is that of two equal individuals involved in a mutual relationship. The conflated interpretation of *kakawari* therefore brings intervention and relationship together, indicating that the practice of remedial education, when stripped of its techniques and methods, can be distilled into personal relationships among the individuals present, be they staff members or children. It is a practice of engaging with the children while enhancing their ability to engage with others. In this sense, remedial education should be open to multitudinous and diverse forms of interaction, not limited to the one-directional endowment of knowledge and care from the giver to the receiver. The increasing awareness about developmental disabilities among the general public may entail the involvement of other experts from unexpected fields and industries in the near future, opening up new and different possibilities of intervention.

NOTES

1. In either case, the presence of the child's father is minimal. In some of the interviews with mothers, I explicitly asked what their husbands were doing about the situation, but was unable to elicit much

information. A typical response was that the father was busy with work, had agreed to send the child to remedial education when his wife brought it up, but there hadn't been any further discussion of the topic. Only once did I see a father pick up his child from remedial education, but he left quickly without talking to the staff members.

2. Adults with developmental disabilities have written about their unique bodily experiences. For example, see Ayaya and Kumagaya 2008.

BIBLIOGRAPHY

Note: Unless noted otherwise the place of publication for Japanese books is Tokyo.

Ayaya Satsuki and Shinichirō Kumagaya. 2008. *Hattatsu shōgai tōjisha kenkyū* [Personal research on developmental disability]. Igakushoin.

Bailey, Anthony, et al. 1995. "Autism as a Strongly Genetic Disorder: Evidence from a British Twin Study." *Psychological Medicine* 25(1): 63–77.

Bettelheim, Bruno. 1967. *The Empty Fortress: Infantile Autism and the Birth of the Self.* New York: The Free Press.

Castles, Anne, et al. 1999. "Varieties of Developmental Reading Disorder: Genetic and Environmental Influences." *Journal of Experimental Child Psychology* 72(2): 73–94.

Itō, Ryuji. 1970. "Seishin hakujakuji no chiryō kyōiku (2) Shinrigakuteki tachiba kara" [Treatment education of children with mental deficiency (2): From a psychological perspective]. *Journal of the Japanese Association for the Scientific Study of Mental Deficiency* 4, no. 2.

Kan, Osamu. 1969. "Seishin hakujakuji no chiryō kyôiku" [Treatment education of children with mental deficiency]. In *Seishin hakujaku no igaku*, edited by Kishimoto Ken'ichi. Kanehara.

Kyūtoku, Shigemori. 1979. *Bogenbyō* [Illnesses caused by mothers]. Kyōiku Kenkyūsha.

Linton, Simi. 1998. *Claiming Disability: Knowledge and Identity.* New York: New York University Press.

Lock, Margaret. 1987. "Protests of a Good Wife and Wise Mother: The Medicalization of Distress in Japan." In *Illness and Medical Care in Japan,* edited by Edward Norbeck and Margaret Lock, 130–57. Honolulu: University of Hawaii Press.

Ohnuki-Tierney, Emiko. 1984. *Illness and Culture in Contemporary Japan: An Anthropological View.* Cambridge: Cambridge University Press.

"Oyagaku Q&A." 2010. *Sankei News.* Series published January to June. http://sankei.jp.msn.com/life/education/.

12

Food, Affect, and Experiments in Care

Constituting a "Household-like" Child Welfare Institution in Japan

Kathryn E. Goldfarb

Chestnut House, a small-scale child welfare institution (what would have been called an "orphanage" or "children's home" in the past), is located on the top of a hill and nestled against a thicket of bamboo, flanked by a chestnut orchard and a neighborhood park, in a suburban part of the greater Tokyo area.[1] "Chestnut" *(kuri)* evokes a cozy and life-sustaining closeness to nature. The city opened the institution in June 2009, responding to a shortage of accommodation for children whose parents, for one reason or other, could not care for them. In their families of origin, many of the children had been maltreated and most were neglected. Staff members and the institution's director were poignantly aware that many of the children needed a supportive and caring family—or a family substitute.

Institutions like Chestnut House are part of a recent movement in Japan to make child welfare facilities smaller-scale and to provide "household-like care" *(katei-teki yōgo)* to state wards. At the time of my research, Chestnut House contained five different "houses," each with six children and (on average) two female and one male residential staff. At least half of child welfare institutions in Japan are large, often dormitory-style buildings with meals taken in a large cafeteria, the staff working on a shift system. Chestnut House's child-staff ratio and small size (thirty total children), the separation into individual houses with discrete dining areas, and the residential staff differentiate it from large-scale residences. In fact, the director, Kitahara Shinobu, conceived of Chestnut House as the antithesis of conventional Japanese child welfare institutions, and emphasized the goal of creating a "household-like atmosphere."

My involvement with Chestnut House dates from October 2008, when I began attending monthly training sessions for the staff, who were preparing for the

FIGURE 14. Architectural model on display at the opening of Chestnut House, June 2009. Courtesy of the author.

institution's opening in June 2009. Shortly after it opened, I began conducting participant-observation ethnographic research at it between two and three days each week, spending time with the children and staff in all five houses. In the course of my research until the end of my doctoral fieldwork in December of 2010, I visited between one and four days each month and focused on one house, usually arriving around 3 p.m. when the children returned from school and staying until the children went to bed around 8 p.m. I have continued to be in contact with the staff and children, and visit whenever I am in Japan.

My analysis in this chapter is deeply informed by the relationships I built with the children at Chestnut House. While research focusing on children often seeks authentic "children's voices," this chapter (as with all my work) conveys accounts of the children mostly through the lens of their caregivers. While I received research ethics clearance to interview children, their status as state wards made me concerned that their participation in my research would entail an element of coercion. I had planned to obtain permission from the institutional director and use a child-friendly "informed consent" script that I had developed in advance, but I quickly came to worry: Were the children really "free" to decide to participate in an informed way, particularly since I knew that time with me in the institution was an object of desire and competition among the children? As state wards, whose lives were documented in so many ways beyond their control, was it ethical that I ask their participation in this project whose scope they could not possibly understand? Further, all of the children had experienced trauma of some sort. I feared that discussions with me about their experiences might trigger flashbacks or other problems that the staff would have to negotiate. Despite my desire to more directly convey elements of their experiences to my readers, I judged the risks to the children—and to my relationship with them—to outweigh the research benefits.

My long-term research at Chestnut House has provided a unique opportunity to examine the director's and staff members' efforts to self-consciously work toward making an institution "household-like." While Chestnut House was designed to be as close to a household as possible, the residents of this household were children who were (for the most part) not related to each other, and salaried staff who, although residential, worked in shifts (although their shifts were counted in days, rather than hours) and struggled to balance relationships with other staff, the children, and their own families. According to one staff member, in an effort to create a household community where there was none before, four bodily interactions between children and staff became of central importance: the children and staff slept together, bathed together, brushed their teeth together, and prepared and ate food together. The children and staff had no past together and their future together was circumscribed by a variety of factors, most notably how long the children would actually live at the institution, and how long the staff continued to work there. Thus a few intensely physical and affective practices came to disproportionately constitute and signify the emergent household.

In this chapter, I consider Chestnut House as a social experiment, motivated by normative ideologies surrounding the concepts of "childhood" and "household" or "home," and beliefs about the proper relationship between a household and the surrounding community.[2] In this experiment, staff members foregrounded the expressive relationships understood to ideally inhere in household membership. National discourses regarding the "proper" care for state wards also informed their work in the institution. Thus, common perceptions about childhood and home articulated with public policy and child welfare scholarship to shape a space in which childhood, itself, was imagined and managed as it is in remedial education facilities (see chapter 11). Concretely, the Chestnut House director and staff engaged with idealized conceptions of childhood and household to create an institution that mimicked but did not actually replicate a household (sometimes to the staff members' great distress). The director's goals were relatively modest, focusing on the material qualities of the institution which was defined in part as a place for the children and staff to eat together, a space for the children to be (re)socialized to learn "ordinary" attitudes toward food and self-expression that would give them embodied and expressive tools as unmarked members of society. The staff embraced these objectives, bringing to bear their own interpretations of what a "household" should be—particularly, an affect-laden grouping of intimates that is separate from the surrounding community. Throughout, the institution's director and the staff negotiated institutional constraints as they grappled with the desire to create a "family-like" community for the children. I discovered that changing institutional practices regarding who cooked the main "household" meal challenged the values at the heart of some of these efforts to make an institution into a household.

CREATING "HOUSEHOLD-LIKE" ENVIRONMENTS: CONTEXT FOR A CHILD WELFARE POLICY OBJECTIVE

In Chestnut House's newsletter, the director, Kitahara Shinobu, documented the first month of operation. "The first children to move into Chestnut House were two- and three-year-old babies," Kitahara wrote. "These children come from baby homes or temporary emergency care at child guidance centers. Up until now they lived in groups of ten or twenty other babies, so at first they were not used to life at Chestnut House, living in little houses with specific staff members . . . but within about a week, they became used to the houses and the staff. From now on, they will form attachment relationships with the staff members that will provide a stable foundation for their lives." The terms Kitahara used here to describe Chestnut House—particularly, the concepts of "little houses," "specific staff members," "attachment relationships," and "stability"—are the central concepts that motivate Japan's current child welfare objectives to provide "household-like" care.

In Japan, almost 90 percent of children in out-of-home care are placed in institutions. As of 2015, there were 602 child welfare institutions in Japan, servicing almost twenty-eight thousand children between the ages of two and eighteen, and 134 baby homes, which provide care to around three thousand infants and toddlers. Around forty-six thousand children are in out-of-home care in Japan, approximately 0.2 percent of the child population. Foster care comprises around 10 percent of out-of-home care, servicing about forty-seven hundred children (MHLW 2016: 1). The 2014 Ministry of Health, Labour and Welfare report on the present state of child welfare in Japan notes that while in 2005, 70 percent of child welfare institutions in Japan were classified as large institutions, serving between 50 and 130 children, the government is working to create smaller institutions. Currently, around 50 percent of institutions are classified as "large" (MHLW 2014: 7).

Those critical of Japan's system of large institutions—including the United Nations Committee on the Rights of the Child, to which Japan became a signatory in 1994 (UNCRC 2009)—point out that characteristic problems center on the child-to-staff ratio. A few staff members care for many children at a time, especially during the night when only a handful of staff remain on duty (sometimes only one staff member during the night at baby homes). Lack of supervision leads to an increased likelihood of violence between children as well as between children and staff (Onchōen 2011). Many institutions are overcrowded and daily life is intensely structured by rules, prohibitions, and time schedules. There is often very little privacy, and in many cases the children share items of clothing, shoes, bedding, and eating utensils (Hinata Bokko 2009; Goodman 2000; Hayes and Habu 2006). Critiques often center on the differences between these large institutions and a "typical" household, including attention to the fact that children lack ownership of individual objects like clothing. Material factors articulate with temporal patterns to make institutional living dissimilar to what is "normal" for children who live with their own families.

The Ministry of Health, Labour and Welfare specifies a goal to eventually increase foster care placements to one third or more, a rate similar to that of Germany, Belgium, or Hong Kong (MHLW 2014). In this long-term plan, another third of children would be placed in small-scale group homes of around six children administrated by three institutional staff, and the final third would be placed in institutions of forty-five children or fewer, broken up into smaller units of six to eight children each. Regardless of the type of care, the stated goal is to provide a "household-like" environment for children.

In a policy context where child welfare placements take place predominantly *outside* an actual household, what social and political work is enacted by this discourse regarding "household-like" care, and how are the children inside these institutions implicated in adult world-making projects (Castañeda 2002)? Through 2012, government documents and public discourse often described both institutional care *and* family-based foster care under the same rubric of "household-like care," a slippage that allowed the Japanese government to report that it was increasing household-like care, without specifying whether this care occurred in an institution or a household (Goldfarb 2011). In 2012 these terms were clarified by an advisory committee, which specified that "household-*like* care" would refer specifically to care occurring in an institution (otherwise identified as institutional care), in which residential groupings approximated, as closely as possible, the physical forms of a household. Family foster care would be called "household care" (MHLW 2012).[3] This clarification recognized the ways linguistic manipulation had simultaneously represented children's "best interests" as at the heart of Ministry policies, while perpetuating frameworks that contravened its stated agreement to decrease institutional placements. Children in care here emerged "both as symbolic figures and as objects of contested forms of socialization" (Stephens 1995: 13). Consistent push-back from the United Nations Committee on the Rights of the Child, as well as Japan's own Federation of Bar Associations, which produced critical alternative reports for the UN, illustrate how care for state wards becomes both an object of international discourse and a reflection on the state itself (UNCRC 2009; JFBA 2009; Goldfarb 2015). "Household-like care" is thus deeply situated within contested ideas surrounding childhood in Japan, particularly the tensions between Western notions of "child rights" and a now ingrained practice of institutional care for state wards in Japan. These tensions played out within Chestnut House, as the director and staff members grappled with contemporary ideas about proper childhoods and households, and the practices that undergird contemporary child welfare policy in Japan.

In official documents, the Ministry's guidelines for "household-like care" portray a continuum from a less- to a more-household-like environment, which the Ministry defines according to particular qualities—both material and affective—that are conventionally understood to index a household (MHLW 2011). On one end of the spectrum is an institution with a merely physical resemblance to a household, and on the other end of the spectrum is an actual household where a family lives. Unit-style care, in which a larger child welfare institution is broken into smaller groups of six to eight children, has "household-like *facilities*," the Ministry document notes: a living room, kitchen, bath, washing machines, bathrooms, et cetera. The physical space looks (and maybe even smells) like a household. Further along the spectrum, group homes that make use of houses in the community, rather than an institutional space, are, by that virtue, considered even more "household-like." According to the Ministry document, a maximally "household-like" quality emerges in a "family home," where the children live in the same location where their caregiver lives, and the caregiver does not work on a shift system. This implies that without a shift system, children have optimal opportunities to develop relationships with their caregivers. As part of the effort to develop a "household-like" atmosphere, Chestnut House's staff members were initially hired to be residential, rather than working in hourly shifts.

The Ministry's report suggests that "household-like" institutions allow deeper attachment relationships between children and staff members. This understanding is echoed in Kitahara's own description of Chestnut House. Signs of a household are understood to index social relationships—a position that does not attend to the banal reality that staff member turnover in child welfare institutions is extremely high, such that staff who have been working for longer than three years are referred to as "veterans" (Goodman 2000). Although many youth maintain connections to the institutions where they were raised (Hinata Bokko 2009), many of my interlocutors—staff members at institutions, foster parents, and people who themselves grew up in state care—note that it is often difficult to develop durable relationships with institutional caregivers.

Having an adult to depend on later in life can be particularly important for young people who experienced state care. Youth may remain in Japanese state care (either institutional care or foster care) until they turn eighteen, at which point they are expected to become independent. However, if a young person does not attend high school, he or she must leave the state care system at age fifteen. In special circumstances—as in the case of developmental disability, or when a youth is pursuing higher education—state care may be extended until age twenty. In 2014 the rate of advancement to high school among young people in child welfare institutions was 95.2 percent, near the national rate of 98.5 percent. However, child welfare system graduates' average level of attendance in two-year or four-year colleges (approximately 11 percent) or professional school (approximately 12 percent) is much lower than nation-wide averages (almost 55 percent and 23 percent, respectively) (MHLW 2016; see also Hinata Bokko 2009: 83; King 2012). These disparities become more poignant given the marked focus on maximizing childhood education among other demographics in Japan (Field 1995), and in light of historical trends in the twentieth century for parents to advance their own class status through their children's education (Jones 2010). One reason the transition to "independence" can be difficult, my interlocutors reminded me many times, is that institutional care is exceptionally regimented and allows children and youth few opportunities to learn to care for their own daily needs. Although there are institutions created to help youth transition to independent living, there are otherwise no government-organized aftercare systems, and few nongovernmental organizations that provide support to youth from state care. There are generally no such resources outside major urban centers. Many youth who leave institutional care feel that they have no one to turn to (CVV and Nagase 2015; Goldfarb 2016a).

The director and staff members of Chestnut House were not blind to the difficulty and importance of creating durable relationships between children and staff in the institution. However, the focus on external signs of "household-ness" at the institution indicated a certain blurring of distinctions between material instantiations of household-like things and behaviors, and the objective to create lasting, deep relationships between children and staff. The intense focus on creating a "household-like" atmosphere at Chestnut House spoke to the concomitant difficulty—indeed, in many cases, the impossibility—of providing these children an actual family.

EATING THE SAME FOOD TOGETHER: THE MEANING OF "HOME"

"We want the children to feel that Chestnut House is their home, their *furusato*," Kitahara Shinobu, Chestnut House's first director, told me. "We want it to be a place to return for holidays, a place to visit when they are sad or happy or need advice." The term *furusato* can be glossed as hometown or original home, and in contemporary culture entails a sense of nostalgia, longing, and a desire for a return to one's origins (Ivy 1995). Kitahara had the habit of sketching as he explained a concept. He reached for a pen and a piece of paper and wrote the character for *sato*, the second character in the term. Below the character he drew another image (see figure 15).

"In the archaic form of the character," Kitahara told me, "you see that on the left, you have a person, and on the right, you also have a person. In the middle is a platform with food placed on it for the gods. But it is also an image of two people

FIGURE 15. Kitahara's drawing of the archaic meaning of the character *sato*. Photo by the author.

eating a meal. You have one table and two people eating the same food together: that is the meaning of this character, *sato.* In each house at Chestnut House, you have the children and the adults sitting at the table eating together." For Kitahara, the institution takes on the meaning of "home" through the temporal extension from many moments of eating together that accumulate over time to produce long-term bonds, ties that bind the children to the place and further index the obligation of the institution to maintain long-term connections with them.

Kitahara's description harkens back to early twentieth-century notions of the "household" *(katei)* that emerged in Meiji-era reform movements to democratize and rationalize a properly "modern" family, in contrast to the older, official concept of the extended family *(ie)* (Nishikawa 1995). The imperative to eat the same food at the same time at the same table—a phrase that was repeated to me many times in discussions at Chestnut House—echoes these turn-of-the-century reform movements that advocated the production of convivial "modern" households and families precisely through dining practices (Sand 2003; Muta 1994). Kitahara's connection of eating with ancestor worship is also historically apropos: Jordan Sand cites a magazine on moral instruction and household management, from 1907, that describes "the house as foundation of the state," including chapters focusing "on ancestor worship and the role of the patriarch," that also "instructed that 'houses of the middle level of society . . . should make a custom whenever possible of gathering the whole family for meals'" (Sand 2003: 34). Sand analyzes images of the dining table to explore the historical specificity of the "family circle," which performed the family as a bounded group, in contrast to previous images of the extended family able to incorporate others (see chapters 2 and 3). While past use of individual dining trays (rather than one single table), with the family arrayed before the patriarch "manifested a strict hierarchy of authority," Sand writes, "it was an open structure, since the ring could be expanded to accommodate any number of participants. A common table, on the other hand, created a focus of limited size for a closed and intimate family circle, delineating inside from out at the same time that it implied greater equality within. Peripheral household members, particularly servants, were placed on the outside" (35; also Nishikawa 1995: 8). Thus early twentieth-century commentaries described how Japanese citizens might constitute this new notion of a household precisely through eating practices, simultaneously delimiting inside from outside and narrowing possible group membership. Kitahara reproduced many of these same concepts in both his belief in the performative power of dining practices to create a feeling of "household," and—as will become clear—in the ways that boundaries between inside and outside were themselves key household characteristics (Makino 2003).

From Kitahara's perspective, eating together did much more than produce a home out of the bonds of shared activity. Kitahara and many of his staff viewed food practices as central to the institution's goal to produce community and a fictive kin network for children who had none, and to resocialize the children as "normal" or "ordinary" members of Japanese society. The notion of middle-class status in Japan is often taken as a gloss for being "normal" or average (Vogel 2013), even as the socioeconomic measures that would mark a person as "middle class" often go undefined. Thus, when the director consistently highlighted the notion of "ordinariness," I interpreted this objective to be classed in a particular way. Children in state care are already at an extreme economic disadvantage, and, as discussed above, a large percentage of young people from institutional care do not go on to secondary education. While Kitahara and his staff might not be able to dramatically influence these two factors, they could help shape the children's social and embodied practices to align more closely with values that could be understood as "ordinary" and of unmarked class status.

In lieu of actually *providing* a family for the children, Kitahara brought together the physical layout of the "household-like" institution and its furniture with the objective of eating together to train the children in proper self-expression. The materiality of the institution cultivated an affect-laden environment that would shape children as "ordinary." Specifically, he depicted daily life at Chestnut House as providing the foundation for positive and future-oriented relationships between staff and children. Kitahara argued that the children who first come to Chestnut House are unable to express themselves positively and have little empathy for other people, a result of problematic relationships with parents or a lack of connection to caregivers. For Kitahara and the other staff members, these children enter the institution far from "innocent," and staff members have to be constantly aware of the ways that children's pasts impacted their present and future lives (Stephens 1994: 7, Jenkins 1998). However, Kitahara believed that by eating home-cooked meals with the staff and exchanging affect-laden interaction, these children would become able to positively express themselves verbally; Chestnut House would become a potent "emotional community" with certain agreed-upon norms about proper emotional communication (Rosenwein 2002). The food that the staff members personally prepared for the children conveys the staff's emotion, Kitahara said, which is then transferred to the children. The children in turn reply with positive, not negative, verbalizations. What goes into a child's mouth, Kitahara seemed to believe, is what comes out.

Kitahara told me, "Through eating together, conversation is born, facial expressions are born. A certain atmosphere is born. Within all that, of course you preserve life, but at the same time the meal itself, the dining table itself, create connections between people. . . . It's about something done together, you know, each connection brings about a huge effect."[4] Although it would be nice if the staff made delicious food for dinner, the taste is less important, he said, than the greater goal of the children coming to understand the feelings of other people through the food and the process of eating together. "While they eat together with the staff, the children and the staff talk, the kids are scolded, praised, and through that process, the children come to understand joy, anger, pathos, and humor," he explained. Kitahara's primary focus was on the children's socioemotional development as part of a community (Lewis 2003), particularly the relationships that emerged out of these reciprocal connections.[5]

Many of the children at Chestnut House have histories of maltreatment and neglect, Kitahara continued, and "because of that trauma their verbal expressions to the staff are unpleasant." He mentioned the siblings in the house where I conducted research, a six-year-old girl, Maiko, and her three-year-old brother, Noriaki. "When those kids came to Chestnut House, their greetings were, you know, not 'ohayo gozaimasu' (good morning) but instead 'baka' (stupid), 'unchi' (poop), and 'oppai' (boobs)." From Kitahara's perspective, these negative expressions were reflections of the patterns within their past lives. Kitahara suggested that it was thus necessary to retrain them, to give them new patterns to form the base of social interactions. He traced out this pattern:

> They wake up in the morning, wash their face, brush their teeth, they begin this way. Then they go to the toilet, eat breakfast, prepare for school, go to school, and when they come back from school, they play, they take a bath . . . . Those daily experiences weren't ordinary for them before, but when this comes to be commonsense for them, then they will be able to say "good morning" and "good day." These kids are Japanese, and they should be able to do those greetings. It is at the dinner table where they will learn to express themselves, to express sadness, anger, and they will become ordinary people that way.

Tellingly, Kitahara did not seem to consider that a three-year-old boy yelling "stupid!" and "poop!" is, perhaps, an age-specific behavior common to three-year-olds in general or that this behavior was an expression of frustration or anger at being removed from family. His understanding of verbalizations as indexing concrete past actions and behavior patterns can be seen as a linguistic ideology (Schieffelin, Wollard, and Kroskrity 1998) that informs a coherent theory of child development and guides a program for resocialization. Further, this resocialization program focused on verbal signs of problematic relationships, which were reshaped into socially acceptable modes of affective communication, a process that was intended to reshape the child's relationship with the world (Jenkins 1998: 25).

The topic of greetings upon returning home is one that many people mentioned to me in connection with life in child welfare institutions. In small-scale institutions with residential staff, the same staff member may both send a child off to school and greet him upon his return, as a parent might. In larger institutions, however, there are so many rotating staff that the notion of announcing one's return is nonsensical. Children from larger institutions often do not have the awareness that a greeting upon return is considered normal in Japan. All these routines at Chestnut House were intended to train the children to embody the disciplines and skills characteristic of an "ordinary" Japanese person.

From the perspective of Kitahara and many of his staff members, cooking and exchanging these cooked foods activated the staff and children's senses through smells, sounds, sights, and tastes, all of which formed the basis for interpersonal communication. Acts of evaluation—"It's salty today, isn't it!"—offered the perception that the intersubjective divide had been transcended, that the children and staff, with their individual and sometimes traumatic pasts, could find a meeting point in the banality of everyday commentary about food, and that children who were as yet unable to express their emotions could speak, instead, about eating. Preparing and then eating the same food at the same time linked their individual embodied experiences, and provided a basis for further communicative acts such as normative greetings. This physical set of senses and the exchanges that emerged had the potential to produce community where there was not one. However, for some of the staff members this was only the case if the staff were properly situated as the creators of the food, ideally with the children's participation. If these stipulations were not met, the fragile sense of "home" threatened to give way.

"THERE'S NO SMOKE, THERE'S NO SMELL": THE PROBLEM OF A FIRELESS KITCHEN

Chestnut House staff members knew all too well how little they were able to provide for the children in their care. After all, staff members had homes and families elsewhere, and they knew they were caring for these children for only a limited amount of time. Being able to prepare food with the children, and knowing about and incorporating children's food preferences into meal preparation, mattered to the staff. To maintain the affective and emotionally laden dinner table, many of the staff members felt strongly that the staff themselves must prepare the food and eat together with the children, such that food preparation and dining practices mapped out the boundaries of the "household."

However, the constraints of the institutional form often conflicted with the staff's ideals. At any given time, there were fifteen residential staff, and within a year of opening in June 2009, seven original staff members had quit with new members replacing them. This was probably to be expected given the emotional intensity of the work and the fact that the staff were required to live onsite during their shifts, which lasted between three and five days at a time. In order to comply with labor laws, the staff were considered off duty while the children were at school or sleeping, but in reality they might end up caring for a sick child, helping with administrative work, attending trainings, and meeting with the children's social workers in their off duty time. Further, some staff came to the Kanto area from hometowns elsewhere and had no nearby home to return to on days off, so they were effectively always at their work site. For Kitahara, creating an institution that made the children's well-being and happiness the top priority meant that the staff's well-being was often sacrificed. Almost every staff member with whom I spoke at length expressed concern about his or her ability to stay at Chestnut House long-term.[6]

Facing these issues, Kitahara and the other administrators decided to hire part-time workers to prepare evening meals on weekdays. Despite understanding Kitahara's difficulties with staff retention, I was surprised by this new policy, given the importance Kitahara himself attached to food practices. However, he pointed out that the most important thing was for the children and staff to eat together: the staff did not have to be the ones preparing the meal. Further, the staff could spend more time with the children, particularly helping them study, if they were not responsible for food preparation. Finally, the staff members were still expected to cook rice and make the miso soup for dinner, and they still made breakfast and prepared lunchboxes.

After this change in policy, I conducted in-depth interviews with two of the staff members in the house where I focused my research.[7] Both women, Miyazaki Yūko and Sakai Marina, felt strongly that the use of part-time cooks was not the solution to staffing issues. As Miyazaki said to me, with a wrinkled brow, "What kind of household doesn't *cook?*" Their narratives express an ideal of intensely physical and emotional exchanges made possible only by way of the staff's labor preparing homemade food, a perspective that aligns ideologically with gendered expectations regarding food preparation and care in Japan (Allison 1991). Of course there was diversity among staff perspectives, and other staff members expressed gratitude for the release from an additional daily obligation. Notably, I felt that age was a more significant factor than gender, as staff who focused on the benefits of doing their own food preparation tended to be older. Enjoyment played a role as well: both Miyazaki and Sakai mentioned that cooking offered relief from the pressure of constantly interacting with the children, and was a chance to relax and reflect on the day.

The majority of staff at Chestnut House were in their mid- to late twenties, and Miyazaki, in her late forties with three children of her own, was perceived by the other staff as motherly and experienced. She was also a certified nurse. I was always impressed by her ability to laugh in the face of stressful situations, and she struck me as pragmatic and not overly emotional. I perceived her as maintaining a healthy balance between her work and home life, and on her days off she commonly took camping trips with her daughter, who was in her early twenties. At the same time, I knew that she was emotionally invested in her work at Chestnut House and had become very close to the children, even as she found the work physically and emotionally taxing.

I interviewed Miyazaki a week after the part-time cooks began preparing the evening meals and asked her how she felt about the change. She replied:

> It's like the kids feel there is no connection between them and the meal anymore. We're just pretending to make food, we just dump it onto a plate. When you're actually cooking, the kids come up and say, "I want to do it!" and such, which is communication. Then when we're eating that food at the table they say, "Mmm, yummy," or "We put in too much sugar, didn't we" or something, and that kind of conversation at the table is fun. It's just, I don't know, if the person who made the food isn't there at the table, it feels weird to talk about the food that way. Well, we're all eating the same food at the same table, so there's meaning in that, but . . . there's no smell or noise of food preparation, there's no sense of anticipation for the food, and then none of that communication, the kids wanting to help . . .

For Miyazaki, if the food was not made by a house resident, who also took part in the meal, there was no point in commenting on it: there was no real exchange of time and labor for emotion, no point in evaluating or complimenting food when the person who made it was not there.

Sakai Marina told me that having an "outsider" do the cooking seemed strange because Chestnut House was supposed to be a home, and preparing food while watching the kids is normal in a normal household. The children were initially confused by the change, and would ask, "Why is this person coming to cook here?" and "I don't want to eat it, it's not made by one of the adults that belong here." Sakai noted that Noriaki, the little boy with the penchant for rude greetings, would always ask, "Who made breakfast today?" and she would say, "I made it today," which would prompt a happy, "Mmmm, Mari-chan's breakfast is *yummy*!!!" Sakai told me, "I know he'd say the same thing if I said that today Miyazaki-san made breakfast. . . . I don't know, I think there's meaning in it being someone who lives with you, who spends time with you, who cooks the food." Sakai sensed that there were boundaries between people who belonged inside the house and people who didn't, and that her understanding of those boundaries was the same as that of the children. Further, if Chestnut House was to be experienced as a home, like any other home it too should draw clear distinctions between interior and exterior.

Miyazaki and Sakai's sentiments, that the affect associated with meals changed after the meal policies changed, accorded with my own experiences eating dinner with the children and staff. When the staff were still cooking for the children, dinner conversations were lively with discussion of each dish's qualities, joking about dishes that did not turn out so well, and loud expressions of appreciation from the children. I myself always made sure to thank the staff member who cooked that night. After the part-time workers started preparing the food, however, food was often served lukewarm, which made it less delicious, and conversation about the food itself all but stopped. The children came to be familiar with the part-time cooking staff, but the children in this particular house were uninvolved in food preparation, and the cooks departed as soon as they prepared the meal.

Miyazaki described the recent changes in food preparation as "a little lonely these days." She reminded me of an event that had occurred one time when I was visiting. Maiko, Noriaki's older sister, threw a tantrum about where I was going to sit as we were setting the table for dinner. She had been positioning everyone's chopsticks at their places when she realized I was not going to be sitting next to her. She began screaming, threw all the chopsticks on the floor, and then sank to the floor herself, her legs splayed indignantly as she grabbed the dinner table and pushed it away from her, sloshing the bowls of soup on the table. Miyazaki picked her up and carried her upstairs, and we could hear Maiko's screaming until it was finally quiet. After twenty minutes or so, the two returned to the table to eat after everyone else had finished. We were having *udon* noodles that had been prepared and then delivered by the cook.

> I took her upstairs until she stopped crying and then once she was quiet, we talked. I said, "You know, it was really a shame tonight that dinner became not delicious anymore. Because you had a tantrum, it made us all feel really bad, even though we had yummy *udon* to eat." Then Maiko-chan said, "There's not any *udon*. There's no smoke." [Miyazaki paused and looked at me, significantly.] Then I said, "But the soup looked really yummy, didn't it?" and Maiko-chan said, "It doesn't smell like anything! There's no smoke." And that's when I thought, wow, the kids really get it, don't they. Because when you boil *udon*, when you make the soup and prepare the broth, if maybe the kids are fighting and everyone's kind of mad or something, if they're in a bad mood, the kids still come up and say, "What are we having today?" The fact that there isn't food preparation right before their eyes anymore, it's incomplete, isn't it. . . . It's just . . . There's no fire in the kitchen, you don't feel any warmth . . . The kitchen isn't living, it's that kind of loneliness.

There are several significant moments in Miyazaki's recollection of this incident. It was actually an isolated event—it was not as though Maiko was constantly complaining about the food lacking a smell or not being delicious. However, for Miyazaki, it held meaning. When Miyazaki reproachfully told the little girl that her behavior had made the food less "delicious" for everyone else, Maiko was able to refute Miyazaki's argument by claiming that the food wasn't "delicious" to begin with. If communication and mutual understanding of another's emotions emerge through the process of cooking and eating together, Maiko seemed to be saying that food brought in from the outside cannot function as this medium, and her statements struck Miyazaki, who appeared to agree, as poignant.

Miyazaki herself elaborated her own sense of "loneliness" associated with a fireless kitchen. When she was a child, her mother was hospitalized for a long period of time and there were many days when no cooking was done. During those times, her family brought in food from the outside. "That feeling of the mother being in the hospital, the mother being out of the house, that lack of warmth—and then the image of no fire in the kitchen, somehow they're connected in my mind. Meals are just really important. . . . It's not like we make anything so gorgeous when we cook, or anything!" she said, laughing.

I earlier noted that in order to produce a "household-like" atmosphere in the institution, some physical, daily practices were understood to produce intimacy and shape the children's bodies and minds. Sleeping on the same *tatami* mats on adjoining futons. Keeping toothbrushes lined up on the same sink and brushing teeth together. With the little children, stripping off clothing and bathing together. Eating the same food, at the same table, at the same time. However, these practices lacked something that Miyazaki and Sakai perceived to be inherent in the process of preparing the food. The process of creating food, flavoring it according to one's own preference and one's knowledge of the children's preference, adding a touch of something leftover from a previous meal, making the room smoky with the richness of sesame oil and soy sauce which tempts the children to come see what is on the stove, asking a child to stir the contents of a pan and taste the dish for flavor, and then serving the dishes, placing them on the table, telling the person who made the food that it is delicious, thanking a child for his help. These exchanges of food and words produced a sense of obligation and intimacy that endured over time, long after the food had been given and consumed. The children at Chestnut House may never have experienced exchanges with caregivers that yielded positive emotional bonds, a sense of stability and the possibility to imagine a secure future. To that degree, Miyazaki and Sakai understood the acts of exchange that occurred in the kitchen and at the table to have unique power to shape a child's subjectivity for a future that transcended a particular meal and a particular dining table.

NOT QUITE A HOUSEHOLD, NOT QUITE A COMMUNITY

The staff at Chestnut House were in a difficult position from the start. The institution was supposed to be as "household-like" as possible, but the "household" was composed of paid staff, most of whom did not know each other before they lived together, and who did not consider Chestnut House their own home. The majority of the children had not met before and most were unrelated. Further, the children's very existence at Chestnut House was in many cases considered liminal, since it was hoped that some of the children would reunite with their parents or move into foster care (although to my knowledge, this latter objective has only been met in the case of one child). Despite Kitahara's desire to retain his staff, the staff's involvement at Chestnut House was even more temporary. Takada Hitoshi, a forty-year-old, unmarried male staff member whose narrative I introduce below, noted that the continued entrance and exit of staff members in the institution, while the children themselves remained, was one of the main reasons Chestnut House would not, indeed could not, be a "household" or a "family." Recall that within child welfare circles, a staff member who has worked continuously for three years is generally considered a "veteran." At Chestnut House, each "house" was defined by the children who lived there, not the adults. The staff might rotate in and out and change postings, but the children stayed.[8]

Delineating the staff's relationship with the children was a constant topic of concern. Sakai told me that she would like to take the role of the noisy older sister in the children's lives, by coming by to say hello and check if their rooms were clean. Miyazaki, on the other hand, had to remind herself never to compare the Chestnut House children with her own, because their behaviors, abilities, and ways of self-expression were shaped by pasts entirely different from those of her own children. Further, as much as the job called for intimacy, she was constantly aware of the need to maintain a professional distance.

Takada repeatedly described his role as a staff member not as a "substitute" for the child's parent but, particularly at first, as essentially *other,* not the child's parent and not the child's kin. His relationship with the staff with whom he lived and worked was similarly strange: "We're not the children's mother and father, we're not a couple, we're not married. We are unrelated, we are strangers to each other. We're careful around each other. But otherwise, living at Chestnut House together, everything is as if we *were* a couple. The children may not notice now, but as they grow older, it will come to them: Those people, they're strangers to each other, aren't they." Takada described small moments of alterity when the children's desire for intimacy or lack of self-consciousness came into tension with his own sense of proper distance. "In the bath, it's always like, 'Close the curtain, okay!' If we were a family, closing the curtain would be irrelevant. But it's the same with the other female staff members. I am not married to one of them, I have to explain to the kids, so we close the curtain too. We don't see each other naked." Takada thought that, if they all lived together for many years, they would become *like* family, but the staff members' real family sphere, with their children and spouses if they had them, would reinforce the fact that Chestnut House itself was the only space where they came together. It was the space where staff members worked, and staff members were not there during their vacation days. The children, of course, were always there.

Takada's perspective, however, suggests another interpretation of the expressive role of food at the institution. Takada himself loved to eat, and he didn't mind not being the one cooking. He thought it important for the children to be involved in the cooking process, however, and described how he welcomed the part-time cooks so the children got to know them and felt interested in cooking with them. "It doesn't matter that the cooks aren't part of the house," he told me. "The children receive things from all sorts of people, and I want them to understand that the cooks have made this food for them. We talk about the food at the dinner table and the children tell the cooks when they next see them that the food was delicious, or that they liked such-and-such a dish. That is reciprocity." Takada knew that other members of the staff disliked the changes to the food preparation policy, but he took up Kitahara's argument, saying that he had more time to spend with the children during the day and he was less burdened with extraneous duties.

Takada's ideal image of childcare was one in which children are raised by a community. In contrast to contemporary perspectives of a household as distinctly separated from surrounding families, Takada had a different understanding. "When I was growing up," he told me, "you'd go to the next house and ask to borrow some soy sauce. No matter who was around, they would scold you, there would be an adult to look after you. If we don't return in some way to that era, nothing about institutional care will change," he asserted. Chestnut House would never be truly "household-like" unless it embraced this precept of community-based care. He had felt frustrated many times when he offered to help staff members from other households by watching children from those households, only to be refused. There was the sense at Chestnut House, he said, that the staff from one house would take care of only that house's children. Similarly, many staff members were reluctant for nonhouse staff members to enter the houses. Takada argued that Kitahara's main objective with the part-time cooks was to open up the houses, to give the staff time to play outside with the children from all of the houses, and to create a community.[9] Takada felt that the staff members' resistance to opening their kitchens to outside workers was an expression of this tendency to self-isolate.

The tensions surrounding food preparation at Chestnut House were, I suggest, expressions of the ways the staff members conceptualized "household." Takada's own welcoming of the cooks meant that they became one more node in a network of individuals who were helping to care for the children, one more resource for the children and one more opportunity for an affective relationship. A particular ideology of a proper household, in which the caregiver prepares food that is eaten at the same time in the same place, is an ideology surrounding boundary production and maintenance. These boundary lines are shifting, shiftable—they move depending on the ways "household" is continuously redefined. The affective importance of these boundaries was expressed in the anxiety and frustration of some of the staff when part-time workers took over the emotional labor of cooking. But I must emphasize that my own involvement with Chestnut House was made possible by the inherent flexibility of these affect-laden boundaries. Miyazaki and Sakai's willingness to welcome me into their house illustrated a generosity of spirit that could incorporate the "other" and motivate a shifting of boundaries within the institutional household.

CONCLUSION

I close here by returning to a question posed at the start of this chapter: what sort of social and political work is enacted in discourses and practices regarding "household-like care" in the Japanese child welfare system? I view Chestnut House as a social experiment, because it distilled indices of "household" that the staff were able to enact (with variable efficacy) in an institutional context. The staff remained perennially frustrated by the little they were able to do to give the children a sense of "home." At the same time, policy makers take up the concept of "household-like care" as a call to action for the child welfare world in a way that still does too little to provide children with long-term interpersonal resources. Signs of a household, like a dining room table, took on outsized meaning as staff members invested in meals their hopes for affectively loaded and emotionally potent interactions with children, whom they taught to express feelings in socially normative ways through daily routines like eating. Bodily interactions were ways for staff members to create a "household" atmosphere, but they were also a source of consternation, as in Takada's analysis of how physical intimacies highlighted the stranger status of staff and children. The children's own pasts constantly reemerged in their verbalizations and problematic behaviors. Their behaviors bumped up against the micropractices within institutional life that in turn articulated with national and international discourses regarding proper care for state wards. The often-closed space of the Japanese child welfare institution is, thus, a window into the ways that the proper management of childhood emerges as a vexed aspirational project for those charged with providing a "household" to children without one.

NOTES

1. All names of institutions and interlocutors in this chapter are pseudonyms.
2. In this chapter, I generally use the word "household," but the Japanese word *katei* can be translated as either "household" or "home," and sometimes also "family."
3. For a transcript of these deliberations, see www.mhlw.go.jp/stf/shingi/2r9852000002226q.html. I was told that this policy change occurred in response to critiques raised in Goldfarb 2011.
4. Kitahara's focus on "connection" articulates with the contemporary emphasis on interpersonal ties as crucial bases for sociality in Japan, in part through anxious representations of increasing social isolation (*Muen Shakai* 2010; for analysis, see Nozawa 2015). See Goldfarb 2016b for discussion of the ways Japanese concepts of "connection" are used in adoption and fostering discourses.
5. Connectedness is often a focus for education in Japan outside of child welfare settings, and is in fact a core element of what Shimahara and Sakai (1995) call Japanese "ethnopedagogy," or a cultural theory of teaching. One of their interlocutors describes the connectedness between teacher and student as "a relationship that reinforces the reciprocity of the emotional commitment to one another" (171).

6. By the summer of 2012, only one residential staff member of the originally hired staff remained as a caregiver at Chestnut House (two staff members had moved to exclusively administrative roles). Within the next year, the caregiver shift requirements were changed and none of the staff members were considered "residential."

7. Sakai Marina, the nutritionist, was placed in this house for most of the first year, then moved into the office to focus on her work as the nutritionist, and then began filling in at another house after a staff member quit. Miyazaki Yūko was the only staff member who had been in this house for the entirety of the children's time at Chestnut House, from June 2009. However, Miyazaki left her job around when I left the field, December 2010.

8. In recent changes to institution policy, children, too, have been moved between houses to alleviate interpersonal or other problems between household members.

9. This perspective mirrors understandings of children as threatened by decreasing connections to community more broadly, and concomitant diminished state support for children (Giroux 1998: 268).

BIBLIOGRAPHY

Allison, Anne. 1991. "Japanese Mothers and Obentōs: The Lunch-Box as Ideological State Apparatus." *Anthropological Quarterly* 64, no. 4: 195–208.

Castañeda, Claudia. 2002. *Figurations: Child, Bodies, Worlds.* Durham, NC: Duke University Press.

Children's Views and Voices (CVV) and Masako Nagase. 2015. *Shakaiteki yōgo no tōjisha shien gaido bukku* [A guidebook for the support of former child welfare recipients]. Osaka: Children's Views and Voices.

Field, Norma. 1995. "The Child as Laborer and Consumer: The Disappearance of Childhood in Contemporary Japan. In *Children and the Politics of Culture,* edited by S. Stephens, 51–79. Princeton, NJ: Princeton University Press.

Giroux, Henry A. 1998. "Stealing Innocence: The Politics of Child Beauty Pagents." In *The Children's Culture Reader,* edited by Henry Jenkins, 265–82. New York: New York University Press.

Goldfarb, Kathryn. 2011. "'Household-Like Care' or 'Care in a Household'? Cultural Factors Shaping the Japanese Foster Care System." Paper presented June 13, 2011, International Foster Care Organization Conference, Victoria, BC.

———. 2013. "Japan." In *Child Protection and Child Welfare: A Global Appraisal of Cultures, Policy and Practice,* edited by Penelope Welbourne and John Dixon, 144–69. London: Jessica Kingsley.

———. 2015. "Developmental Logics: Brain Science, Child Welfare, and the Ethics of Engagement in Japan." *Social Science and Medicine* 143: 271–78.

———. 2016a. "'Self-Responsibility' and the Politics of Chance: Theorizing the Experience of Japanese Child Welfare." *Japanese Studies* 36(2): 173–89.

———. 2016b. "'Coming to Look Alike': Materializing Affinity in Japanese Foster and Adoptive Care." *Social Analysis* 60(2): 47–64.

Goodman, Roger. 2000. *Children of the Japanese State: The Changing Role of Child Protection Institutions in Contemporary Japan.* Oxford: Oxford University Press.

Hayes, Peter, and Toshie Habu. 2006. *Adoption in Japan: Comparing Policies for Children in Need.* New York: Routledge.

Hinata Bokko. 2009. *Shisetsu de sodatta kodomotachi no ibasho "Hinata Bokko" to shakaiteki yōgo* [A place to belong for children who were raised in institutional care: Hinata Bokko and social protective care]. Akashi Shoten.

Ivy, Marilyn. 1995. *Discourses of the Vanishing: Modernity, Phantasm, Japan.* Chicago: University of Chicago Press.

Japan Federation of Bar Associations (JFBA). 2009. "The Japan Federation of Bar Associations' Report on the Japanese Government's Third Report on the Convention on the Rights of the Child and the Initial Reports on OPAC & OPSC." www.crin.org/docs/Japan%20Federation%20of%20Bar%20Association%20report%20on%20the%20CRC&OPs.doc.

Jenkins, Henry. 1998. "Introduction: Childhood Innocence and Other Modern Myths." In *The Children's Culture Reader,* edited by Henry Jenkins, 1–40. New York: New York University Press.

Jones, Mark A. 2010. *Children as Treasures: Childhood and the Middle Class in Early Twentieth-Century Japan.* Cambridge, MA: Harvard University Asia Center.

King, Michael Maher. 2012. "Who cares? Exploring the disparity in contemporary Japanese rates of tertiary education progression between children from child welfare institutions and the general population." Master's thesis, University of Oxford.

Lewis, Catherine C. 2003. *Educating Hearts and Minds: Reflections on Japanese Preschool and Elementary Education.* Cambridge: Cambridge University Press.

Makino, Seiichi. 2003. "The Space of Culture." *Association of Departments of Foreign Languages Bulletin* 34(3): 10–14.

Ministry of Health, Labour and Welfare (MHLW). 2011. *Jidō yōgo shisetsu nado no shakaiteki yōgo no kadai ni kansuru kentō iinkai* [Investigative commission report on issues concerning child welfare institutions and social welfare]. June 30.

———. 2012. '*Katei teki yōgo*' to '*katei yōgo*' *no yōgo no seiri ni tsuite* [Putting into order the use of the terms, "household-like care" and "household care"]. Materials distributed at the Social Security Commission of Inquiry, Children's Section, Social Protective Care Advisory Committee meeting, Jan. 16.

———. 2014. *Shakaiteki yōgo no genjyō ni tsuite* [Present conditions in social protective care]. March. www.mhlw.go.jp/bunya/kodomo/syakaiteki_yougo/dl/yougo_genjou_01.pdf.

———. 2016. *Shakaiteki yōgo no genjyō ni tsuite* [Present conditions in social protective care]. November. www.mhlw.go.jp/file/06-Seisakujouhou-11900000-Koyoukintoujidou kateikyoku/0000143118.pdf.

Muen Shakai—"Muenshi" 32000-nin no Shōgeki [Society of no-relation: 32,000 "Muen deaths"]. 2010. Nippon Hōsō Kyōkai.

Muta Kazue. 1994. "Images of the Family in Meiji Periodicals." *U.S.-Japan Women's Journal English Supplement* 7: 53–71.

Nishikawa Yuko. 1995. "The Changing Form of Dwellings and the Establishment of the Katei (Home) in Modern Japan." *U.S.-Japan Women's Journal English Supplement* 8: 3–36.

Nozawa, Shunsuke. 2015. "Phatic Traces: Sociality in Contemporary Japan." *Anthropological Quarterly* 88(2): 373–400.

Onchōen Children's Support Group. 2011. *Jidō shisetsu no jidō gyakutai* [Abuse within child welfare institutions]. Akashi Shoten.

Rosenwein, Barbara H. 2002. "Worrying about Emotions in History." *American Historical Review* 107, no. 3 (June): 821–45.

Sand, Jordan. 2003. *House and Home in Modern Japan: Architecture, Domestic Space, and Bourgeois Culture, 1880–1930.* Cambridge, MA: Harvard University East Asia Center.

Schieffelin, Bambi, Kathryn Woollard, Paul Kroskrity, eds. 1998. *Language Ideologies: Practice and Theory.* New York: Oxford University Press.

Shimahara, Nobuo K., and Akira Sakai. 1995. *Learning to Teach in Two Cultures: Japan and the United States.* New York: Garland Publishing.

Stephens, Sharon. 1995. "Children and the Politics of Culture in 'Late Capitalism.'" In *Children and the Politics of Culture,* edited by Sharon Stephens, 3–48. Princeton, NJ: Princeton University Press.

United Nations Committee on the Rights of the Child (UNCRC). 2009. *Consideration of Reports Submitted by States Parties under Article 44 of the Convention on the Rights of the Child: Japan.* www.refworld.org/docid/4afae5bf2.html.

Vogel, Ezra F. 2013. *Japan's New Middle Class.* 3rd ed. Plymouth, UK: Rowman and Littlefield.

13

Monju-kun

Children's Culture as Protest

Noriko Manabe

Hello! I'm Monju-kun. I've just started tweeting. Public interest in my exis-tence has been fading because of the accident at Fukushima Daiichi, but I don't want people to forget about me. Up to now, I haven't generated a single watt of electricity, yet I've used up 900 billion yen. Some people are inconsid-erate enough to say that I'm a waste of money, but isn't it all for the develop-ment of science? As my dad, JAEA [Japan Atomic Energy Agency], says, "As we attend to our research, we'll hold dear in our hearts that we are using the invaluable taxes taken from everyone in this country." (@monjukun, Twitter, May 4, 2011)

With this self-introduction, Monju-kun—a cartoon character modeled on the Monju fast-breeder reactor (FBR) in Fukui prefecture—made his debut on Twit-ter. He garnered over one hundred thousand followers and published four books, regular newspaper columns, and interviews with key antinuclear figures while posing as a problematic nuclear reactor, personified as a cherubic but sickly boy. Through this character, Monju-kun's creator (hereafter "M.C.") informed citizens about nuclear power, news sources, and antinuclear events, as well as encouraged them to raise their voices in demonstrations.

Monju-kun resembles characters in *manga* (comics) and *anime* (animation) for children, with a fully developed personality and life story that recall those of Tetsuwan Atomu (Iron-Strength Atom, known in the United States as Astro Boy) and Nobita of *Doraemon*, characters from two of Japan's best-loved anime. But both Atomu (derived from "atom") and Doraemon (the cat-robot from the future) are powered by internal nuclear reactors; they were part of the media-intensive process of naturalizing nuclear power into a part of everyday Japanese life (Kine-fuchi 2015: 452). Much of this pronuclear media was directed at children and their mothers, often through the deployment of cute characters like Denko-chan, Tokyo

Electric Power (TEPCO)'s mascot, and Pluto-kun, JAEA's stand-in for plutonium. By harnessing character culture, Monju-kun's creator played on the same methods used by pro-industry bodies to present an alternative take on the nuclear industry, nuclear accidents, and radiation, so that mothers and children could learn about the issues in a friendly, approachable, nontechnical way. This chapter explores the ways in which Monju-kun plays on the tropes of Japanese characters and children's culture, and how these tropes are harnessed in propaganda and oppositional movements alike, much in the same way that children once humanized soldiers (see chapter 9).

WHY MONJU-KUN?

On March 11, 2011, a magnitude 9.0 earthquake and tsunami led to an electricity blackout, precipitating the Fukushima Daiichi nuclear accident. The cores of three nuclear reactors melted down, setting off hydrogen explosions, and the roof of a fourth reactor blew off, exposing spent fuel. As Japanese residents watched the explosions on television, the lack of information caused many to panic over the safety of air, water, food, and land. Government officials—relying on TEPCO, the operator of the troubled plant, for information—played down concerns about radiation, only to report higher numbers months later. As M.C. recounted in anger, "The officials would say it wasn't dangerous, but later on, they'd say, 'Well, actually, a meltdown did occur. Actually, all this cesium and iodine got into the tap water.' It was useless to find out after the fact" (M.C., interview with the author, Tsuruga, October 15, 2013).[1]

But even under such frustrating circumstances, most Japanese could not show their anger, fear, or any emotion other than sympathy for the victims of the disaster, which became known as 3/11; an atmosphere of self-restraint (*jishuku*) had fallen on the country. The nuclear accident became a particularly sensitive topic. Mothers were particularly worried about the impact of radiation on young children's health, but they could not say anything about it. "Radiation became a taboo topic that no one could mention, even among mothers' groups. Everyone, including the press, was censoring him or herself. Physicians held a range of opinions on radiation and health, but the press would quote only those who said, 'It's all fine,' while ignoring the ones who said it was dangerous, 'in order not to worry people.' It made me sad that people couldn't say what they truly thought, or even that they were scared. The accident was having a highly negative psychological impact as well as a physical one" (M.C. interview).

M.C. also recognized that the media, particularly television, was reinforcing this spiral of silence (see Noelle-Neumann 1993) by repeating pronuclear positions such as, "There's not enough electricity," so constantly on television and in newspapers that these positions became de facto "truths."[2] Information was actually being reported, but the most crucial information was being treated like a minor detail:

"It didn't stand out and would go by in an instant. There was a lot of information you'd miss if you weren't reading the newspapers very, very carefully" (M.C. interview). M.C. decided to act as a sort of translator, making the news easy to understand. In doing so, M.C. served a function akin to independent journalism sources like Iwakami Yasumi's IWJ Internet news network, alternative information blogs like *Fukushima Diary*, and blogs and newspapers by popular musicians like Gotō Masafumi of rock band Asian Kung-Fu Generation; such independent content was instrumental in educating the population about radiation, the collusion among the nuclear industry and government officials, and alternative energy solutions. But M.C. had a different orientation: "I'm taking information that looks very difficult to understand and putting it into *childlike* language, *simple enough for even a child to understand,* so that more people would want to read it" (M.C. interview; emphasis mine).

In other words, M.C. purposefully targeted Monju-kun toward mothers and their small children. Historically, Japanese children's culture has had propagandistic elements, allowing the country's leadership to mold its citizens from an early age. For example, school songbooks up to 1945 included many songs that encouraged a pro-military stance—encouraging children to play war games, glorifying self-sacrifice for the emperor, and promoting adulation of the war dead—for the purpose of grooming boys to be prepared for war (Manabe 2012; see also chapters 8 and 9). Furthermore, children's culture is embraced and absorbed into adult culture, partly because it is part of adults' activities with children. Parents and grandparents read children's stories to them, watch children's movies and television programs with them, and sing children's songs with them. As such, much of children's culture is formulated to stimulate adults as well as children—a point which is true for *dōyō*, a type of children's song, many of which are composed for adults to sing to children. Such songs are popular among adults, featuring in concert halls and recordings.

Furthermore, children and their mothers had been among the biggest targets of pronuclear propaganda and needed to hear the counterarguments. During the drive to domesticate nuclear power as safe, modern, and necessary for economic growth, Japanese children's culture became filled with stories that made nuclear power seem natural or even heroic. Nuclear reactors were internalized into the bodies of Astro Boy and Doraemon; they powered the cyclones of Kamen Rider and the mobile suits of Gundam. Godzilla, which had debuted in 1954 as a feared by-product of nuclear testing, had by the mid-1960s become a kiddie hero, protecting mankind using atomic powers. Nuclear power plants often built public relations facilities in their host towns, to which schoolchildren would be taken. Children's characters often adorned these facilities: a stuffed replica of Studio Ghibli's Totoro once welcomed children to the PR facility near the Fukushima Daini plant.[3] Rock star Gotō Masafumi, who visited the nearby Hamaoka PR facility as a child, said that he grew up thinking it was completely normal to live near this plant, which lies near the intersection of tectonic plates. Poster contests sponsored through schools or government ministries encouraged children to reiterate the mantra that nuclear power was safe, modern, and clean. The now infamous sign on the entry to Futaba, the host town for the Fukushima Daiichi plant—"Bright energy of the future"—was the result of one such contest; the winner was a sixth-grade boy. Pictured often after Futaba was evacuated, it became an index of pronuclear propaganda. Mothers, too, not only absorbed this positioning through children's culture, but were also specifically targeted in pronuclear television advertisements, which emphasized the environmental friendliness and necessity of nuclear power. They often pictured children, linking nuclear power with protecting them. Monju-kun was a counterpunch to these pronuclear arguments directed at children and mothers.

Second, mothers were concerned about radiation, which has the most serious effects on babies and young children. Sources of contamination could be anywhere—school lunches, drinking water, milk, playgrounds, puddles on the way home, et cetera. However, mothers were ill equipped to inform themselves. As M.C. told this author, "Mothers with young children are extremely busy, taking care of children all day. They don't have the time to look for information on a PC. Their only tool might be their mobile phones, and they can only gather fragments of information. Their Internet literacy may be low, and they may have difficulty reading through a long essay. For them, a Twitter message of 140 characters and a link to further information is just right. I thought it would be useful to them if I could hand them the information one [data] packet at a time" (M.C. interview).

M.C. also decided to speak in the guise of a cartoon-like character. First, M.C. wished to retain anonymity, likely to avoid the backlash that is commonly directed at antinuclear activists, who are humiliated publicly, lose professional opportunities, and receive physical threats.[4] In addition, M.C. may have wished to avoid disagreements: M.C.'s own family did not know about Monju-kun. Indeed, Japanese are far more likely to use the Internet anonymously than Americans (Morio and Buchholz 2009), which accounts for the more rapid acceptance in Japan of Twitter, which allows multiple accounts, over Facebook, which prefers users to register under their own names. In 2010, only 22.5 percent of Japanese Twitter users held an account under their real names; 70 percent held a pseudonymous account, and 8.5 percent had multiple accounts (Kin 2010: 75). Another survey in 2011 showed that in Japan only 7 percent of Twitter users and 21 percent of social network users (mixi, Facebook) held accounts in their real names (Orita 2014). Through anonymity, more Japanese are able to hold frank discussions that are rare in day-to-day life; some users speak more openly on Twitter than with friends (Kin 2010: 43). Anonymity on Twitter helped not only M.C. to speak out, but also Monju-kun's followers to speak.

The guise of a *character* was also beneficial. As M.C. explained to me: "People are familiar with characters and have friendly feelings toward them. They would prefer to listen to a neutral, cute character chatting away [than to a person] . . . . If the person behind it becomes known, many people will want to attack him. The more conspicuous a person becomes, the more people he will infuriate. On the other hand, it's hard to get angry at this soft, fluffy thing. After all, people really love cute things" (M.C. interview).

THE LOVE OF CHARACTERS

That many Japanese would prefer to learn from a fictional character than a person is hardly strange in a country where children regularly learn about history, politics, Buddhism, and other complex issues through manga. Indeed, cartoons and characters are ubiquitous in contemporary Japanese culture and have a long history. During the Asia-Pacific War, the protagonist of the Momotarō (Peach Boy) fable was made into a character symbolizing the quintessential brave Japanese male. In the 1960s, Tezuka Osamu's *Astro Boy* enjoyed television ratings as high as 40 percent (Aihara 2007: 14). Hello Kitty—perhaps Japan's most famous character—underwent a big boom in the 1990s, when adult women began buying more character goods (Aihara 2007: 43; Yano 2013). According to a survey by toy maker Bandai's Character Research Institute in 2004, character goods (e.g., stuffed toys, pencils, or other items with an imprint of the character) were popular among not only children but also adults, with 90 percent of women and 60 percent of men in their forties owning them (Aihara 2007: 19–21). The Bandai survey found that adults owned character goods to help them relax from the stresses of the day. Characters were substitute mothers that comforted and protected their owners by their sheer presence, allowing some to regress to a childlike state (Aihara 2007, 27–28, 39–41; Yano 2013).

This affection for characters has led corporations to use them to foster intimacy between their goods and consumers (Allison 2006: 14). For example, Peko-chan, a pigtailed girl licking her lips, has been the character mascot of candy retailer Fujiya since the 1950s (Aihara 2007: 14). Local governments and organizations also employ *yuru kyara*—"loose" or "wobbly" characters—as mascots to create a favorable image of towns, local products, or events (Occhi 2012). These characters have personalities and stories that explain how they are related to what they represent. In addition to cartoon logos or animated characters, these characters have a live version (a person in a fluffy costume) that walks around events and greets people, who pose for pictures with them.

The nuclear industry has also had its share of characters. TEPCO, the company in charge of the troubled Fukushima Daiichi Nuclear Power Plant, had a cartoon spokeswoman in Denko-chan (Electric Girl). Pictured as a ponytailed housewife, she appeared in pamphlets, websites, and a series of television commercials encouraging efficient use of electricity and promoting nuclear power. In one 2004 commercial, Denko is shopping at a supermarket and remarks that everything is imported. Suddenly a professor appears, telling her that energy is also imported. He says that electric power companies are importing the source that generates the most energy out of the least amount of raw materials—uranium. He argues that nuclear power raises Japan's self-sufficiency in energy.[5] Denko-chan was decommissioned in March 2012, following the Fukushima Daiichi accident.

Pluto-kun was a mascot character of JAEA, representing plutonium—the radioactive element used in the bomb dropped on Nagasaki and as part of fuel in the Monju fast-breeder nuclear reactor (FBR). He appears in Atom Plaza, JAEA's public-relations building in Tsuruga, Fukui prefecture, where the Monju FBR is located; he also appears on its website. The character looks like a cute little boy from outer space, with a round, smiling face and a helmet with the letters "Pu," the chemical symbol for plutonium. In an eleven-minute video made in 1993, Pluto-kun speaks in a cute, high-pitched, innocent little boy's voice, attempting to dispel all the "negative rumors" about him.[6] In a hurt tone, he says, "Some people exaggerate and talk about me as if I were something really terrible . . . They say I'm highly poisonous and can be the cause of cancer, but they misunderstand." To cheery, soothing music, he enthuses, "No one has ever gotten cancer from plutonium! If you drink plutonium, your body will just get rid of it." This video was shown in the public-relations facilities of several nuclear power plants. After 3/11, it stopped being used.

The industry's use of characters for promoting nuclear power inspired M.C. to come up with another take on corporate characters and wobbly mascots: "If you can use characters to say that a dangerous thing isn't dangerous, then why not have a counterpart say that a dangerous thing is actually dangerous? After all, to say that nuclear power is safe is a lie. If you need a cute character to cover up a lie, you can conversely use one to undo the lie and dissolve it" (M.C. interview).

M.C. also decided to use the Monju FBR as the basis for the character, "because it's dangerous, and it's not that well known, despite its great significance and hazardousness. It hadn't attracted that much interest or protests against it . . . It's the devil-child [oni-go] of Japan's nuclear policy" (M.C. interview). Monju was a key node in the nuclear fuel cycle, in which the spent fuel of ordinary nuclear reactors was to be reprocessed into mixed oxide (MOX) fuel at the Rokkashō Nuclear Fuel Reprocessing Facility in Aomori prefecture, and MOX was used as fuel for the Monju FBR. However, both Rokkashō and Monju had had several accidents, and as of 2017, neither seemed close to being commercially viable. As M.C. said:

> The plan is to have ordinary nuclear power plants, Monju, and Rokkasho, operate the nuclear cycle among them. If they admit two of those nodes don't work, then you really wouldn't be able to use nuclear power anymore, because there won't be any place to take the spent fuel. But they won't admit it, and keep saying that it will succeed one day. They started planning it in the 1960s, and fifty years later in the 2010s, it's still not done. They're now saying it will be completed in 2050. It's a dream that's taking ninety years to fulfill. How much can you trust that? It's like a comedy. And it wasn't

known about at all. It's emblematic of Japanese nuclear policy, and it's very critical. For that reason, I featured Monju. (M.C. interview)

Monju-kun constantly reminded followers that Monju, the plant, cost Japanese taxpayers 20 billion yen ($180 million) every year. Despite its many problems, including an order from the Nuclear Regulatory Authority (NRA) in 2013 to remain shut due to lax safety inspections, it remained an ongoing entity, supported by taxes, until September 2016. While Monju-kun often referred to his friend Fukuichi-kun—the troubled Fukushima Daiichi plant—M.C. believed it would be in poor taste to feature Fukuichi-kun as the primary character, given that 160,000 people had had to evacuate from their homes as a result of the nuclear accident (M.C. interview).

While M.C. said that much of the character's genesis and development was spontaneous and driven by emotional response, the character of Monju-kun shares many of the features of well-formed Japanese characters. As Itō (2007), Aihara (2007), Condry (2009), Yano (2013), and others have pointed out, creators of anime, manga, and character goods take great care in developing the personalities, premises, and world-settings for their characters, whose formation often precedes and receives more emphasis than plotlines. Let us now examine how Monju-kun, the character, was constructed in terms of appearance, personality, and premise.

Monju-kun appears as a very young boy, with a round face and rotund figure. That he is a boy rather than a girl fits partly into character convention—most nuclear-powered characters, such as Astro Boy, are boys, as they are meant to be strong. Indeed, nuclear power is often depicted in masculine terms, as a representation of Japan's technological and economic might. Perceiving this depiction as a hangover of Nakasone's desire to possess the technology behind the atom bomb, the rapper ECD declares in "Straight Outta 138" (Dengaryū 2012) that nuclear power is the "penis substitute of those old men who wanted to keep fighting the war" but were prohibited from having nuclear weapons.

Hence, Monju-kun's gender is deeply ironic. He is anything but an Astro Boy-like hero. He is a little boy who is physically fragile—"Even though I haven't worked, I'm falling apart, and my body hurts everywhere" (Monju-kun 2012b: 12)—an apt personification of the actual reactor, which had proved prone to accidents. The Monju FBR's vulnerability to sodium leakage is translated into the kid-friendly metaphor of a boy susceptible to diarrhea ("If there's a big earthquake, would I be able to hold it in?" Monju-kun 2012b: 68). This depiction of Monju-kun as a helpless boy, in need of continuous minding, emasculates the Monju FBR, and with it, Japan's nuclear power program, as incapable and powerless. Monju-kun's youth and rotund figure also symbolize that the reactor has hardly worked; in contrast, Fukuichi-kun (Fukushima Daiichi) is an *ojii-chan* (grandpa) because before its collapse the plant was old, having operated for over forty years.

The appearance of characters often has symbolic meaning. To formulate Monju-kun's, M.C. took aspects of Monju the FBR, as well as of Monju, the Mañjuśrī bodhisattva of wisdom after whom the nuclear reactor is named. Like Mañjuśrī, Monju-kun has a bindi on his forehead, elongated ears, and a headband bordering a crown, with a flower in its center (see figure 16).[7] In place of Mañjuśrī's crown, Monju-kun sports a dome resembling a nuclear reactor with a pointed top that looks like the exhaust tower of the Monju FBR. To make him child-friendly, M.C. limited colors to four basic ones that toddlers could name—baby blue, pink, skin color, and yellow. On book covers and in the stuffed costume, much surface area is colored in yellow to make the objects brighter (M.C. interview). This coloring helps the books and characters to stand out in public and attract attention. Monju-kun's costume sports a band-aid on his bottom "to prevent sodium from leaking."

Many characters come with an origin story that explains who the character is and how he or she has become this way. For Monju-kun, the most dramatic version of his origin story is given in his "autobiography," *Goodbye Monju-kun* (Sayōnara, Monju-kun; Monju-kun 2012b). The first chapter is a recounting of the December 8, 1995 accident at the Monju plant and subsequent cover-up, where actual events are told from the anthropomorphic perspective of the reactor himself:

> I still remember that accident clearly . . . It was past 7 pm, and the *oji-san* ("uncles," men) were raising the output of the reactor . . . I started to feel a little sick. My stomach started to twitch. Hmm, what is this awful feeling? Then something burst open. I suddenly felt pangs of pain at the bottom of my stomach, as if I were being squeezed . . . Suddenly, I saw a hole in the sodium pipe, and sodium was flowing out. I thought, oh no! If hot sodium touches the air, it will burst into flame . . . The white smoke of burning sodium filled the room, and I couldn't see anymore in the haze . . . Beep! Beep! The fire alarms started to go off. I was *so* scared (Monju-kun 2012b: 13–16).

Much to Monju-kun's disappointment, the uncles of Dōnen (Power Reactor and Nuclear Fuel Development Corporation, forerunner to JAEA) were slow to react in his hour of need: "They didn't stop the sodium pump, so I couldn't stop wetting my pants. It was so embarrassing and painful. I was very sad" (19). In the actual accident, ninety minutes passed by before Dōnen halted the reactor, allowing 650 kilograms of sodium to leak.

At a press conference the following day, Dōnen claimed that the accident wasn't serious, even though the total amount of sodium leaked was substantial, and that it had no knowledge of conditions at the site of the accident, although it had already taken a video of it. In the autobiographical narrative, an appalled Monju-kun yelled, "The uncles are lying! . . . The pipe room is completely covered in white," but none of the reporters heard him (26–28). Subsequently, Dōnen edited the video to make the accident look minor and held another press conference. Monju-kun was again horrified by the lies: "I was so surprised, I almost wet my pants with sodium

FIGURE 16. Images of Monju-kun, from @monjukun, Twitter. Courtesy @monjukun, Instagram, April 29, 2012.

again" (31). Fed up with Dōnen's vague responses, the people of Fukui prefecture demanded to see the site themselves. The visit revealed the lie, and the resulting scandal was well covered in the media. Nishimura Shigeo, the assistant manager in charge of investigating the accident, was found dead, and his death was ruled a suicide; his wife, who had previously worked for Dōnen, claimed he was murdered.[8] Pressure from intense media coverage was blamed for his death, and the media backed off from Monju.

This event, which happened in real life, is set up as a defining moment for Monju-kun, the character, who begins to question his identity and worth.

> As a fast-breeder reactor, exactly what am I? Until then, I had always been told, "You are the reactor of dreams." "If you succeed, Japan no longer has to worry about energy" . . . I thought I was supporting the ambitions of Japanese science . . .
>
> But the sodium accident made me realize three important points. First, I break easily and I'm dangerous . . . It hurt, it was hot, it was scary. I don't ever want to experience that again.
>
> Second, I make everyone worry . . . After I had the accident, residents in the area were asking fearfully, "Should we evacuate?" . . .
>
> Third, I started to wonder if Dad, Dōnen, were really all right. I had always trusted Dad, because he was Dad . . . But during the accident, I kept saying, "It's hot, it's hot!" but no one came to extinguish the fire. The uncles didn't stop the nuclear reactor right away. They hesitated to drain the sodium so I continued to wet my pants. I wondered if they really intended to take care of me. . . .
>
> They lied, they hid the video, they piled lies upon lies, and they use everyone's tax money for research but can't explain it properly to outsiders. That's dishonest. They drive someone in their organization into a corner and don't protect him . . . Since then, I have continued to wonder if my existence is really necessary. (Monju-kun 2012b: 36–40)

MONJU-KUN'S PERSONALITY

This origin story highlights the key elements in Monju-kun's character. First, he is a child, and as a child, he is helpless: he is dependent on the uncles to prevent accidents. As a child, Monju-kun (and by analogy, the Monju FBR) is blameless: the accident is clearly the fault of the technological uncles of Dōnen, who have designed him badly and cover it up.

Second, he possesses the basic human goodness attributed to children (Malkki 2010; see chapter 5): he is an honest boy with a sense of morality and social responsibility. He feels outrage at the cover-up of the Monju accident and is deeply saddened by the reported suicides of the manager in charge of communicating Monju's accident in 1996 and the manager who was organizing repairs in 2011.[9] He laments that the Nuclear and Industrial Safety Agency had just been rubber-stamping Dōnen's materials: "I felt sad that people weren't paying adequate attention. It scared me" (Monju-kun 2012b: 100). Fukuichi-kun's accident also makes him wonder if he's really safe. When the uncles at the plants or the government claim, "It's safe," he feels more unsettled.

Thirdly, he has the child's ability to see the truth: he doubts the moral integrity of his father and creator, Dōnen, and its successor, JAEA. Dependent on Dōnen, Monju-kun feels betrayed by his uncles' inability to "take care of him" by dealing quickly with the accident. And as a seer of truth (Malkki 2010), Monju-kun recognizes that he is not the future of nuclear energy as he is purported to be. Like some children unable to deal with unrealistic expectations, he retreats into a somewhat nihilistic dream of retiring and being reborn as a solar cell in the Sahara.

This depiction of a technology-based character in a moral conflict with his father/creator locates Monju-kun in a tradition of character-types created by Tezuka Osamu, the author of *Astro Boy* and considered the father of Japanese postwar manga and animation. At the beginning of *Astro Boy*, Tobio, the son of Dr. Tenma, the director-general of the Institute of Science, is killed in a turbo-car accident. The bereaved father summons all the resources of the Institute to build Astro Boy, a boy robot with an atomic generator as a source of energy, as a substitute for his son. Tenma becomes disappointed when he doesn't grow like a human boy. Dismissing him as "just a robot," he sells him to a cruel circus owner who makes Astro Boy fight gladiator-style with other robots. Astro Boy recharges cast-off robots and mobilizes them to rescue people from a circus fire. The passage of a robot bill of rights frees him from the circus. Meanwhile, Dr. Tenma has been forced to resign from his position, and the kindly Dr. Ochanomizu has replaced Dr. Tenma as the director of the Institute. Ochanomizu adopts Astro Boy, who goes on to fight villains.[10]

Astro Boy shares with Monju-kun the attributes associated with children: like Monju-kun, Astro Boy is an honest boy who seeks righteousness and truth. Moreover, both embody an anxiety about technology and those who wield its power. They are both powered by atomic energy and billed as technological marvels (although Monju-kun's wonders remain unmaterialized). Both father-creators are powerful figures in science, the director-general of the Institute of Science mirroring Dōnen's position at the heart of Japanese research on nuclear power. Both fathers are also deeply flawed: the director-general eventually loses his position, and Dōnen, reorganized as Japan Atomic Energy Agency (JAEA), has been censored by the new NRA for underreporting problems. Astro Boy is betrayed and abandoned by his father, while Monju-kun is betrayed and misled by Dōnen/JAEA; both harbor conflicting feelings about "dad." Anne Allison surmises that Astro Boy's abandonment resonated with many in postwar Japan, who felt that military leaders had betrayed and sacrificed them (Allison 2006: 57). Similarly, Monju-kun's betrayal and doubt over the leadership of nuclear power—and with it, the underlying assumptions behind Japan's technological and economic policies—echo the feelings of many Japanese in the wake of the Fukushima Daiichi accident. For Astro Boy, the emotional dissonance is resolved when the kindly Dr. Ochanomizu adopts him. For Monju-kun, no such adoptive parent materialized—just as in real life, in which no organization stepped up to replace JAEA as the manager for the Monju FBR.

Szasz and Takechi have noted that "in Tezuka's world, the robots, such as Astro Boy, are often more human than humans themselves, as they deal with sadness, fear, sorrow, and even remorse. Humans cause most of the problems in his stories" (Szasz and Takechi 2007: 737). In other words, the technology-based character (also a child) is socially responsible: it is the human (adult) who begets evil out of technology. Similarly, Monju-kun and his nuclear-reactor friends—Fukuichi-kun, Hamaoka-kun, Ōi-kun, etc.—are worried that they are not truly safe; they are disappointed in the humans who lie and engage in cover-ups. Fukuichi-kun deeply regrets the consequences of his accident, for which Monju-kun blames the Nuclear Village: "Fukuichi-kun . . . , I can see your tears. You can't see them on television because they're mixing and disappearing with the continuing flow of contaminated water, but I can see that you are crying tears of apology. You're not the one who's bad! It's the over-lenient plans and fraudulent inspections that are bad!" (@monjukun, Twitter, May 13, 2011). Hence, Monju-kun, the innocent boy, asserts that the technology of nuclear power is not inherently evil, but that humans handle it in a problematic manner.

Like Astro Boy, whose liminal position between the robot and human worlds brings on an identity crisis, Monju-kun is highly anxious about his identity as a nuclear reactor and the meaning of his existence. He laments when the *Yomiuri* newspaper writes that nuclear power allows Japan to have plutonium, which is the raw material for nuclear weapons (September 8, 2011). Unlike Astro Boy, who responds heroically by fighting injustice, Monju-kun is remorseful about his very existence. As mentioned previously, he wants his existence as Monju to end. This pessimistic, unheroic withdrawal differentiates him from Astro Boy and other nuclear-powered commercial characters. However, the social and economic difficulties in the current society have led to an increase of NEETs—a person who is not pursuing employment, education, or training—and *hikikomori,* or extreme social withdrawal (Borovoy 2008; Furlong 2008). Monju-kun's desire to withdraw may have resonated with many young Japanese people.

Indeed, Monju-kun's depiction as a weakling may have made his character more appealing. Childlike weakness and helplessness are key components of the cuteness *(kawaii)* aesthetic, as they invite others to take care of that person or character (Kinsella 1995). Monju-kun tends to highlight his physical weakness, which draws the motherly attention of his followers. When Monju-kun tweeted extensively about his "operation" in June 2011 (mirroring a real-life effort to remove fallen equipment from the FBR), so many followers tweeted "get well soon" messages that M.C.'s Twitter app crashed.

As M.C. observed, "The Japanese prefer something flawed or weak over something perfect, like Nobita from *Doraemon*" (M.C. interview). In this long-running manga and anime series, Nobita is a boy who is always failing: he receives poor grades at school, performs poorly at athletic activities, and can't do anything right. His descendant sends the robot cat Doraemon to protect Nobita from a hapless future. Whenever Nobita gets into a bind, Doraemon tries to rescue him by pulling out a gadget, which Nobita misuses. Schilling (1993) notes that many children, who are under extreme pressure to succeed in school and elsewhere, identify with Nobita. And like Nobita, Monju-kun is under pressure to work, although he simply can't. According to Monju-kun's author, "People can empathize more with an incompetent kid like Nobita [than with a perfect kid]. Monju-kun, too, is very weak physically, and he's always failing, like the actual Monju FBR . . . Those types of characters feel friendly and familiar to many people" (M.C. interview). And as Monju-kun fit into this recognizable type, he appealed to more people, making them more willing to listen to his explanations of nuclear power.

Nobita has a marked lazy streak—another characteristic Monju-kun shares with him. Building on the fact that the Monju FBR only operated for about six months since its completion in 1991, Monju-kun calls himself "Japan's number one NEET" (@monjukun, Twitter, May 22, 2011). On his resume, he lists his special skills as "loafing" and "using up a lot of money" (Monju-kun 2012b: 2). His T-shirts and illustrations show Monju-kun hula-dancing and hunting for insects (a favorite summer pastime for children) with the caption, "Every day is summer vacation"— a biting remark for the many Japanese who hardly get any vacation from their jobs.

Another endearing element to Monju-kun's character is his distinctive language. He greeted followers in the morning with an "*oha-oha*" tagline to the common greeting, "*ohayō gozaimasu*" (good morning). He also uses the distinctive "*desu-dayo*" sentence ending, combining two auxiliary verbs when either one alone would suffice—the kind of mistake a child would make. M.C. explained that this pattern was a form of *keigo* (polite language) when addressing evacuees and people of higher status on Twitter.[11] That is to say, Monju-kun is a polite, well-behaved child.

Like Astro Boy, Monju-kun sought kinship outside of his original "family." He made his most frequent references to his nuclear reactor friends, comprised of all the other reactors in Japan and pictured as a mutually supportive network of coworkers in difficult environments. When the Hamaoka Nuclear Plant, which sits directly over the subduction zone of two tectonic plates that are overdue for a major earthquake, was taken off-line, Monju-kun tweeted, "I tried to call Hamaoka-kun to congratulate him on being taken off-line, but I couldn't get through! There's a flood of congratulatory calls from Tsuruga-kun, Kashiwazaki-kun, Shimane-kun—all the nuclear reactors in Japan. We all put on a brave face, but we're actually scared of earthquakes" (@monjukun, Twitter, May 9, 2011).

Hence, Monju-kun's cute personality, classic conflicts of father versus son and technology versus humans, and multiplicity of associated subcharacters made him both familiar and distinctive to Japanese, enhancing his acceptance. Let us now explore how his popularity grew and how he was received in various forms.

MONJU'S SPREAD ACROSS MEDIA PLATFORMS

Monju-kun began his life as a Twitter account on May 4, 2011, tweeting little-known stories about the Monju FBR in humorous, often sarcastic tones that resonated with the angry mood at the time:

> Hello from atop an active fault! It's me, Monju-kun (May 6, 2011).
> I don't drink mother's milk. I grew this big from everyone's hard-earned taxpayer money! (May 10, 2011)

Monju-kun's amusing manner quickly attracted the attention of the Twittersphere, where many Japanese had congregated for news in those first few months after 3/11. He was quickly retweeted by influential tweeters such as musicians Soul Flower Union, Gotch (Asian Kung-Fu Generation), Ōtomo Yoshihide, and Sakamoto Ryūichi, resulting in a rapid increase in followers (M.C. interview). These endorsements encouraged musicians' fans to follow Monju-kun and increased his perceived trustworthiness. In ten weeks, he had over fifty thousand followers, and in a year, he had nearly one hundred thousand.

Monju-kun was chatty and interactive with his followers, who asked him "personal" questions, in language similar to the way in which adults engage with children. Noting that Monju-kun had referred to his dad, a follower asked, "What about your mom?" He responded, "The energy industry is a male-dominated world, so there aren't many moms. It doesn't have any mom-oriented ideas either" (June 14, 2011). When another asked, "What are your hobbies?" he responded, "I wanted to try the tea ceremony, but [the water] would react with the sodium and make it explode, so I gave it up" (September 10, 2011).

But amid all the fun, Monju-kun's easily understood messages quickly made him a trusted authority to whom adults, particularly parents, could ask questions. He corrected misunderstandings, gently telling one follower that he couldn't use his Geiger counter to measure radiation in food ("A Geiger counter measures sieverts; when you eat vegetables, you want to know about bequerels," May 13, 2011). When a follower asked, "Is it all right to drink plutonium? . . . Ōhashi Hiroshi, a distinguished professor from Tokyo University, said it's fine to drink it" (@benntenn5283, June 6, 2011), he emphatically replied, "Even if a professor says it's all right, good children must never drink it! If you choke, and it goes down your windpipe into your lungs, you'd receive continuous doses of internal radiation" (June 6, 2011).

Eventually M.C. was unable to keep up with the barrage of questions, and Monju-kun moved into the authorship of books and blogs. First Monju-kun solicited questions from his followers under the hashtag #oshiete_monju. This Q&A on topics relating to nuclear policy and radiation formed the basis for his first book, *Teach Me, Monju-kun* (Oshiete! Monju-kun; Monju-kun 2012a).

Monju-kun found that while Twitter was good for transmitting sound bites, its 140 characters were not sufficient for discussing complicated issues. Furthermore, many Japanese still put greater trust in print media than in Internet sources: a digital divide existed between regular Internet users and flip-phone users, and the Internet, while less prone to censorship, suffered from an image of unreliability. M.C. thus felt that Monju-kun would seem more trustworthy if the information were packaged into a physical book from a reputable publisher (M.C. interview). With the longer book format, M.C. was able to explain complex concepts in nuclear science, give advice on avoiding radiation, debunk pronuclear arguments, and present renewable energy as a viable alternative to nuclear power.

In the guise of Monju-kun, M.C. published four books: *Teach Me, Monju-kun* (Oshiete! Monju-kun, March 2012), an FAQ on nuclear power and radiation; *Goodbye, Monju-kun* (Sayonara, Monju-kun, March 2012), an "autobiography" explaining the accidents and problems of the Monju FBR; *Energy of the Future for Everyone* (Monju-kun to miru! Yomu! Wakaru! Minna no mirai no enerugii, July 2012), describing renewable energy sources; and *Have We Changed Since 3/11?* (Monju-kun taidan-shū: 3.11 de bokura wa kawatta ka, 2014), a book about cultural responses to 3/11 featuring interviews with Sakamoto Ryūichi, artist Nara Yoshitomo, photographer Suzuki Shin, philosopher Kokubun Kōichirō, and martial arts researcher Kōno Yoshinori. Each of the first three books was supervised by an expert in the field: environmental economics professor Ōshima Ken'ichi and science education professor Samaki Takeo for *Teach Me, Monju-kun;* nuclear physicist Kobayashi Keiji for *Goodbye, Monju-kun;* and Iida Tetsunari, director of the Institute for Sustainable Energy Policies, for *Energy of the Future for Everyone.*

M.C. wrote the books with mothers in mind, using simple, clear language so that they could read them quickly and read them aloud to their children. So that upper-elementary-school children would be able to read them on their own, the books are printed in large letters with *kana* (phonetic spellings) for nearly all Chinese characters. They also include a plethora of kid-friendly illustrations that explain complicated concepts (e.g., the nuclear fuel cycle) or anthropomorphize actual situations (e.g., Monju-kun bent over with a stomachache while leaked sodium catches fire).

The books have been received well, the first two books having sold more than twenty thousand copies within the first month.[12] Many readers tweeted that their children were reading them: "Not satisfied with just having the book read to him, our first grader is reading it himself, dictionary in hand" (@lovelovebonchan, March 7, 2012).

LIVE APPEARANCES

Given Monju-kun's popularity, it seemed only a matter of time before he appeared live in stuffed costume, like a true wobbly mascot. In particular, he had already been helping to spread information about demonstrations; in Twitter conversations with individual followers, he sometimes gave them the extra push of courage

FIGURE 17. Monju-kun at the TwitNoNukes demonstration, Shibuya, Tokyo, 29 April 2012.
Courtesy @monjukun, Instagram, April 29, 2012.

they needed to participate in a public protest. As early as June 2011, demonstrators were already carrying hand-drawn images of his likeness. Monju-kun then uploaded placards and round fans, which protesters downloaded and took to demonstrations. When he finally appeared at a TwitNoNukes antinuclear demonstration in Shibuya, Tokyo, on April 29, 2012, protesters, particularly those with children, were delighted to be greeted by him and posed for pictures with him (see figure 17).

Monju-kun was also a big hit at the Sayonara Genpatsu (Goodbye, Nuclear Power Plants) rally and demonstration on July 16, 2012, which attracted 170,000 protesters. Fans of all ages—both adults and children—came up to hug him and take pictures with him.[13] He entertained protesters in a skit with journalist Tsuda Daisuke on a big stage, declaring himself the King of NEETs for receiving an "allowance" of 55 million yen a day ("I took a taxi from Tsuruga! . . . Not even a dent in my allowance!").[14]

Monju-kun also participated in a number of music festivals, such as No Nukes, Project Fukushima Festival, and Fuji Rock Festival's Atomic Café stage. At the Atomic Café in 2013, Monju-kun performed in a skit with Suishinger—the comedy unit Okome Takeru no Ichiza's "superhero" trio representing pronuclear forces—TEPCO (in red leotards), METI (blue), and mass media (white); "suishin" means "to promote" (in this case, nuclear power).[15] Monju-kun told them that he didn't want to work, reminding the audience that the sodium in him will explode if combined with water—"If I start sweating from working, it'll be dangerous!" Suishinger bullied him, saying, "Just pretend you're going to work at some point." As Monju-kun cried, his tears of sodium generated smoke, causing Suishinger to flee. Tsuda Daisuke joined Monju-kun onstage, mentioning the moves by the Liberal Democratic Party, which had just returned to power, to restart twelve "nuclear reactor friends," all of which Monju-kun named. Monju-kun reported that the NRA had forbidden restarting him because the JAEA had failed to conduct safety checks on ten thousand pieces of equipment. The skit entertained children while updating adults on the current status of nuclear power.[16] A child was overheard asking his mother, "Do we not need nuclear power?"

Monju-kun finished the skit by dancing to his theme song, "Monju-kun ondo," based on a common Japanese song style (explained below). Music is usually part of a character's packaging: many characters are identified with the theme songs of their anime (e.g., Astro Boy) or videogame (e.g., Nintendo's Super Mario). Typically these songs summarize the premise and highlight the personality of characters; e.g., "I'm Doraemon" (Boku Doraemon) introduces the robot cat as one that can solve any problem.

M.C. felt that the Monju FBR was so "patently absurd" that "only a song could make people learn about it." M.C. chose the ondo style because it "is the most common type of Japanese song. Everyone knows it. It doesn't have to be trendy or cool" (M.C. interview). Originally a type of traditional call-and-response song and dance associated with particular localities and summertime bon festivals, the ondo was commercialized into a popular song form played with Western instruments in the 1920s. Today, many places, situations, personalities, and characters (e.g., Doraemon) have their own ondo. M.C. was familiar with the music of traditional ondo, having participated in many bon festivals, and found the lyrical pattern of ondo, which alternates lines of seven and five morae (short syllables) like haiku, straightforward to write. The cheery music of Monju-kun's theme song sports the pentatonic melody and dotted rhythm characteristic of a commercial ondo. The song was made available for download on the Project Fukushima site and for streaming on Soundcloud and YouTube.[17]

Audiences have responded positively, with bemusement, to the song at live performances. M.C. attributed this reception to the sheer familiarity of the form:

> When you play it at an event, that ondo has a devastating impact. . . . with an ondo, everyone is on the same page, because everyone knows the ondo. Everyone can sing

it and has danced to it before. It's something everyone has in common, something the body remembers . . .

[The *ondo*] also embarrasses the Japanese. In their daily lives, Japanese people tend to hide anything in the culture that seems Japanese. *Ondo* is definitely one of those things . . . You wouldn't sing one at a karaoke bar. Because you've hidden it away in a closet, you giggle when you hear an *ondo*. Just when you're smirking, the lyrics grab you. (M.C. interview)

Another reason for this reception may be the absurdity of having a giant stuffed character dance, jump at the word "explosion," and cover his mouth at "plutonium," all to lyrics that describe a dead-serious situation; the incongruity itself is enough to make one laugh, just as incongruous mash-ups do. The song's three verses succinctly explain the issues with the Monju FBR: that both the sodium it uses for cooling and the plutonium it uses for fuel are extremely dangerous; that it remains unfinished despite fifty years of planning and testing; that a serious accident was covered up; that the FBR is more difficult to control than other nuclear reactors; and that every other developed country has already given up on this technology. Its chorus begins by reminding us that "the annual budget is 20 billion yen," that "it's called the reactor of dreams, but it's a nightmare from which we haven't awakened," and that it would "ruin Lake Biwa if there were an accident." In simple words that a child could mostly understand, coupled with a familiar *ondo* melody, the song is catchy and easy to learn. It replicates the long-held Japanese practice of using music to teach children, as in the case of Meiji-era school songs that teach Confucian values or the recent wobbly mascot Kumamon's song, which teaches children to overcome difficulties. But the recording also replicates the mother-child dynamic seen throughout the Monju-kun character: a woman-mother is singing, while a sprightly boy yelps the response pattern: "*Mon, Mon, Mon-ju, hai, hai, hai-ro*" (Monju, shut it down).

CONCLUSION

Through the tropes of Japanese character culture—a cute, fuzzy being, with the father-son conflicts and technology-human ambiguities that shape *Astro Boy* or *Doraemon*—Monju-kun provided a nonthreatening and fun conduit to inform citizens, particularly mothers, about nuclear power and radiation. He exemplified the political usefulness of children's culture, whose friendly, familiar, and comforting associations made it a perfect foil for transmitting technically difficult information like nuclear fission or contentious situations like the problematic Monju reactor. In addition, Japanese children's culture also permeates adult culture, due not only to the participation of parents in their children's culture but also to the Japanese attraction to cuteness. Children's culture has historically been used in public relations (e.g., Denko, Pluto-kun) or outright propaganda, as with children's songs during World War II. Other antinuclear activists and musicians also used children's culture, such as Saitō Kazuyoshi's antinuclear songs based on Aesop tales, Acid Black Cherry and Coma-chi's concept albums written as children's stories, and Scha Dara Parr and Hikashū's references to Godzilla, while visual artists such as Sayonara Atom applied the cuteness aesthetic to banners for demonstrations. As M.C. inferred, most Japanese may find it hard to discuss the nuclear crisis, but they also find it hard to get mad at cute, childlike things or reminders of childhood. And like a child without social filters (see chapter 5), Monju-kun was able to speak the truth about nuclear power and get away with it.

Monju-kun's beginnings and primary existence on the Internet also illustrate how important the anonymity of cyberspace has been in disseminating information and sustaining discussion outside of mainstream-media narratives. Anonymity allowed not only both M.C. and Monju-kun's followers to speak out. Having amassed a large following on Twitter, M.C., under the Monju-kun *nom de plume*, wrote informative and accessible books that a child could read, while the character, in stuffed costume, attracted parents, children, and fans to antinuclear demonstrations and festivals. The combination of the cute, approachable character and timely dissemination made Monju-kun a crucial source of information under a spiral of silence.

In November 2015, the NRA announced that JAEA could no longer manage the Monju plant. It instructed the education and science ministry (MEXT) to find a new manager or consider closing the plant. After a ministry report failed to lay out a reform plan or identify a new operator, Cabinet members agreed in September 2016 to decommission Monju, at an estimated cost of 375 billion yen ($3.3 billion) over thirty years, and the government formally confirmed this decision in December 2016. However, the Cabinet did not shift policy away from nuclear fuel recycling: the government plans to build a demonstration fast-breeder reactor in Fukui, the same prefecture that hosted Monju. Japan has a forty-eight-ton plutonium stockpile, which it has justified through the nuclear fuel recycling program.

Meanwhile, Monju-kun's creator appears to have gone on with life. Monju-kun stopped tweeting shortly after the fifth anniversary of 3/11, without a goodbye. In his last tweets, he sounded optimistic over Monju's potential decommissioning but resigned over Japan's inability to give up nuclear power; asked by an inquisitive child as to why the nuclear accident had to happen, he said he still did not have simple words to explain.

But Monju-kun hadn't disappeared from the minds of his fans. As the news on Monju flowed, they revisited his books, articles, and songs, reposting them on Twitter as quick refreshers on the problematic reactor. Monju-kun had entered the discourse on this reactor: in discussing its potential decommissioning, many Twitter users referred to it as Monju-kun, discussing the reactor as if it actually were the little boy of the character. They credited him for making them aware of the Monju controversy. As Monju-kun remained inactive in the face of decommissioning news, fans became increasingly mystified by his silence; they tweeted that they missed his wry, friendly commentary. They were also concerned for the creator's well-being; as one might with an ill or lost friend, they tweeted to other antinuclear avatars—Pluto-kun and the Zeronomics bear—to ask after him. They showed their affection for him by posting their personal memories of him, such as their own photos of Monju-kun badges or Monju-kun in stuffed costume, or imitating his characteristic *desu-dayo* speech pattern. When Monju's decommission was confirmed, fans again poured out their affection, posting pictures of him with the caption, "Good-bye Monju-kun," sometimes with a wistful comment about the character's disappearance: "He must be happy that he can retire" (@mem_no_koe, December 21, 2016). Like a lost lover in an *enka* lyric, Monju-kun was gone, but the feelings of his fans lingered.

Through the trope of children's culture, Monju-kun's funny, biting, and oftentimes absurd manner attracted people to his Twitter feed and books, bringing attention to the issue of Monju, which had become obscure and forgotten at the time of 3/11. He engaged them not only intellectually but also affectively, inviting them to learn, think, discuss, and become passionate about the future of nuclear energy.

NOTES

1. My research on Monju-kun is part of a larger project involving five years of ethnographic work. While M.C. and I had additional correspondence, all M.C. quotes in this article are taken from our interview of October 15, 2013.

2. Monju-kun, 2012, "Monju-kun intabyū: Genpatsu zero uttae, Tōkyō no demo ni shutsubotsu," interview by *Shimbun Akahata,* May 14, www.jcp.or.jp/akahata/aik12/2012–05–14/2012051414_01_1. html.

3. Ghibli asked for its products to be removed from the facility after receiving customer complaints that its characters should not be tied to nuclear power.

4. See Manabe 2015, chapter 3, for stories of musicians and activists who have suffered after expressing antinuclear opinions.

5. "Otsuha CM, Denko no denki nikki: 'Enerugii jikyū ritsu' hen," YouTube video, 0:31, from televised commercials in the Kantō area, posted by "fitone10001" on December 24, 2009, http://youtu.be/wOTuafkP-RY.

6. "Japanese Nuclear Propaganda Cartoon," YouTube video, 10:54, from 1993 Dōnen (JAEA) public relations film, uploaded by "WHENDASHTF1," August 28, 2013, https://www.youtube.com/watch?v=sOFg8oWMHRM.

7. A photo of the Manjusri bodhisattva can be seen here: http://bit.ly/2gxNI3U. A photo of the Monju FBR can be seen here: http://bit.ly/2vRLTkh.

8. Nishimura's reasoning was as follows: while her husband was said to have leaped from a hotel room, the X-rays showed no sign of skull or neck fracture, the deep body temperature did not match the reported time of death, the hotel room held no signature of registration, the police only took one photo of the scene, and parts of the suicide note, which was on official company stationery, were not in her husband's handwriting. She published an exposé in the magazine *Shinchō 45,* to which the company never responded (Nishimura 2005; Nishimura Toshiko, 2013, "Homicide by JPN Nuclear Village!?" interview by Mari Takenouchi, April 14, http://takenouchimari.blogspot.com/2013/04/blog-post_1741.html).

9. The section manager in charge of overseeing this repair was found dead in the woods around Tsuruga in February 2011, as the repair was being attempted. The death was ruled a suicide.

10. This story is the version given in the first episode of the 1963 television anime. In that version, Tobio is riding on "the safest highway in the world," where "all you have to do is press a button, and the road does everything for you," when a car appears from around a corner; the incident warns against putting too much faith in technology.

11. Monju-kun, 2012, "Monju-kun intabyū: Genpatsu zero uttae, Tōkyō no demo ni shutsubotsu," interview by Shimbun Akahata, May 14, http://www.jcp.or.jp/akahata/aik12/2012-05–14/2012051414_01_1.html.

12. Nakamura Mariko, 2012, "Monju-kun, yuruuku wakariyasuku: Genpatsu hon ga wadai ni," *Asahi Shimbun,* April 2, afternoon edition.

13. "2012.07.16 Sayonara genpatsu 10 man nin shūkai NNMH demo (10/11) Monju-kun," YouTube video, 2:31, from Sayonara genpatsu demonstration, uploaded by "ken23qu," July 16, 2012, https://www.youtube.com/watch?v=4weuQaXSxIk.

14. "Monju-kun wairudoda ze ~e! Tsuda Daisuke Sayonara Genpatsu 10 man-nin shūkai," YouTube video, 6:14, Monju-kun's skit from Sayonara genpatu demonstration, uploaded by "fitop1go," July 16, 2012 https://www.youtube.com/watch?v=jK9OM4RZFSU.

15. Suishinger's self-introductory video, designed as a parody of an opening sequence to a superhero television series, can be seen on Okome Takeru no Ichiza's website, www.okometakeru.com and at https://www.youtube.com/watch?v=8P2iQyyArwo

16. The skit can be seen at "Tsuda Daisuke, Monju-kun, Okome Takeru no Ichiza @ Fuji Rock Festival '13, New Power Gear Stage/Gypsy Avalon," uploaded by Sakai Satoru, July 30, 2013, 28:48, https://www.youtube.com/watch?v=RE8MVuVFr7A.

17. "Monju-kun ondo," available at Project Fukushima, April 29, 2012, www.pj-fukushima.jp/download/diy_list_details026.php; SoundCloud, April 29, 2012, https://soundcloud.com/monjukun/monjukun-ondo-diy; YouTube, with English subtitles, from a July 2012 performance at Fuji Rock, https://www.youtube.com/watch?v=KP01MtE6Q4c.

BIBLIOGRAPHY

Note: Unless noted otherwise the place of publication for Japanese books is Tokyo.

Aihara, Hiroyuki. 2007. *Kyara-ka suru Nippon.* Gendai Shinsho. Kōdansha.
Allison, Anne. 2006. *Millennial Monsters: Japanese Toys and the Global Imagination.* Berkeley: University of California Press.
Borovoy, Amy. 2008. "Japan's Hidden Youths: Mainstreaming the Emotionally Distressed in Japan." *Culture, Medicine, and Psychiatry* 32(4): 552–76.
Condry, Ian. 2009. "Anime Creativity Characters and Premises in the Quest for Cool Japan." *Theory, Culture and Society* 26(2–3): 139–63.
Dengaryū. 2012. *B-kyū eiga no youni.* Mary Jay Recordings, MJCD-059.
Furlong, Andy. 2008. "The Japanese Hikikomori Phenomenon: Acute Social Withdrawal among Young People." *The Sociological Review* 56(2): 309–25.
Itō, Gō. 2007. *Manga wa kawaru: "Manga katari" kara "Manga ron" e.* Seido-sha.
Kin Masanori. 2010. *Tsuittaa shakai shinkaron: Ichiman nin shijō chōsa de yomitoku.* Asahi Shinsho.
Kinefuchi Etsuko. 2015. "Nuclear Power for Good: Articulations in Japan's Nuclear Power Hegemony." *Communication, Culture and Critique* 8(3): 448–65.
Kinsella, Sharon. 1995. "Cuties in Japan." In *Women Media and Consumption in Japan,* edited by Lise Skov and Brian Moeran. Richmond, UK: Curzon Press.

Malkki, Liisa H. 2010. "Children, Humanity, and the Infantilization of Peace." In *In the Name of Humanity: The Government of Threat and Care*, edited by Ilana Feldman and Miriam Ticktin, 58–85. Durham, NC: Duke University Press.

Manabe, Noriko. 2012. "Songs of Japanese Schoolchildren during World War II." In *The Oxford Handbook of Children's Musical Cultures*, edited by Patricia Shehan Campbell and Trevor Wiggins, 96–113. New York: Oxford University Press.

———. 2015. *The Revolution Will Not Be Televised: Protest Music after Fukushima*. New York: Oxford University Press.

Monju-kun. 2012a. *Oshiete! Monju-kun: Koredake wa shitte okō, genpatsu to hōshanō*. Edited by Ōshima Ken'ichi and Samaki Takeo. Heibonsha.

———. 2012b. *Sayōnara, Monju-kun: Kōsoku zōshoku-ro ga kataru genpatsu no honto no o hanashi*. Edited by Kobayashi Keiji. Kawade Shobō Shinsha.

———. 2012c. *Monju-kun to miru! Yomu! Wakaru! Minna no mirai no enerugii*. Edited by Iida Tetsunari. Kawade Shobō Shinsha.

———. 2014. *Monju-kun taidan-shū: 3. 11 de bokura wa kawatta ka*. Heibonsha.

Morio, Hiroaki, and Christopher Buchholz. 2009. "How Anonymous Are You Online? Examining Online Social Behaviors from a Cross-Cultural Perspective." *AI and Society* 23: 297–307.

Nishimura Toshiko. 2005. "Watashi no otto wa Dōnen ni korosareta! 'Monju jiko' no kaibu o otta 9-nenkan." *Shinchō* 45 (March): 78–89.

Noelle-Neumann, Elisabeth. 1993. *The Spiral of Silence: Public Opinion—Our Social Skin*. Chicago: University of Chicago Press.

Occhi, Debra J. 2012. "Wobbly Aesthetics, Performance, and Message: Comparing Japanese Kyara with Their Anthropomorphic Forebears." *Asian Ethnology* 71(1): 109–32.

Orita, Akiko. 2014. "Name, Identity, and Privacy on the Internet." *Journal of Information Processing and Management* 57(2): 90–98.

Schilling, Mark. 1993. "Doraemon: Making Dreams Come True." *Japan Quarterly* 40(4): 405–17.

Szasz, Ferenc M., and Issei Takechi. 2007. "Atomic Heroes and Atomic Monsters: American and Japanese Cartoonists Confront the Onset of the Nuclear Age, 1945–80." *Historian* 69(4): 728–52.

Yano, Christine. 2013. *Pink Globalization: Hello Kitty's Trek across the Pacific*. Durham, NC: Duke University Press.

CONTRIBUTORS

ELISE EDWARDS is an associate professor of anthropology and chair of the Department of History and Anthropology at Butler University in Indianapolis, Indiana. She recently authored "Fields of Individuals and Neoliberal Logics: Japanese Soccer Ideals and the 1990s Economic Crisis" in the *Journal of Sport and Social Issues* (2014), and "The Promises and Possibilities of the Pitch: 1990s Ladies League Soccer Players as Fin-de-siècle Modern Girls" in Christine Yano and Laura Miller, eds., *Modern Girls on the Go: Gender, Mobility, and Labor in Japan* (2013). She is currently completing a book manuscript about soccer, corporate sport, the 1990s recession, and national identity in Japan, which is tentatively titled *Fields for the Future: Soccer and Citizens in Japan at the Turn of the Twenty-First Century*. She also is pursuing a new project on the intersections between Japan's "hometown" soccer movement, grassroots activism, volunteerism, and ever-evolving relationships between public and private entities in contemporary Japan. Edwards both played and coached soccer in the Japanese women's "L-League" in the mid-1990s and continued to work as a goalkeeping coach with Butler University's women's soccer team until 2016.

SABINE FRÜHSTÜCK is a professor of modern Japanese cultural studies at the University of California, Santa Barbara. She is mostly concerned with the history and ethnography of modern Japanese culture and its relations to the rest of the world. Her book publications include *Colonizing Sex: Sexology and Social Control in Modern Japan* (2003), *Uneasy Warriors: Gender, Memory, and Popular Culture in the Japanese Army* (2007), and *Playing War: Children and the Paradoxes of Modern Militarism in Japan* (2017). She coedited with Anne Walthall, *Recreating Japanese*

Men (2011) and is currently writing a book, *Gender and Sexuality in Modern Japan* (Cambridge University Press).

KATHRYN E. GOLDFARB is an assistant professor of cultural anthropology at the University of Colorado at Boulder. Her research explores the effects of social inclusion and exclusion on well-being, and how social relationships shape bodily experience. In Japan, she conducts research on the stakes of disconnection from family networks, focusing specifically on children and caregivers within the Japanese child welfare system. Her research explores how kinship ideologies articulate with discourses of Japanese national and cultural identity, and how these discourses shape understandings of what is "normal." Her research further examines how these concepts of normalcy are caught up in global circuits of knowledge surrounding human development, child rights, and concepts of "care" under the rubric of social welfare.

JINNŌ YUKI earned her doctorate from the Institute of Art and Design at the University of Tsukuba. She is professor of modern design and cultural history of Japan at the Department of Interhuman Symbiotic Studies, Kanto Gakuin University. Among other books and articles, she is the author of *Shumi no tanjō* (The birth of taste, Keisō Shobo 1994), *Kodomo o meguru desain to kindai* (Design and modern times of the child, Sekai Shisō-sha 2011), and *Hyakkaten de shumi o kau* (Buying a hobby at a department store, Yoshikawa Kobun Kan 2015). She has also coauthored *Hyakkaten no bunkashi* (A cultural history of the department store, Sekai Shisō-sha 1999), and *Arts and Crafts to Nihon* (Arts and crafts and Japan, Shibunkaku Shuppan 2004).

KORESAWA HIROAKI graduated from Tōyō University and is currently a professor in the Department of Childhood Studies at Otsuma Women's University. He specializes in the cultural history of everyday life and of children and childhood. The author of many books, he has written *Nihon ningyō no bi* (The beauty of Japanese dolls, Tankōsha 2008), *Kyōiku gangu no kindai: Kyōiku taishō toshite no kodomo tanjō* (The modern history of educational toys: The birth of children as object of education, Seori shobō 2009), and *Aoi me no ningyō to kindai Nihon* (Blue-eyed dolls and modern Japan, Seori shobō 2011), among others.

NORIKO MANABE is associate professor of music studies at Temple University. Her monograph, *The Revolution Will Not Be Televised: Protest Music after Fukushima* (Oxford 2015) won the John Whitney Hall Book Prize from the Association for Asian Studies and Honorable Mention for the Alan Merriam Prize from the Society for Ethnomusicology. Her monograph, *Revolution Remixed: Intertextuality in Protest Music,* and two coedited volumes, *Nuclear Music* (with Jessica

Schwartz) and *Oxford Handbook of Protest Music* (with Eric Drott), are forthcoming from Oxford University Press. She has published articles on Japanese rap, hip-hop DJs, online radio, the music business, wartime children's songs, and Cuban music in *Ethnomusicology, Popular Music, Asian Music, Asia-Pacific Journal, Oxford Handbook of Children's Musical Cultures, Oxford Handbook of Mobile Music Studies,* among other volumes. She is series editor for 33-1/3 Japan, a book series; contributing editor for the *Asia-Pacific Journal;* and editorial board member for *Music and Politics* and *Twentieth-Century Music.* Her research has been supported by fellowships from NEH, Kluge, Japan Foundation, and SSRC/JSPS.

AARON WILLIAM MOORE (PhD Princeton, 2006) is a senior lecturer in the History Department at the University of Manchester, where he teaches the comparative history of East Asia. He has published on diary-writing practices among combat soldiers in Japan, China, and the United States, including his first monograph, *Writing War: Soldiers Record the Japanese Empire* (Harvard University Press, 2013). He has recently completed a book on civilian narratives of aerial bombing in Britain and Japan (*Bombing the City,* Cambridge University Press, 2017), and is developing a new manuscript on the history of wartime childhood and youth in Britain, Japan, China, and the Soviet Union. His research on childhood and youth has been published in *Japanese Studies* and *Modern China,* and has included funding awards from the Leverhulme Trust and the Arts and Humanities Research Council. In 2014 he was awarded the Philip Leverhulme Prize.

L. HALLIDAY PIEL is an assistant professor of history at Lasell College in Massachusetts. She received her doctorate from the University of Hawai'i at Manoa, focusing on the history of childhood in Japan. Piel spent two years as a research associate with the project "Remembering and Recording Childhood Education and Youth in Japan, 1925–1945," codirected by Peter Cave and Aaron Moore at the University of Manchester in the United Kingdom. Piel's papers for this project, currently in press, include "Japanese Adolescents and the Wartime Labor Service, 1941–1945: Service or Exploitation?" *Japanese Studies;* "The School Diary in Wartime Japan: Cultivating Morale and Self-discipline through Writing," *Modern Asian Studies;* and "Recruiting Japanese Boys for the Pioneer Youth Core of Manchuria and Mongolia," a chapter in Mischa Honek and James Marten, eds., *More than Victims: War and Childhood in the Age of the World Wars* (Cambridge University Press). Her previously published articles on childhood and war in Japan include "Food Rationing and Children's Self-Reliance in Japan, 1942–1952," *Journal of the History of Childhood and Youth* 5, no. 3 (Fall 2012): 393–418, and "The Family State and Forced Youth Migrations in Wartime Japan, 1937–1945," *Revue d'histoire de l'enfance irrégulière* 15 (October 2013).

OR PORATH is a doctoral candidate in the Department of Religious Studies at the University of California, Santa Barbara. His research centers on medieval Japanese religion and its conceptualization of sexual norms, specifically, the figure of the acolyte *(chigo/dōji)* and its role as an object of sexual longing in the Tendai Eshin lineage, and the way in which the acolyte's divine status was affirmed and contested by medieval Buddho-Shinto doctrine, ritual, and narrative in general. Porath has published an article on the topic of monastic male-male sexuality in medieval Japan, "The Cosmology of Male-Male Love in Medieval Japan: Nyakudō no Kanjinchō and the Way of Youths," *Journal of Religion in Japan* 4, no. 2: 241–71, and is currently translating several articles on medieval Japanese religion and culture. Porath is also the recipient of a Japan Foundation Dissertation Fellowship (2015–16), and an American Counsel of Learned Societies, Robert H. N. Ho Family Foundation Program in Buddhist Studies dissertation fellowship (2017–18). He is currently a visiting research fellow at the Nanzan Institute for Religion and Culture, and a collaborative research fellow in the Research Center for Cultural Heritage and Texts at Nagoya University, Japan.

LUKE S. ROBERTS earned his doctorate in East Asian studies at Princeton University in 1991 and is currently a professor of early modern Japanese history at the University of California, Santa Barbara. He is author of *Mercantilism in a Japanese Domain: The Merchant Origins of Economic Nationalism in Eighteenth Century Tosa* (1998), and *Performing the Great Peace: Political Space and Open Secrets in Tokugawa Japan* (2012), and coauthor with Sharon Takeda of *Japanese Fisherman's Coats from Awaji Island* (2001). His current book project is called *A Samurai's Life*, a biography of an eighteenth-century samurai of no particular repute pursued as a form of social history.

HARALD SALOMON studied modern history and Japanese studies at the University of Tübingen and Rikkyō University, Tokyo. He conducted his doctoral research at Waseda University and the German Institute for Japanese Studies, Tokyo, and completed his doctorate at Humboldt University, Berlin. His research interests focus on the history of interactions between Japan and Europe during the transition to modernity, Japanese film and media culture, and the history of family and childhood. He is the director of the Mori Ogai Memorial Center and a lecturer at the Seminar for East Asian Studies of Humboldt University, Berlin. His publications include *Views of the Dark Valley: Japanese Cinema and the Culture of Nationalism, 1937–45* (Wiesbaden: Harrassowitz, 2011). He coedited the volume *Kindheit in der japanischen Geschichte: Vorstellungen und Erfahrungen / Childhood in Japanese History: Concepts and Experiences* (Wiesbaden: Harrassowitz, 2016).

EMILY B. SIMPSON is a doctoral candidate in the Department of East Asian Languages and Cultural Studies at the University of California, Santa Barbara. Her research centers on medieval reinterpretations of the legend of Empress Jingū and their role in the formation of late medieval and early modern women's cults. Her fields of interest include Japanese religious syncretism, shamanism, Japanese folklore, and women and gender in premodern East Asia. In addition to her multiple translations of academic articles, Simpson has also authored a book chapter, "An Empress at Sea: Sea Deities and Divine Union in the Legend of Empress Jingū" in the forthcoming volume *Sea Religion in Japan*, edited by Fabio Rambelli, and several entries on women and Shinto for the *Encyclopedia of Women in World Religions: Faith and Culture Across History*, ABC-CLIO, 2017.

JUNKO TERUYAMA earned her doctorate in anthropology from the University of Michigan and is currently an assistant professor of cultural and medical anthropology at the University of Tsukuba. She has conducted fieldwork on the community of individuals with learning disabilities, ADHD, and autism spectrum disorder and their family members in Tokyo. Her recent publications include "Politics of Care and Ethics of Intervention in Treatment Programs for Children with Developmental Disability," in *Ecologies of Care: Innovations through Technologies, Collectives and the Senses* (Osaka University Institute for Academic Initiatives 2014).

ANNE WALTHALL is Professor emerita at the University of California, Irvine. She has published extensively on many topics in Edo-period history, ranging from peasant uprisings to guns to steamships. Her publications include *Social Protest and Popular Culture in Eighteenth-Century Japan* (1986), *Peasant Uprisings in Japan: A Critical Anthology of Peasant Histories* (1991), *The Weak Body of a Useless Woman: Matsuo Taseko and the Meiji Restoration* (1998), and *Japan: A Cultural, Social, and Political History* (2006). She has edited or coedited a number of volumes, most recently *Recreating Japanese Men* (2011) with Sabine Frühstück and *Politics and Society in Japan's Meiji Restoration: A Brief History with Documents* (2017) with M. William Steele.

INDEX

Godzilla, 266, 282
Goldfarb, Kathryn E., 7
Goodbye Monju-kun (Sayōnara, Monju-kun, 2012), 271, 278
Good Child's Play, The [Yoi ko no asobi] (Kurosaki, 1941), 164
Gordon, Andrew, 176
Gotch, 277
Gotō Masafumi, 266–67
Greater Japanese Youth Association (Dai Nippon Seinendan), 111
Great Japan Youth Association, 170
Great Kantō Earthquake (1923), 122, 123
Grilli, Peter, 162
Grimm's Fairy Tales, 94
Grossman, Eike, 3
guessing games, 173
Gulick, Sidney, 121

Hachiman festival and shrine, 23, 172
Haggerty, Timothy, 8
hajiki (girls' game), 169
hakama (pleated boys' pants), 35, 43, 62, 63, 64, 74, 78n2
"half-adulthood" ceremony, 41
Hata Hidetarō, 66
Hatano Kanji, 163
Have We Changed Since 3/11? (Monju-kun taidan-shū: 3.11 de bokura wa kawatta ka, 2014), 278
Hayashi Fumiko, 106
Hayashi Fumio, 106, 110
Hayashi Seigo, 55
Hayashi Shihei, 68
Health Reader for Daughters, Wives, and Mothers, The (Musume to tsuma to haha no eisei dokuhon), 187
Heart Sutra, 25
Heian period (794–1185), 3, 24, 25
Heisei period (1989 to present), 3
Hello Kitty (cartoon character), 268
Hendry, Joy, 176
heterosexuality, 9, 55
hide-and-seek games, 165, 167–68, 170
Hikashū, 282
hikikomori ("acute social withdrawal"), 210, 275
Hinduism, 22–23
Hirakawa Tadaichi, 195
Hirata Atsutane, 61; childhood of, 75–77; letters sent by, 62; love for children in letters of, 68–75; rituals recorded in diary of, 62, 64–68; sickness and death of granddaughter, 60

Hirata Fuki, 60, 65, 67, 68
Hirata Kanesaburō, 65, 66, 67, 69, 72
Hirata Kanetane, 64, 73, 76
Hirata Kaneya, 65, 66, 68, 70, 72
Hirata Mika, 65, 66–67, 70, 71, 72
Hirata Nobutane, 64, 65, 66, 69, 72, 73, 76
Hirata O-Chō, 62, 70, 71
Hirata Orise, 68, 70, 71, 72, 74, 75
Hirata Shin'ichirō, 73, 74, 77
Hirata Sutematsu, 72
Hirata Suzu, 65, 67, 70, 71
Hirayama Keisuke, 69
Hirose Takeo, 99n6
History of Japanese Film (Satō), 103
Hitler, Adolf, 181–82
Hokkeji temple, 38n2
"Holding Hands" (poem by Japanese fourth grader), 131
Home Life [Hōmū Raifu] (magazine), 188
Honjō Shigeru, 126
honne (private self), 233
Horibe Chieko, 141, 143
horseback riding, 52, 65, 66
house, playing, 169, 170
"household-like care" (*katei-teki yōgo*), 243, 260
Housewife's Friend, The [Shufu no tomo] (magazine), 84, 109
Housing [Jūtaku] (magazine), 99n4
Housing and Architecture [Jūtaku to kenchiku] (Kogure, 1928), 86
"Housing and Ornamentation" (Kogure, 1928), 87

Ibuka Masaru, 223n7
identity, Japanese, 168, 171, 173, 177
Iida Tetsunari, 278
Ikeda Giichi, 162
illness, cultural notions of embodying, 239–40
Illustrated Children in the War (Yamanaka, 1989), 164
Imada Erika, 10
Imperial Grandchild's Birthday Children's Exhibition (1926), 97
Imperial Japanese Army (IJA), 187, 190, 193, 194, 195
Improving One's Home [Wagaya o kairyō shite] (Kogure, 1930), 86, 88, 89
indentured servitude, 45
individualism, 85, 163, 168, 169, 177
infanticide, 45, 61, 77
Infinite Stratos [Infinitto Sutoratosu] (manga/anime, 2009–present), 198